LAW RELATING TO CENTRAL ARMED POLICE FORCES & AR

SHAKTI PRAKASH & HIMANSHU GAUTAM

FOREWORD BY
HON'BLE JUSTICE REKHA PALLI,
JUDGE, DELHI HIGH COURT

BLUEROSE PUBLISHERS
India | U.K.

Copyright © Shakti Prakash and Himanshu Gautam 2024

All rights reserved by author. No part of this publication may be reproduced, stored in a retrieval system or transmitted in any form or by any means, electronic, mechanical, photocopying, recording or otherwise, without the prior permission of the author. Although every precaution has been taken to verify the accuracy of the information contained herein, the publisher assume no responsibility for any errors or omissions. No liability is assumed for damages that may result from the use of information contained within.

BlueRose Publishers takes no responsibility for any damages, losses, or liabilities that may arise from the use or misuse of the information, products, or services provided in this publication.

For permissions requests or inquiries regarding this publication, please contact:

BLUEROSE PUBLISHERS
www.BlueRoseONE.com
info@bluerosepublishers.com
+91 8882 898 898
+4407342408967

ISBN: 978-93-6452-770-5

Cover design: Daksh
Typesetting: Tanya Raj Upadhyay

First Edition: October 2024

Justice Rekha Palli  *High Court of Delhi*
Sher Shah Road
New Delhi-110 503
Ph. : 011-43010101 (Off.)

FOREWORD

1. In the vast and dynamic realm of public service, few institutions are as critical to the maintenance of national security and internal stability as the Central Armed Police Forces (CAPFs) and the Assam Rifles. These Forces, through their unwavering dedication and professionalism, ensure the safety and security of our nation's borders and internal frontiers. However, as the interest of the State has to be harmonized with the rights of the Force personnel, the legal framework that governs these services is intricate and often challenging to navigate.

2. The provisions that regulate the functioning of the CAPFs and the Assam Rifles are not merely procedural but are foundational to the effective functioning and discipline of these Forces. They provide the structure within which these organizations operate and ensure that their members are well-equipped to perform their duties with integrity. Given the unique nature of their roles ranging from counter-insurgency operations to disaster response, they must be treated with fairness and therefore, clarity and precision in these legal provisions is of paramount importance.

3. As someone who has spent a significant part of her career witnessing the growth of law relating to Armed Forces and the CAPFs in India, I can say that this branch of law requires striking a delicate balance between duty, discipline, and national security, while simultaneously safeguarding individual rights. This book offers a detailed and systematic exploration of this branch of law, blending

Resi. : 7, Teen Murti Lane, New Delhi-110011
Ph. : 011-21410820

Justice Rekha Palli  High Court of Delhi
Sher Shah Road
New Delhi-110 503
Ph. : 011-43010101 (Off.)

statutory analysis with practical insights. The author's methodical approach to distilling complex legal texts will undoubtedly be a valuable asset for readers.

4. It will, therefore, serve as a guide for those within the Forces as well as legal practitioners who seek to understand the nuances of the rules and regulations that govern the service in these Forces. I extend my heartfelt congratulations to the author for this comprehensive work and hope that the book will become an indispensable resource for everyone associated with the CAPFs and the Assam Rifles.

23/9/2024

REKHA PALLI

Resi. : 7, Teen Murti Lane, New Delhi-110011
Ph. : 011-21410820

TINU BAJWA, ADVOCATE
DELHI HIGH COURT

2024

FOREWORD

In an era where the need for effective governance and the preservation of public order have never been more critical, the role of the Central Armed Police Forces (CAPF) and the Assam Rifles has come to the forefront of national security and civil administration. These esteemed institutions not only uphold the law but also embody the spirit of duty, discipline, and dedication to the nation. Understanding the intricate legal frameworks that govern their operations is crucial for ensuring that these forces continue to serve with integrity and effectiveness.

This book on the Service Law of CAPF and Assam Rifles arrives at a pivotal moment, providing a comprehensive exploration of the legal and administrative principles that underpin the functioning of these crucial organizations. It delves into the complex tapestry of service regulations, employment rights, disciplinary procedures, and administrative practices that govern the personnel of CAPF and the Assam Rifles. Such an examination is essential for practitioners, policymakers, and members of these forces themselves, as it offers clarity and guidance on navigating the legal landscape that shapes their professional lives.

The authors, with their expertise and deep understanding of the subject matter, have crafted a work that not only serves as an invaluable reference for legal scholars and practitioners but also provides practical insights for the personnel who rely on these

CH NO. 610 BLOCK III
DELHI HIGH COURT, SHER SHAH SURI ROAD
NEW DELHI 1100503

regulations daily. Their meticulous research and clear presentation make this book a significant contribution to the field of service law.

As we continue to face complex security challenges and evolving administrative demands, it is imperative that those who serve in CAPF and Assam Rifles are well-versed in the legal frameworks that govern their service. This book stands as a testament to the commitment to ensuring that justice, fairness, and accountability remain at the heart of these esteemed institutions. It is my hope that this work will not only enhance understanding but also contribute to the ongoing evolution and strengthening of service laws, ultimately supporting those who work tirelessly to safeguard our nation

— [TINU BAJWA]
[Advocate]
[Former Member, Police Complaints Authority, New Delhi]
[25.09.2024]

CH NO. 610 BLOCK III
DELHI HIGH COURT, SHER SHAH SURI ROAD
NEW DELHI 1100503

ACKNOWLEDGEMENT

- Hon'ble Justice Rekha Palli, Judge, Delhi High Court, for reviewing chapters and providing her valuable insights.

- **Acknowledgement by Sh. Himanshu Gautam**

I would like to express my deepest gratitude to my father, Late Shri Sanjay Kumar Mishra, My mother Smt. Sudha Mishra and my teacher and Guide Hon'ble Justice Jyoti Singh for their unwavering support and guidance throughout. Their selfless love and encouragement have been a constant source of inspiration and strength. I further acknowledge the constant support of Ms. Tinu Bajwa, Mr. Padma Kumar S., Mr. Rahul Sharma, Ms. Jyoti Dutt Sharma, Sri Amandeep Joshi, Sri Kishan Gautam, Anuradha Gautam, Sri Lokesh Sharma, Sri Navneet Mishra, Kalyani Mishra, Sri Narendra Deo Pandey, Sri Pramod Upadhyay, Sri Dinesh Yadav, Vaishali Pandey and Sri C.K. Bhatt. I am lucky to have them all as my constant support and guide.

-**Acknowledgement by Sh. Shakti Prakash**

I would like to express my deepest gratitude to my wife Dr. Pallavi Rana, for her constant encouragement and to my sweet little daughter Siddhi Singh Rana. I would like to extend my gratitude to my grand father, Late Uday Bhan Singh, my father, Sh. S.P. Singh and to my mother, Smt. Renu Singh, Sh. V.P. Singh Rana and Smt. Shashi Rana, in-laws parents. I would like to express my sincere thanks to my sisters Dr. Amrita Rana, Dr. Payal Rana, Dr. Mehak Rana and my brother-in-law Dr. Deepak Sengar. I would like to express my sincere gratitude and special thanks to Sh. Satpal Chouhan, DG(Awards), MHA, Sh. Sanjeev Kumar Jindal, Additional Secretary, MHA, Sh. G. Parthasarathi, Joint Secretary, MHA, Sh. Anil Subramaniam, Joint Secretary, MHA for constantly guiding and encouraging me. I would also like to appreciate the support received from

Smt. Seema Dhundia, IG, CRPF, Sh. S.K. Shahi, Joint Secretary (Retd.), MHA, Sh. Shri Prakash, Joint Secretary (Retd.), MHA, Sh. Krishan Kumar, Director (Retd.), MHA, Smt. Renu Sarin, Director (Retd.), MHA, Sh. Lalit Kapoor, Director, MHA, Sh. Ashok Samyal, DIG, CRPF, Sh. Praveen Yadav, Deputy Secretary, MHA, Sh. B.C. Patra, DIG, CRPF & JAG, NSG, Anil Kumar Chaturvedi, DIG & CSO, MHA, Sh. R. Jayakumar, Commandant, CRPF, Sh. Amitabh Gupta, Commandant, BSF and Legal Officer, MHA, Sh. Anil Yadav, 2IC, CRPF, Sh. Vivek Kumar Singh, 2IC, CRPF, Sh. Maheshwar Rai, 2IC, CRPF, Sh. Manish Kumar, 2IC, CRPF, Md. Raji, 2IC, CRPF, Sh. K.S. Bhandari, Ex-IG, CRPF, Sh. Arun Kumar, Ex-IG, CRPF, Sh. Sandeep Gokel, Ex- DIG, CRPF, Sh. Kislaya Upadhyaya, DC, SSB, Sh. Vinod Trivedi, DC, CRPF, Sh. Vimal Singh, DC, CRPF, Sh. Amit Sharma, AC, CRPF, Sh. Amit Sankholia, Deputy Director, I4C, MHA, Mervyn Mathews Rajan, AC, MHA, Sh. Nilesh Pandey, AC, CRPF, Sh. Dipankar Nagar, AC, CRPF, Sh. Manoj Khajotiya, AC, CRPF, Sh. Sabyasachi Saha, Associate Professor, RIS(MEA), Sh. Mrutyunjay Tripathy, US, MHA, Sh. Deendayal Shivhare, SO, Sh. Paritosh Yadav, SO, MHA, Sh. Puneet, SO, MHA, Sh. Pankaj Verma, SO, MHA, Sh. Kundan Kumar, SO, MHA, Sh. Atul Shukla, SO, MHA, Sh. Rohit Goyal, ASO, MHA and Sh. Mohit Ahuja.

The views expressed by the authors in this book are of their own and not that of the Government of India.

Table of Contents

CHAPTER-I 1
   CONSTITUTIONAL/STATUTORY PROVISIONS AND
   CASE LAWS 1

CHAPTER-II 24
   CENTRAL RESERVE POLICE FORCE- LAW
   INCLUDING LEADING CASE LAWS 24

CHAPTER III 198
   INDO – TIBETAN BORDER POLICE-LAW
   INCLUDING LEADING CASE LAWS 198

CHAPTER IV 237
   BORDER SECURITY FORCE -LAW INCLUDING
   LEADING CASE LAWS 237

CHAPTER V 330
   SASHASTRA SEEMA BAL (SSB) -LAW INCLUDING
   LEADING CASE LAWS 330

CHAPTER VI 344
   ASSAM RIFLES -LAW INCLUDING LEADING CASE
   LAWS 344

CHAPTER VII 365
   CENTRAL INDUSTRIAL SECURITY FORCE -LAW
   INCLUDING LEADING CASE LAWS 365

INDEX

1. **CHAPTER-I - CONSTITUTIONAL / STATUTORY PROVISIONS AND CASE LAWS**
    i. Introduction
        a. *Maj. Reena Goswami and Ors. versus Union of India*
        b. *Pawan Kumar and Ors. and other Vs Union of India & Ors*
        c. *Union of India & Ors. vs Sri Harananda & Ors*
        d. *Nigude Ashok Dasharath & Ors. vs. Union of India & Ors*
        e. *Dev Sharma vs Indo Tibetan Border Police & Anr.*
    ii. Constitution of the Force
    iii. Coverage under Central Civil Services (Pension) Rules in place of National Pension System, of those Central Government employees who were recruited against the posts/vacancies advertised /notified for recruitment, on or before 22.12.2003
        a. *Shyam Kumar Choudhary & Ors. vs. Union of India & Ors.*
        b. *Parmanand Yadav v. Union of India*
        c. *M.R. Gurjar and Ors.vs. Union of India & Ors.*
        d. *Patil Gopal Babulal &Ors. vs. Union of India &Ors*
    iv. Effect of not having undergone pre-promotional course due to Non-Detailment by the department
        a. *Tribhuwan Pratap Singh and Ors vs UOI And Ors*
        b. *Suraj Bhan and Ors vs UOI And Ors*

  c. *Union of India and Others vs. Ex. HC/GD Virender Singh*
 v. Legal Protection available to Members of Force

2. **CHAPTER-II - CENTRAL RESERVE POLICE FORCE-LAW INCLUDING LEADING CASE LAWS**
 i. Constitutionality and *vires* of the CRPF Act, 1949
  a) *Tarun Kumar Sengupta vs Union of India And Anr.*
  b) *State Of West Bengal And Anr. vs Tarun Kumar Sen Gupta And Anr*
 ii. Judgments on Persons with Disabilities
  a. *Union of India & Ors. vs. Dileep Kumar Singh*
  b. *Ravinder Kumar Dhariwal & Anr. Versus The Union of India &Ors.*
 iii. Departmental Proceedings: Inquiring Authority not to act as Presenting Officer – Enquiry Vitiated
  a. *Union of India & Ors. vs. Ram Lakhan Sharma and other*
 iv. Section 9, 10 & 12 of the CRPF Act, 1949 and Disciplinary Proceedings under Rule 27 of the CRPF Rules, 1955
  a. *Union of India and Ors. Versus Const Sunil Kumar*
  b. *Commandant, 22 Battalion, CRPF Srinagar, C/o 56/APO & Ors. Vs. Surinder Kumar*
  c. *Jagannath Naik Vs Inspector General of Police & Ors*
 v. Criminal proceedings and departmental proceedings
  a. *Union of India & Ors. Vs. Dalbir Singh*
  b. *Union of India & Ors. Versus Santosh Kumar Tiwari*
  c. *Ex Ct GD Prem Kumar Vs Union of India & Ors*

- vi. Disciplinary Cases-Requirement of Advice of UPSC to Impose Penalties
    - a. Prakash Kumar Dixit vs. Union of India &Ors.
    - b. Union of India &Ors Vs Prakash Kumar Dixit
- vii. Judicial Trial in CRPF– Case Laws
    - a. State (Union Of India) vs Ram Saran
- viii. Interpretation Of Standing Order For Giving Benefits of Promotion
    - a. Venkatesh Versus Union Of India & Ors.
    - b. Srikand Prasad vs Union Of India [7(2007)1GLR221]
    - c. Shri Suresh Kumar vs Union OOf India & Ors
- ix. Accommodation Rules In CRPF
    - a. WPC 1824 of 2015 titled Neeraj Kumar Singh Vs Union of India & Ors
- x. Recovery when impermissible
    - a. WP(C) No. 3232/2019 Dilshad Ali Vs. UOI & Ors
- xi. Role of Presenting Officer
    - a. Union Of India vs Ram Lakhan Sharma
- xii. Medical Requirements In Recruitment Process (Tattoo Mark)
    - a. Union of India vs Sanyogita
- xiii. Requirement Of Mandatory Field Service For Promotion
    - a. Rakesh Sethi vs Union Of India And Anr.
- xiv. Requirement Of Headquarter For Entitlement Of HRA to Officers In CRPF
    - a. J S Chauhan vs The Union Of India

3. **CHAPTER-III INDO TIBETAN BORDER POLICE- LAW INCLUDING LEADING CASE LAWS**
    - i. Requirement of Consultation with UPSC
        - a. Saurabh Dubey & Ors. vs Union Of India &Ors.

- ii. Regarding Pre-Promotional training for Promotion
  - a. Force No. 937040966 Ram Charan Singh vs. Union of India vs. Ors.
- iii. Relevant judgements interpreting ITBP Act
  - a. S.Kannan V. The Director General (Madras High Court, 2024)
  - b. Bharosi Lal Vs Union of India & Ors SWP No. 2449/2012 High Court of Jammu & Kashmir
- iv. General Security Force Court Under ITBP Act
  - a. Commandant/Gd Rajesh Kumar Tomar vs Union Of India & Ors.

4. **CHAPTER-IV BORDER SECURITY FORCE- LAW INCLUDING LEADING CASE LAWS**
   - i. Case laws related to Security Force Courts
     - a. B. S. Hari Commandant Versus Union of India &Ors.
     - b. Union Of India Vs L/Nk Vishav Priya Singh Civil Appeal No. 8360 Of 2010
     - c. Union Of India & Others Versus Jogeshwar Swain
     - d. Director General, Border Security Force Vs Iboton Singh
   - ii. GSFC- Finding, Conviction and Sentence Awarded by GSFC modified by Supreme Court
     - a. Ex. Ct. Mahadev Vs The Director General Bsf Civil Appeal No. 2606 Of 2012
     - b. Union of India & Ors vs Ashok Kumar & Ors on 18 October, 2005 Civil Appeal 4792 of 1999
   - iii. Non Compliance Of Rule 45 B of BSF Rules
     - a. Union Of India (Uoi) And Ors. vs B.N. Jha Case No.: Appeal (civil) 2054 of 2002
   - iv. Definition of Active Duty under the BSF Act and Rules

- a. State of J&K vs Lakhwinder Kumar & Ors on 25 April, 2013
- b. Union of India and Ors. vs Mudrika Singh Civil Appeal 6859 of 2021
  v. Relevant Judgements under the BSF Act
- a. Ex-BSF Personnel Welfare Association V. Union Of India (Kerala High Court, 2018)

5. **CHAPTER-V SASHASTRA SEEMA BAL (SSB)- LAW INCLUDING LEADING CASE LAWS**
   i. Seniority Dispute Direct Recruits vis-a-vis Promotees
      - a. B.S. Jaswal And Ors. vs Union Of India & Ors. WP (C) 7939/2012 (Delhi High Court)
   ii. Request For Resignation
      - a. Rakesh Kumar Bhartiya Versus Union Of India, Through Its Secretary, Ministry Of Home Affairs & Anr. W.P.(C) 8500/2021 (Delhi High Court)

6. **CHAPTER-VI ASSAM RIFLES- LAW INCLUDING LEADING CASE LAWS**
   i. Trial for offences under the PC Act, 1988 may be undertaken by the Assam Rifles Court under the Assam Rifles Act, 2006
      - b. Civil Appeal No. 5136 Of 2019 Union Of India, Represented By The Secretary, Ministry Of Home Affairs & Ors. Versus Ranjit Kumar Saha & Anr
   ii. Effect of red ink entries under the Assam Rifles Act, 1941
      - a. Supreme Court Of India Civil Appeal Nos. 11473-11474 Of 2018 Amarendra Kumar Pandey Versus Union Of India & Ors

     iii. Pay Parity With BSF And CRPF
          a. Union Of India & Ors Vs Dineshan K.K

7. CHAPTER-VII CENTRAL INDUSTRIAL SECURITY FORCE- LAW INCLUDING LEADING CASE LAWS

     i. House Rent Allowance for Officers in CISF
          a. *Civil Appeal No.4967/2023 Union Of India & Ors. Versus Paramisivan M*
     ii. Disciplinary Proceedings under the CISF Act
          a. *Civil Appeal Nos._7939-7940 Of 2022 Union Of India And Others Versus Subrata Nath*

CHAPTER-I

CONSTITUTIONAL/STATUTORY PROVISIONS AND CASE LAWS

INTRODUCTION

In Constitution of India, 'public order' and 'police' are State subjects. Article 355 of the Constitution enjoins the Union to protect every State against external aggression and internal disturbance and to ensure that the Government of every State is carried on in accordance with the provisions of the Constitution.

2. Article 355 of the Constitution of India assigns the Central Government the responsibility of protecting every part of India from external aggression and internal disturbances. Under items 1 to 2A of List I (Union List) of the Seventh Schedule to the Constitution, the deployment of naval, military & air forces; and any other armed forces of Union are vested in the Central Government.

3. To fulfill its constitutional responsibilities, the Central Government has raised five Central Armed Police Forces (CAPFs) of which three are Border Guarding Forces (BGFs) viz., Sashastra Seema Bal (SSB), Indo-Tibetan Border Police (ITBP) and Border Security Force (BSF) and two Non-Border Guarding Forces used for internal security including Central Reserve Police Force (CRPF) and Central Industrial Security Force (CISF). Apart from the aforesaid CAPFs, Assam Rifles also has peace keeping role in North Eastern Areas of India.

4. SEVENTH SCHEDULE

(Article 246)

List I—Union List *1. Defence of India and every part thereof including preparation for defence and all such acts as may be conducive in times of war to its prosecution and after its termination to effective demobilisation.*

2. Naval, military and air forces; any other armed forces of the Union.

2A. Deployment of any armed force of the Union or any other force subject to the control of the Union or any contingent or unit thereof in any State in aid of the civil power; powers, jurisdiction, privileges and liabilities of the members of such forces while on such deployment.

List II—State List

1. Public order (but not including the use of any naval, military or air force or any other armed force of the Union or of any other force subject to the control of the Union or of any contingent or unit thereof in aid of the civil power).

2. Police (including railway and village police) subject to the provisions of entry 2A of List I.

5. The Ministry of Home Affairs, Government of India, vide Circular dated 6th August, 2004 clarified that the following Central Forces under the administrative control of the Ministry of Home Affairs have been declared as Armed Forces of the Union:

(i) Border Security Force vide Section 4 of the Border Security Force Act, 1968

(ii) Central Industrial Security Force Vide section 3 of the Central Industrial Security Force Act, 1968 (Amended by Act 14 of 1983).

(iii) Central Reserve Police Force vide Section 3 of the Central Reserve Police Force, Act, 1949

(iv) Indo Tibetan Borden Police vide Section 4 of the Indo Tibetan Border Police Force Act, 1992.

(v) SSB

(vi) Assam Rifles

6. The provisions of Section 3(1) of the CRPF Act, 1949 stipulate that the CRPF is a part of armed forces. It reads as under:-

"CONSTITUTION OF THE FORCE

3. Constitution of the Force-(1) There shall continue to be an armed force by the Central Government and called the Central Reserve Police Force."

7. The Supreme Court in Judgment dated 11.2.1981 in Criminal Appeal No. 439/1980 in the matter of Akhilesh Prasad Vs. Union Territory of Mizoram **(1981) 2 SCC 150** has held that CRPF is an Armed Force of the Union.

8. In exercise of the powers conferred by sub-section (1) of Section 43 of the Arms Act, 1959 (54 of 1959), the Ministry of Home Affairs vide Gazette Notification No. G.S.R. 904(E) dated 11th November, 2010 directed that the officers of the rank of Assistant Commandant and above and the subordinate officers of the rank of Sub-Inspector and above in the Central Para Military Forces shall exercise the powers conferred on the Central Government under Section 24 of the Arms Act, 1959 (54 of 1959) in all the areas where they are deployed or called upon to perform any duty. In this Gazette notification, "Central Para Military Forces" means—

(i) the Central Reserve Police Force constituted under Section 3 of the Central Reserve Police Force Act, 1949 (66 of 1949);

(ii) the Border Security Force constituted under Section 4 of the Border Security Force Act, 1968 (47 of 1968);

(iii) the Central Industrial Security Force constituted under Section 3 of the Central Industrial Security Force Act, 1968 (50 of 1968);

(iv) the National Security Guard constituted under Section 4 of the National Security Guard Act, 1986 (47 of 1986);

(v) the lndo-Tibetan Border Police Force constituted under Section 4 of the lndo-Tibetan Border Police Force Art, 1992 (35 of 1992);

(vi) the Assam Rifles constituted under Section 4 of the Assam Rifles Act, 2006 (47 of 2006); and

(vii) the Sashastra Seema Bal constituted under Section 4 of the Sashastra Seema Bal Act, 2007 (53 of 2007).

9. Further, the Ministry of Home Affairs, Govt. of India in exercise of the powers conferred by sub-section (I) of Section 19, sub-section (2) of Section 22 and Section 23 of the Arms Act, 1959 (54 of 1959)vide Gazette Notification No. G.S.R. 905(E)dated 11th November, 2010, empowered the officers of the rank of Assistant Commandant and above and the Subordinate officers of the rank of Sub-Inspector and above in the Central Para Military Forces to exercise the powers and perform the duties conferred under Section 19, sub-section (2) of Section 22 and Section 23 of the Arms Act, 1959 (54 of 1959) in all the areas where they are deployed or called upon to perform any duty.

10. Ministry of Home Affairs vide OM No. I-45020/2/2011-Pers-II dated 18.3.2011 adopted a uniform nomenclature of Central Armed Police Forces (CAPFs) in respect of following Central Forces:

(i) Border Security Force

(ii) Central Reserve Police Force

(iii) Central Industrial Security Force

(v) lndo-Tibetan Border Police Force

(vi) Sashastra Seema Bal

11. Ministry of Home Affairs vide OM No. 27011/100/2012-R&W dated 23.11.2012 communicated that Cabinet Committee on Security has approved the proposal to declare retired Central Armed Police

Force personnel in respect of following Central Forces as "Ex Central Armed Police Force personnel(Ex-CAPF Personnel):

(i) Border Security Force

(ii) Central Reserve Police Force

(iii) Central Industrial Security Force

(v) lndo-Tibetan Border Police Force

(vi) Sashastra Seema Bal

12. The High Court of Delhi in W.P.(C) 2754/2015 titled Maj. Reena Goswami and Ors. versus Union of India vide Judgment & Order 11.08.2015 held as under:

"3. The petitioners are governed by the National Cadet Corps (Whole Time Lady Officers) Recruitment Rules, 1995 which were made in exercise of power conferred under Section 9 and 13 of the Act. Although the cadre structure closely resembles that of the Indian Army, **we observe that enactments which concededly provide for raising of the armed forces units – such as the Central Reserve Police Force Act, Border Security Force Act, Central Industrial Security Force Act and Assam Rifles Act etc. – each contain provisions declaring the respective force(s) to be an armed force of the Union.** *The provisions of the NCC Act are lacking in this respect, and state nothing in that regard."*

13. Delhi High Court in W.P.(C) No. 12712/2021 in the matter of Pawan Kumar and Ors. and other connected tagged petitions vide Judgment dated 11.1.2023 declared CAPFs as Armed Forces of the Union of India and all the personnel of CAPFs are entitled to be covered under Old Pension Scheme in terms of Department of Economic Affairs, Ministry of Finance Notification dated 22.12.2003 as well as Department of Pension and Pensioner's Welfare OM dated 17.02.2020 in essence. The Judgment dated 11.1.2023 of Delhi High Court has been stayed by Supreme Court in Special Leave Petition

(Civil) Diary No. 19815/2023 vide Order dated 5.7.2023. There is a stay of operation of the impugned judgment of Delhi High Court to the extent it directs that the Old Pension Scheme would be applicable to the para-military forces.

14. The Supreme Court vide Judgment dated 5.2.2019 in Civil Appeal No. 1474/2019 in the matter of Union of India & Ors. vs Sri Harananda & Ors. and other connected matters upheld the Judgment dated 3.9.2015 of Delhi High Court in W.P(C) 153/2013 in the matter of G.J. Singh &Ors. vs. Union of India & Ors. and other connected matters. The Delhi High Court vide Judgment dated dated 3.9.2015 in W.P(C) 153/2013 held that officers in PB-3 and PB-4 in the Group A Executive Cadre of CAPFs have been categorised under Organised Group "A" Service ever since the year 1986. Hence, the benefits contemplated by the 6th CPC by way of NFFU to remove disparity between All India Services and other Organised Central Group "A" Services, ought to be granted to them. Further, the Supreme Court in the Judgment dated 5.2.2019 in Civil Appeal No. 1474/2019 held as under:

"24.2 Considering the aforesaid facts and circumstances and the objects and reasons of the grant of NFFU as recommended by the 6th Pay Commission, when the High Court has observed and consequently directed that the officers in PB-III and PB-IV in the CAPFs are Organized Group "A" Service and, therefore, entitled to the benefits recommended by the 6th Pay Commission by way of NFFU and thereby has directed the Appellants to issue a requisite notification granting the benefits of NFFU as recommended by the 6th Central Pay Commission, it cannot be said that the High Court has committed any error which calls for the interference by this Court. We are in complete agreement with the view taken by the High Court."

15. Press Information Bureau, Government of India in its press note dated 3.7.2019 stated that the Union Cabinet has approved the proposal for Grant of Organized Group 'A' Service (OGAS) status to Group 'A' Executive Cadre Officers of Central Armed Police Forces (CAPFs) and

extension of benefit of Non-Functional Financial Upgradation (NFFU) and Non-Functional Selection Grade (NFSG).

16. The High Court of Delhi vide Judgment dated 26.2.2024 in W.P.(C) 3445/2020 in the matter of Nigude Ashok Dasharath & Ors. vs. Union of India & Ors and other connected matter held as under:

1. Petitioner Nigude Ashok Dasharath & 16 others have filed Writ Petition 3445/2020 with the following prayer: -

(i) Issue a writ of certiorari for quashing the orders dated 03.02.2020 to the extent that the petitioners have not been considered for grant of NFSG despite fulfilling all the conditions as laid down by the above OMs and by wrong calculation of Senior Duty Post;

(ii) Issue a writ of mandamus directing the respondents to calculate 30% of Senior Duty Post properly by including the posts held by Assistant Commandants already granted to STS (Grade Pay 6600/-) as well as post held by IPS for calculation of Senior Duty Post (SDP) and thereafter consider the petitioners for grant of NFSG and if found eligible then grant the same to the petitioners from the dates as shown in the above table in the petition with all consequential benefits;

(iii) Issue a writ of mandamus to enhance ceiling of Senior Duty Post (SDP) from 30% to 100% as a one-time measure to address acute stagnation to left out Second-in-Command (2ICs) those who are not covered by counting AC (STS) if any, and grant them NFSG with consequential benefits.

....

23. Moreover, the Monograph published by the DoPT in the year 2010 clearly defines Senior Duty post as "SDP (Total strength-Reserves Number of post at junior time scale)." As per the definition, only posts at Junior Time Scale and reserves are to be subtracted for calculation of SDP. Also, DoPT vide its OM dated 25.06.2014 clarified that Senior Duty Posts means all cadre posts at Senior Time Scale (Rs.6600/-) and above Senior Time Scale. Thus, the officers who are in Senior Time Scale are to be considered for calculation of SDP.

24. We do not find any real logic for excluding the posts held by Assistant Commandants who have been granted Senior Time Scale as well as the posts held by IPS. We say so because in above noted clarification issued by DoPT way back on 25.06.2014, it was specifically clarified that Senior Duty Post would mean all cadre posts at Senior Time Scale (GP Rs. 6600/-) and above the Senior Time Scale. Merely because, the Assistant Commandants have been granted Senior Time Scale and are not formally promoted and merely because several posts are held by deputationists would not mean that they cannot be reckoned to be part of SDP, at least in context of present service which is faced with acute stagnation.

25. We need not lay emphasis that NFSG is a benefit given to those employees who do not get promoted to the high rank/post due to the unavailability of the vacancy. The spirit of this benefit is employee centric as it motivates those employees who do not get promoted despite putting in enough years of service. Thus, for the purpose of grant of NFSG, there is no reason for excluding them. Respondents cannot be heard claiming that posts held by IPS also do not belong to the cadre and, therefore, they cannot be calculated for the purposes of Senior Duty Post and thus the formula adopted by the respondents does not seem to be correct.

26. Fact, however, remains that the petitioners have not been able to place on record the requisite data which may, at the moment, compel us to increase the ceiling of SDP from 30% to 100%.

27. In view of our foregoing discussion, we hereby partly allow the present Writ Petition and direct the respondents to re-calculate the grant of NFSG while including the posts held by Assistant Commandants (STS) as well as the posts held by IPS on deputation. Needless to say, NFSG would be given to those officers only who are

otherwise found eligible and meet the prescribed conditions and parameters.

28. As regards enhancement of ceiling of Senior Duty Post from 30% to 100% as a one-time measure, petitioners would be at liberty to file appropriate representation and the respondents would be at liberty to consider the same as expeditiously as possible. If aggrieved by the outcome thereof, they would certainly be at liberty to take recourse to law."

17. The High Court of Delhi vide Judgment dated 31.1.2019 in W.P.(C) No. 1951/2012 in the matter of Dev Sharma vs Indo Tibetan Border Police & Anr. and other connected matters held as under:

"59. This Court is of the view that the Petitioners have made out a case of discrimination, that is violative of Articles 14 and 16 of the Constitution, based on empirical data that the fixing of the age of superannuation of members of the ranks of Commandant and below in the ITBP, CRPF, BSF and SSB different from those in the ranks above that of the Commandant is not based on a rational criteria and that such differentiation has no nexus to the object sought to be achieved. Also, the expert body that was required to examine the matter and make its recommendations, i.e. the CPC, by a majority of 2:1 favoured the enhancement of the retirement age. The concerned CAPFs themselves i.e. the BSF, CRPF, ITBP and SSB have also favoured the removal of the discrimination. The following test laid down by the Supreme Court in Air India v. Nergesh Meerza (supra) stands fully satisfied in the present case:

*"There **can be no cut and dried formula for fixing age of retirement. It is to be decided by the authorities concerned after taking into consideration various factors such as the nature of the work, the prevailing conditions, the practice prevalent in other establishments and the like. But the factors to be considered must be relevant and should bear a close nexus to the nature of the organisation and the duties of the employees. So where the authority concerned takes into***

account factors or circumstances which are inherently irrational or illogical or tainted, the decision fixing the age of retirement is open to serious scrutiny." (emphasis supplied)

60. There appears to be no justification whatsoever put forth by the Respondents in discriminating amongst the CAPFs particularly when the retirement age of all members of the CISF and AR is 60 years and whereas the retirement age of those of the rank of Commandant and below in BSF, CRPF, SSB and ITBP is 57 years. The above classification has no rational nexus to the object sought to be achieved, which is keeping high the morale of the CAPFs, who are performing yeoman service and supplementing the efforts of the armed forces and the police throughout the country. The CAPFs have become an indispensable part of the security apparatus in the country. It is difficult to think that the Government whether at the Centre or at the States would be able to combat the serious challenges of safety and security and of its people without the participation and the sacrifices made by members of the CAPFs. Their morale definitely needs to be preserved. Discrimination in the matter of the age of retirement amongst members of two wings of the CAPFs will contribute to lowering the morale rather than bolstering it. Accordingly, it is held that Rule 43 (a) of the CRPF Rules which presently states that "Retirement of member of the Force shall take effect from the afternoon of the last day of the month in which such member attains the age of 57 years" is held to be discriminatory and violative of Article 14 of the Constitution vis-à-vis members of the CRPF of the rank of Commandant and below. The OM dated 1st April 2013 issued by the MHA rejecting the plea of the Petitioners is hereby quashed.

61. In the present petitions, while the primary challenge is to Rule 43 (a) of the CRPF Rules, the corresponding challenge is in effect to separate rules applicable to each of the three CAPFs in question i.e. the CRPF, the BSF, and the ITBP. To recapitulate, Rule 14 of the CRPF Group (A) General Duty Officers Recruitment Rules, 2001 stipulates that officers holding post higher than the rank of

Commandants shall retire from service "on the afternoon of the day of the month in which they attained the age of 60 years and officers of other ranks shall retire from the service on the afternoon of the last day of the month in which they attained the age of 57 years." Rule 8 (a) of the ITBP General Duty in Group „A" Posts Rules stipulates that officers holding the rank of Deputy Inspector General (General Duty) (DIG), Inspector General Duty and Inspector General Duty shall retire when they attained the age of 60 years. For officers holding the rank of AC, DC, Second-in-command and Commandant the age of retirement is 57 years. Likewise Rule 12 of the BSF (General Duty Officers) Recruitment Rules, 2001 stipulates that officers of the BSF holding post higher than the rank of Commandant shall retire when they attained the age of 60 years and officers of other ranks will retire from service when they attained the age of 57 years.

62. In view of the above conclusion of this Court that Rule 43 (a) of the CRPF Rules, 1955 as it presently stands is unconstitutional and liable to be struck down, correspondingly Rule 14 of the CRPF Group (A) General Duty Officers Recruitment Rules, 2001, Rule 8 (a) of the ITBP General Duty in Group A Posts Rules and Rule 12 of the BSF (General Duty Officers) Recruitment Rules, 2001 to that extent are also held to be unconstitutional and liable to be struck down."

18. Ministry of Home Affairs (MHA) issued Order No. F.N.45020/1/2019/Legal-I dated 19.8.2019 in compliance to Judgment & Order dated 31.1.2019 in WP(C) No. 1951/2012 in the matter of Dev Sharma, Dy. Comdt. of ITBP Vs UOI & Anr. and Order dated 04.02.2019 in WP(C) No.695/2019 in the matter of Ram Chander Kasania & Anr Vs UOI &Ors of High Court of Delhi. In the MHA Order dated 19.8.2019, it has been conveyed that the Competent Authority has decided age of retirement irrespective of rank in CRPF, BSF,ITBP,SSB , CISF& AR to be 60 years. It was also directed that the Forces may amend provisions of Rules as applicable.

19. Coverage under Central Civil Services (Pension) Rules in place of National Pension System, of those Central Government

employees who were recruited against the posts/vacancies advertised /notified for recruitment, on or before 22.12.2003:

19.1 The High Court of Delhi vide Judgment dated 9.4.2019 in W.P. (C) 1358/2017in the matter of Shyam Kumar Choudhary & Ors. vs. Union of India & Ors. held as under:

"1. This petition has been filed by 14 Petitioners all of whom are Assistant Commandants in the Central Reserve Police Force ('CRPF'). All of them applied pursuant to the notification dated 10th - 16th May, 2003 which was advertised by the UPSC and qualified in the Central Police Forces (Assistant Commandant) Examination, 2003. On the date of the advertisement, the Old Pension Scheme under the CCS (Pension) Rules, 1972 was applicable.

2. The new Contributory Pension Scheme was introduced by a notification dated 22nd December, 2003 and implemented with effect from 1st January, 2004. By a notification dated 22nd December 2003, it was stated that the new scheme would not be applicable to Armed Forces and that they would be governed by the Old Pension Scheme. It is further pointed out that the Ministry of Home Affairs ('MHA') by a communication dated 6th August, 2004, clarified that the CRPF was an Armed Force of the Union of India under the administrative control of the MHA. It is accordingly contended that the Petitioners were entitled to the Old Pension Scheme.

3. The Petitioners relied on the decision dated 12th February, 2015 of this Court in W.P. (C) No. 3834 / 2013 (Parmanand Yadav v. Union of India) wherein, in relation to the BSF, it was held that those who had participated in the examination of 2003, would be covered by the Old Pension Scheme, even if they had been offered letters of appointment only after 1st January, 2004. When the representations made by the Petitioners, that the old pension scheme should be extended to them was rejected, the present petition was filed.

4. Pursuant to the notice issued in the present petition, the Respondents have filed their counter affidavit and an additional affidavit.

5. The issue is no longer res integra. In the case of certain constables of the BSF, this Court by its judgment dated 12th February, 2019 in Tanka Ram v. Union of India 2019 (174) DRJ 146 (DB) allowed the prayer of those Petitioners and permitted them to avail of the benefit of the Old Pension Scheme. It was held that the option to continue the Old Pension Scheme should be extended to all those who had been selected in the examination conducted in 2003, but were issued call letters in only in January or February, 2004. 6. In the present case also, the reason the Petitioners not joining prior to 1st January, 2004 is entirely due to the Respondents. The Petitioners cannot bedeprived of the benefit of the Old Pension Scheme, as they qualified even prior to the notification of the New Pension Scheme.

7. For the above reasons, the petition is allowed........................".

19.2   Union of India filed Special Leave Petition bearing no. 31539/2019 in Supreme Court against the Judgment dated 9.4.2019 of the High Court of Delhi in W.P. (C) 1358/2017 which was dismissed by Supreme Court vide Order dated 27.9.2019. The Union of India thereafter chose to file a Review Petition bearing no.2188/2020 before the Supreme Court in the abovementioned matter and the Review petition was also dismissed on merits Vide Order dated 24.11.2020.

19.3   The High Court of Delhi vide Judgment dated 9.4.2019 in W.P. (C) 8208/2020 in the matter of M.R. Gurjar and Ors. Vs. Union of India & Ors. and other connected tagged matters held as under:

1. These Petitions have been filed by Petitioners who are Personnel Below Officer Rank (PBOR) in the Central Reserve Police Force (CRPF), Border Security Force (BSF), Sashastra Seema Bal (SSB) and Indo-Tibetan Border Police (ITBP). All the petitioners applied pursuant to the notification dated September 2003 and June 2003 for the post of Constable/GD in Central Armed Police Forces and Sub-Inspectors through Staff Selection Commission and qualified in the said examination of 2003. On the basis of the advertisement, the Old Pension Scheme under the CCS (Pension) Rules, 1972 was applicable.

The New Contributory Pension Scheme was introduced by a notification dated 22nd December, 2003 and implemented with effect from 1st January, 2004.

2. Learned counsel for the petitioners state that by a notification dated 22nd December 2003, it was stipulated that the new scheme would not be applicable to Armed Forces and that they would be governed by the Old Pension Scheme. They point out that the Ministry of Home Affairs ('MHA') by a communication dated 6th August, 2004, has clarified that the CRPF and ITBP is an Armed Force of the Union of India under the administrative control of the MHA and that even the Section 3(i) of the CRPF Act and Section 4 (i) of the ITBP Act clearly provides that there shall continue to be an Armed Force maintained by the Central Government and called the 'CRPF', 'BSF', 'SSB' and 'ITBP'.

3. They submit that even Article 246 read with List I Entry II of the Seventh Schedule of the Constitution of India clearly envisages Armed Forces of Union of India and includes Naval, Military and Air Force, any other Armed Force of the Union. They further submit that the Apex Court in the case of Akhilesh Prasad v Union Territory of Mizoram; 1981 (2) SCC 150, has categorically held that the sub-section itself declares in no uncertain terms that CRPF is an Armed Force of the Central Government which is the same thing as saying that it is a part of the Armed Force of the Union and that being the position, even as per the notification dated 22nd December, 2003, the scheme of New Pension Scheme has been excluded from the Armed Forces of the Union.

4. They also contend that batchmates of most of the petitioners have been given benefit of Old Pension Scheme under various judgements passed by this Court in Patil Gopal Babulal &Ors. vs. Union of India &Ors., W.P.(C) 11646/2018; Tanaka Ram &Ors. vs. Union of India & Ors., 2019 (174) DRJ 146 (DB); Shyam Kumar Choudhary and Ors. vs. Union of India being W.P.(C) No.1358 of 2017 and Niraj Kumar Singh & Ors. vs. Union of India & Ors.,W.P.(C) No.13129/2019.

5. *Pursuant to the notice issued in the present petitions, the Respondents despite having been given adequate time, have not filed reply in most of the matters till date. On behalf of the Respondents, further time has been sought for the purpose of filing Counter Affidavit. It is urged that because of the large number of petitioners, their factual details could not be verified and a last opportunity be given to them. Learned counsel for the respondents submit that without their counter-affidavits being on record, they will be handicapped in approaching the Supreme Court because they will not be able to give the mandatory undertaking that the facts stated therein were part of records before this Court.*

6. *However, in the counter affidavit filed in W.P.(C) 12083/2019 it is stated that admittedly since the entire recruitment process was initiated in the year 2004 and the appointment letters were issued between the months of June – July 2004, the New Pension Scheme would be applicable and the petitioners would therefore not be entitled to the Old Pension Scheme. It is further urged on behalf of Respondents that in W.P.(C) No. 5075/2020, the chart mentioned in the petition shows that the Written Examinations were itself held on different dates of January 2004 and therefore, the Petitioners cannot legally exercise lien over a post from the date of advertisement i.e. from a date even prior to the Written Examination.*

7. *Learned counsel for respondents submit that none of the earlier judgements including Patil Gopal Babulal & Ors. vs. Union of India & Ors., W.P.(C) 11646/2018 and Tanaka Ram &Ors. vs. Union of India &Ors., 2019 (174) DRJ 146 (DB) are applicable to the present case inasmuch as in those cases the recruitment process had started in the year 2003 and some of the incumbents had been issued appointment letters in the year 2003 itself before the New Pension Scheme was made effective from 01 st January, 2004. Therefore, according to them, on facts, the present batch of matters is different and the petitioners in the present case are not entitled to any relief as prayed for.*

8. The issue in the present batch of matters is no longer res integra. Consequently, the request for additional time to file counter-affidavit is declined.

9. In the case of certain constables of the BSF, this Court by its judgment dated 12th February, 2019 in Tanaka Ram (supra) allowed the prayer of those Petitioners and permitted them to avail of the benefit of the Old Pension Scheme. It was held that the option to continue the Old Pension Scheme should be extended to all those who had been selected in the examination conducted in 2003, but were issued call letters only in January or February, 2004. It is also pertinent to mention that the Respondents aggrieved by the said judgment filed an SLP bearing No. 25228/2019 before the Apex Court. The said SLP has been dismissed by the Supreme Court vide order dated 02nd September, 2019. 10. This Court in Shyam Kumar Choudhary and Ors. vs. Union of India being W.P.(C) No.1358 of 2017 allowed similar petitions vide judgment dated 09th April, 2019 against which the Respondents had again filed SLP bearing no. 31539/2019 which was again dismissed on 27th September, 2019. The Respondents thereafter chose to file a review petition bearing no.2188/2020 before the Apex Court in the said matter and the said Review petition was also dismissed on merits vide order dated 24th November, 2020.

11. Following the judgment of Shyam Kumar Choudhary (supra), the learned predecessor Division Bench in Niraj Kumar Singh &Ors. vs. Union of India &Ors.,W.P.(C) No.13129/2019 granted similar benefit to 17 petitioners who had applied to the post of Sub-Inspector in Central Police Organisations pursuant to an advertisement dated 21st June, 2003 even when the written examination and physical efficiency test were held in November, 2003, medical examination was held in January-February, 2004 and final result was declared in May, 2004. The said 17 petitioners were issued offer of appointment on 02nd June, 2005 and on accepting the same, the appointment letter was issued on 14th July, 2005 for joining the Sashastra Seema Bal.

12. Another Coordinate Bench vide judgment dated 06th November, 2020 in W.P.(C) No. 6548 of 2020 as well 6989/2020 was pleased to allow the said petitions for grant of Old Pension Scheme by following the judgment in Shyam Kumar Choudhary (supra).

13. Having regard to the fact that in the present batch of cases also the advertisement/notification was issued in September, 2003 and June, 2003 i.e. prior to coming into force of the present contributory pension scheme on 22nd December, 2003, this Court is of the view that petitioners cannot be deprived of the benefit of the Old Pension Scheme.

14. This is more so when the batchmates of the petitioners are getting this benefit under various judgements passed by this Court.

15. For the above reasons, the petitions are allowed......................"

20. EFFECT OF NOT HAVING UNDERGONE PRE-PROMOTIONAL COURSE DUE TO NON-DETAILMENT BY THE DEPARTMENT

20.1 The High Court of Delhi vide Judgment dated 25.07.2024 in W.P.(C) 10174/2024 in the matter of Tribhuwan Pratap Singh and Ors vs UOI And Ors held as under:

"Learned counsel for the petitioner submits that the only grievance of the petitioners is that the benefit of NFFU has been extended to the petitioners from 01.01.2020/01.012021 as against their eligibility in the year 2016 itself. This he submits on account of the premise that the petitioners had qualified the Junior Commander Management (JCM) (Pre Promotional Course) Course only in the year 2019. He submits that while taking the said decision, the respondents have failed to appreciate that the petitioners were never detailed for the JCMC (Pre Promotional Course) Course any time prior to December 2019 and therefore, they cannot be faulted for not having qualified the JCMC (Pre Promotional Course) Course from August 2016- 2019. He submits that this issue is no longer res integra that in a case where the

employees are for administrative reasons not detailed in the JCMC (Pre Promotional Course) Course, they cannot be deprived of promotion on the ground that they had not qualified in the JCMC (Pre Promotional Course) Course.

He therefore submits that the petitioners are entitled to the benefit of NFFU from the due date and not merely after they had qualified the JCMC (Pre Promotional Course) Course.

Issue notice. Mr. Mayank Sharma, learned counsel accepts notice on behalf of the respondents and does not deny that the issue has been settled in favour of the petitioners by way of number of decisions passed by this Court. He however submits that it is still required to be ascertained whether the petitioners were not detailed for the JCMC (Pre Promotional Course) Course prior to December 2019.

In the light of this stand taken by the respondents, we are of the view that the writ petition deserves to be allowed by directing the respondent to examine the service record of the petitioners. In case, it is found that they were never detailed for the JCMC (Pre Promotional Course) Course, the respondent will extend the benefit of NFFU to them from the due date i.e., the date when they completed the eligibility period. However, in the event if it is found that the petitioners were detailed for the JCMC (Pre Promotional Course) Course and either could not qualify or did not undergo the same due to personal reasons, no benefit from the due date in terms of this Court's order will be extended to the petitioners."

20.2 The High Court of Delhi vide Judgment dated 11.10.2013 in W.P.(C) 6550/2013 in the matter of Suraj Bhan and Ors Vs. UOI And Ors. held as under:

"11. This very contention is urged before us just as in the present case the petitioner Hargovind Singh also did not get an opportunity to undergo the PCC course on the date he became eligible for grant of further financial up-gradation which was withdrawn. On this aspect in Hargovind Singh (supra) the Court has ruled on the respondent's

contention urged before us as well, and commented upon the responsibility of the department to detail the person for undertaking the promotional course. In this regard observations made in Para 8 to 14 of the judgment are being relied upon which reads as under:

"8..

12. It is an admitted position that the department has to detail persons for undertaking the promotion cadre course and attending said courses is not at the option of the officers concerned.

13. If that be so, the respondents cannot take advantage of not discharging their obligation which precedes the obligation of the incumbent to clear the promotion cadre course. The prior obligation of the department is to detail the person concerned to undertake the promotion cadre course."

....

16. Admittedly it is the responsibility of the respondents to detail the individual for the pre promotional cadre course. Having not done so the respondents cannot be allowed to withhold the benefits entitled to an individual for their own faults."

20.3 The Supreme Court vide Judgment dated 22.8.2022 in Special Leave Petition (Civil) No. 16442 of 2021 in the matter of Union of India and Others Vs. Ex. HC/GD Virender Singh held as under:

"2. These appeals by way of special leave raise three issues, all of which are connected and relate to the Modified Assured Career Progression Scheme, namely:

"(a) Whether the MACP Scheme is applicable and to be implemented with effect from 1st January 2006, the date from which the Central Civil Service (Revised Pay) Rules, 2008 were enforced, or in terms of O.M. dated 19th May 2009 with effect from 1st September 2008?

(b) Whether under the MACP Scheme the respondents are entitled to financial upgradation equivalent to the pay scale/grade pay of the next

promotional post in the hierarchy, or the immediate next grade pay in the hierarchy of the pay bands as stated in Section 1, Part A of the First Schedule to the Central Civil Services (Revised Pay) Rules, 2008?

(c) Whether the respondents, who belong to the Central Armed Police Forces, are entitled to grant of financial upgradation under the MACP Scheme, if for administrative reasons they were unable to fulfil the pre-promotional norms?

....

10. Learned counsel for the government employees, inspite of being correct that M.V. Mohanan Nair (supra) does not refer to Balbir Singh Turn (supra) and does not overrule it specifically, misses the point that the entire ratio and reasoning given in M.V. Mohanan Nair (supra), as rightly observed in R.K. Sharma (supra), cannot be reconciled with the ratio in Balbir Singh Turn (supra). M.V. Mohanan Nair (supra) has examined the MACP Scheme in depth and detail to settle the controversy, inter alia holding that supersession of the ACP Scheme by the MACP Scheme is a matter of government policy, and that "after accepting the recommendation of the Sixth Central Pay Commission, the ACP Scheme was withdrawn and the same was superseded by the MACP Scheme with effect from 1.9.2008. The ACP Scheme and MACP Schemes were held to be in the nature of incentive schemes to relieve stagnation and not as a part of pay structure, which had revised the pay and the dearness allowance with effect from 1.1.2006. In these circumstances, we do not think a case for reference to a larger Bench of three Judges to reconsider the ratio in the decision of R.K. Sharma (supra) is made out. Therefore, we reject the contention of the learned counsel for the respondents/government employees for reference of the matter.

11. On the third aspect, we should record the concession rightly made by the Additional Solicitor General during the course of the hearing that the personnel working in the Central Armed Forces would be granted financial benefit under the MACP Scheme on completion of prescribed years of regular service by relaxation in cases where, on account of administrative or other reasons, they could not be sent for participation in pre-promotional course. The appellant-Union of India has agreed to accept the directions given by the Delhi High Court in the case of Ram Avtar Sharma v. Director General of Border Security Force9 in this regard. A liberal, pragmatic and ameliorative approach is required to succour genuine grievances of the personnel doing duty for the nation, owing to which they forgo participation in pre-promotional courses. Accordingly, the third question is answered against the appellant-Union of India.

12. In view of the aforesaid discussion, the appeals filed by the Union of India are partly allowed and impugned judgments, to the extent they hold that the MACP Scheme applies with effect from 1.1.2006 and that under the MACP Scheme the employees are entitled to financial upgradation equivalent to the next promotional post, are set aside. MACP Scheme is applicable with effect from 1.9.2008 and as per the MACP Scheme, the entitlement is to financial upgradation equivalent to the immediate next grade pay in the hierarchy of the pay bands as stated in Section 1, Part A of the First Schedule to the Central Civil Services (Revised Pay) Rules, 2008. The third issue, which relates to the fulfilment of pre-promotional norms for grant of financial upgradation, is decided against the appellant-Union of India to the extent that this would not be insisted in the case of the Central Armed Forces personnel where, for administrative or other reasons, they could not be sent or undergo the pre-promotional course."

21. **Legal Protection available to Members of Force are as under:**

a. Section 45 of Cr PC: Protection of Members of the Armed Forces from arrest (Section 42, BNSS, 2023)

b. Section 197 of Cr PC: Prosecution of Judges and Public Servants (Section 218, BNSS, 2023)

c. Section 17 of CRPF Act, 1949: Protection for acts of Members of the Force

d. Section 132 of Cr PC: Protection against Prosecution for acts done under Sections 129, 130 and 131 relating to dispersal of unlawful assembly (Section 151 BNSS, 2023)

e. Section 6 of Armed Forces Special Powers Act, 1958: Against Prosecution for acts under the Act

f. Section 76 of Indian Penal Code: General Exceptions-Act done by a person bound, or by mistake of fact believing himself bound by law (Section 14 BNS, 2023)

The aforesaid protection has further been incorporated in the three new Laws viz., the Bharatiya Nyaya Sanhita, 2023, Bharatiya Nagarik Suraksha Sanhita, 2023 and Bharatiya Sakshya Adhiniyam, 2023.

22. Ministry of Home Affairs, Govt. of India vide Gazette Notification dated 27.7.1976 in exercise of the powers conferred by Sub- Section (1) of Section 16 of the Central Reserve Police Force Act, 1949(66 of 1949) and in supersession of the Notification of the Ministry of Home Affairs No.10/127/57-P.II dated 22nd April, 1958 directed as under:

"(1) That the powers conferred and duties imposed on a Police Officer by Sections 41(1), 46,47,49, 51(1), 52, 74, 102, 149, 150, 151 and 152 of the Code of Criminal Procedure 1973(2 of 1974), or in the State of Jammu and Kashmir by the corresponding Sections of the Code of Criminal Procedure, 1889, shall be powers and duties, respectively of every Member of the Central Reserve Police Force; and

(2) That the powers conferred and duties imposed on a Police Officer by Section 53, 100 and 129 of the Code of Criminal Procedure 1973(2 of 1974), and in the State of Jammu and Kashmir by the corresponding Sections of the Jammu and Kashmir Code of Criminal Procedure, 1889, shall be the powers and duties, respectively of every Member of and above the rank of Sub-Inspector of the Central Reserve Police Force."

23. Powers to NCOs and above under Armed Forces (Special Powers) Act, 1958

"Section 4: Any commissioned officer, warrant officer, non-commissioned officer or any other person of equivalent rank in the armed forces may, in a disturbed area-

(a) if he is of opinion that it is necessary so to do for the maintenance of public order, after giving such due warning as he may consider necessary, fire upon or otherwise use force, even to the causing of death, against any person who is acting in contravention of any law or order for the time being in force in the disturbed area prohibiting the assembly of five or more persons or the carrying of weapons or of things capable of being used as weapons or of fire-arms, ammunition or explosive substances;

(b) if he is of opinion that it is necessary so to do, destroy any arms dump, prepared or fortified position or shelter from which armed attacks are made or are likely to be made or are attempted to be made, or any structure used as training camp for armed volunteers or utilised as a hide-out by armed gangs or absconders wanted for any offence;

(c) arrest, without warrant, any person who has committed a cognizable offence or against whom a reasonable suspicion exists that he has committed or is about to commit a cognizable offence and may use such force as may be necessary to effect the arrest;

(d) enter and search without warrant any premises to make any such arrest as aforesaid or to recover any person believed to be wrongfully restrained or confined or any property reasonably suspected to be stolen property or any arms, ammunition or explosive substances believed to be unlawfully kept in such premises, and may for that purpose use such force as may be necessary.

Section 5. Arrested persons to be made over to the police: Any person arrested and taken into custody under this Act shall be made over to the officer in charge of the nearest police station with the least possible delay, together with a report of the circumstances occasioning the arrest".

CHAPTER-II

CENTRAL RESERVE POLICE FORCE- LAW INCLUDING LEADING CASE LAWS

1. Constitutionality and *vires* of the CRPF Act, 1949

1.1 The single Judge Bench of the Calcutta High Court vide Judgment dated 18.4.1972 in the matter of Tarun Kumar Sengupta vs Union of India AndAnr. [AIR1973CAL56, AIR 1973 CALCUTTA 56] held as under:

"1. Two questions are involved in this application under Article 226 of the Constitution namely,--

(i) whether the Central Reserve Police Force Act, 1949 is valid law and

(ii) whether the petitioner has any locus standi to maintain this application. The Central Reserve Police Force Act, 1949 was enacted by the Constituent Assembly by virtue of Section 8 (1) of the Indian Independence Act, 1947. Under Sub-section (2) of Section 8 of the said Act, the Constituent Assembly while exercising the powers of legislation had only the powers that the Federal Legislature had under the Government of India Act, 1935. Under Article 372 of the Constitution all laws in force prior to the Constitution would continue until repealed or altered by competent authority. Therefore, in order to be law in force, the said law must have been valid law when it was enacted. The main question, therefore, that requires consideration is whether the Federal Legislature had the powers under the Government of India Act, 1935 to enact the Central Reserve Police Force Act, 1949.

....

(vii) It should be observed that the essential functions and duties of the Police Officers under the Police Act as well as the members of the Central Reserve Police Force under the Central Reserve Police Act 1949 are identical, namely, (i) to obey and execute all orders and warrants lawfully issued to them by any competent authority, (ii) to detect and bring offenders to justice, (iii) to apprehend all persons whom they are legally authorised to apprehend and for whose apprehension sufficient grounds exist. All these duties arc essential duties for the detection and prevention of crimes and maintenance of public law and order. As mentioned, hereinbefore, the Central Reserve Police Force Act, 1949 also authorised the Central Government to confer all the powers of the Police Officers of any Grade on the members of the Central Reserve Force. It appears to me that in pith and in substance, the Central Reserve Police Force Act, 1949 was an Act dealing with the subject of Police. The aim, object and purpose of the said Act were to create a body of men for performance of the functions which are performable by the members of the Police. The only difference is that all the members of the Central Reserve Police Force are armed and the various sections of the Act authorised and imposed a strict military discipline for the members of the Central Reserve Police Force. But the object for their creation appears to be the performance of the functions perform-able by the police in a more efficient manner. Police, as mentioned, hereinbefore, was a Provincial subject under the Government of India Act, 1935. It has been held and, with respect in my opinion rightly, in the case of Pooran v. U. P. State, that the word "police" was wide enough to empower the State Legislature to create an armed constabulary.

11. It has to be emphasised that the question might have been different if the impugned legislation had been passed by the Parliament under the Constitution of India. It has to be remembered that the Article 248 of the Constitution gives the residuary powers of the Constitution (sic) is significantly differently worded from the Section 104 of the

Government of India Act, 1935 which dealt with the residuary powers of legislation. My attention was not drawn to any notification empowering the Federal Legislature in terms of the Section 104 of the Government of India Act, 1935 to enact the impugned legislation. It has to be noted, further, that Entry 97 of the List I of the Constitution of India deals with the residuary powers of the Parliament There was no such corresponding entry in the Government of India Act, 1935. It is therefore not necessary for me to consider the principles which the Supreme Court had occasion to consider in the case of Union of India v. Harbasan Singh Dhillon, . It is also necessary to point out that under the Constitution of India Entry I of List II of the 7th Schedule deals with the public order but excludes from the concept of public order the use of naval, military or armed force or any other armed force of the Union in aid of the civil powers. But in Entry I of List II of the Government of India Act, 1935 the concept of public order did not exclude the use of "any other armed force". In view of the fact that the Central Reserve Police Act, 1949 applies to the whole of India the question whether the impugned legislation was otherwise valid under Sub-section (4) of Section 100 of the Government of India Act 1935 does not fall for consideration.

....

16. For the reasons mentioned hereinbefore I must hold that the Central Reserve Police Force Act, 1949 was ultra vires the Government of India Act, 1935 and as such was not law in force within the meaning of Article 372 of the Constitution. The respondents are, therefore, directed to forbear from giving effect to the Central Reserve Police Force Act, 1949 in West Bengal, and further directed not to enforce the said Act in the State. Let writ in the nature of mandamus issue accordingly. The Rule is made absolute to the extent indicated above. There will be no order of the costs of this application. In view of the fact that this legislation has continued for a considerable length of time, I stay the operation of the order passed today for a period of twelve weeks to enable the respondents to take such steps as they may be advised."

1.2 Union of India and the State of West Bengal filed appeal against the above Judgment of Single Judge Bench of Calcutta High Court and the Division Bench of Calcutta High Court vide its Judgment dated 25.7.1972 in the matter of the State Of West Bengal And Anr. vs Tarun Kumar Sen Gupta AndAnr. [AIR 1974 CAL 39, AIR 1974 CALCUTTA 39] held as under:

"1. These are two appeals, one by the State of West Bengal and the other by the Union of India. The appeals are against the judgment and order of Mr. Justice Sabyasachi Mukharji dated the 18th April, 1972.

2. The learned Judge held that the Central Reserve Police Force Act, 1949, was ultra vires the Government of India Act, 1935, and as such was not law in force within the meaning of Article 372 of the Constitution. He, therefore, directed the two appellants the Governments or rather the Union of India and the State of West Bengal to forbear from giving effect to the Central Reserve Police Force Act, 1949, in West Bengal and further directed them not to enforce the said Act in the State. He issued a writ in the nature of mandamus accordingly and made the Rule absolute. It is against this judgment that the appeals have been filed. Although there are two separate appeals, they are from the same judgment and order. I, therefore, propose to deal with the questions in the appeals in one judgment.

..

4. The central question in both the appeals is whether the Central Reserve Police Force Act, 1949, is a valid law. The Act was passed by the Constituent Assembly by virtue of Section 8(1) of the Indian Independence Act, 1947. Under Sub-section (2) of Section 8 of the said Act, the Constituent Assembly while exercising the powers of legislation had only the powers that the Federal Legislature had under the Government of India Act, 1935. Under Article 372 of the Constitution, all existing laws in force prior to the Constitution were to continue until repealed, altered or amended by competent legislature or other competent authority. Therefore, in order to be law in force, the said law must have been a valid law validly passed when it was enacted. The core of the question, therefore, is whether the federal legislature had the powers under the Government of India Act, 1935, to enact the Central Reserve Police Force Act, 1949, There is a further Article in the Constitution, namely, Article 372-A of the Constitution which gives power to the President to adopt laws.

....

31. Having come to that conclusion, on the merits of the case, I shall examine whether on the technical interpretation of the Legislative Lists, the creation of such an armed force of the nature which I have described above is permissible under the Constitution or under the Government of India Act, 1935 for the Federal Legislature to pass such an Act. The Government of India Act, 1935, described the List I as the Federal Legislative List and used the following material expression in Item 1:

"His Majesty's naval, military and air forces borne on the Indian establishment and any other armed force raised in India by the Crown, not being forces raised for employment in Indian States or military or armed police maintained by Provincial Governments."

Apparently it did not include Armed Police maintained by the Provincial Government of the time. Apparently the Government of India was contemplating an Armed Force for the Indian Government. It cannot therefore be said that because Item 3 in the Legislative List II, State List, the word "Police" is used, it includes Armed and Unarmed Police and therefore it impinges on the State List Item 1 of List I should be harmonised with Item 3 of List II of the Government of India Act, 1935, in the Seventh Schedule. The intention obviously was not to interfere with the Armed Police maintained by the Provincial Government. Therefore, that an Armed Police was maintained by the Provincial Government was well known to the India Government. At the same time, the question of Armed Police being considered in connection with "any other Armed Force" would indicate that Armed Police will come within the meaning of "any other Armed Force". This is the essential raison detre and not merely the statement in the Objects and Reasons of the statute which I have quoted above. It is true that by India (Provisional Constitution) Order, 1947, a slight amendment was made in Entry 1 of List I in the Federal List, but it does not, in my opinion, affect the essential core of the meaning, because it still Used the words "The naval, military and air forces of the Dominion and any other armed forces raised or maintained by the Dominion". Besides the point is to be emphasised that this is not in replacement of the State Police, not in replacement of the Police Act of 1861 but in addition to and supplementary to the same in so far as their operation within the State is concerned. This construction of the Legislative Lists is in consonance with the residual powers of legislation with the Federal Legislature or with the Union Government in case it is held that it does not come under "any other armed force" within List I, Item 1, Seventh Schedule, of the Government of India Act, 1935. That is also the provision in Article 248 of the Constitution of India.

....

35. I hold, therefore, that the <u>Central Reserve Police Force Act, 1949</u>, was not ultra vires the <u>Government of India Act, 1935</u> and that it was a law validly in force within the meaning of <u>Article 372</u> of the Constitution. I hold further that there should be no writ in the nature of mandamus in these appeals.

36. In the result, I set aside the Judgment and order of the learned trial Judge, discharge the Rule and dismiss the petition. The appeals are allowed."

2. Entry 2A of List I of the Seventh schedule to the Constitution which deal with the subject matter of the *deployment of any armed force of the Union or any other force subject to the control of the Union or any contingent or unit thereof in any State in aid of the civil power; powers,*

jurisdiction, privileges and liabilities of the members of such forces while on such deployment, has been inserted by the Constitution (Forty-second Amendment) Act, 1976.

3. Entry 1 of List II of the Seventh Schedule to the Constitution dealing with the subject matter *of Public order (but not including [the use of any naval, military or air force or any other armed force of the Union or of any other force subject to the control of the Union or of any contingent or unit thereof] in aid of the civil power)* and Entry 2 dealing *with Police (including railway and village police) subject to the provisions of entry 2A of List I* were the result of Substitution by the Constitution (Forty-second Amendment) Act, 1976.

4. Judgments on Persons with Disabilities:

4.1 The Supreme Court in its Judgment dated 26.2.2015 in Civil Appeal Nos. 2466-2467 OF 2015 in the matter of Union of India & Ors. vs. Dileep Kumar Singh held as under:

....

2. These appeals raise an interesting question as to the interpretation of a proviso contained in Section 47 of the Persons with Disabilities (Equal Opportunities, Protection of Rights and Full Participation) Act, 1995 (in short the "1995 Act").

3. The facts giving rise to these appeals are as follows:-

On 1st January, 1998, the respondent was enlisted in the CRPF as Assistant Commandant. While on duty, on 19th October, 2001, he sustained grievous injuries in his spinal cord and legs while he was out on a visit checking night guards. Thereafter, he was provided with specialized treatment in various hospitals, but nothing worked and, ultimately, a medical board in its report dated 22nd July, 2004 categorized the respondent as PEE-5, i.e., a person who is permanently incapacitated and stated that he has 100% disability and recommended that he be relieved from service on medical grounds. On 27th October, 2004, a show cause notice was served on the respondent along with a copy of the report of the medical board with a direction to submit his representation, if any, against the proposed invalidation from service on medical grounds. Instead of representing against the show cause notice, the respondent filed writ petition No.30278/2004 challenging the said show cause notice. By an interim order passed on 19th January, 2005, the appellants were directed not to pass any order pursuant to the report given by the medical board against the respondent.

4. Pursuant to an order modifying the stay application, by an order dated 1st July, 2011, the respondent was relieved from service and given invalidation pension as admissible under Rule 38 of the CCS (Pension) Rules of 1972. The respondent filed a second writ petition No.42101 of 2011 challenging the aforesaid order.

5. By the impugned judgment dated 8th January, 2014, the Allahabad High Court held on a construction of Section 47 of the said Act that a Notification dated 10th September, 2002 issued under Section 47 insofar as the CRPF is concerned, (exempting the CRPF from the rigours of Section 47) would have to be read with reference to the field occupied by Section 47(2) only. Thus, the High Court made it clear that the exemption provision would apply only to promotion and not to continuing the respondent in service. As a consequence, the order dated 1st July, 2011, was set aside and the Union was directed to treat the petitioner in service and to adjust him against any suitable post or against a supernumerary post until a suitable post is available or until he attains the age of superannuation, whichever is earlier.

....

28. Apart from the plea of the disabled officers mentioned being vague, for no particulars are given as to the extent of their disability, the Union has made it clear that Standing Order No.7/99 will not apply and that since the job requirements demand a high level of fitness and ability CRPF is exempted from the provisions of Section 47 of the Act. Not only has this plea not been raised before the High Court, but the plea raised before us is lacking in particulars and has to be dismissed for this reason also.

....

30. The appeals are, therefore, allowed. The judgment of the Allahabad High Court is set aside."

4.2 The Supreme Court in in its Judgment dated 17.12.2021 in Civil Appeal No.6924 of 2021 in the matter of Ravinder Kumar Dhariwal & Anr. Vs. The Union of India & Ors. held as under:

"1. *The Division Bench of the Gauhati High Court* allowed an *appeal against the judgment of the Single Judge of the High Court in a petition under Article 226 of the Constitution challenging the disciplinary proceedings initiated against the appellant. The Single Judge had directed the State to consider the case of the petitioner in view of Section 47 of the Persons with Disabilities (Equal Opportunities, Protection of Rights and Full Participation) Act 1995 . Allowing the appeal against the order of the Single Judge, the Division Bench set aside the enquiry report and restored the proceedings to the stage of evidence. A Factual Background*

2. The appellant joined the Central Reserve Police Force2 in November 2001. In 2003, he was appointed as Assistant Commandant and served in the Darrang and Haflong Districts of Assam. Between the years 2005 to 2007, he served as Assistant Commandant in Chhattisgarh, and between 2007 to 2008, he served in Srinagar. Subsequently, he was transferred to Ajmer where he was serving till 2010. On 18 April 2010, while the appellant was serving in Ajmer, the Deputy Inspector General of Police3 lodged a complaint against him in the Alwar Gate police station alleging that the appellant had stated that he was obsessed with either killing or being killed and made a threat that he could shoot...

3. An enquiry was initiated against the appellant. A memorandum was issued on 8 July 2010 whereby the President proposed to hold an enquiry against the appellant under Rule 14 of the Central Civil Services (Classification, Control and Appeal) Rules 1965. Six charges were framed against him which were that he remained absent from morning marker, used unparliamentary language, appeared in television channels and other print media without the prior approval of the Department, did not give parade report, tried to intentionally cause an accident, and assaulted a Deputy Commandant. The appellant was placed under suspension with effect from 8 October 2010 with the declared headquarter. The departmental enquiry was completed, and the enquiry officer submitted the enquiry report dated 3 October 2013. Pursuant to the enquiry report, notice was issued to the appellant on 7 August 2015.

4. A second enquiry was initiated against the appellant through a memorandum dated 6 April 2011 on the charge that the petitioner without depositing the pistol and ammunition proceeded to Mukhed. The enquiry has been completed and the punishment of withholding two increments was awarded.

5. A third enquiry was initiated against the appellant. The memorandum was issued on 17 February 2015 on the charges that when the appellant was placed under suspension with the declared headquarter pursuant to the initiation of the first enquiry report, he remained absent without obtaining permission............................

...

Submissions of Counsel

13. Mr Rajiv Raheja, learned counsel appearing on behalf of the appellant, has made the following submissions:

(i) The appellant was continuously posted in areas where anti-insurgency operations were being conducted from 2003 to 2010. As a consequence, he developed mental health issues in 2008;

(ii) The appellant is diagnosed with OCD, secondary major depression, and bipolar affective disorder, which he developed during

service. Dr Ram Manohar Lohia Hospital categorized the appellant as having a permanent disability in the range of 40-70 percent;

(iii) The appellant started taking treatment from a psychiatrist in 2009-2010. He has taken treatments from Apollo Hospital Delhi, Rohtak Medical College, Government Hospital Chandigarh, Dr Ram Manohar Lohia Hospital Delhi, and Gauhati Medical College;

(iv) The events which led to the initiation of departmental enquiries took place between April 2010 and July 2012. An FIR was registered against the appellant at the behest of the DIGP under whom the appellant was serving in Ajmer. It was alleged in the complaint that the appellant's mental state is not sound, and he threatened to kill people and commit suicide. Instead of sending the appellant for medical treatment, the DIGP initiated criminal action against him. Thereafter, three enquiries were instituted against the appellant;

(v) The departmental enquiries were initiated against the appellant for acts committed by him after developing severe mental illnesses;

(vi) The first and third enquiries against the appellant are pending. The first enquiry has been restored to the stage of evidence by the High Court in the impugned judgment. The second enquiry is completed and the punishment of withholding two increments has been awarded to the appellant;

(vii) Section 18 (5) (b) and (d) of the Mental Healthcare Act 2017 mandates that persons with mental illness should be posted in their native places and where good treatment facilities are available. The appellant was being treated in Delhi in 2010 but was posted to Mudkhed in Maharashtra making it impossible for him to avail of medical care every fortnight or even every month. In October 2014, the appellant was first posted in Gauhati and thereafter in Silchar. These locations are far from his hometown and treatment centers;

(viii) The Composite Hospital, CRPF, Delhi admitted that the appellant has OCD and secondary major depression. Further, it

acknowledged that the appellant has taken various treatments and was subjected to anti-anxiety agents, anti-depressants, anti-psychotics, sedatives, hypnotics, psychotherapy, behavior therapy, and electroconvulsive therapy;

(ix) The appellant showed only partial response to the treatment and is still symptomatic. He was categorized as S-3 but was eventually classified as S-5 (permanent disability from the psychiatric side, 100 percent unfit) by the Medical Directorate of CRPF;

(x) On 14 April 2019, even the Court of Enquiry noted that the appellant has been diagnosed with OCD and secondary major depression. The appellant was directed to appear for review before medical officers;

(xi) The behavior report issued by DIG, GC, CRPF, Gauhati dated 9 January 2019 stated that no duty was assigned to the officer due to "mental disorder" and that the "officer caught mental disorder on duty". In another behavior report dated 27 January 2018, it was noted that the "officer has not been performing any duties since he is psychiatric patient". DIG, GC, CRPF, Silchar in the behavior report dated 5 January 2019 observed that the "officer lacks proper reasoning and in making proper conclusive opinion [sic]". Thus, while the CRPF concluded that the appellant has a severe mental illness, it still chose to proceed with departmental enquiries;

(xii) The appellant made several requests for being transferred to the place where he was undergoing treatment. The last such request was made on 16 March 2020;

(xiii) The principles of natural justice were not followed in the departmental enquiries. Further, it is unreasonable to expect a person undergoing severe mental health issues to lead evidence and defend himself;

(xiv) The appellant is entitled to the protection granted under Section 20 of the RPwD Act, which is pari materia to Section 47 of the PwD Act;

(xv) The exemption granted to CRPF from the application of provisions of Section 47 under the PwD Act in terms of the notification dated 10 September 2002 does not have any effect once the RPwD Act 2016 came into force; and

(xvi) The order of the Department of Personnel and Training dated 25 February 2015 nullifies the exemption granted to the CRPF by the 2002 notification.

14. Ms Madhavi Divan, the learned Additional Solicitor General appearing on behalf of the respondents, has urged that:

(i) The appellant was involved in various acts of misconduct during 2010 and 2011, for which three different departmental enquiries were initiated against him;

(ii) Both the pending departmental enquiries have been put on hold till the appellant's mental condition improves;

(iii) The appellant was transferred from time to time following the transfer policy. The good work done by the appellant in the past has no relevance to the specific charges of misconduct against him;

(iv) Exposure to insurgency does not result in the development of mental health issues. Innumerable officers are posted in such areas and are performing their duties;

v) The acts of misconduct were committed by the appellant when he was posted at a peaceful station in Ajmer. He was residing near his hometown and was availing of static/home posting. Rajasthan is his home state. If he had any grievance against a senior officer, he should have followed proper procedure for registering such a grievance;

(vi) The DIG, Ajmer CRPF was constrained to register an FIR against the appellant because there was an apprehension that the appellant will commit an untoward act;

(vii) The appellant did not produce himself before the medical officer of the force for treatment. There is no indication from the reports of medical officers that he has any mental ailment;

(viii) According to AMR reports dated 20 October 2008, 28 October 2009 and 26 June 2014, the appellant was placed in the medical category S-1 and was declared fit for duty. These reports do not indicate that the appellant has any mental illness;

(ix) The appellant actively participated in the first and second departmental enquiries which were conducted from 2010 to 2014. He cross-examined witnesses and submitted a defence. He never claimed that he had a mental health disorder. When the first departmental enquiry was completed by the Investigating Officer and the Union Public Service Commission advised that he be removed from service, the appellant claimed that he had mental illnesses to avoid the penalty;

(x) The Mental Healthcare Act was enacted in 2017, while the acts of misconduct relate to 2010 and 2011 when he was posted in Ajmer;

(xi) The appellant has been deployed in peaceful stations since 2014. He was posted in Gauhati from 2014 to 2018 and in Silchar from 2018 onwards. Adequate medical facilities are available in these areas. Family accommodation is also available;

(xii) The appellant was sent for Review Medical Examination in Composite Hospital, CRPF, Delhi where he was placed in the S-5 category on 31 August 2016. He was declared unfit for duty on account of being diagnosed with OCD and secondary depression. It was recommended that his service be invalidated. To avoid such invalidation, the appellant produced two medical certificates issued by Gauhati Medical College and Hospital, which declared him fit for any activity stating that he had no symptoms of a mental illness;

(xiii) The appellant has taken contradictory stands. In the first enquiry, he claimed that he had a mental illness to avoid a penalty but when he was declared unfit for duty, he claimed to be medically fit. It is clear that the ploy of mental illness is being used to mislead the department and the Court;

(xiv) On the order of the High Court dated 15 November 2018, a Review Medical Examination was conducted which placed the appellant in the medical category of S-3 because of OCD and secondary depression. At the time, the appellant was asymptomatic and was not on any medication. However, because he had a record of mental illness, he was placed under observation in medical category S-3 for 24 weeks. Thereafter, Review Medical Examinations were conducted from 23 December 2019 to 30 December 2019 in Composite Hospital, CRPF. The appellant was placed in medical category S-3 on 31 December 2019;

(xv) The appellant has been evading Review Medical Examinations because he is aware that if he is upgraded to the S-1 category, then the pending departmental enquiries will recommence and if he is downgraded to S-5 category, he will be boarded out of service;

(xvi) The Review Medical Examinations conducted from 20 January 2021 to 29 January 2021 place him in medical category S-2;

(xvii) The contention of the appellant that the exemption granted to the CRPF from the application of Section 47 of the PwD Act was overruled by order of Department of Personnel and Training dated 25 February 2015 is incorrect;

(xviii) After the enactment of the RPwD Act, a proposal was submitted to the Central Government to exempt the CRPF from the provisions of Section 20 of the RPwD Act. A notification to this effect was issued in 2021; and

(xix) According to the department standing orders, when CRPF personnel with mental illness are placed in medical category S-3 for a

maximum of 48 weeks and are not upgraded to S-2 within 48 weeks, they are downgraded to S-5 and declared permanently unfit for service. Under the rehabilitation policy relating to disabled force personnel, persons having a mental illness are immediately invalidated from service irrespective of their fitness at the time of recruitment. They cannot be retained or rehabilitated within the force since the job profile of the CRPF personnel involves handling firearms.

....

101. In light of Section 20(4) and the general guarantee of reasonable accommodation that accrues to persons with disabilities, the appellant is entitled to be reassigned to a suitable post having the same pay scale and benefits. The CRPF may choose to assign him a post taking into consideration his current mental health condition. The suitability of the post is to examined based on an individualised assessment of the reasonable accommodation that the appellant needs. The authorities can ensure that the post to which the appellant is accommodated does not entail handling or control over firearms or equipment which can pose a danger to himself or to others in or around the workplace.

....

106. In view of the discussion above, we summarise our findings below:

(i) The validity of the disciplinary proceedings shall be determined against the provisions of the RPwD Act 2016 instead of the PwD Act 1995 for the following reasons:

(a) The respondent holds a privilege under the 2002 notification to not comply with the principles of non-discrimination and reasonable accommodation provided under Section 47 of the PwD Act. However, for a privilege to accrue in terms of Section 6 of the GCA, mere expectation or hope is not sufficient. Rather, the privilege-holder must have done an act to avail of the right. The privilege provided by the 2002 notification would accrue only when one of the punishments provided under Section 47 has been imposed. However, in the instant

case, the disciplinary proceedings were challenged even before the punishment stage could be reached. Therefore, the privilege available to the respondent under the 2002 notification was not accrued in terms of Section 6 of the GCA;

(b) Section 47 of the PwD Act is not the sole source of the right of equality and non-discrimination held by persons with disability. The principle of non-discrimination guides the entire statute whose meaning and content find illumination in Article 5 of the CRPD. An interpretation that furthers international law or gives effect to international law must be preferred. Therefore, even though the PwD Act does not have an express provision laying down the principle of equality vis-à-vis disabled persons, it will have to be read into the statute; and

(c) The 2002 notification is not saved by Section 102 of the RPwD Act since Section 20 of the RPwD Act is not corresponding to Section 47 of the PwD Act;

(ii) The disciplinary proceedings are discriminatory and violative of the provisions of the RPwD for the following reasons:

(a) A person with a disability is entitled to protection under the RPwD Act as long as the disability was one of the factors for the discriminatory act; and

(b) The mental disability of a person need not be the sole cause of the misconduct that led to the initiation of the disciplinary proceeding. Any residual control that persons with mental disabilities have over their conduct merely diminishes the extent to which the disability contributed to the conduct. The mental disability impairs the ability of persons to comply with workplace standards in comparison to their able-bodied counterparts. Such persons suffer a disproportionate disadvantage due to the impairment and are more likely to be subjected to disciplinary proceedings. Thus, the initiation of disciplinary proceedings against persons with mental disabilities is a facet of indirect discrimination.

107. The disciplinary proceedings against the appellant relating to the first enquiry are set aside. The appellant is also entitled to the protection of Section 20(4) of the RPwD Act in the event he is found unsuitable for his current employment duty. While re-assigning the appellant to an alternate post, should it become necessary, his pay, emoluments and conditions of service must be protected. The authorities will be at liberty to ensure that the assignment to an alternate post does not involve the use of or control over fire-arms or equipment which may pose a danger to the appellant or others in or around the work-place."

5. In exercise of Power conferred under Section 16(2) of the CRPF Act, 1949, the Central Government may invest the Commandant or an Assistant Commandant with the powers of a Magistrate of any class for the purpose of inquiring into or trying any offence committed by a member of the force and punishable under the Act or any offence committed by a member of the force against the person or property of another member.

6. Departmental Proceedings: Inquiring Authority not to act as Presenting Officer – Enquiry Vitiated

6.1 The Supreme Court vide Judgment dated 2.7.2018 in Civil Appeal No. 2608 of 2012 in the matter of Union of India & Ors. Vs. Ram Lakhan Sharma and other connected matters held as under:

"These appeals have been filed by the Union of India questioning the judgments of the Gauhati High Court by which writ petitions filed by the respondents challenging their orders of removal were allowed by setting aside the removal/dismissal orders and the respondents were directed to be reinstated. The High Court had allowed the writ petitions filed by the respondents on more or less similar grounds, 2018 INSC 558 2 hence, it shall be sufficient to notice the facts and pleadings in detail in Civil Appeal No.2608 of 2012 for deciding this batch of appeals.

2. The respondent- Ram Lakhan Sharma was appointed as constable in the Central Reserve Police Force (hereinafter referred to as "CRPF") on 10.04.1991. On 23.10.1999 while he was posted as constable 11 Bn., CRPF at Agartala, Tripura he went out from Guard duty at 09.00 a.m. and returned back at 09.50 a.m. In the afternoon, an allegation was made by one lady Smt. Gita Paul making allegation of rape against the respondent and First Information Report was registered on 23.10.1999 at the Police Station under Section 376 IPC.

3. On 23.10.1999 the appellant was placed under suspension. On 04.12.1999 chargesheet was issued to the respondent containing articles of charges I and II. First charge was that the appellant remained absent without proper permission of competent authority with consent of his Guard Commander from his duty on 23.10.1999 from 0900 hrs. to 0930 hrs.

3. Second charge was that he while functioning as constable (Guard) has committed an act of misconduct in his capacity as a member of the force in that he tried to do sexual intercourse with a woman with mutual consent by giving money which amounts to indiscipline/moral turpitude.

4. The disciplinary authority appointed one Shri S.S. Bisht, Second-in-Command, 11 Bn CRPF as Inquiry Officer. The Inquiry Officer recorded the prosecution evidence. The Inquiry Report was submitted which was also supplied to the delinquent vide letter dated 07.02.2000 asking the respondent to submit reply within 15 days. The Commandant, 11 Bn passed an order on 19.03.2000 imposing penalty of removal from service w.e.f. 19.03.2000 under Section 11(1) of the Central Reserve Police Force Act, 1949 read with Rule 27 of the Central Reserve Police Force Rules, 1955.

5. On the basis of First Information Report registered against the respondent a chargesheet was submitted in the Court of Sessions Judge, Tripura, Agartala. Learned Sessions Judge after completing the trial on 20.09.2001 acquitted the respondent from 4 charges levelled against him. After acquittal from criminal case the respondent filed a

Writ Petition No.6778 of 2000 in the High Court of Allahabad challenging his order of removal. The High Court by order dated 20.05.2004 disposed of the writ petition giving liberty to the respondent to file an appeal under CRPF Rules, 1955 within two weeks. In pursuance of the order of the High Court an appeal was filed before D.I.G.P., CRPF, Patna. The Appellate Authority rejected the appeal by its order dated 22.07.2004 against which order a revision was filed before the Inspector General of Police, CRPF which too was rejected on 02.03.2005. Challenging the order of removal as well as orders passed in appeal and revision the respondent filed Writ Petition (C) No.14 of 2006. Learned Single Judge vide judgment dated 12.04.2010 allowed the writ petition by setting aside the removal order and directed for reinstatement of the respondent. The learned Single Judge also permitted the appellant to initiate the disciplinary inquiry afresh from the stage of appointing Presenting Officer. It was further directed that if the departmental proceeding is required to be started afresh, the respondent shall be placed under suspension and during the period of suspension, subsistence allowance should be paid. It was left to the wisdom of the authority to decide on arrear pay and allowances of the respondent.

6. Union of India filed an appeal against the judgment of the learned Single Judge being Writ Appeal No.25 of 2010. The Division Bench of the High Court by its judgment dated 10.01.2011 dismissed the writ appeal aggrieved by which order Civil Appeal No.2608 of 2012 has been filed by the Union of India.

7. The facts and pleadings in other civil appeals being more or less similar they need to be only briefly noted. Civil Appeal No.6745 of 2013

8. Union of India has filed this appeal challenging the judgment of the Division Bench dated 18.01.2013 by which Writ Appeal No.1 of 2013 filed by the Union of India questioning the judgment of the learned Single Judge was dismissed. The respondent, Shri T. Lupheng while posted at Manipur on 24.03.2008 sought 6 permission from his senior during his duty hours for going to the Bank to withdraw his salary. He was allowed to go and directed to report back to his duties. On his return he was found under the influence of alcohol. On 07.04.2008 the personnel was suspended. On four articles of charges inquiry was held. The Inquiry Officer recorded the evidence of prosecution. The inquiry was completed and report was submitted on 19.06.2008. The disciplinary authority vide its order dated 05.07.2008 awarded the punishment of dismissal from service. An appeal was filed which was dismissed by DIG, CRPF on 07.11.2008. The revision was also dismissed by IGP-C/S, CRPF on 05.06.2009. Writ Petition No.556 of 2009 was filed in the Gauhati High Court which was allowed by the learned Single Judge by judgment dated 04.08.2012. A writ appeal was filed by the Union of India which was dismissed by the Division Bench on 18.01.2013 against which this appeal has been filed. Civil Appeal Nos.9373-74 of 2013

9. These appeals have been filed by the Union of India against the Division Bench judgment dated 24.08.2012 by which the appeal filed by the Union of India questioning the judgment dated 08.02.2012 has been dismissed. The respondent was serving as constable in F/27 Bn CRPF. It was alleged that on 13.04.2000 he left lines without seeking prior permission, consumed liquor and created nuisance in the market. The chargesheet was issued to the respondent containing two articles of charges. The Inquiry Officer was appointed. Inquiry Officer recorded the statement of 12 prosecution witnesses. By an order dated 30.08.2000 the respondent was dismissed from services. There were two other delinquents apart from the respondent who were proceeded with and dismissed by the common order. Learned Single Judge relying on an order of the High Court in Writ Petition (C) No.297 of 2002 (Sri Mutum Shanti Kumar Singh vs. Union of India) on 08.02.2012 set aside the order of the dismissal and directed reinstatement of the respondent. Union of India filed Writ Appeal No.32 of 2012 challenging the order of Learned Single Judge before the Gauhati High Court. The Division Bench of the High Court by order dated 24.08.2012 dismissed the writ appeal. Review petition was filed by the Union of India which too was dismissed on 18.01.2013. Consequently, these appeals have been filed by the Union of India.

10. This appeal has been filed by the Union of India against the Division Bench judgment of the High Court dated 29.05.2013 by which writ petition filed by the respondent challenging the disciplinary proceedings for dismissal of the respondent was allowed. The respondent while serving at Chothegaon, Bishnupur (Manipur) on 12.03.2007 deserted from line without permission of competent authority. Subsequently, an FIR was lodged on 12.03.2007. A warrant was issued to apprehend him on 29.07.2007 but he could not be apprehended. A Court of Inquiry was conducted and the respondent was declared "DESERTER" w.e.f. 12.03.2007 vide order dated 13.07.2007. A Departmental proceeding was initiated with articles of charges on 12.11.2007. Since, the respondent had not reported in the Unit, the inquiry proceeded ex parte. Charges levelled against the respondent were found proved. An order dated 20.05.2008 was passed awarding dismissal from service to the respondent. Thereafter, he submitted appeal before DIG, CRPF. A writ petition was filed by the respondent. The writ petition was disposed of on 29.05.2013 setting aside the dismissal order and directing for reinstatement. The appeal has been filed against the above said judgment.

11. The Gauhati High Court had allowed the writ petition filed by the respondents on the ground that in the disciplinary inquiry the principles of natural justice were violated. The High Court found that no Presenting Officer was appointed and the Inquiry Officer acted as prosecutor which violates the principles of natural justice and the entire inquiry was set aside on the aforesaid ground with liberty to the respondent to hold afresh inquiry from the stage of appointing of the Presenting Officer.

12. All the appeals filed by the Union of India raises almost similar question of law and facts and the learned counsel for the Union of India has also raised common submission in all the appeals.

13. Learned counsel for the appellant, Shri Vikramjit Banerjee, Addl. Solicitor General contends that the High Court committed error in setting aside the dismissal order on the ground of non-appointment of Presenting Officer. It is submitted that Rule 27 of CRPF Rules, 1955 which provides for holding of disciplinary inquiry does not provide for appointment of Presenting Officer. The appellants have followed the requirement of Rule 27 in holding disciplinary inquiry in consonance with principles of natural justice, hence, there was no occasion to set aside the dismissal order. It is submitted that the respondents were given full opportunity in the disciplinary inquiry including serving chargesheet, giving opportunity to cross-examine the witnesses, opportunity to lead evidence and submit a reply to the Inquiry Report.

14. Learned counsel for the appellant submits that Rule 27 does not mandate the appointment of Presenting Officer to hold disciplinary inquiry. It is further submitted that even if it is assumed that while non-appointment of Presenting Officer, principles of natural justice have been violated, respondents have to show what prejudice has been caused due to non-appointment of the Presenting Officer in the department enquiry. No prejudice having been caused to any of the respondents, they were not entitled for grant of relief as has been granted by the High Court.

15. Learned counsel appearing for the respondents refuting the above submissions contends that the High Court has rightly set aside the dismissal/removal orders of the respondents. In the facts and circumstances of the present case, appointment of Presenting Officer was necessary to ensure compliance of principles of natural justice which having not been done the respondents have been seriously prejudiced. It is submitted that Inquiry Officer himself acted as prosecutor by putting questions to the prosecution witnesses. Inquiry Officer having become prosecutor with entire approach towards inquiry was tainted with bias and has rightly been interfered by the High Court. It is submitted that Inquiry Officer having acted as a prosecutor no further prejudice needs to be proved.

16. We have considered the submissions of the learned counsel for the parties and perused the records.

17. Before we proceed to consider the rival submissions of the learned counsel for the parties, it is relevant to look into the reasons given by the High Court for allowing the writ petitions filed by the respondents.

18. In Civil Appeal No.2608 of 2012 (leading appeal) judgment of learned Single Judge allowing the writ petition is dated 12.04.2010 which is filed at Annexure P-7 to the appeal. After elaborately considering the facts of the case, the nature of charges and affidavit filed in the writ petition, learned Judge proceeded to decide the writ petition. Learned Single Judge had directed to make available the proceedings of the disciplinary inquiry and on perusal of the proceedings of the disciplinary inquiry Learned Single Judge came to the conclusion that no Presenting Officer was appointed in the said proceedings and the Enquiry Officer himself led the examination in chief of the prosecution witness by putting questions. The High Court further came to the conclusion that Enquiry Officer acted himself as prosecutor and Judge in the said disciplinary enquiry. It is useful to extract paragraphs 9 and 10 of the judgment which are to the following effect:

"(9) This Court directed the learned Asstt. S.G. appearing for the respondents to make available the proceedings of the disciplinary enquiry against the petitioner. On perusal of the proceeding, it is crystal clear that no Presenting Officer was appointed in the said proceedings and the Enquiry Officer himself led the examination in chief of the prosecution witness by putting questions. This fact is not disputed by the learned Asstt. S.G. appearing for the respondents, but his only submission is that all opportunities were given to the writ petitioner to put up his defence case and also the writ petitioner had pleaded guilty for both the charges levelled against him.

(10) It is, therefore, crystal clear that the Enquiry Officer acted himself as Prosecutor and Judge in the said disciplinary enquiry against the

writ petitioner. From this admitted fact, it may not be wrong to infer that there were no fair procedures in the disciplinary proceedings as a result of which principle of natural justice was undisputedly denied to the writ petitioner."

19. The Division Bench of the High Court in writ appeal against the aforesaid judgment also affirmed the aforesaid view of the learned Single Judge while dismissing the writ appeal.

20. As noted above there are two principal submissions raised by the learned counsel for the appellant, they are:

(i) The disciplinary inquiry is required to be conducted under Rule 27 of 1955 Rules which does not contemplate appointment of a Presenting Officer. Hence, the inquiry proceedings are not vitiated by the non-appointment of Presenting Officer.

(ii) The disciplinary inquiry has been held against the respondents by complying with the principles of natural justice. No principle of natural justice is violated by non-appointment of Presenting Officer. No prejudice has been caused to the respondents by non-appointment of Presenting Officer.

21. Rule 27 sub-rule (c) of the CRPF Rules, 1955 provides for the procedure for conducting a departmental enquiry which is as follows: "Rule 27(c) The procedure for conducting a departmental enquiry shall be as follows:-

(1) The substance of the accusation shall be reduced to the form of a written charge which should be as precise as possible. The charge shall be read out to the accused and a copy of it given to him at least 48 hrs. before the commencement of the enquiry.

(2) At the commencement of the enquiry the accused shall be asked to enter a plea of Guilty or Not Guilty after which evidence necessary to establish the charge shall be let in. The evidence shall be material to the charge and may either be oral or documentary, if oral: (i) it shall be direct: (ii) it shall be recorded by the Officer conducting, the

enquiry himself in the presence of the accused: (iii) the accused shall be allowed to cross examine the witnesses.

(3) When documents are relied upon in support of the charge, they shall be put in evidence as exhibits and the accused shall, before he is called upon to make his defence be allowed to inspect such exhibits.

(4) The accused shall then be examined and his statement recorded by the officer conducting the enquiry. If the accused has pleaded guilty and does not challenge the evidence on record, the proceedings shall be closed for orders. If he pleads "Not guilty", he shall be required to file a written statement and a list of such witnesses as he may wish to cite in his defence within such period, which shall in any case be not less than a fortnight, as the officer conducting enquiry may deem reasonable in the circumstances of the case. If he declines to file a written statement, he shall again be examined by the officer conducting the enquiry on the expiry of the period allowed.

(5) If the accused refuses to cite any witnesses or to produce any evidence in his defence, the proceedings shall be closed for orders. If he produces any evidence the officer conducting the enquiry shall proceed to record the evidence. If the officer conducting the enquiry considers that the evidence of any witness or any document which the accused wants to produce in his defence is not material to the issues involved in the case he may refuse to call such witness or to allow such document to be produced in evidence, but in all such cases he must briefly record his reasons for considering the evidence inadmissible. When all relevant evidence has been brought on record, the proceedings shall be closed for orders.

(6) If the Commandant has himself held the enquiry, he shall record his findings and pass orders where he has power to do so. If the enquiry has been held by any officer other than the Commandant, the officer conducting the enquiry shall forward his report together with the proceedings to the Commandant who shall record his findings and pass order where he has power to do so.".

22. *A perusal of the aforesaid Rule does not indicate that Rule contemplates appointment of Presenting Officer. Service conditions including punishment and appeal procedure of an employee are governed by statutory rules. The CRPF Act, 1949 has been enacted by the Parliament for the constitution and regulation of an armed Central Reserve Police Force. Section 18 of the Act empowers the Central Government to make rules for carrying out the purposes of this Act.*

23. *The disciplinary proceedings are quasi-judicial proceedings and Inquiry Officer is in the position of an independent adjudicator and is obliged to act fairly, impartially. The authority exercises quasi-judicial power has to act in good faith without bias, in a fair and impartial manner.*

24. *Rules of natural justice have been recognised and developed as principles of administrative law. Natural justice has many facets. Its all facets are steps to ensure justice and fair play. This Court in Suresh Koshy George vs. University of Kerala and others, AIR 1969 SC 198 had occasion to consider the principles of natural justice in the context of a case where disciplinary action was taken against a student who was alleged to have adopted malpractice in the examination. In paragraph 7 this Court held that the question whether the requirements of natural justice have been met by the procedure adopted in a given case must depend to a great extent on the facts and circumstances of the case in point, the constitution of Tribunal and the rules under which it functions. Following was held in paragraphs 7 and 8:*

"*7....The rules of natural justice are not embodied rules. The question whether the requirements of natural justice have been met by the procedure adopted in a given case must depend to a great extent on the facts and circumstances of the case in point, the constitution of the Tribunal and the rules under which it functions.*

8. In Russel v. Duke of Norfolk, Tucker, L. J. observed: "There are, in my view, no words which are of universal application to every kind of inquiry and every kind of domestic tribunal. The requirements of *natural justice must depend on the circumstances of the case, the nature of the inquiry, the rules under which the tribunal is acting, the subject matter that is being dealt with, and so forth. Accordingly, I do not derive much assistance from the definitions of natural justice which have been from time to time used, but, whatever standard is adopted, one essential is that the person concerned should have a reasonable opportunity of presenting his case."*

25. A Constitution Bench of this Court has elaborately considered and explained the principles of natural justice in A.K. Kraipak and others vs. Union of India and others, AIR 1970 SC 150. This Court held that the aim of the rules of natural justice is to secure justice or to put it negatively to prevent miscarriage of justice. The concept of natural justice has undergone a great deal of change in recent years. Initially recognised as consisting of two principles that is no one shall be a judge in his own cause and no decision shall be given against a party without affording him a reasonable hearing, various other facets have been recognised. In paragraph 20 following has been held:

"20. The aim of the rules of natural justice is to secure justice or to put it negatively to prevent miscarriage of justice. These rules can operate only in areas not covered by any law validly made. In other words they do not supplant the law of the land but supplement it. The concept of natural justice has undergone a great deal of change in recent years. In the past it was thought that it included just two rules namely (1) no one shall be a judge in his own case (Nemo debetesse judex propria causa) and (2) no decision shall be given against a party without affording him a reasonable hearing (audi alteram partem). Very soon thereafter a third rule was envisaged and that is that quasi-judicial enquiries must be held in good faith, without bias and not arbitrarily or unreasonably...."

26. In State of Uttar Pradesh and others vs. Saroj Kumar Sinha, 2010 (2) SCC 772, this Court had laid down that inquiry officer is a quasi-judicial authority, he has to act as independent adjudicator and he is

not a representative of the department/ disciplinary authority/ Government. In paragraphs 28 and 30 following has been held:

"28. An inquiry officer acting in a quasi-judicial authority is in the position of an independent adjudicator. He is not supposed to be a representative of the department/disciplinary authority/ Government. His function is to examine the evidence presented by the Department, even in the absence of the delinquent official to see as to whether the unrebutted evidence is sufficient to hold that the charges are proved. In the present case the aforesaid procedure has not been observed. Since no oral evidence has been examined the documents have not been proved, and could not have been taken into consideration to conclude that the charges have been proved against the respondents. 30. When a departmental enquiry is conducted against the government servant it cannot be treated as a casual exercise. The enquiry proceedings also cannot be conducted with a closed mind. The inquiry officer has to be wholly unbiased. The rules of natural justice are required to be observed to ensure not only that justice is done but is manifestly seen to be done. The object of rules of natural justice is to ensure that a government servant is treated fairly in proceedings which may culminate in imposition of punishment including dismissal/removal from service."

27. When the statutory rule does not contemplate appointment of Presenting Officer whether non-appointment of Presenting Officer ipso facto vitiates the inquiry? We have noticed the statutory provision of Rule 27 which does not indicate that there is any statutory requirement of appointment of Presenting Officer in the disciplinary inquiry. It is thus clear that statutory provision does not mandate appointment of Presenting Officer. When the statutory provision does not require appointment of Presenting Officer whether there can be any circumstances where principles of natural justice can be held to be violated is the broad question which needs to be answered in this case. We have noticed above that the High Court found breach of principles of natural justice in Inquiry Officer acting as the prosecutor

against the respondents. The Inquiry Officer who has to be independent and not representative of the disciplinary authority if starts acting in any other capacity and proceed to act in a manner as if he is interested in eliciting evidence to punish an employee, the principle of bias comes into place.

28. Justice M. Rama Jois of the Karnataka High Court had occasion to consider the above aspect in Bharath Electronics Ltd. vs. K. Kasi, ILR 1987 Karnataka 366. In the above case the order of domestic inquiry was challenged before the Labour and Industrial Tribunal. The grounds taken were, that inquiry is vitiated since Presenting Officer was not appointed and further Inquiry Officer played the role of prosecutor. This Court held that there is no legal compulsion that Presenting Officer should be appointed but if the Inquiry Officer plays the role of Presenting Officer, the inquiry would be invalid. Following was held in paragraphs 8 and 9:

"8. One other ground on which the domestic inquiry was held invalid was that Presenting Officer was not appointed. This view of the Tribunal is also patently untenable. There is no legal compulsion that Presenting Officer should be appointed. Therefore, the mere fact that the Presenting Officer was not appointed is no ground to set aside the inquiry See : Gopalakrishna Reddy v. State of Karnataka (ILR 1980 Kar 575). It is true that in the absence of Presenting Officer if the Inquiring Authority plays the role of the Presenting Officer, the inquiry would be invalid and this aspect arises out of the next point raised for the petitioner, which I shall consider immediately hereafter.

9. The third ground on which the Industrial Tribunal held that the domestic inquiry was invalid was that the Inquiry Officer had played the role of the Presenting Officer. The relevant part of the findings reads : "The Learned Counsel for the workman further contended that the questions put by the Enquiry Officer to the Management's witnesses themselves suggest that he was biased and prejudiced against the workman. There has been no explanation as to why no Presenting Officer was appointed and as to why the Enquiry Officer took upon

himself the burden of putting questions to the Management witnesses. The enquiry proceedings at Ext. A-6 disclose that after the cross-examination of the Management's witnesses by the defence, the Enquiry Officer has further put certain questions by way of explanation, but from their nature an inference arises that they are directed to fill in the lacuna. The Learned Counsel for the Management contended that the Enquiry Officer has followed the principles of natural justice and that the domestic enquiry is quite valid. I am of the view that the fact that the Enquiry Officer has himself taken up the role of the Presenting Officer for the management goes to the root of the matter and vitiates the enquiry," As far as position in law is concerned, it is common ground that if the Inquiring Authority plays the role of a Prosecutor and cross-examines defence witnesses or puts leading questions to the prosecution witnesses clearly exposing a biased state of mind, the inquiry would be opposed to principles of natural justice. But the question for consideration in this case is : Whether the Inquiry Officer did so ? It is also settled law that an Inquiring Authority is entitled to put questions to the witnesses for clarification wherever it becomes necessary and so long the delinquent employee is permitted to cross-examine the witnesses after the Inquiring Authority questions the witnesses, the inquiry proceedings cannot be impeached as unfair. See :Munchandani Electric and Radio Industries Ltd. v. Their Workman."

29. This Court had occasion to observe in Workmen of Lambabari Tea Estate vs. Lambabari Tea Estate, 1966 (2) LLJ 315, that if Inquiry Officer did not keep his function as Inquiry Officer but becomes prosecutor, the inquiry is vitiated. Following was observed: "The inquiry which was held by the management on the first charge was presided over by the manager himself. It was conducted in the presence of the assistant manager and two others. The enquiry was not correct in its procedure. The manager recorded the statements, cross-examined the labourers who were the offenders and made and recorded his own statements on facts and questioned the offending labourers about the truth of his own statements recorded by himself.

The manager did not keep his function as the enquiring officer distinct but became witness, prosecutor and manager in turns. The record of the enquiry as a result is staccato and unsatisfactory."

30. A Division Bench of the Madhya Pradesh High Court speaking through Justice R.V. Raveendran, CJ (as he then was) had occasion to consider the question of vitiation of the inquiry when the Inquiry Officer starts himself acting as prosecutor in Union of India and ors. vs. Mohd. Naseem Siddiqui, ILR (2004) MP 821. In the above case the Court considered Rule 9(9) (c) of the Railway Servants (Discipline & Appeal) Rules, 1968. The Division Bench while elaborating fundamental principles of natural justice enumerated the seven well recognised facets in paragraph 7 of the judgment which is to the following effect:

"7. One of the fundamental principles of natural justice is that no man shall be a judge in his own cause. This principle consists of seven well recognised facets: (i) The adjudicator shall be impartial and free from bias, (ii) The adjudicator shall not be the prosecutor, (iii) The complainant shall not be an adjudicator, (iv) A witness cannot be the Adjudicator, (v) The Adjudicator must not import his personal knowledge of the facts of the case while inquiring into charges, (vi) The Adjudicator shall not decide on the dictates of his Superiors or others, (vii) The Adjudicator shall decide the issue with reference to material on record and not reference to extraneous material or on extraneous considerations. If any one of these fundamental rules is breached, the inquiry will be vitiated."

31. The Division Bench further held that where the Inquiry Officer acts as Presenting Officer, bias can be presumed. In paragraph 9 is as follows:

"9. A domestic inquiry must be held by an unbiased person who is unconnected with the incident so that he can be impartial and objective in deciding the subject matters of inquiry. He should have an open mind till the inquiry is completed and should neither act with bias nor

give an impression of bias. Where the Inquiry Officer acts as the Presenting Officer, bias can be presumed. At all events, it clearly gives an impression of bias. An Inquiry Officer is in position of a Judge or Adjudicator. The Presenting Officer is in the position of a Prosecutor. If the Inquiry Officer acts as a Presenting Officer, then it would amount to Judge acting as the prosecutor. When the Inquiry Officer conducts the examination-in- chief of the prosecution witnesses and leads them through the facts so as to present the case of the disciplinary authority against the employee or cross- examines the delinquent employee or his witnesses to establish the case of the employer/disciplinary authority evidently, the Inquiry Officer cannot be said to have an open mind. The very fact that he presents the case of the employer and supports the case of the employer is sufficient to hold that the Inquiry Officer does not have an open mind."

32. The Division Bench after elaborately considering the issue summarised the principles in paragraph 16 which is to the following effect: "16. We may summarise the principles thus: (i) The Inquiry Officer, who is in the position of a Judge shall not act as a Presenting Officer, who is in the position of a prosecutor. (ii) It is not necessary for the Disciplinary Authority to appoint a Presenting Officer in each and every inquiry. Non- appointment of a Presenting Officer, by itself will not vitiate the inquiry. (iii) The Inquiry Officer, with a view to arrive at the truth or to obtain clarifications, can put questions to the prosecution witnesses as also the defence witnesses. In the absence of a Presenting Officer, if the Inquiry Officer puts any questions to the prosecution witnesses to elicit the facts, he should thereafter permit the delinquent employee to cross-examine such witnesses on those clarifications. (iv) If the Inquiry Officer conducts a regular examination-in-chief by leading the prosecution witnesses through the prosecution case, or puts leading questions to the departmental witnesses pregnant with answers, or cross-examines the defence witnesses or puts suggestive questions to establish the prosecution case employee, the Inquiry Officer acts as prosecutor thereby vitiating the inquiry. (v) As absence of a Presenting Officer by itself will not vitiate the inquiry and it is recognised that the Inquiry Officer can put questions to any or all witnesses to elicit the truth, the question whether an Inquiry Officer acted as a Presenting Officer, will have to be decided with reference to the manner in which the evidence is let in and recorded in the inquiry. Whether an Inquiry Officer has merely acted only as an Inquiry Officer or has also acted as a Presenting Officer depends on the facts of each case. To avoid any allegations of bias and running the risk of inquiry being declared as illegal and vitiated, the present trend appears to be to invariably appoint Presenting Officers, except in simple cases. Be that as it may."

33. We fully endorse the principles as enumerated above, however, the principles have to be carefully applied in facts situation of a particular case. There is no requirement of appointment of Presenting Officer in each and every case, whether statutory rules enable the authorities to make an appointment or are silent. When the statutory rules are silent with regard to the applicability of any facet of principles of natural justice the applicability of principles of natural justice which are not specifically excluded in the statutory scheme are not prohibited. When there is no express exclusion of particular principle of natural justice, the said principle shall be applicable in a given case to advance the cause of justice. In this context reference is made of a case of this Court in Punjab National Bank and others vs. Kunj Behari Misra, 1998 (7) SCC 84. In the above case, this Court had occasion to consider the provisions of Punjab National Bank Officer Employees' (Discipline and Appeal) Regulations, 1977. Regulation 7 provides for action on the enquiry report. Regulation 7 as extracted in paragraph 10 of the judgment is as follows:

"7. Action on the enquiry report.—(1) The disciplinary authority, if it is not itself the enquiring authority, may, for reasons to be recorded by it in writing, remit the case to the enquiring authority for fresh or further enquiry and report and the enquiring authority shall thereupon proceed to hold the further enquiry according to the provisions of Regulation 6 as far as may be.

(2) The disciplinary authority shall, if it disagrees with the findings of the enquiring authority on any article of charge, record its reasons for such disagreement and record its own findings on such charge, if the evidence on record is sufficient for the purpose.

(3) If the disciplinary authority, having regard to its findings on all or any of the articles of charge, is of the opinion that any of the penalties specified in Regulation 4 should be imposed on the officer employee, it shall, notwithstanding anything contained in Regulation 8, make an order imposing such penalty.

(4) If the disciplinary authority having regard to its findings on all or any of the articles of charge, is of the opinion that no penalty is called for, it may pass an order exonerating the officer employee concerned."

34. The question which was debated before this Court was that since Regulation 7(2) does not contain any provision for giving an opportunity to the delinquent officer to represent before disciplinary authority who reverses the findings which were in favour of the delinquent employee, the rules of natural justice are not applicable. This Court held that principle of natural justice has to be read in Regulation 7(2) even though rule does not specifically require hearing of delinquent officer. In paragraph 19 following was held: "19. The result of the aforesaid discussion would be that the principles of natural justice have to be read into Regulation 7(2). As a result thereof, whenever the disciplinary authority disagrees with the enquiry authority on any article of charge, then before it records its own findings on such charge, it must record its tentative reasons for such disagreement and give to the delinquent officer an opportunity to represent before it records its findings. The report of the enquiry officer containing its findings will have to be conveyed and the delinquent officer will have an opportunity to persuade the disciplinary authority to accept the favourable conclusion of the enquiry officer. The principles of natural justice, as we have already observed, require the authority which has to take a final decision and can impose a penalty, to give an opportunity to the officer charged of misconduct to file a representation before the disciplinary authority records its findings on the charges framed against the officer."

35. Thus, the question as to whether Inquiry Officer who is supposed to act independently in an inquiry has acted as prosecutor or not is a question of fact which has to be decided on the facts and proceedings of particular case. In the present case we have noticed that the High Court had summoned the entire inquiry proceedings and after perusing the proceedings the High Court came to the conclusion that Inquiry Officer himself led the examination in chief of the prosecution witness by putting questions. The High Court further held that the Inquiry Officer acted himself as prosecutor and Judge in the said disciplinary enquiry. The above conclusion of the High Court has already been noticed from paragraphs 9 and 10 of the judgment of the High court giving rise to Civil Appeal No.2608 of 2012.

36. The High Court having come to the conclusion that Inquiry Officer has acted as prosecutor also, the capacity of independent adjudicator was lost which adversely affecting his independent role of adjudicator. In the circumstances, the principle of bias shall come into play and the High Court was right in setting aside the dismissal orders by giving liberty to the appellants to proceed with inquiry afresh. We make it clear that our observations as made above are in the facts of the present cases.

37. In result, all the appeals are dismissed subject to the liberty as granted by the High Court that it shall be open for the appellants to proceed with the inquiry afresh from the stage as directed by the High Court and it shall be open for the appellant to decide on arrear pay and allowances of the respondents."

7. Section 9, 10 & 12 of the CRPF Act, 1949 and Disciplinary Proceedings under Rule 27 of the CRPF Rules, 1955:

7.1 The Hon'ble Supreme Court vide Judgment dated 19.1.2023 in Civil Appeal No. 219 of 2023 in the matter of Union of India and Ors. Vs. Const Sunil Kumar held as under:

"1. Feeling aggrieved and dissatisfied with the impugned judgment and order dated 01.09.2017 passed by the High Court of Judicature for Rajasthan Bench at Jaipur in D.B. Special Appeal Writ No. 303/2005, by which, the High Court has allowed the said appeal preferred by the respondent herein and has set aside the penalty imposed by the disciplinary authority and has directed the appellant(s) to reinstate him in service with notional benefits without any back wages, the Union of India and others have preferred the present appeal.

....

3.4 It is further submitted by learned ASG that in the case of **Commandant, 22nd Battalion, CRPF Vs. Surinder Kumar; (2011) 10 SCC 244**, it is observed and held by this Court that even in a case when a CRPF personnel is awarded imprisonment under Section 10(n) for an offence which though less heinous he can be dismissed from service after holding departmental enquiry if his conduct is found to be prejudicial to good order and discipline of CRPF. It is submitted that in the aforesaid decision, it is observed and held by this Court that the High Court in exercise of powers of judicial review, Courts should be slow in interfering with the punishment of dismissal on the ground that it was disproportionate. It is submitted that punishment should not be merely disproportionate but should be strikingly disproportionate to warrant interference by the High Court under Article 226 of the Constitution of India and it is only in an extreme case, where on the face of it there is perversity or irrationality that there can be judicial review under Articles 226 or 227 or under Article 32 of the Constitution of India.

....

6.2 Even otherwise, the Division Bench of the High Court has materially erred in interfering with the order of penalty of dismissal passed on proved charges and misconduct of indiscipline and insubordination and giving threats to the superior of dire *consequences on the ground that the same is disproportionate to the gravity of the wrong. In the case of* **Surinder Kumar** *(supra) while considering the power of judicial review of the High Court in interfering with the punishment of dismissal, it is observed and held by this Court after considering the earlier decision in the case of* **Union of India Vs. R.K. Sharma; (2001) 9 SCC 592** *that in exercise of powers of judicial review interfering with the punishment of dismissal on the ground that it was disproportionate, the punishment should not be merely disproportionate but should be strikingly disproportionate. As observed and held that only in an extreme case, where on the face of it there is perversity or irrationality, there can be judicial review under Article 226 or 227 or under Article 32 of the Constitution.*

6.3 Applying the law laid down by this Court in the aforesaid decision(s) to the facts of the case on hand, it cannot be said that the punishment of dismissal can be said to be strikingly disproportionate warranting the interference of the High Court in exercise of powers under Article 226 of the Constitution of India. In the facts and circumstances of the case and on the charges and misconduct of indiscipline and insubordination proved, the CRPF being adisciplined force, the order of penalty of dismissal was justified and it cannot be said to be disproportionate and/or strikingly disproportionate to the gravity of the wrong. Under the circumstances also, the Division Bench of the High Court has committed a very serious error in interfering with the order of penalty of dismissal imposed and ordering reinstatement of the respondent.

6.4 At this stage, it is required to be observed that even while holding that the punishment/penalty of dismissal disproportionate to the gravity of the wrong, thereafter, no further punishment/penalty is imposed by the Division Bench of the High Court except denial of back wages. As per the settled position of law, even in a case where the punishment is found to be disproportionate to the misconduct committed and proved the matter is to be remitted to the disciplinary authority for imposing appropriate punishment/penalty which as such is the prerogative of the disciplinary authority. On this ground also, the impugned judgment and order passed by the Division Bench of the High Court is unsustainable.As observed hereinabove as the order of penalty/punishment cannot be said to be disproportionate, there is no question of remanding the matter back to the disciplinary authority.

7. In view of the above and for the reasons stated above the present appeal succeeds. The impugned judgment and order passed by the High Court setting aside the order of penalty of dismissal and reinstating the respondent is hereby quashed and set aside."

7.2 The Supreme Court vide Judgment dated 20.10.2011 in Civil Appeal No. 2177 of 2006 in the matter of the Commandant, 22 Battalion, CRPF Srinagar, C/o 56/APO & Ors. Vs. Surinder Kumar held as under:

"This is an appeal against the order dated 12.02.2004 of the Division Bench of the Jammu and Kashmir High Court in L.P.A. No.600-A 1999 (for short 'the impugned order').

2. The facts very briefly are that the respondent was working as a Constable in the Central Reserve Police Force (for short 'the CRPF'). A complaint was lodged against the respondent. It was alleged in the complaint that he was detailed with vehicle no.25 to carry patrolling party on Chandel Palel Road but he left the vehicle unattended and absented himself without permission of his superior officer and reported on his own after 20 minutes. It was also alleged in the complaint that while he was on duty, he consumed illicit alcohol and in an inebriated state of mind misbehaved with his superior officer H.N. Singh, snatched his AK-47 rifle and pointed the barrel of the rifle to him and on the intervention of Lachhi Ram, Assistant Commandant, the barrel of the rifle was pointed upward and an untoward incident was avoided. A copy of the complaint was served on the respondent and a disciplinary enquiry was conducted and the Assistant Commandant-cum-Magistrate First Class in his order dated 10.06.1993 found the respondent guilty of charges and convicted him and sentenced him to imprisonment till the rising of the Court. By a separate order dated 10.06.1993, the Commandant also dismissed the respondent from service.

3. Aggrieved, the respondent challenged the order dated 10.06.1993 passed by the Assistant Commandant-cum Magistrate First Class as well as the order of dismissal dated 10.06.1993 passed by the Commandant in Writ Petition No.555 of 1994 before the High Court. The Learned Single Judge dismissed the writ petition on 09.11.1998. The respondent challenged the order of the learned Single Judge in L.P.A. No. 600-A 1999 and by the impugned order, the Division Bench held that the punishment of dismissal of the respondent was disproportionate in as much as his conviction was till the rising of the court for having committed a less heinous offence. By the impugned order, the Division Bench of the High Court directed the appellants to reconsider the nature and quantum of punishment awarded to the respondent and accordingly grant him consequential benefits.

4. Mr. Ashok Bhan, learned counsel for the appellants, submitted that the respondent was punished with imprisonment for one day by the judgment dated 10.06.1993 of the Assistant Commandant-cum-Magistrate First Class for having committed a less heinous offence under Section 10(n) of the Central Reserve Police Force Act, 1949 (for short 'the Act'). He submitted that Section 12(1) of the Act provides that every person sentenced under the Act to imprisonment may be dismissed from the CRPF and in exercise of this power the Commandant 22 Battalion, CRPF, dismissed the respondent from service by order dated 10.06.1993. He submitted that the findings in the judgment of the Assistant Commandant cum-Magistrate in the order under Section 10(n) of the Act would show that the respondent was guilty of grave charges of indiscipline and therefore the Division Bench of the High Court was not right in coming to the conclusion in the impugned order that the punishment of dismissal from service was disproportionate.

5. Mr. J.P. Dhanda, learned counsel appearing for the respondent, on the other hand, submitted that Section 10 of the Act is titled 'Less heinous offences' and it is under Section 10(n) that the respondent has been punished for imprisonment till the rising of the court. He argued that for a less heinous offence and for an imprisonment till rising of the Court, the respondent could not have been dismissed from service. He submitted that in Union of India vs. Parma Nanda (AIR 1989 SC 1185), this Court has held that even in cases where an enquiry is dispensed with under the proviso (b) to Article 311(2) of the Constitution if the penalty impugned is apparently unreasonable or uncalled for, having regard to the nature of the criminal charge, the Administrative Tribunal may step in to render substantial justice and may remit the matter to the competent authority for reconsideration or itself substitute one of the penalties. He submitted that the High Court has relied upon the decision in Union of India vs. Parma Nanda (supra) and has set aside the order of dismissal without going into the merits of the findings of the Assistant Commandant-cum Magistrate on the charges against the respondent.

6. We have considered the submissions of the learned counsel for the parties and we find that the respondent has been imprisoned by the judgment of the Assistant Commandant-cum Magistrate under Section 10(n) of the Act and has been dismissed from service by a separate order of the Commandant, 22 Battalion, CRPF passed under Section 12(1) of the Act. Sections 10(n) and 12(1) of the Act are extracted hereinbelow:

"10. Less heinous offences:- Every member of the Force who

(n) is guilty of any act or omission which, though not specified in this Act, is prejudicial to good order and discipline; or

shall be punishable with imprisonment for a term which may extend to one year, or with the fine which may extend to three months' pay, or with both.

12. Place of imprisonment and liability to dismissal on imprisonment.- (1) Every person sentenced under this Act to imprisonment may be dismissed from the Force, and shall further be liable to forfeiture of pay, allowance and any other moneys due to him as well as of any medals and decorations received by him."

It will be clear from Section 10(n) of the Act that a member of the CRPF who is guilty of any act or omission which is prejudicial to good order and discipline is punishable with imprisonment for a term which may extend to one year or with fine which may extend to three months' pay, or with both. Section 12(1) of the Act provides that every person sentenced under this Act to imprisonment may be dismissed from the CRPF. The word "may" in Section 12(1) of the Act confers a discretion on the competent authority whether or not to dismiss a member of the CRPF from service pursuant to a sentence of imprisonment under the Act and while exercising the discretion, the competent authority has to consider various relevant factors including the nature of the offence for which he has been sentenced to imprisonment.

7. In the present case, the acts of indiscipline of the respondent which have been established beyond doubt by the Assistant Commandant-cum-Magistrate are that the respondent left his party without permission while on duty in 6 the operational area for 20 minutes and returned on his own and he got enraged when H.N. Singh, Assistant Commandant, decided to take him for medical examination when he found him to be in a state of intoxication and he snatched the AK-47 rifle of H.N. Singh and pointed the barrel towards him and due to the intervention of Lachhi Ram, Assistant Commandant, an untoward incident was avoided. These acts of indiscipline were obviously prejudicial to the good order and discipline and when committed by a member of a disciplined force like the CRPF were serious enough to warrant dismissal from service.

8. The Division Bench of the High Court has taken a view in the impugned order that as the respondent has been punished for imprisonment for a less heinous offence and only till the rising of the court, the punishment of dismissal was disproportionate. The Division Bench of the High Court failed to appreciate that for less heinous offences enumerated in Section 10 of the Act, a person was liable for punishment with imprisonment and under Section 12(1) of the Act every person sentenced under the Act to imprisonment was liable to be dismissed from the CRPF. In other words, the legislative intent was that once a member of the CRPF was sentenced for imprisonment under the Act, he was also liable for dismissal from service. The Division Bench of the High Court, in our considered opinion, should have looked into the acts of indiscipline proved against the respondent for which he has been sentenced to imprisonment and then decided whether the dismissal of the respondent from service was disproportionate to the gravity of acts of indiscipline. As we have already held, the acts of indiscipline for which the respondent had been sentenced for imprisonment were serious and grave for a disciplined force. Therefore, the competent authority was right in imposing the punishment of dismissal from service.

9. Moreover, it appears from the impugned order that the High Court has in exercise of power of judicial review interfered with the punishment of dismissal on the ground that it was disproportionate. In Union of India vs. R.K. Sharma (AIR 2001 SC 3053), this Court has taken the view that the punishment should not be merely disproportionate but should be strikingly disproportionate to warrant interference by the High Court under Article 226 of the Constitution and it was only in an extreme case, where on the face of it there is perversity or irrationality that there can be judicial review under Articles 226 or 227 or under Article 32 of the Constitution. Since this is not one of those cases where the punishment of dismissal was strikingly disproportionate or where on the face of it there was perversity or irrationality, the Division Bench of the High Court ought not to have interfered with the order of dismissal from service.

10. We, accordingly, allow this appeal and set aside the impugned order of the Division Bench of the High Court."

7.3 Delhi High Court in WP(C) 4839 of 2018 titled Jagannath Naik Vs. Inspector General of Police & Ors. while interpreting the mandate of CRPF Act, 1949 and Rule 27 of the CRPF Rules, 1955 held that *"The CRPF Act, 1949 do not prescribe for punishment of stoppage of increments. However, subsequently, CRPF Rules, 1955 came into force. Section 27 (a) of Chapter – VI DISCIPLINE, of the CRPF Rules, 1955 provides for Procedure for Award of Punishments, whereunder punishment of 'stoppage of increment' has been mentioned but the words 'with cumulative effect' do not find any place. In our considered opinion, the punishment of 'stoppage of three increments' inflicted upon the petitioner is just and proper and as per law. However, 'with cumulative effect' is against the prescribed law and so, deserves to be and is, accordingly set aside."*

8. CRIMINAL PROCEEDINGS AND DEPARTMENTAL PROCEEDINGS

8.1 The Supreme Court vide Judgment dated 21.9.2021 in Civil Appeal No.5848 Of 2021 in the matter of Union of India & Ors. Vs. Dalbir Singh held as under:

"1. Leave granted.

2. The order dated 11.4.2019 passed by the Division Bench of the High Court of Delhi at New Delhi is the subject matter of challenge in the present appeal whereby the order of dismissal passed by the Competent Authority on 24.5.2014, appellate order dated 9.10.2014, and revisional order dated 13.2.2015 were set aside. The respondent was hence directed to be reinstated and also was found entitled to arrears of pay from the date of dismissal of service till the date he actually joins the duty.

3. The writ petitioner was a General Duty Constable in the Central Reserve Police Force (CRPF). An FIR No. 16/1993 was lodged against the writ petitioner for an offence under Section 302, 307 of the Indian Penal Code, 18602 and Section 27 of the Arms Act, 1959 when the writ petitioner was accused to have fired from his service revolver on Head

Constable Shri Harish Chander and Deputy Commandant Shri Hari Singh resulting in the death of Shri Harish Chander and injuries to Shri Hari Singh. The writ petitioner was convicted by the learned trial court on 11.3.1996 and sentenced to life imprisonment. However, in appeal, the High Court of Punjab and Haryana acquitted him of the charges framed against him by giving benefit of doubt for the reason that 20 cartridges were fired but only 7 empties were recovered whereas none of the bullets have been recovered. In view of the said finding, the High Court doubted the prosecution version as the Investigating Agency had failed to collect the evidence. Criminal Appeal No. 117 of 2006 filed by the State was dismissed by this Court relying upon the aforesaid finding of the High Court.

4. The writ petitioner was initially served with a chargesheet on 27.6.1993. Article-I from the Statement of Article of charges reads thus:

"ARTICLE-I That the said No.880957136 Ct. Dalbir Singh of D/36 BN CRPF while functioning as CT(GD) at BN HQ Fatehbad on 11.04.1993 has committed an act of misconduct in his capacity as member of the force U/s 11(1) of CRPF Act, 1949 in that he has committed misconduct and disobedience of lawful orders and refused to perform fatigue duty between 0900 hrs. to 1000 hrs."

5. In the statement of imputation of misconduct or misbehaviour in support of the above said Article of charge, it was stated that the writ petitioner returned to the Unit Headquarter after 60 days of earned leave on 10.4.1993 and was detailed for fatigue duty. Instead of performing such fatigue duty, the writ petitioner sat at the tailor shop. BHM Harish Chandra asked for non-compliance of the orders, the writ petitioner however arrogantly misbehaved with the officers. It is admitted that the proceedings of the chargesheet were not concluded.

6. The writ petitioner was dismissed from service on 21.12.1996 on account of his conviction in the criminal trial in pursuance of the FIR lodged. However, since he was granted benefit of doubt in appeal by

the High Court and was subsequently acquitted, the writ petitioner was reinstated vide order dated 20.7.2012 by the Deputy Inspector General of Police, CRPF, Patna. The following were the directions issued in the order of reinstatement:

"(i) The punishment of dismissal from service awarded to No. 880957136 CT/GD Dalbir Singh of 36BN, CRPF by disciplinary authority i.e. Commandant 36 BN vide order No. I-X-2/93-EC-II dated 21.12.1996 is hereby set aside. (ii) The appellant No. 880957136 CT/GD Dalbir Singh of 36BN, CRPF is reinstated into service immediate effect (i.e. from the date of reporting in 36BN). (iii) Since the appellant i.e. Ex. CT/GD Dalbir Singh has been acquitted by criminal court, he shall not be punished departmentally on the same charge or similar charge upon the evidence cited in the criminal case Rule 27 (ccc) of CRPF Rules, 1955. If some other misconduct on other ground is made out then it is upto disciplinary authority to decide whether any Departmental Enquiry is called for or not under Rule GOI decisions No. 5 below Rule 19 of CCS (CCA) 1965."

7. The writ petitioner was served with another chargesheet on 27.8.2012. The said chargesheet was withdrawn when the writ petition filed by the writ petitioner was pending before the High Court of Delhi. Consequently, the Writ Petition (C) No. 6354 of 2012 was disposed of on 21.11.2012, giving liberty to the appellant to charge sheet the writ petitioner. The relevant extract from the order reads as thus:

"15. However, learned counsel for the respondents submits that the issue pertaining to the departmental instructions with reference to safe custody of arms and ammunition issued to force personnel while on duty, which was not the subject matter of a criminal trial can always be gone into at a departmental inquiry. Learned Counsel submits that an official arm and ammunitions issued to a force personnel if found to be used in an incident resulting in the death of force personnel would certainly require an accountability to be given by the officer concerned who was issued the arm and ammunitions.

16. The offending chargesheet which has been challenged in the writ petition has been withdrawn by the respondents and therefore the writ petition is disposed of as infructuous observing that it would be permissible for the respondents to issue a chargesheet but not in relation to the death of Battalion Havaldar Major Harish Chander and the injuries caused to Dy. Comdt. Hari Singh. The respondents would be entitled to hold an inquiry with respect to the arm and ammunitions issued to the writ petitioner on day of incident and seek petitioner's accountability in relation thereto."

....

8. It is thereafter that another chargesheet was issued on 25.2.2013. Article I of the said chargesheet reads thus:

" ARTICLE 1

That during his posting at Amritsar Punjab No. 880957136 CT/GD Dalbir Singh of 36, BN, CRPF, on 11.04.1993 without having the order from Competent Officer fired from his service rifle (SLR Butt No. 417 Body No. 150410-59), issued for his Govt. duties and hence misused the Government weapon and ammunition and committed remissness of duties. The above said misconduct is a serious offence U/s 11(1) of CRPF Act read with Rule 27 of CRPF Rules. Therefore, the constable while being the member of the force has misused his service rifle and ammunition without having the order of competent officer which is a serious offence and misconduct and the same is also against the discipline and management of the force and is also a punishable offence."

9. In the enquiry proceedings, the appellants had examined six witnesses. The first departmental witness was Havaldar Dayamai Banerjee (PW-1). He had deposed that on 11.4.1993 around 11 o' clock, when he was doing camp maintenance work, he heard the sound of firing coming from the Head Office. He reached the place of firing which was 150 meters away from his place of work and found some persons were holding the writ petitioner. There is nothing substantial in the cross-examination conducted. He had reached the place of firing after the incident but had deposed about the time of incident of firing.

10. PW-2 Havaldar Bal Singh deposed that he heard the noise of about 15-20 fire shots at around 11 o' clock on 11.4.1993. He reached the place of occurrence and found Constable Dilip Mishra holding the writ petitioner as the latter was trying to free himself. He further deposed that people around the writ petitioner were saying that the writ petitioner fired inside the camp by his personal weapon. Nothing material has come out in the cross-examination. He also however reached the place of firing after the incident but both the above witnesses have deposed regarding of timing of firing i.e., around 11 o' clock.

11. PW-3 Havaldar Hetlal Deepankar was deployed for quarter guard duty from 10-12 o' clock on 11.4.1993. Around 11 o' clock, he heard the sound of gunfire. The firing stopped after 15-20 minutes. The writ petitioner was immobilized and was brought to the quarter guard. In the cross-examination, he stated that the firing took place at about 11:45 and that the distance between the quarter guard and the Head Office was about 70-80 yards.

12. PW-4 Havaldar J.N. Tripathi was working in the mess of the Headquarters, which was about 50 meters away from the place of firing. He also saw some persons immobilizing the writ petitioner. In the cross-examination, he stated that the firing was done by the writ petitioner near the Head Office. The location of firing may be 10 meters away from the Head Office.

13. PW-5 Brij Kishore Singh deposed that at about 11:00 am, after he handed over his charge to the writ petitioner, who was the runner of Deputy Commandant Shri Hari Singh as he wanted to have his food. He heard the sound of firing of about 15-20 bullets continuously while he was eating his food. After the firing went off, he ran towards the control room and saw 4-5 people were holding the writ petitioner and Constable Dilip Mishra was also one of them. 3-4 soldiers had taken the Self-Loading Rifle (S.L.R.) of the writ petitioner in their possession. He also stated that people were saying that the writ petitioner had fired from his personal weapon. He further deposed that the writ petitioner fired with his weapon without any meaningful purpose inside the camp.

14. The most important witness is PW-6 Constable D.K. Mishra. He was performing the duty of runner on 11.4.1993. He heard firing when he had gone to get the documents signed by the officer in the Head Office. He saw from lope hole that the writ petitioner was in a kneeling position and was firing. He caught hold of the writ petitioner from behind when he was changing the magazine. He was then handed over to guard commander and three sentries of quarter guard. In the cross-examination, he deposed that he caught the writ petitioner alone and later the guard commander and three sepoys from quarter guard came for help.

15. The Commandant, punishing authority, returned a finding considering the evidence led by the Department that the writ petitioner has misused his service weapon and is thus not entitled to be retained in the disciplinary force. Such order was affirmed by the appellate and the revisional authority.

16. The High Court in the writ petition filed by the writ petitioner examined the question as to whether service rifle was issued on 11.4.1993. The High Court found that on 27.6.1993, when the first chargesheet was issued, the writ petitioner was not on duty as he was to perform fatigue duty but he sat in a tailor shop instead. The Court found that this contradicts with the charges mentioned in the chargesheet dated 25.2.2013 that while on duty, he misused the 'government weapon'. The High Court returned the following finding:

"14. While it is possible that notwithstanding the pendency of a criminal case there could be disciplinary proceedings on the same issue, in the present case it is seen that Respondents are confused on facts. On the one hand, they charge-sheeted the Petitioner on 27th June 1993 for not performing his fatigue duty but instead sitting at a tailor's *shop, while nearly two decades later on 25th February 2013 they have charged him with misusing the service weapon issued to him. This contradiction in the stand of the Respondents is fatal to the disciplinary proceedings. The charge that he misused the weapon issued to him falls flat if he was in fact not even present at the place of duty. This was a case based on no evidence. The Respondents had to prove that the weapon which was issued to the Petitioner was misused by him. This it has failed to do by credible evidence."*

17. We find that the High Court has exceeded its jurisdiction while exercising the power of judicial review over the orders passed in the disciplinary proceedings which were conducted while adhering to the principles of natural justice.

....

18. The High Court failed to notice the fact that in the charge sheet issued on 27.6.1993, the allegation was that the writ petitioner failed to perform his fatigue duty from 9 to 10 am and was disobedient to the lawful orders issued to him. There was no allegation of use of a fire arm leading to death of Shri Harish Chander and injuries to Shri Hari Singh.

19. The writ petitioner completed his fatigue duty at 10 am and then reported for duty at the Headquarters. In the later Charge Sheet dated 25.2.2013, the departmental witnesses have uniformly deposed that the noise of firing of 15-20 gun shots was heard around 11 am on 11.4.1993. In fact, PW-6 Constable D.K. Mishra is the one who immobilized the writ petitioner when he was in the process of loading another magazine in the self-loading rifle. Still further, PW-5 Brij Kishore Singh has deposed that 3-4 soldiers had taken the self-loaded rifle of the writ petitioner. Such self-loaded rifle is the one which was issued to the writ petitioner.

20. The statement of some of the departmental witnesses was that they heard that the writ petitioner used his personal weapon but such part of the statements is hearsay evidence. It was open to the writ petitioner

to lead evidence that he was not using the official weapon but a personal weapon to rebut the stand of the Department.

21. A three-Judge Bench of this Court in State of Haryana & Anr. v. Rattan Singh 3 was dealing with the issue of non-examination of passengers when the allegation against the conductor was non issuance of the tickets. This Court held that in a domestic enquiry, strict and sophisticated rules of evidence under the Indian Evidence Act may not apply and that all materials which are logically probative for a prudent mind are permissible. There is no allergy to hearsay evidence provided it has reasonable nexus and credibility. This Court held as under:

"4. It is well settled that in a domestic enquiry the strict and sophisticated rules of evidence under the Indian Evidence Act may not apply. All materials which are logically probative for a prudent mind are permissible. There is no allergy to hearsay evidence provided it has reasonable nexus and credibility. It is true that departmental authorities and Administrative Tribunals must be careful in evaluating such material and should not glibly swallow what is strictly speaking not relevant under the Indian Evidence Act. For this proposition it is not necessary to cite decisions nor text books, although we have been taken through case-law and other authorities by counsel on both sides. The essence of a judicial approach is objectivity, exclusion of extraneous materials or considerations and observance of rules of natural justice. Of course, fairplay is the basis and if perversity or arbitrariness, bias or surrender of independence of judgment vitiate the conclusions reached, such finding, even though of a domestic tribunal, cannot be held good. However, the courts below misdirected themselves, perhaps, in insisting that passengers who had come in and gone out should be chased and brought before the tribunal before a valid finding could be recorded. The 'residuum' rule to which counsel for the respondent referred, based upon certain passages from American Jurisprudence does not go to that extent nor does the passage from Halsbury insist on such rigid requirement. The simple

point is, was there some evidence or was there no evidence — not in the sense of the technical rules governing regular court proceedings but in a fair commonsense way as men of understanding and worldly wisdom will accept. Viewed in this way, sufficiency of evidence in proof of the finding by a domestic tribunal is beyond scrutiny. Absence of any evidence in support of a finding is certainly available for the court to look into because it amounts to an error of law apparent on the record. ...."

22. This Court in Union of India & Ors. v. P. Gunasekaran had laid down the broad parameters for the exercise of jurisdiction of judicial review. The Court held as under:

"12. Despite the well-settled position, it is painfully disturbing to note that the High Court has acted as an appellate authority in the disciplinary proceedings, reappreciating even the evidence before the enquiry officer. The finding on Charge I was accepted by the disciplinary authority and was also endorsed by the Central Administrative Tribunal. In disciplinary proceedings, the High Court is not and cannot act as a second court of first appeal. The High Court, in exercise of its powers under Articles 226/227 of the Constitution of India, shall not venture into reappreciation of the evidence. The High Court can only see whether:

(a) the enquiry is held by a competent authority;

(b) the enquiry is held according to the procedure prescribed in that behalf;

(c) there is violation of the principles of natural justice in conducting the proceedings;

(d) the authorities have disabled themselves from reaching of fair conclusion by some considerations extraneous to the evidence and merits of the case;

(e) the authorities have allowed themselves to be influenced by irrelevant or extraneous considerations;

(f) the conclusion, on the very face of it, is so wholly arbitrary and capricious that no reasonable person could ever have arrived at such conclusion;

(g) the disciplinary authority had erroneously failed to admit the admissible and material evidence;

(h) the disciplinary authority had erroneously admitted inadmissible evidence which influenced the finding;

(i) the finding of fact is based on no evidence.

13. Under Articles 226/227 of the Constitution of India, the High Court shall not:

(i) reappreciate the evidence;

(ii) interfere with the conclusions in the enquiry, in case the same has been conducted in accordance with law;

(iii) go into the adequacy of the evidence;

(iv) go into the reliability of the evidence;

(v) interfere, if there be some legal evidence on which findings can be based.

(vi) correct the error of fact however grave it may appear to be;

(vii) go into the proportionality of punishment unless it shocks its conscience."

23. In another Judgment reported as B.C Chaturvedi v. Union of India &Ors. , it was held that the power of judicial review is meant to ensure that the individual receives fair treatment and not to ensure that the conclusion which the authority reaches is necessarily correct in the eye of the court. The Judicial review is not an appeal from a decision but a review of the manner in which the decision is made. The Court is to examine as to whether the inquiry was held by a competent officer or

whether rules of natural justice are complied with. This Court held as under:-

"12. Judicial review is not an appeal from a decision but a review of the manner in which the decision is made. Power of judicial review is meant to ensure that the individual receives fair treatment and not to ensure that the conclusion which the authority reaches is necessarily correct in the eye of the court. When an inquiry is conducted on charges of misconduct by a public servant, the Court/Tribunal is concerned to determine whether the inquiry was held by a competent officer or whether rules of natural justice are complied with. Whether the findings or conclusions are based on some evidence, the authority entrusted with the power to hold inquiry has jurisdiction, power and authority to reach a finding of fact or conclusion. But that finding must be based on some evidence. Neither the technical rules of Evidence Act nor of proof of fact or evidence as defined therein, apply to disciplinary proceeding. When the authority accepts that evidence and conclusion receives support therefrom, the disciplinary authority is entitled to hold that the delinquent officer is guilty of the charge. The Court/Tribunal in its power of judicial review does not act as appellate authority to reappreciate the evidence and to arrive at its own independent findings on the evidence. The Court/Tribunal may interfere where the authority held the proceedings against the delinquent officer in a manner inconsistent with the rules of natural justice or in violation of statutory rules prescribing the mode of inquiry or where the conclusion or finding reached by the disciplinary authority is based on no evidence. If the conclusion or finding be such as no reasonable person would have ever reached, the Court/Tribunal may interfere with the conclusion or the finding, and mould the relief so as to make it appropriate to the facts of each case.

13. The disciplinary authority is the sole judge of facts.

Where appeal is presented, the appellate authority has coextensive power to reappreciate the evidence or the nature of punishment. In a disciplinary inquiry, the strict proof of legal evidence and findings on that evidence are not relevant. Adequacy of evidence or reliability of evidence cannot be permitted to be canvassed before the Court/Tribunal. In Union of India v. H.C. Goel [(1964) 4 SCR 718 : AIR 1964 SC 364 : (1964) 1 LLJ 38] this Court held at p. 728 that if the conclusion, upon consideration of the evidence reached by the disciplinary authority, is perverse or suffers from patent error on the face of the record or based on no evidence at all, a writ of certiorari could be issued."

This Court in Management of Tamil Nadu State Transport Corporation (Coimbatore) Limited v. M. Chandrasekaran 6 held that in exercise of power of judicial review, the Labour Commissioner exceeded his jurisdiction in reappreciating the evidence adduced before the enquiry officer and in substituting his own judgment to that of the disciplinary authority. It was not a case of no legal evidence. The question as to decision of the disciplinary authority of dismissing the respondent is just and proper could be assailed by the respondent in appropriate proceedings. Considering the fact that there was adequate material produced in the departmental enquiry evidencing that fatal accident was caused by the respondent while driving the vehicle on duty, the burden to prove that the accident happened due to some other cause than his own negligence was on the respondent. The doctrine of res ipsa loquitur squarely applies to the fact situation. The Court held as under:

"11. The respondent on the other hand contends that the Commissioner has applied the well-settled legal position that there can be no presumption of misconduct by the employees. That, charge must be proved by the Department during the inquiry. Non-examination of the material witnesses such as eyewitnesses present on the spot, conductor and passengers, travelling on the same bus was fatal. For, it entails in not substantiating the charges against the respondent and failure to discharge the initial onus resting on the Department to prove the charge as framed. According to the respondent, no fault can be found with the tangible reasons recorded by the Commissioner as noticed by

the Single Judge (reproduced above); and resultantly, the conclusion of the Commissioner of not according approval to the order of dismissal is just and proper. It is submitted that the Single Judge was justified in allowing the writ petition preferred by the respondent and issuing direction to the appellant to reinstate him with back wages andcontinuity of service and all attendant benefits accrued to him."

25. *This Court in Ajit Kumar Nag v. General Manager (PJ), Indian Oil Corpn. Ltd., Haldia & Ors. 7 held that the degree of proof which is necessary to order a conviction is different from the degree of proof necessary to record the commission of delinquency. In criminal law, burden of proof is on the prosecution and unless the prosecution is able to prove the guilt of the accused "beyond reasonable doubt", he cannot be convicted by a court of law. In a departmental enquiry, on the other hand, penalty can be imposed on the delinquent officer on a finding recorded on the basis of "preponderance of probability". It was held as under:*

"11. As far as acquittal of the appellant by a criminal court is concerned, in our opinion, the said order does not preclude the Corporation from taking an action if it is otherwise permissible. In our judgment, the law is fairly well settled.Acquittal by a criminal court would not debar an employer from exercising power in accordance with the Rules and Regulations in force. The two proceedings, criminal and departmental, are entirely different. They operate in different fields and have different objectives. Whereas the object of criminal trial is to inflict appropriate punishment on the offender, the purpose of enquiry proceedings is to deal with the delinquent departmentally and to impose penalty in accordance with the service rules. In a criminal trial, incriminating statement made by the accused in certain circumstances or before certain officers is totally inadmissible in evidence. Such strict rules of evidence and procedure would not apply to departmental proceedings. The degree of proof which is necessary to order a conviction is different from the degree of proof necessary to record the commission of delinquency. The rule relating to

appreciation of evidence in the two proceedings is also not similar. In criminal law, burden of proof is on the prosecution and unless the prosecution is able to prove the guilt of the accused "beyond reasonable doubt", he cannot be convicted by a court of law. In a departmental enquiry, on the other hand, penalty can be imposed on the delinquent officer on a finding recorded on the basis of "preponderance of probability". Acquittal of the appellant by a Judicial Magistrate, therefore, does not ipso facto absolve him from the liability under the disciplinary jurisdiction of the Corporation. We are, therefore, unable to uphold the contention of the appellant that since he was acquitted by a criminal court, the impugned order dismissing him from service deserves to be quashed and set aside."
(Emphasis Supplied)

26. This Court in *Noida Entrepreneurs Association v. NOIDA &Ors.* held that the criminal prosecution is launched for an offence for violation of a duty, the offender owes to the society or for breach of which law has provided that the offender shall make satisfaction to the public, whereas, the departmental inquiry is to maintain discipline in the service and efficiency of public service. It was held as under:

"11. A bare perusal of the order which has been quoted in its totality goes to show that the same is not based on any rational foundation. The conceptual difference between a departmental inquiry and criminal proceedings has not been kept in view. Even orders passed by the executive have to be tested on the touchstone of reasonableness. [See Tata Cellular v. Union of India [(1994) 6 SCC 651] and Teri Oat Estates (P) Ltd. v. U.T., Chandigarh [(2004) 2 SCC 130] .] The conceptual difference between departmental proceedings and criminal proceedings have been highlighted by this Court in several cases. Reference may be made to Kendriya Vidyalaya Sangathan v. T. Srinivas [(2004) 7 SCC 442 : 2004 SCC (L&S) 1011] , Hindustan Petroleum Corpn. Ltd. v. Sarvesh Berry [(2005) 10 SCC 471 : 2005 SCC (Cri) 1605] and Uttaranchal RTC v. Mansaram Nainwal [(2006) 6 SCC 366 : 2006 SCC (L&S) 1341] .

"8. ... The purpose of departmental inquiry and of prosecution are two different and distinct aspects. The criminal prosecution is launched for an offense for violation of a duty, the offender owes to the society or for breach of which law has provided that the offender shall make satisfaction to the public. So crime is an act of commission in violation of law or of omission of public duty. The departmental inquiry is to maintain discipline in the service and efficiency of public service. It would, therefore, be expedient that the disciplinary proceedings are conducted and completed as expeditiously as possible. It is not, therefore, desirable to lay down any guidelines as inflexible rules in which the departmental proceedings may or may not be stayed pending trial in the criminal cases against the delinquent officer. Each case requires to be considered in the backdrop of its own facts and circumstances. There would be no bar to proceed simultaneously with departmental inquiry and trial of a criminal case unless the charge in the criminal trial is of grave nature involving complicated questions of fact and law. Offense generally implies infringement of public duty, as distinguished from mere private rights punishable under criminal law. When the trial for a criminal offense is conducted it should be in accordance with proof of the offense as per the evidence defined under the provisions of the Indian Evidence Act, 1872 [in short 'the Evidence Act']. The converse is the case of departmental inquiry. The inquiry in a departmental proceeding relates to conduct or breach of duty of the delinquent officer to punish him for his misconduct defined under the relevant statutory rules or law. That the strict standard of proof or applicability of the Evidence Act stands excluded is a settled legal position. ... Under these circumstances, what is required to be seen is whether the departmental inquiry would seriously prejudice the delinquent in his defense at the trial in a criminal case. It is always a question of fact to be considered in each case depending on its own facts and circumstances."

27. This Court in Depot Manager, A.P. State Road Transport Corporation v. Mohd. Yousuf Miya &Ors. 9 held that in the disciplinary proceedings, the question is whether the respondent is

guilty of such conduct as would merit his removal from service or a lesser punishment. It was held as under:

"7. ...There is yet another reason. The approach and the objective in the criminal proceedings and the disciplinary proceedings is altogether distinct and different. In the disciplinary proceedings, the question is whether the respondent is guilty of such conduct as would merit his removal from service or a lesser punishment, as the case may be, whereas in the criminal proceedings the question is whether the offences registered against him under the Prevention of Corruption Act (and the Penal Code, 1860, if any) are established and, if established, what sentence should be imposed upon him. The standard of proof, the mode of enquiry and the rules governing the enquiry and trial in both the cases are entirely distinct and different. Staying of disciplinary proceedings pending criminal proceedings, to repeat, should not be a matter of course but a considered decision. Even if stayed at one stage, the decision may require reconsideration if the criminal case gets unduly delayed." (Emphasis Supplied)

28. Mr. Yadav, learned counsel for the writ petitioner has submitted that during the pendency of the writ petition before the High Court, the appellants were given opportunity to produce the registers of the entrustment of S.L.R. to the writ petitioner. But it was stated that record was not available being an old record as the incident was of 1993. The enquiry was initiated in 2013 after the acquittal of the writ petitioner from the criminal trial. Therefore, in the absence of the best evidence of registers, the oral evidence of use of official weapon stands proven on the basis of oral testimony of the departmental witnesses.

29. The burden of proof in the departmental proceedings is not of beyond reasonable doubt as is the principle in the criminal trial but probabilities of the misconduct. The delinquent such as the writ petitioner could examine himself to rebut the allegations of misconduct including use of personal weapon. In fact, the reliance of the writ petitioner is upon a communication dated 1.5.2014 made to the Commandant through the inquiry officer. He has stated that he has not fired on higher officers and that he was out of camp at the alleged time of incident. Therefore, a false case has been made against him. His further stand is that it was a terrorist attack and terrorists have fired on the Camp. None of the departmental witnesses have been even suggested about any terrorist attack or that the writ petitioner was out of camp. Constable D.K. Mishra had immobilized the writ petitioner whereas all other witnesses have seen the writ petitioner being immobilized and being removed to quarter guard. PW-5 Brij Kishore Singh deposed that 3-4 soldiers had taken the Self-Loading Rifle (S.L.R.)of the writ petitioner in their possession. Therefore, the allegations in the chargesheet dated 25.2.2013 that the writ petitioner has fired from the official weapon is a reliable finding returned by the Departmental Authorities on the basis of evidence placed before them. It is not a case of no evidence, which alone would warrant interference by the High Court in exercise of power of judicial review. It is not the case of the writ petitioner that there was any infraction of any rule or regulations or the violation of the principles of natural justice. The best available evidence had been produced by the appellants in the course of enquiry conducted after long lapse of time.

30. Consequently, we find that the order passed by the High Court is not sustainable. Hence, the same is set aside and the order of punishment of dismissal passed on 21.12.1996 as affirmed in appeal and revision stands restored. Accordingly, the appeal is allowed."

8.2 Rule 27 of the CRPF Rules, 1955 to the extent it provides for punishments other than those specified in Section 11 of the CRPF Act, 1949 is *intra-vires* the CRPF Act, 1949

The Supreme Court vide Judgment dated 8.5. 2024 in Civil Appeal No.6135 of 2024 in the matter of Union of India & Ors. Versus Santosh Kumar Tiwari held as under:

"1. Leave granted.

2. This appeal is against the judgment and order of the High Court of Orissa at Cuttack dated 10.12.2020, whereby the Writ Appeal No.

435/2020, preferred by the appellants against the judgment and order of the learned Single Judge dated 14.01.2020, has been dismissed and the order of the learned Single Judge has been affirmed.

Factual Matrix

3. The respondent was a Head Constable in Central Reserve Police Force. He was charge-sheeted on allegations of assaulting and abusing his fellow colleague. In the ensuing enquiry, the charges were found proved against the respondent. As a result thereof, the respondent was compulsorily retired from service vide order dated 16.02.2006. Aggrieved therewith, the respondent filed a departmental appeal, which was dismissed by the Deputy Inspector General (P), CRPF vide order dated 28.07.2006.

4. Assailing the order of compulsory retirement and dismissal of his appeal, the respondent filed a Writ Petition (C) No.17398/2006 before a Single Judge Bench of the High Court. The learned Single Judge vide order dated 14.01.2020 allowed the writ petition, inter alia, on the ground that the punishment of compulsory retirement was not one of the punishments specified in Section 11 (1) of the Central Reserve Police Force Act, 19494. The operative portion of the order of the learned Single Judge is extracted below:

"Thus, this court is of the opinion that the award of punishment by the order vide Annexure 5 not only remains bad, but in the circumstances, the consequential order vide Annexure 7 also becomes bad. In such view of the matter and as the Disciplinary Authority is to reconsider the question of punishment, this matter is relegated back to the Disciplinary Authority to hear the question of punishment, giving opportunity of hearing to the petitioner and pass the final order involving the disciplinary proceeding. For a remand of the matter to the Disciplinary Authority, this court observes, the Disciplinary Authority, while reconsidering the matter will also consider other grounds raised herein. For the setting aside of the order vide Annexure 5 and as the matter is relegated back to the authority, the position of *the petitioner before passing of the final order shall be restored and for interference of this court with the order vide Annexures 5 and 7 release of the arrears, if any, involving the petitioner shall be dependent on the ultimate outcome involving fresh disposal of the proceeding by the Disciplinary Authority in terms of the directions of the apex court in paragraph 24 of the judgement in the case of Ranjit Singh versus Union of India as reported in (2006) 4 SCC 153."*

5. Aggrieved with the order of the learned Single Judge, the appellants preferred writ appeal before the Division Bench of the High Court, inter alia, on the following grounds:

(i) The charges against the respondent were found proved in the enquiry. They were of serious nature warranting penalty including that of dismissal or removal from service. Compulsory retirement is nothing but a species of removal from service and, therefore, being a lesser penalty than dismissal or removal from service, was an imposable punishment.

(ii) Section 11 of the CRPF Act provides that, subject to the rules made under the Act, the Commandant or any other authority or officer, as may be prescribed, award in lieu of, or in addition to, suspension or dismissal, anyone or more of the punishments specified therein to any member of the Force whom he considers to be guilty of disobedience, neglect of duty or remissness in the discharge of duty or of other misconduct in his capacity as a member of the Force. Sub-section (1) of Section 18 empowers the Central Government to notify rules for carrying out the purposes of the CRPF Act. Sub-section (2) of Section 18 provides that without prejudice to the generality of the foregoing power, rules may provide for all or any of the matters specified therein, which includes regulating the award of minor punishment under Section 11, and providing for appeals from, or the revision of, orders under that section, or remission of fines imposed under that section. Rule 27 of the Central Reserve Police Force Rules, 19555, specifies the procedure for the award of punishments. Clause (a) of Rule 27 enumerates in a tabular form the punishments which could be imposed

and the authority competent to impose such punishments. At serial no.4, under column no.2, in the table, the punishment of compulsory retirement is mentioned as being one of the punishments that may be imposed by the Commandant after a formal departmental enquiry. Thus, in light of the provisions of Section 11 of the CRPF Act read with Rule 27 of the CRPF Rules, and by taking into consideration that charges were duly proved in the enquiry, the punishment of compulsory retirement was fully justified.

6. The Division Bench of the High Court, however, found no merit in the writ appeal and dismissed the same accordingly.

7. In these circumstances, the appellants are before this Court questioning the impugned judgment and order of the High Court.

8. We have heard Ms. Aishwarya Bhati, learned Additional Solicitor General, appearing for the appellants, and Mr. Anand Shankar, learned counsel, appearing for the respondent.

Submissions on behalf of the appellants

9. Ms. Bhati, learned counsel for the appellants, inter alia, submitted:

(i) The only ground pressed by the original petitioner was that the punishment of compulsory retirement is not imposable as it is not provided for in Section 11 of the CRPF Act, which is nothing but misconceived;

(ii) The High Court while accepting the above ground failed to consider:

(a) Section 11 of the CRPF Act is expressly made subject to any rules made under the Act. Section 18 of the CRPF Act empowered the Central Government to make rules for carrying out the purposes of the Act and without prejudice to the generality of the foregoing power, rules could be made regulating the award of punishment under Section 11. CRPF Rules, 1955 were notified by the Central Government. Rule 27 specifically provided for compulsory retirement as one of the *punishments imposable on a non-gazetted officer, like the respondent. Thus, the impugned order of the High Court is in ignorance of the relevant provisions of the Act as well as the rules.*

(b) Section 11 empowers the Commandant or any other competent authority to award in lieu of, or in addition to, suspension or dismissal anyone or more of the specified punishments. The specified punishments include removal from any office of distinction or special emolument in the Force. Dismissal is the highest of those punishments. Removal is a lesser punishment. Section 11 uses the word removal as an expression of wide amplitude so as to include any punishment that has the effect of terminating the service. As compulsory retirement also entails in termination of service, it is nothing but a species of removal, which is permissible under the CRPF Rules. Therefore, once an enquiry is held, charge of gross indiscipline is found proved, bearing in mind that the original petitioner was a member of a disciplined force, the punishment awarded, being one of the punishments imposable, was not liable to be interfered with by the High Court.

10. In support of her submissions, Ms. Bhati relied on two decisions of this Court, namely, (a) Union of India &Ors. v. Ghulam Mohd. Bhat ; and (b) Union of India &Ors. v. Diler Singh.

Submissions on behalf of the respondent

11. Mr. Anand Shankar, learned counsel for the respondent, defending the impugned order submitted:

(i) Punishment of compulsory retirement as specified in Rule 27 of the CRPF Rules is ultra vires the provisions of Section 11 of the CRPF Act, which is exhaustive, and no punishment beyond what is specified therein can be imposed;

(ii) Decision of this Court in Ghulam Mohd. Bhat (supra) is of no help to the appellants as it relates to the punishment of removal from service and not compulsory retirement from service;

(iii) Rule 27 was framed in exercise of power delegated to the Central Government under clause (d) of sub-section (2) of Section 18 of the CRPF Act, which is only to regulate the award of minor punishment not to introduce any other species / kind of punishment. Therefore, a punishment which is not contemplated under the statute cannot be introduced by way of a rule, particularly in absence of specific delegation of power in this regard. Dismissal and compulsory retirement are two different kinds of punishment and cannot be treated as interchangeable. Thus, in absence of any delegation of power to frame rules introducing a new punishment, Rule 27, to the extent it introduces the punishment of compulsory retirement, is ultra vires the CRPF Act;

(iii)The charge levelled on the original petitioner was not established, as no eyewitness was presented to prove it. Otherwise also, Hawaldar M. Devnath, who was allegedly assaulted by the original petitioner, was inimical to the original petitioner and made a false complaint. The Disciplinary Authority and the Appellate Authority acted in a mechanical manner.

12. In support of his submissions, Mr. Anand Shankar relied on a decision of this Court in General Officer Commanding-in-Chief & Anr. v. Subash Chandra Yadav & Anr.

13. Having taken note of the rival submissions, the issues that arise for our consideration in this appeal are as follows:

(i) Whether the punishment of compulsory retirement from service could have been imposed upon the respondent by relying upon the provisions of Rule 27 of the CRPF Rules?

(ii) Whether Rule 27 of the CRPF Rules to the extent it provides for punishments other than those specified in Section 11 of the CRPF Act, ultra vires the CRPF Act and as such inoperable and void?

(iii)Whether the punishment of compulsory retirement imposed upon the respondent suffers from any procedural infirmity and / or is

shockingly disproportionate to the proven misconduct of the respondent?

An Overview of the CRPF Act and the Rules

14. Before we address the above issues it would be useful to have an overview of the relevant provisions of the CRPF Act and the rules made thereunder. The CRPF Act is "an Act to provide for the constitution and regulation of an armed Central Reserve Police Force (for short the Force)". Section 3 provides for constitution of the Force. Subsection (2) of Section 3 provides that the Force shall be constituted in such manner, and the members of the Force shall receive such pay, pension and other remuneration, as may be prescribed. The word "prescribed" is defined in Section 2 (f) as prescribed by rules made under the Act. Section 8 vests the superintendence, control and administration of the Force in the Central Government. It declares that the Force shall be administered by the Central Government in accordance with the provisions of the Act and of any rules made thereunder, through such officers as the Central Government may from time to time appoint in that behalf. Section 9 enumerates "more heinous offences", whereas Section 10 enumerates "less heinous offences", both punishable under the Act. For "more heinous offences", the punishment is of transportation for life or for a term of not less than seven years or with imprisonment for a term which may extend to 14 years or with fine which may extend to three months' pay, or with fine to that extent, in addition to such sentence of transportation or imprisonment. The punishment for "less heinous offences" is imprisonment for a term which may extend to one year, or with fine which may extend to three months' pay or with both. Section 11 deals with minor punishments. According to it, the Commandant or any other authority or officer as may be prescribed, may, subject to any rules made under the Act, award in lieu of, or in addition to, suspension or dismissal anyone or more of the punishments specified therein to any member of the Force whom he considers to be guilty of disobedience, neglect of duty, or remissness in the discharge of any duty or of other misconduct in his capacity as a member of the Force. One of the minor punishments specified in Section 11, other than dismissal or suspension, is "removal from any office of distinction or special emolument in the Force".

15. Section 18 confers rule-making power on the Central Government. Sub-section (1) of Section 18 states that the Central Government may, by notification in the Official Gazette, make rules for carrying out the purposes of the Act. Sub-section (2) of Section 18 provides that without prejudice to the generality of the foregoing power, such rules may provide for all or any of the matters specified therein. Amongst other matters specified therein, clause (d) inter alia, empowers the Central Government to make rules for regulating the award of minor punishment under Section 11, and providing for appeals from, or the revision of, orders under that section.

16. An overview of the CRPF Act would make it clear that the Central Government has overall superintendence and control over the Force and the Force is to be administered by the Central Government in accordance with the provisions of the CRPF Act and of any rules made thereunder through such officers as the Central Government may from time to time appoint.

Discussion/ Analysis

17. The rule-making power of the Central Government found in Section 18 is in broad terms. sub-section (1) of Section 18 empowers the Central Government to make rules for carrying out the purposes of the CRPF Act. Rule-making power under sub-section (2) of Section 18 is without prejudice to the generality of the power conferred by sub-section (1) thereof. Thus, the Central Government is not only empowered to make rules for regulating the award of minor punishment under Section 11 but also to carry out the purposes of the Act which includes superintendence of, and control over, the Force as well as its administration.

Punishment of compulsory retirement is intra vires the CRPF Act

18. Ordinarily a person in service cannot be visited with a punishment not specified in the contract of service or the law governing such service. Punishments may be specified either in the contract of service or in the Act or the rules governing such service. In State Bank of India and Ors. v. T.J. Paul this Court had occasion to deal with a situation where, for a proven charge of gross misconduct, punishment of removal was not one of the punishments specified in the extant rules though, punishment of dismissal was imposable. This Court set aside the punishment of removal and remitted the matter to the Appellate Authority for considering imposition of one or the other punishment as specified in the extant rules.

19. In the case on hand the CRPF Rules provide for imposition of the punishment of compulsory retirement though the CRPF Act itself does not provide for it in specific terms. Therefore, the argument on behalf of the respondent is that the CRPF Rules are ultra vires the CRPF Act. In support of this submission reliance has been placed on a decision of this Court in **Subash Chandra Yadav (supra)** *where it was observed:*

"14....... It is well settled that rules framed under the provisions of a statute form part of the statute. In other words, rules have statutory force. But before a rule can have the effect of a statutory provision, two conditions must be fulfilled, namely, (1) it must conform to the provisions of the statute under which it is framed; and (2) it must also come within the scope and purview of the rule-making power of the authority framing the rule. If either of these two conditions is not fulfilled, the rule so framed would be void." (Emphasis supplied)

20. The CRPF Act while dealing with offences and punishments, categorizes offences in two parts. One "more heinous offences" (vide Section 9) and the other "less heinous offences" (vide Section 10). These two categories of offences entail a punishment of imprisonment and/or fine. The usual disciplinary action which befalls on a delinquent employee is envisaged as a minor punishment under Section 11 of the

CRPF Act even though many of the punishments specified therein, such as dismissal, reduction in rank and removal from office of distinction, in common service jurisprudence are considered major punishment. That apart, Section 11 which describes minor punishments declares: (a) that the minor punishments specified in Section 11 may be awarded "in lieu of, or in addition to, suspension or dismissal"; and (b) that the power of the Commandant or any other authority or officer, as may be prescribed, to award the specified punishment "is subject to any rules made under the CRPF Act". Another important feature is that Section 11 does not use common expressions such as "dismissal from service" or "removal from service" while describing the punishments. Though, Rule 27 (vide Table) uses those expressions.

21. The question which would therefore arise for our consideration is whether Section 11 is exhaustive as far as minor punishments imposable under the CRPF Act are concerned or it merely provides for a skeletal framework to be supplemented by the rules framed under the Act.

22. **In Ghulam Mohd. Bhat (supra)**, a question arose whether punishment of removal from service could be awarded to a Constable in the Force. The argument against the award of punishment of removal from service was that it is not one of the punishments specified in Section 11 of the CRPF Act. The Union of India defended the said punishment on the ground that it is a species of dismissal and permissible under Rule 27 of the CRPF Rules. After examining the provisions of Section 11 of the CRPF Act and Rule 27 of the CRPF Rules, this Court observed:

"5. A bare perusal of Section 11 shows that it deals with minor punishment as compared to the major punishments prescribed in the preceding section. It lays down that the Commandant or any other authority or officer, as may be prescribed, may, subject to any rules made under the Act, award any one or more of the punishments to any member of the Force who is found guilty of disobedience, neglect of duty or remissness in the discharge of his duty or of other misconduct *in his capacity as a member of the Force. According to the High Court the only punishments which can be awarded under this section are reduction in rank, fine, confinement to quarters and removal from any office of distinction or special emolument in the Force. In our opinion, the interpretation is not correct, because the section says that these punishments may be awarded in lieu of, or in addition to, suspension or dismissal. 6. The use of the words "in lieu of, or in addition to, suspension or dismissal", appearing in subsection (1) of Section 11 before clauses (a) to (e) shows that the authorities mentioned therein are empowered to award punishment of dismissal or suspension to the member of the Force who is found guilty and in addition to, or in lieu thereof, the punishment mentioned in clauses (a) to (e) may also be awarded. 8. It is fairly well-settled position in law that removal is a form of dismissal. This Court in Dattatraya Mahadev Nadkarni (Dr.) v. Municipal Corpn. of Greater Bombay [(1992) 2 SCC 547 : 1992 SCC (L&S) 615 : (1992) 20 ATC 275 : AIR 1992 SC 786] explained that removal and dismissal from service stand on the same footing and both bring about termination of service though every termination of service does not amount to removal or dismissal. The only difference between the two is that in the case of dismissal the employee is disqualified from future employment while in the case of removal he is not debarred from getting future employment. Therefore, dismissal has more serious consequences in comparison to removal. In any event, Section 11(1) refers to the Rules made under the Act under which action can be taken. Rule 27 is part of the Rules made under the Act. Rule 27 clearly permits removal by the competent authority. In the instant case the Commandant who had passed the order of removal was the competent authority to pass the order." (Emphasis supplied)*

23. The learned counsel for the respondent seeks to distinguish the above decision, inter alia, on the ground that removal may be a species of dismissal or vice versa but compulsory retirement is not, because in common service jurisprudence compulsory retirement is not considered a punishment. Therefore, according to him, Rule 27 prescribes an altogether new punishment which is not contemplated by

the CRPF Act. Hence, according to him, Rule 27 to that extent is ultra vires the CRPF Act and as such void.

24. To determine whether the punishment of compulsory retirement prescribed in Rule 27 is ultra vires the CRPF Act, it would be apposite to first examine the scope of rule-making power conferred on the Central Government by the statute. The CRPF Act, vide sub-section (1) of Section 18, grant the power to make rules in general terms, that is, "to carry out the purposes of this Act". And, vide subsection (2) of Section 18, "in particular and without prejudice to the generality of the foregoing power", to make rules for all or any of the matters enumerated therein. Interpreting such a rule-making provision, in State of Jammu and Kashmir v. Lakhwinder Kumar and Ors., a two-Judge Bench of this Court, relying on a Constitution Bench decision in Rohtak & Hissar Districts Electric Supply Co. Ltd. v. State of U.P. &Ors., held:

"23. In our opinion, when the power is conferred in general and thereafter in respect of enumerated matters, as in the present case, the particularization in respect of specified subject is construed as merely illustrative and does not limit the scope of general power. Reference in this connection can be made to a decision of this Court in Rohtak and Hissar Districts Electric Supply Co. Ltd. v. State of UP, in which it has been held as follows:

"18......... Section 15 (1) confers wide powers on the appropriate government to make rules to carry out the purposes of the Act; and Section 15 (2) specifies some of the matters enumerated by clauses (a) to (e) in respect of which rules may be framed. It is well settled that the enumeration of the particular matters by sub-section (2) will not control or limit the width of the powers conferred on the appropriate government by sub-section (1) of Section 15; and so, if it appears that the item added by the appropriate government has relation to conditions of employment, its addition cannot be challenged as being invalid in law." (Emphasis supplied)

This would imply that the intention of the legislature, as indicated in the enabling Act, must be the prime guide to the extent of delegate's power to make rules. However, the delegate must not travel wider than the object of the legislature rather it must remain true to it.

25. In St. Johns Teachers Training Institute v. Regional Director, National Council for Teacher, a three-Judge Bench of this Court observed:

"10. .... The power to make subordinate legislation is derived from the enabling act and it is fundamental that the delegate on whom such a power is conferred has to act within the limits of authority conferred by the Act. Rules cannot be made to supplant the provisions of the enabling act but to supplement it. What is permitted is the delegation of ancillary or subordinate legislative functions, or, what is fictionally called, a power to fill up details. The legislature may, after laying down the legislative policy confer discretion on an administrative agency as to the execution of the policy and leave it to the agency to work out the details within the framework of policy....................

12. The question whether any particular legislation suffers from excessive delegation has to be decided having regard to the subject matter, the scheme, the provisions of the statute including its preamble and the facts and circumstances in the background of which the statute is enacted........It is also well settled that in considering the vires of subordinate legislation one should start with the presumption that it is intra vires and if it is open to two constructions, one of which would make it valid and the other invalid, the courts must adopt that construction which makes it valid and the legislation can also be read down to avoid its being declared ultra vires." (Emphasis supplied)

26. Francis Bennion in his treatise on Statutory Interpretation (Fifth Edition, page 262, Section 69) has written:

"There are various types of delegated legislation, but all are subject to certain fundamental factors. Underlying the concept of delegated

legislation is the basic principle that the legislature delegates because it cannot directly exert its will in every detail. All it can in practice do is lay down the outline. This means that the intention of the legislature, as indicated in the outline (that is the enabling Act), must be the prime guide to the meaning of delegated legislation and the extent of the power to make it."

27. As discussed above, since the rule-making power under Section 18 of the CRPF Act is in broad terms, that is to carry out the purposes of the Act as well as to regulate the award of minor punishment under Section 11, in order to determine whether Rule 27 of the CRPF Rules, insofar as it prescribes an additional punishment of compulsory retirement, is intra vires or ultra vires the CRPF Act, we would have to consider: (a) whether the intention of the legislature, as borne out from the provisions of the CRPF Act, was to leave it open for the Central Government to prescribe any other minor punishment than what has already been prescribed in Section 11 of the Act; and (b) whether it is in conflict with any of the provisions of the CRPF Act.

28. As regards Section 11 being exhaustive of the minor punishments which could be imposed, the intention of the legislature appears to the contrary. Section 11 expressly uses the phrase "subject to any rules made under this Act" before "award in lieu of, or in addition to, suspension or dismissal any one or more of the following punishments". Importantly, while prescribing punishment for "more heinous offences" and "less heinous offences" in Sections 9 and 10 respectively, the phrase "subject to any rules made under this Act" is not used. The expression "subject to" conveys the idea of a provision yielding place to another provision or other provisions subject to which it is made.

29. G.P. Singh in his treatise "Principles of Statutory Interpretation" (13th Edition, Chapter 12 at page 1019, published by LexisNexis) writes: "The delegate cannot override the Act either by exceeding the authority or by making provisions inconsistent with the Act. But when the enabling Act itself permits its modification by rules, the rules made

prevail over the provision in the Act. When provision A in the Act is subject to other provisions of the Act, a valid notification issued under any other provision in the Act would in case of conflict with section A override its provisions."

30. In light of the discussion above, we are of the view that while enacting the CRPF Act the legislative intent was not to declare that only those minor punishments could be imposed as are specified in Section 11 of the CRPF Act. Rather, it was left open for the Central Government to frame rules to carry out the purposes of the Act and the punishments imposable were subject to the rules framed under the Act.

31. In that context, one of the purposes of the Act could be gathered from Section 8, which vests the superintendence and control over the Force in the Central Government. The concept of "control", as per P. Ramantha Aiyer's Advanced Law Lexicon (4th Edition), inter alia, implies that the controlling authority must be in a position to dominate the affairs of its subordinate19. In State of West Bengal v. Nripendra Nath Bagchi, a Constitution Bench of this Court had occasion to explore the true import of the expression 'control' as used in Article 235 of the Constitution of India. After considering the submissions, it was held that the word 'control' must include disciplinary jurisdiction. In Madan Mohan Choudhary v. State of Bihar &Ors. it was reiterated that the expression 'control,' as used in Article 235 of the Constitution, includes disciplinary control. It was also observed that transfers, promotions, and confirmations including transfer of District Judges or the recall of District Judges posted on ex-cadre post or on deputation or on administrative post etc. is also within the administrative control of the High Court. So also, premature and compulsory retirement is within the control of the High Court.

32. From above, it is clear that 'control' is a word of wide amplitude and includes disciplinary control. Therefore, in our view, if the CRPF Act envisages vesting of control over the Force in the Central Government and the various punishments imposable under Section 11 are subject to the rules made under the Act, the Central Government

in exercise of its general rule-making power, to ensure full and effective control over the Force, can prescribe punishments other than those specified in that section, including the punishment of compulsory retirement.

33. It cannot be gainsaid that compulsory retirement is a well-accepted method of removing dead wood from the cadre without affecting his entitlement for retirement benefits, if otherwise payable. It is another form of terminating the service without affecting retirement benefits. Ordinarily, compulsory retirement is not considered a punishment. But if the service rules permit it to be imposed by way of a punishment, subject to an enquiry, so be it. To keep the Force efficient, weeding out undesirable elements therefrom is essential and is a facet of control over the Force, which the Central Government has over the Force by virtue of Section 8 of the CRPF Act. Thus, to ensure effective control over the Force, if rules are framed, in exercise of general rule-making power, prescribing the punishment of compulsory retirement, the same cannot be said to be ultra vires Section 11 of the CRPF Act, particularly when sub-section (1) of Section 11 clearly mentions that the power exercisable therein is subject to any rules made under the Act. We, therefore, hold that the punishment of compulsory retirement prescribed by Rule 27 is intra vires the CRPF Act and is one of the punishments imposable. Issues (i) and (ii) are decided in the above terms."

8.3 Further the Hon'ble Delhi High in WP(C) 11051/2017 titled Ex Ct/GD Prem Kumar Singh Vs Union of India & Ors while interpreting the mandate of Rule 27 (ccc) of CRPF Rules 1955 observed that *"In the present case too, the acquittal was not on technical grounds. In fact the present case stands on an even stronger footing from the point of view of the Petitioner. It is seen that there is no provision in the CRPF Rules which is in pari materia with Rule 12 of the Delhi Police Rules which permits departmental punishment of a delinquent officer on the same charge as in a criminal case where the criminal charge fails on technical grounds. On the other hand Rule 27 (ccc) of the CRPF Rules,*

1955 specifies that when a member of the force has been tried and acquitted by a criminal Court, he shall not be punished departmentally under this rule on the same charge or on a similar charge upon the evidence cited in the criminal case, whether actually led or not, without the prior approval of the Inspector General. Here even without waiting for the outcome of the criminal trial, the Petitioner was dismissed from service.

28. The Court finds that the article of charge on which the Petitioner was proceeded against departmentally is a combination of two alleged acts of misconduct. One part of it concerns his having left the campus without permission for a day and the other pertains to the charge of theft of a motorcycle. As far as the latter part is concerned, with the Petitioner having been acquitted by the trial Court honourably and not on technical grounds, the finding of guilt of the Petitioner for that charge in the department enquiry is clearly unsustainable in law. Rule 27 (ccc) of the CRPF Rules further supports this conclusion."

9. DISCIPLINARY CASES-REQUIREMENT OF ADVICE OF UPSC TO IMPOSE PENALTIES

9.1 High Court of Delhi in Judgment dated 4.12.2019 in W.P.(C) 1525/2019 in the matter of Prakash Kumar Dixit vs. Union of India & Ors. observed as follows

"31. Having perused the file notings and the correspondence placed on record, the Court is of the view that there has been a serious error in the manner in which the Petitioner"s case has been dealt with. The UPSC had, by its letter dated 1st September, 2016, made it clear that it had nothing to add and that it was open to the DA to take an independent view in the matter. To recapitulate, the advice of the UPSC was sought, after the DA decided to impose a minor penalty. The UPSC did not disagree with this. It simply stated that it was not even required to be consulted and that it was open to the DA to take an independent view. The Court is not able to view the above sequence of

events as representing a *"disagreement"* between the UPSC on the one hand, and the DA on the other.

32. The Under Secretary, who had earlier initiated an erroneous noting dated 4th May 2017, despite the decision of the DA, needlessly persisted in placing the matter again for the opinion of the DoPT. After receiving the advice of the MoLJ and the DoPT, the Under Secretary once again referred the file to the DoPT, which reiterated that there is "no denying that the DA can take his independent decision on the quantum of penalty irrespective of the advice of the UPSC". Despite noting thus, the DoPT proceeded on the premise that the case was one of "disagreement", and forwarded the file to the PMO. At the PMO, without giving any reasons, a decision was taken to impose the penalty of removal from service, which was considered to be the advice of the UPSC, when in fact that was not the advice of the UPSC in its letter dated 1st September, 2016. By that letter the UPSC declined to give advice on the basis that "no new material had come to light". It limited itself to advising that the DA could take an independent view, and further, that since the DA had already proposed to impose "another penalty", it was not "appropriate to comment further in the matter".

33. The above sequence of events points clearly to an erroneous procedure having being adopted by the Respondents in dealing with the case of the Petitioner. This primarily was owed to the erroneous note of the Under Secretary in the MHA that there was a "disagreement" between the DA and the UPSC, when there was none. The matter ought not to have been placed before the PM, who, as far as the Petitioner was concerned, was not the DA. The impugned order dated 16th October 2018, removing the Petitioner from service, has come about as a result of the above erroneous procedure, which was entirely unnecessary considering that the DA was at liberty to take a decision independent of the UPSC and did take such a decision, imposing a minor penalty.

34. For all of the aforementioned reasons, the order dated 16th October, 2018, passed by the DIG (CR&VIG) in the Directorate

General, CRPF, imposing the penalty of removal from service on the Petitioner, is hereby set aside. The minor penalty as decided by the DA viz., "reduction to a lower stage in the scale of pay by one stage for a period not exceeding 3 years, without cumulative effect and adversely affecting pension" will be the penalty in the Petitioner"s case.

35. Consequently, the Petitioner is directed to be forthwith reinstated in service, with all consequential benefits, but without any back wages. The date of reinstatement will relate back to the date of his having been originally removed from service i.e. 10th July 1995, for the purposes of pay fixation, seniority and all other consequential benefits including promotions. The consequential orders by way of implementation of this judgment be issued not later than 8 weeks from today.

36. The writ petition is allowed in the above terms. The pending application is disposed of."

The aforesaid judgement was further challenged by the CRPF before the Hon'ble Supreme Court of India

SUPREME COURT

9.2 Supreme Court vide Judgment dated 7.12.2020 in Civil Appeal No 3970 of 2020 in the matter of Union of India &Ors Vs Prakash Kumar Dixit held as under:

OM No 39023/02/2006-Estt (B)

".....If in the opinion of the Secretary of the Ministry of Personnel, Public Grievances and Pensions, there is a case for disagreement with the advice of UPSC in a disciplinary or other matter (other than appointment cases) in respect of services/posts for which it is the controlling authority, a proposal will be placed before the Committee of Secretaries for its consideration. Thereafter, the case will be submitted to the Minister-in-charge/Prime Minister, as the case may be, along with the opinion of the Committee of Secretaries. In cases of appointment, however, the matter will be placed before the Minister-in-charge/Prime Minister directly and if the decision of Minister

involves non-acceptance of the advice of the Commission, the case would be referred to the ACC for a final decision."

"....Hence, in the above factual situation, as it has emerged before the Court, we are in agreement with the ultimate conclusion of the High Court that there was no disagreement between the advice of the UPSC so as to invoke the application of the above OM. We are confining our opinion to the ultimate conclusion which has been arrived at by the High Court on the facts of the present case. However, it needs to be clarified that the impugned judgment and order shall not be construed in any other case as having interpreted the OM dated 5 December 2006 since the decision has turned on the above facts.

The appeal is disposed of, with the above clarification."

10 JUDICIAL TRIAL IN CRPF – CASE LAWS

10.1 Vires of Judicial Trial in CRPF Act

The Supreme Court vide Judgment dated 4.12.2023 in Criminal Appeal No. 410 of 1997 in the matter of State (Union Of India) vs Ram Saran observed as under "*...Questioning conviction made by the Assistant Commandant of Central Reserve Police Force (in short the 'CRPF') made under Section 10(m) of the Central Reserve Police Force Act, 1949 (in short the 'Act') and consequential sentences imposed, the respondent filed an appeal before the Sessions Judge, Solan and Sirmaur. The Sessions Judge held that the Assistant Commandant had no jurisdiction to record conviction and impose sentence. The said judgment was questioned before the High Court of Himachal Pradesh by a revision petition filed by the Union of India. The revision was also dismissed. Both the Sessions Judge and the High Court held that the Assistant Commandant, III Battalion, ITBP, Nahan could not have exercised powers of Judicial Magistrate Ist Class and, therefore, the trial and conviction of the accused-respondent were illegal. The High Court held that combined reading of Sections 11, 12 and 13 of the Code of Criminal Procedure, 1973 (in short the 'Code') clearly rule out the* *appointment of any person exercising powers of Judicial Magistrate, Ist Class in the absence of conferment of powers by the High Court. This, according to the Sessions Judge and the High Court stemmed from the fact that there was separation of judiciary from the Executive in 1973 and thereafter the powers of appointment and conferment for functioning as Judicial Magistrate either of First Class or Second Class could only be done by the High Court and the Central Government or the State Government had no power to invest any person with powers of Judicial Magistrate of any class. Reference was also made to Section 5 of the Code and observed that the expression "in the absence of a specific provision to the contrary" used therein did not render Section 16(2) of the Act redundant.*

At this juncture, it would be necessary to take note of the factual position. The respondent while functioning as a Constable (Sweeper) in the III Battalion, ITBP, Nahan did not join duty after expiry of the leave granted to him. Though he was granted leave for the period from 9.4.1987 to 24.5.1987, he did not join after expiry of the period. There was no intimation to the competent authority or request for extension of leave. The respondent accepted that he had stayed beyond the period of leave, but indicated several reasons as to why the same was necessitated. Complaint was lodged by the concerned authorities and the Assistant Commandant exercising powers of Judicial Magistrate, Ist Class in terms of Section 10 (m) of the Act, issued notice in terms of Section 251 of the Code and after trial found him guilty and sentenced him to undergo imprisonment for three months. The said order as noted above was questioned before the Sessions Judge by the respondent and in view of the relief granted to him by the Sessions Judge, the matter was carried in revision by the Union of India. But the same having been rejected, this appeal has been filed.

In support of the appeal, learned senior counsel for the appellant submitted that the Sessions Judge and the High Court clearly lost sight of Section 16(2) of the Act and Rule 36 (a), (b), (e) and (f) of the Central Reserve Police Force Rules, 1955 (in short the 'Rules') as well as

Sections 4 and 5 of the Code. Section 16(2) of the Act clearly indicates that notwithstanding anything contained in the Code, the provisions of the Act could be applied. Section 4(2) of the Code permits action under any law other than the Indian Penal Code, 1860 (for short the 'IPC'). Section 5 refers to absence of a specific provision to the contrary in any special or local law. The Act was a special law which operated in a specified field. These aspects were not considered in their proper perspective by the Sessions Judge and the High Court.

Per contra, learned counsel for the respondent submitted that the Sessions Judge and the High Court were justified in interfering with the order passed by the Assistant Commandant as he had no jurisdiction to function and his appointment by a Notification issued by the Central Government could not have conferred on him any power to act as a Judicial Magistrate when the sole repository of the power to so notify is the High Court after the Code was enacted in 1973. The position may have been different under the Code of Criminal Procedure, 1898 (in short the 'Old Code'), but the present position is entirely different and the Ministry of Home Affairs' Notification dated 25.1.1978 was really of no consequence.

The Courts below have overlooked certain essential and vital aspects necessary to appreciate the relevant issues arising in their proper perspective. Under Section 3(1) of the Act, CRPF is constituted to be an 'armed force' maintained by the Central Government, and consequently it would be 'any other armed forces of the union' as envisaged in Entry 2 of List I of the VII Schedule to the Constitution of India. Entry 93 of List I enables Parliament also to provide for offences against laws with respect to any of the matters enumerated in List I. Sections 9 and 10 create by enumerating what are stated to be 'more heinous offences' and 'less heinous offences' respectively and many of such specially created offences for the purposes of this Act cannot constitute or amount to be offences under the ordinary criminal law of the land. To that extent they are new class of offences created with punishments therefor, which are unknown to ordinary criminal law in force. Section 16 provides for empowering Competent Authorities in the hierarchy of the force itself with powers or duties conferred or imposed on a police officer of any class or grade by any law for the time being in force and by further enacting a provision with a specific "non obstante" clause stipulates that notwithstanding anything contained in the Code, the Central Government may invest the Commandant or Assistant Commandant with the powers of a Magistrate of any class for the purpose of inquiring into or trying any offence committed by a member of the force and punishable "under this Act" or any offence committed by a member of the force against the person or property of another member. Consequently, what is purported to be done by these provisions are merely to refer to the nature and extent of powers possessed by such authorities under the other laws being made available to the authorities designated under this Act, for discharging their duties under this Act, without exhaustively enumerating the details of all such powers or without re-enacting all such provisions in detail as part and parcel of this law the Act, and not to constitute them to be or empower them as Magistrates as such for all or any of the purposes for which Courts of ordinary criminal justice have been constituted under the Code. Section 5 of the Code sufficiently protects the authorities empowered to function and exercise powers under the Act, from any such challenge as are directed against them, in this case. The fallacy in the reasoning of the Courts below lies in their superficial and cursory nature of consideration undertaken therein, without reference to the competence and powers of the Parliament to specifically and specially provide for trial and punishment of offences separately created under a special enactment of Parliament, in a manner distinct and separate from the method of trying other ordinary criminal offences under the general criminal law of the country.

At the outset, it must be noted that certain infractions which are relatable to service broadly fall within the spectrum of disciplinary proceedings. Section 10(m) is an infraction which though normally would have attracted departmental proceedings, keeping in view the essentiality of force and imminent and ever alert situation in which with high sense of morale and duty consciousness the member of this service is expected to be demonstrate at all times, a serious view of the same is being taken. But the CRPF, the Army, the Navy and the Air Force are disciplined forces and even any infraction which otherwise would not be an offence is deemed to be an offence under certain provisions like Section 10(m) of the Act. Unauthorised absence of an employee staying beyond the sanctioned period of leave is not an offence in the normal course under the ordinary criminal law of the land. But as noted above, disciplined forces with the intention of enforcing discipline have made them punishable considering them as offences and have prescribed various sentences. For such particular purposes the designated officials have been conferred with magisterial powers. The Assistant Commandant who passed the order undisputedly acted as a Judicial Magistrate in view of the powers conferred on him under the Act. The conferment of such power has not been distinctly questioned and could not have been questioned in a proceeding, appeal or a revision under the Code. As long as the specific provision in Act exists enabling the competent Authority to pass the order under challenge, the same will have full force and efficacy. It is well settled that creature of any statute cannot consider the vires of a particular provision in that statute or any other statute as well. Exclusive power for such purposes are vested under the Constitution of India, 1950 (in short 'the Constitution') only on Courts exercising powers of judicial Review under Articles 32/226 of the Constitution alone. While exercising appellate or revisional jurisdiction under the Code it is impermissible for any Court to decide on the vires of the provision. That is precisely what the Sessions Judge and the High Court have done in the present case. The vires of a provision can only be questioned in a writ proceeding before the Constitutional Court. That being the position, neither the Sessions Judge nor the High Court could have found fault with the exercise of jurisdiction by the Assistant Commandant in exercising magisterial powers. It will also be relevant to note that in List I of Seventh Schedule to the Constitution in Union List, Entry 2 makes the position clear that members of CRPF are part of the armed forces of the Union Government. The punishments to be imposed under the Act for various offences are defined by Sections 9 and 10, which have been created by statute. As noted earlier, they are deemed offences and in the scheme of enforcing discipline they have been treated as infractions unbecoming of members belonging to disciplined forces like the CRPF That being the position, the Sessions Judge and the High Court were not justified in holding that the Assistant Commandant had no jurisdiction to deal with the respondent in the concerned trial.

It would also be necessary to take note of Sections 10(m), 16(2) of the Act and Sections 4 and 5 of the Code: Act "Section 10 (m)- Every member of the Force who absents himself without leave, or without sufficient cause overstays leave granted to him shall be punishable with imprisonment for a term which may extend to one year, or with fine which may extend to three months' pay, or with both".

Section 16(2)- Notwithstanding anything contained in the Code of Criminal Procedure, 1898 (5 of 1898) the Central Government may invest the Commandant or an Assistant Commandant with the powers of a Magistrate of any class for the purpose of inquiring into or trying any offence committed by member of the Force and punishable under this Act, or any offence committed by a member of the Force against the person or property of another member:

Provided that-

when the offender is on leave or absent from duty, or

when the offence is not connected with the offender's duties as a member of the Force, or

(iii)when it is a petty offence, even if connected with the offender's duties as a member of the Force, the offence may, if the prescribed authority within the limits of whose jurisdiction the offence has been

committed, so directs, be inquired into or tried by an ordinary criminal court having jurisdiction in the matter".

Code Section 4: Trial of offences under the Indian Penal Code and other laws- (1) All offences under the Indian Penal Code (45 of 1860) shall be investigated, inquired into, tried, and otherwise dealt with according to the provisions hereinafter contained.

(2) All offences under any other law shall be investigated, inquired into, tried, and otherwise dealt with according to the same provisions, but subject to any enactment for the time being in force regulating the manner or place of investigating, inquiring into, trying or otherwise dealing with such offences.

Section 5:Saving- Nothing contained in this Code shall, in the absence of a specific provision to the contrary, affect any special or local law for the time being in force, or any special jurisdiction or power conferred, or any special form of procedure prescribed, by any other law for the time being in force".

Provisions of the Code would be applicable to the investigations, inquiries into and trials of cases by criminal Courts of various descriptions, being the parent statute, in the absence of any contrary provision in any special statute or special provision excluding jurisdiction or applicability of the Code. Sub-section (1) of Section 4 deals with offences under the IPC. Second limb of sub-section (2) deals with the exclusion, reading ".........but subject to any enactment for the time being in force regulating the manner or place of investigating, inquiring into, trying or otherwise dealing with such offences". (See Directorate of Enforcement v. Deepak Mahajan and Anr. (1994 (3) SCC

440). In a case involving Bombay Prevention of Gambling Act, 1887 it was held that the Act was a special law providing special procedures for the manner or place of investigating or inquiring into the offences under it, and therefore the provisions thereof must prevail and no provisions of the Code can apply. (See Nilratan Sircar v. Lakshmi Narayan Ram Niwas (AIR 1965 SC 1).

Section 5 consists of three components, and as observed in Maru Ram etc.etc. v. Union of India and Ors. (1981 (1) SCC 107), they are as follows:

"(1) The Code covers matters covered by it;

If a special or local law exists covering the same area, the said law is saved and will prevail;

If there is a special provision to the contrary, that will override the special or local law. A "special law", as observed in Kaushalya Rani v. Gopal Singh (AIR 1964 SC 260), means a law enacted for special cases, in special circumstances, as distinguished from the general rules of law laid down as being applicable to all cases dealt with by the general law. The Act fits the description.

Additionally, Section 16(2) of the Act begins with a non obstante clause relating to the Code."

There are parallel provisions to Section 10(m) of the Act in the Army Act, 1950 (hereinafter referred to as the 'Army Act'). In fact Section 39 of the Army Act deals with 'absence without leave'. The maximum period of imprisonment may extend to three years or with such less punishment as is mentioned in the said Act itself.

The inevitable conclusion is that the Assistant Commandant was clothed with necessary jurisdiction for trial of the matter.

Residual question is what would be an appropriate sentence. It is not disputed and rather fairly conceded that for a person in a disciplined service like the CRPF, any act of indiscipline deserves adequate and stringent punishment under the Act. In terms of Section 10(m) an employee who absents himself without leave or without sufficient cause overstays leave granted to him can be punished with imprisonment for a term which may extend to one year or with fine which may extend to three months pay or with both. The offence has been treated as one of "less heinous offences". More heinous offences are provided in Section 9. The Assistant Commandant has found the explanation given by the respondent to be not acceptable. Therefore, he has been rightly held to have committed a less heinous offence. Taking note of the relevant aspects, we feel the fine of two months pay which respondent was drawing at the time when the proceedings were initiated would meet the ends of justice. By altering the punishment we are not belittling the gravity of offence but, in our view deterrent punishment must be resorted to when such absence is resorted to avoid and evade undertaking a testing or trying venture or deployment essential at any given point of time, and not as a routine in the normal course. The appeal is allowed to the extent indicated above.

Comments: It is further stated that Section 2(d) of the CRPF Act, 1949 excludes Gazetted Officers from the Purview of Section 9, 10 & 11 of the CRPF Act. The law is well settled in this regard. Only such proceeding may be initiated against a non gazetted official. Proceedings contemplated under CCS(CCA) Rules, 1965 applies for Group A Gazetted Officers in CRPF. The Commandant enjoys the magisterial power as per Sec 16(2) of CRPF Act only for the offences committed by a Non Gazetted Personnel punishable under CRPF Act and further any Rule made under this Act i.e. Rule 27. The offences exclusively mentioned in Sec 9 to 11 of the CRPF Act are not applicable on Gazetted Officers as per the definition in Sec 2(d) of the CRPF Act, 1949 and Rule 110 of CRPF Rules, 1955.

11. INTERPRETATION OF STANDING ORDER FOR GIVING BENEFITS OF PROMOTION

11.1 High Court of Delhi vide Judgment dated 13.12.2018 in W.P.(C) 11263/2015 in the matter of Venkatesh versus Union of India & Ors. held as under:

"11. At the outset, it requires to be notice that while a SHAPE-I medical category is certainly a requirement for consideration for

promotion in terms of SO No.4/2008 dated 15th December 2008, the same SO No.4/2008 recognizes certain medical categories that are eligible for relaxation. Para 4.17 reads as under:

"4.17. Relaxation in SHAPE-1 Medical Category

The relaxation in SHAPE-I Medical Category will be admissible to the following two categories of CPMFs personnel to the extent detailed below:- a. Official/Personnel wounded/injured during war or while fighting against the enemy/militant/intruders/armed hostiles/insurgents due to an act of these in India or abroad will be eligible for promotion while placed in one of the following medical classification:-

i) Individual low Medical Factors

(aa) H2 or E2 opr P2 (Dental) which will be considered at par with SHAPE-1; and;

(ab) A2 or P2 or A3 ii) Combined Low Medical Factors

(aa) H2 and E2 combined and

(ab) H2 or E2 combined with A2, A3 or P2

b) Officers/men who are wounded/injured during field firings/accidental firings/explosion of mines or other explosive devices and due to accidents while on active Government duty in India or abroad will be eligible for promotion in the following

SHAPE Categories:-

i) SIHlA2PlE1 (ii) SIHlAlP2E1 (iii) S1H2A1P1E1

(iv) SIHlAlPlE2 (v)SlH2AlPIE2

12. *Therefore, it is seen that in terms of para 4.17 (B) (v), a permanent E2 medical category, which is the categorization as far as the Petitioner is concerned, is recognized as one of those medical categories which would be viewed as a relaxation in the Shape-I*

medical category. The Further question that arises is whether the Petitioner fulfills the requirement to be considered eligible for such relaxation. In other words is the accident suffered by the Petitioner, as a result of which his medical category is E2, "while on active government duty in India".

13. Section 2 (a) of the CRPF Act defines „active duty" means the duty to restore and preserve order in any local area in the event of any disturbance therein.

14. The stand of the Respondents is that this expression „active duty" has to be read as administrative genres with the circumstances mentioned in para 4.17 B i.e. a duty which could envisage "field firings, accidental firings, explosion of mines or other explosive devices". In other words, the Respondents want to narrow down the expression "accidents" to only those accidents of the aforementioned kind and not just about any accident.

15. There is a difficulty in accepting the submission on behalf of the Respondents. A member of the CRPF does not cease to be on active duty only because he is not actually in the line of firing or dealing with mines or other explosive devices. A member of the CRPF continues to remain on duty in whichever post he is - whether it is an anti-insurgency station posting or a peace posting. He is expected to be ready to perform his duty "to restore and preserve order in any local area in the event of any disturbance there". To elaborate even in a peace station when members of the CRPF are engaged in an activity which is formed part of their assigned duties and suffered an accident, that accident cannot be characterized as not big incurred while on „active duty". It is the preparedness to participate in all activities to restore and preserve order in any local area that is determinative of whether a person is on „active duty" or not.

16. For instance, if in a peace station as part of a regular drill that the officers have to undertake for maintaining their fitness, an accident takes place which reduces an officer medical category from Shape-I to

Shape-II and to be more precise to the E2 permanent medical category. It cannot be said that this is on account of an accident that was not suffered one being on "active duty". At any point in time as long as the officer in that station and in that posting, he may be called upon to perform active duties and therefore to restrict the expressions "accidents" to only those incurred during "field firings, accident firings, explosion of mines" will not do justice to the intention behind providing for such relaxation.

17. Another situation could be that while an officer is in his dormitory or barrack or quarters and there is an accident which occurs and reduces his medical category from Shape-I to Shape-II, can it be said that it was an accident while he was not on "active duty". In the considered view of the Court, the answer has to be in the negative. An officer continues to remain on "active duty" even in such a situation and it will not be justified in characterizing such an accident as having been incurred while not on activity.

18. In a somewhat similar situation in the BSF where a member of the BSF while being posted as a Company Commander was injured while playing a volley ball match with the company troops deployed under him and sustained an injury on his head, this Court held that he had suffered such injury while on duty. In **Ramesh Fonia v. Union of IndiaILR 2014 1 Del 171**, this Court rejected the contention of the Respondents that the Petitioner in that case had not suffered the injury while on "bona fide government duty" attributed to his service. The Court observed as under:

"38. From the above discussion, the inevitable and only possible conclusion is that the evening games were the integral part of the petitioner"s duties. It is also a fact that the petitioner was not exempted from performance of any part of the assigned duty. The respondents have themselves not treated the petitioner as any special case of low medical category. He was being assigned postings and positions just as any other BSF personnel who was not a low medical category including the hard postings. The respondents recognized the *leadership required by a person in the position of a commander. There is no dispute that the petitioner had to motivate the troops towards the acquisition of physical fitness by participation in the games. The same is only possible by the officer leading from the front. It therefore, has to be held that the injuries suffered by the petitioner on 14th of August, 2006 while playing volleyball at the Border Out Post (BOP) Barapansuri (Mizoram) was suffered by him while he was on duty."*

19. Learned counsel for the Respondents then pointed out that the medical condition of the Petitioner might worsen since it was progressive in nature and therefore he may be found unfit for discharging the duties of the DC.

20. The Court clarifies that it is not expressing any opinion on what category the Petitioner should be placed under. The Court is proceeding on the basis that at present the Petitioner has been placed in the E2 permanent category. If in future point in time that medical category gets revised, then obviously it will be open to the Respondents to proceed on the basis of such revised medical category. However, as of now the Petitioner continues to be in the E2 permanent category and in the considered view of the Court, he is entitled to the relaxation which is provided under para 4.17 (B) (v) of SO No.4/2008.

21. In that view of the matter, rejection of the Petitioner"s representation by the orders dated 1st April 2015 and 26th August 2015 is hereby set aside by the Court and a mandamus is issued to the Respondents to pass a fresh order within four weeks giving the Petitioner the relaxation in terms of para 4.17 (b) (v) of SO No.4/2008. The Respondents will also pass the consequential orders for promotion of the Petitioner to the rank of DC from 19th December 2014 the date on which the batch mates were promoted as DC received the said promotion.

22. The consequential orders for fixing the Petitioner's be now issued within a period of four weeks. The Petitioner's pay will also be revised

and notionally fixed in the above terms along with his batch mates with all consequential benefits.

23. The Petition is allowed in the above terms."

12. JUDICIAL TRIAL

12.1 The Gauhati High Court vide Judgment dated 19.7.2006 in the matter of Srikand Prasad vs Union Of India **[7(2007)1GLR221]** held as under:

"1. The matter has been referred to this Bench, as per the order of hon'ble the Chief Justice, to consider the question as to whether in the matter of conviction under Section 10 of the Central Reserve Police Force Act, 1949 ('the Act'), an appeal lies against the order of conviction passed under the above section of law.

2. Facts (in Crl. Revn. No. 472/03) leading to the present reference, may be noted in brief.

The petitioner Shri A.K. Mishra was tried before Shri C.J.S. Behra, Commandant, 114 Bn. Central Reserve Police Force, Rani, Kamrup, who has also been empowered and conferred the powers of Judicial Magistrate 1st Class under the Act, for commission of the offence under Section 10(n)(p) of the Act in Case No. 04/01 and the petitioner was convicted under the above section of law sentencing him to imprisonment for six months, vide order dated 19.2.2001. The said order was challenged by the petitioner in Criminal Appeal No. 36/01 and, vide impugned order dated 5.5.2003 the ad hoc Additional Sessions Judge, Kamrup, Guwahati dismissed the said appeal holding, inter alia, that the appeal is not maintainable under Section 28 of the Central Reserve Police Force Rules, 1955 (hereinafter referred to as 'the Rules'). The appellate court also relied on the decision of this Court in Union of India v. Hari Ram reported in 2003 (2) GLT 365 to hold that no appeal lies to Sessions Court.

3. Section 10 of the Act provides that for commission of offence under Section 10 of the Act a member of the force may be punished with imprisonment for a term which may extend to one year or with fine which may extend to three months' pay or with both.

4. The Central Reserve Police Force Rules, 1955 was enacted by virtue of powers provided in Section18 of the Act. There is no dispute at the Bar that the trial of an accused under Section 10 of the Act is a judicial trial and a Judicial Magistrate appointed under the Criminal Procedure Code has jurisdiction and power to try offences under Section 10 of the Act. Moreover, Section 16(2) of the Act reads as follows:

Section 16(2). Notwithstanding anything contained in the Code of Criminal Procedure, 1898 (now II of 1974), the Central Government may invest the Commandant or an Assistant Commandant with the powers of a Magistrate of any class for the purpose of inquiring into or trying any offence committed by a member of the Force and punishable under this Act, or any offence committed by a member of the force against the person or property of another member. Provided that-

(i) When the offender is on leave or absent from duty, or

(ii) When the offence is not connected with the offender's duties as a member of the Force, or

(iii) When it is a pretty offence, even if connected with the offender's duties as a member of the Force, the offence may, if the prescribed authority within the limit of whose jurisdiction the offences has been committed, so directs, be inquired into or tried by an ordinary criminal Court having jurisdiction in the matter.

5. We find that both Judicial Magistrate as well as in a given case, the Commandant, who has been specifically empowered as provided under Section 16(2) of the Act have jurisdiction to try cases under the above provisions of law.

6. Rule 36 of the Rules, reads as under-

36. Judicial Trials. - (a) All trials in relation 'to any one of the offences specified in Sections 9 and 10 shall be held in accordance with the procedure laid down in the Code of Criminal Procedure, 1898 (1973).

(b) All persons sentenced to imprisonment under the Act shall be confined in the nearest jail.

Provided that if the sentence of imprisonment is for one month or less, "or where the Commandant is satisfied that due to the difficulty of transport and escort of the person sentenced to imprisonment to the nearest jail, it is so desirable, such persons shall be confined in the Quarter Guard of the Force.

36(B) Definition. - For the purpose of this chapter, "Magistrate" means a Magistrate other than the Commandant or an Assistant Commandant on whom the powers of a Magistrate have been conferred under Sub-section (2) of Section 16.

7. Learned Additional Sessions Judge, Kamrup has referred to Rule 28 of the Rules, but in our considered opinion this reference was not relevant as Rule 28 apply in the matter of awarding punishment in disciplinary proceedings whereas the trial under Section 10 of the Act itself is a judicial proceedings and Rule 36 applies in judicial trial.

8. In case of Hari Ram (supra), this Court held-

11. On perusal of the provisions of law above noted, it is noticed that offences prescribed under Section 10(m) and 10(n) of the Act are triable by the Assistant Commandant/Judicial Magistrate 1st Class being invested with the power of Magistrate according to the provisions of Section 16(2) of the Act. The said section has clearly enshrined that the Central Govt. may invest the Commandant or Assistant Commandant with the power of Magistrate of any Class for the purpose of inquiring into or trying any offence committed by a Member of the Force and punishable under this Act. There is no dispute as regards such investing powers of Magistrate upon the Commandant as for such purpose the Central Govt. had already notified, vide GSR 161(E) dated 30.3.1974 which was published in Gazette of India dated 30.3.1974 (see foot note A of Section 16 of the Act). The Rule 36(B) which was mainly relied upon by the Appellate Court, has been incorporated under Chapter VIA under the heading of "Place of trial and adjustment of jurisdiction of ordinary courts". The expression 'Magistrate' occurring in Rule 36B under this Chapter VIA of the rules has been defined in the context of place of trial and adjustment of jurisdiction of only ordinary courts and not in the context of power conferred upon the Central Government under Section 16(2) of the Act to invest the Commandant or Assistant Commandant to exercise power of a Magistrate to try offence under the Act. That being so, the appellate court it appears, misconstrued and misinterpreted this provision of Rule 36B which has clearly referred to ordinary courts other than Special Courts constituted under the Act. In Section 16(2) of the Act some special power of duties have been conferred or imposed on members of the Force entrusting special judicial powers for inquiry or trial of any offences committed by a member of the Force and also for resultant punishment under the Act. Therefore, the magisterial power so invested by the Central Govt, on the Commandant or the Asstt. Commandant for trial of any offence under the Act cannot be taken away by Rule 36B wherein the meaning of Magistrate has been defined in relation to the ordinary courts only. It is clearly provided under Section 16(2) of the Act, that in case of offences like-

(i) When the offender is on leave or absent from duty ; or

(ii) When the offence is not connected with the offender's duty as a member of the force or ;

(iii) When it is a petty offence, even if connected with the offender's duties as a member of the Force.

The prescribed authorities like Commandant or Asstt. Commandant within the limit of whose jurisdiction such offence has been committed may direct that such offence may be inquired into or tried by an ordinary criminal court having jurisdiction in this matter. In case of trial of such offences by the ordinary courts only, the definition of Magistrate as per the Rule 36B is significant. In that view of the matter, I unhesitatingly hold that the Assistant Commandant exercising the power of Magistrate under Section 16(2) of the Act has the legal authority to try the offences which are exclusively covered under this Special Act enacted for the purpose of constitution of regulation of an Armed Central Reserve Police Force and the learned Addl. District Magistrate was absolutely wrong in holding that the Assistant Commandant, Judicial Magistrate has no power to convict the respondent.

9. A conjoint reading of the provisions of the Act and the Rules made thereunder clearly show that for alleged commission of offence under Section 10 of the Act, an accused person, i.e., a member of the force may be tried by a Judicial Magistrate 1st Class or in a given case, by the Commandant or Assistant Commandant on whom powers of Judicial Magistrate have been conferred under Section 16(2) of the Act. The question whether trial shall be conducted by a Judicial Magistrate or Commandant or Assistant Commandant specially conferred with the powers of Judicial Magistrate has been left in the discretion of the competent authority. When both the forums are available, as a matter of fact, it is only one forum, i.e., the Judicial Magistrate 1st Class, but instead of sending the case to the ordinary court of Judicial Magistrate 1st Class for the exigency of service the Central Government has been authorized to invest the Commandant or Assistant Commandant the powers of Judicial Magistrate 1st Class exclusively for the purpose of holding trial under Section 10 of the Act. A Commandant or Assistant Commandant who is so empowered can try offences allegedly committed by the members of the force only in relation to the 'Act' only.

10. The Act, as well as the Rules framed thereunder, has not laid down any special procedure as regards holding of an enquiry or trial for the offences under Section 9 or 10 of the Act by the Judicial Magistrate 1st Class or Assistant Commandant specially empowered in this behalf.

Under Rule 36 of the Rules a trial is to be held in the accordance with the procedure laid down in the Criminal Procedure Code. Sections 4 and 5 of the Criminal Procedure Code reads as under:

4. Trial of offences under the Indian Penal Code and other laws. - (1) All offences under the Indian Penal Code (45 of 1860) shall be investigated, inquired into, tried, and otherwise dealt with according to the provisions hereinafter contained.

(2) All offences under any other law shall be investigated, inquired into, tried and otherwise dealt with, according the same provisions, but subject to any enactment for the time being in, force regulating the manner or place of investigating, inquiring into, trying or otherwise dealing with such offences.

5. Saving - Nothing contained in this Code shall, in the absence of a specific provision to the contrary, affect any special or local law for the time being in force, or any special jurisdiction or power conferred, or any special form of procedure prescribed, by any other law for the time being in force.

11. There cannot be any distinction in the matter of trial or procedure of trial, where the accused, admittedly a member of the force, is tried by a Judicial Magistrate 1st Class or Commandant or Assistant Commandant conferred with the powers for the above purpose. As stated above, no separate procedure for trial is laid in the Act or the Rules framed thereunder. Rule 36 of the Rules provides that the trial shall be in accordance with the Criminal Procedure Code. Provisions of Criminal Procedure Code are applicable in respect of any other law, which, in our opinion, includes the Central Reserve Police Force Act. As regards maintenance of appeal before the appellate Court, i.e., the Additional Sessions Judges appointed under the provisions of the Criminal Procedure Code, learned Single Judge in Hari Ram (supra) observed as follows:

12. As regards the question of jurisdiction of the appellate Court, i.e., the learned Addl. District Magistrate, Aizawl who entertain the appeal in question, raised by the learned Counsel for the appellant, on plain reading of the provisions of the Act and Rules, it is seen that there is no provision for appeal prescribed under the Act and the Rules to be preferred before learned District Judge/District Magistrate under the ordinary court against the conviction and sentence under Section 10 of the Act. Rule 36 only prescribing judicial trials does not speak of any provision of such appeal. In that view of the matter I find enough force in the submissions of the learned CGSC and accordingly it is held that the learned District Magistrate/Addl. District Magistrate in the present case, lacks jurisdiction to entertain the appeal in question arising out of conviction and sentence passed under this Special Act.

13. In the case of R.S. Nayak V.A.R. Antuley reported in AIR 1984 SC 684, a similar question, though in a different context, was raised before the Constitution Bench. It was rotated to the constitution of the Court of Special Judge for trying offences under the Prevention of Corruption Act and the question raised was whether the Court of Special Judge is a Court of Magistrate or a Court of Sessions and what will be its power and procedure for trial, the Apex Court held-

27. ...Shorn of all embellishment, the court of special Judge is a court of original criminal jurisdiction. As a court of original criminal jurisdiction in order to make it functionally oriented some powers were conferred by the statute setting up the court. Except those specifically conferred and specifically denied, it has to function as a court of original criminal jurisdiction not being hidebound by the terminological status description of Magistrate or a Court of Session. Under the Code it will enjoy all powers which a Court of original criminal jurisdiction enjoys save and except the once specifically denied.

29. Once the position and power of the court of special Judge in the hierarchy of Criminal Courts under the High Court is clearly and unambiguously established, it is unnecessary to roam into an enquiry examining a large number of decisions laying down in the context of each case that the court of a special Judge is a Court of Session and the contrary view taken in some other decisions. Reference to those judgments would be merely adding to the length of this judgment without achieving any useful purpose.

15. So far the Act and Rules under consideration are concerned, we find that the Act does not create any special Court, but merely provides that the offences under Section 10 of the Act are required to be a Judicial Magistrate 1st Class and the procedure will be that of the Cr.P.C. It also provides that even the Commandant or the Assistant Commandant may be conferred with the powers of Judicial Magistrate 1st Class to try offences under the Act. This is. mere a conferment of powers of Judicial Magistrate 1st Class on a Commandant or Assistant Commandant for limited exercise of jurisdiction and powers of Judicial Magistrate. However, whether trial is held by ordinary Court of Judicial Magistrate 1st Class or by specially empowered Commandant or Assistant Commandant, the procedure remain the same.

16. So far the question of investment of powers of Judicial Magistrate 1st Class on Commandant or Assistant Commandant is concerned, the matter was examined by the Supreme Court in State Union of India v. Ram Saran and the Apex Court observed that the offence under Sections 9 and 10 of the Act are new classes of offence created with punishment therefor which is unknown to the ordinary criminal law in force. The Apex Court further observed-

Section 16 provides for empowering competent authorities in the hierarchy of the force itself with powers of duties conferred or imposed on a police officer or any class or grade by any law for the time being in force and by further enacting a provision with a specific "non-obstante" clause stipulating that notwithstanding anything contained in the Code, the Central Government may invest the Commandant or Assistant Commandant with the powers of a Magistrate of any class for the purpose of inquiring into or trying any offence committed by a member of the force and punishable "under this Act" or any offence committed by a member of the force against the person or property of another member. Consequently, what is purported to be done by these *provisions is merely to refer to the nature and extent of powers possessed by such authorities under the other laws being made available to the authorities designated under this Act, without exhaustively enumerating the details of all such powers or without re-enacting all such provisions in detail as part and parcel of this, law, the Act, and not to constitute them to be or empower them as Magistrates as such for all or any of the purposes for which courts of ordinary criminal justice have been constituted under the Code. Section 5 of the Code sufficiently protects the authorities empowered to function and exercise powers under the Act from any such challenge as are directed against them in this case.*

17. The Apex Court, therefore, held that the Assistant Commandant specially empowered on that behalf, who is specially conferred with the powers of Judicial Magistrate, by the Central Government had jurisdiction to deal with the members of the force in a trial under Section 10 of the Act.

18. Although the question whether any appeal/revision lies before the Sessions Judge or High Court against an order of the Assistant Commandant did not arise for consideration directly, but as a matter of fact the order of conviction by the Assistant Commandant was challenged before the Sessions Judge on the ground that the Assistant Commandant has no jurisdiction to try the C.R.P.F. Constable and when the appeal was allowed the matter was taken to the High Court in Division Bench and the High Court also agreed with the findings of the Sessions Judge, i.e., the appellate court that conferment of powers of Judicial Magistrate 1st Class by the Central Government on the Assistant Commandant is bad in law. The Apex Court did not find fault with Sessions Judge for entertaining the appeal observing that no appeal lies under the Act.

19. The right of the accused to prefer an appeal under Section 374 Cr.P.C. in the matter of conviction under Section 10 of the Act was denied by the learned Single Judge solely on the ground that the Act is a special Act and it does not provide for any forum of appeal. A

submission was made before us that the appeal is a creation of statute and when the statute is silent and does not provide for an appeal, it cannot be entertained. In Durga Sahankar Mehta v. Raghuraj Singh, Apex Court observed-

It is well known that an appeal is a creature of statute and there can be no inhere right of appeal from any judgment or determination unless an appeal is expressly provided for by the law itself." In Mustaq Ahmed Mohammed Hussain and Anr. v. State of Gujarat AIR 1973 1222, the Apex Court observed - "The right of appeal conferred by Section 410 read with Section 418 Cr.P.C. entitled the appellants to question the conclusions of the trial court both on matters of fact and law. They had a right to ask for a review of the entire evidence and to challenge the appraisal of the evidence by the trial court and its conclusions based on such appraisal.

20. In view of the above discussions we have no hesitation to hold that the Act is a special Act providing for trial of particular classes of offence, the offences are "more heinous offence" and "less heinous offence" defined under the Act so far the trial of above offence is concerned, the' procedure will be as per the provisions of the Criminal Procedure Code. In view of provision of Section 4(2) and Section 5 of the Criminal Procedure Code the procedure is applicable in case of special laws also. In Maru Ram v. Union of India the Apex Court held:

33. The anatomy of this savings section is simple, yet subtle. Broadly speaking, there are three components to be separated. Firstly, the Procedure Code generally governs matters covered by it. Secondly, if a special or local law exists covering the same area, this latter law will be saved and will prevail. The short-sentencing measures and local laws and must override. Now comes the third component which may be clinching. If there is a specific provision to the contrary, then that will override the special or local law. Is Section 433Aa specific law contra? If so, that will be the last word and will hold even against the special or local law.

The above views were reiterated in the case of Director of Enforcement v. Deepak Mahajan, which reads-

"122. Section 4(2) of the Code corresponds to Section 5(2) of the old Code. Section 26(b) of the Code corresponds to Section 29 of the old Code except for a slight change. Under the present Section 26(b) any offence under any other law shall, when any court is mentioned in this behalf, may be tried by the High Court or other court by which such offence is shown in the First Schedule to be triable. The combined operation of Sections 4(2) and 26(b) of the Code is that the offence complained of should be investigated or inquired into or tried according to the provisions of the Code where the enactment which creates the offence indicates no special procedure.

123. We shall now consider the applicability of provisions of Section 167(2) of the Code in relation to Section 4(2) to a person arrested under FERA or the Customs Act and produced before a Magistrate. As we have indicated above, a reading of Section 4(2) read with Section 26(b) which governs every criminal proceeding as regards the course by which an offence is to be tried and as to the procedure to be followed, renders the provisions of the Code applicable in the field not covered by the provisions of the FERA or Customs Act.

128. To sum up, Section 4 is comprehensive and that Section 5 is not in derogation of Section 4(2) and it only relates to the extent of application of the Code in the matter of territorial and other jurisdiction but does not nullify the effect of Section 4(2). In short, the provisions of this Code would be applicable to the extent in the absence of any contrary provisions of this Code would be applicable to the extent in the absence of any contrary provision in the Special Act or any special provision excluding the jurisdiction or applicability of the Code. In fact, the second limb of Section 4(2) itself limits the application of the provisions of the Code reading, "... But subject to any enactment for the time being in force regulating the manner or place of investigating, inquiring, into, trying or otherwise dealing with such offences.

21. The learned Single Judge in Hari Ram (supra) however held that the provisions of Section 16(2) of the Act shall apply or shall stand restricted in the matter, place and trial of the offence under the Act. But, there is no provision for appeal. Under the Act or Rules framed thereunder there is no specific provision or bar that no appeal will lie against the order of conviction. As stated above, the trial under Sections 9 and 10 of the Act is a judicial trial and is held as per the Criminal Procedure Code before a Judicial Magistrate 1st Class or a Commandant or Assistant Commandant who has been specially conferred with the powers of Judicial Magistrate 1st Class. A submission was made before us that in a given case where trial has been conducted by a Judicial Magistrate 1st Class, an appeal may lie under Section 374 Cr.P.C. but in case of trial by a Commandant or Assistant Commandant, who has been specially conferred with the powers of Judicial Magistrate 1st Class, in absence of any specific provision in the Act or the Rules framed thereunder no appeal will lie. The above proposition may led to serious question of discrimination between two members of the same force. If a member is tried by an ordinary criminal court he is entitle to the right to appeal, revision etc. whereas in case he is tried by a Commandant or Assistant Commandant, he will lose the right to appeal. Whether a member of force has been tried by a Judicial Magistrate 1st Class or Commandant or Assistant Commandant the procedure of trial will be same and their rights and privileges of appeal/revision, etc., cannot vary and must remain same.

22. Chapter XXIX Cr.P.C. provides for appeals. We may have a look at the provisions of Section 372 and Sub-clause (3) of Section 374 Cr.P.C which provides:

372. No appeal to lie unless otherwise provided, - No appeal shall lie from any judgment or order of a Criminal Court except as provided for by this Code or by any other law for the time being in force.

374(3). Save as otherwise provided in Sub-section (2), any person,-

convicted on a trial held by a Metropolitan Magistrate or Assistant Sessions Judge or Magistrate of the first class, or of the second class, or

sentenced under Section 325, or

in respect of whom ah order has been made or a sentence has been passed under Section 360 by any Magistrate, may appeal to the Court of Session.

23. The forum for appeal is provided by virtue of Section 372 Cr.P.C. Section 374 Cr.P.C. provides for appeal for conviction and in Sub-clause (3) provides specific provision as regards conviction by the Judicial Magistrate. The Act or the Rules does not contain any provision that in case of conviction entered in to by the Commandant in exercise of power of Judicial Magistrate 1st Class no appeal will lie. In view of Section 5 of the Code, if there is any specific provision in the Act the same would have prevail over the provisions of Sections 372 and 374 Cr.P.C. Section 375 Cr.P.C. further provides that in certain cases no appeal is maintainable.

24. In the case of Atiq-ur-Rehman v. Municipal Corporation of Delhi and Anr. 1996 SCC (Crl.) 457,the Apex Court held - "Prom a plain reading of Section 4 Cr.P.C. (supra) it emerges that the provisions of Criminal Procedure Code are applicable where an offence under the Indian Penal Code or under any other law is being investigated, inquired into, tried or otherwise dealt with." In the case of H.N. Bhavsar v. State of Gujarat 1976 Crl. 84 the Full Bench of Gujarat High Court, relying on held that right of appeal under Section 372 Cr.P.C. is a substantive right which crystallizes at the date of the institution of action and this right includes a right to go on appeal to the Supreme Court.

25. In view of the foresaid discussions we hold that the decision in Hari Ram (supra) at para 13 does not lay down the correct position of law. We accordingly hold as follows:

(1) A member of the Central Reserve Police Force may be tried either by a Judicial Magistrate 1st Class or Commandant or Assistant Commandant who has been specially conferred with the powers of Judicial Magistrate;

(2) Trial will be a judicial trial and the procedure to be followed shall be as per the Criminal Procedure Code ;

(3) Appeal/revision will lie against the order of the trial Court i.e. Judicial Magistrate1st Class or Commandant or Assistant Commandant; and (4) Sessions' Judge shall have the power and jurisdiction to entertain appeal/revision against such orders.

The criminal revision may be listed before the appropriate Bench for hearing.

12.2 Shri Suresh Kumar vs Union Of India & Ors. on 27 July, 2010 in W.P.(C) No.442/1995 & CM No.773/1995

1. *That the petitioner had filed the writ petition assailing the order dated 30th May, 1994 passed by Shri D.C. Dey, Commandant, 42nd Battalion, Khonsa, Central Reserve Police Force (hereinafter referred to as `CRPF' for brevity) exercising powers of the Chief Judicial Magistrate under Section 16(2) of the Central Reserve Police Force Act, 1949 (hereinafter referred to as `CRPF Act, 1949' for brevity). By this judgment, the petitioner was found guilty of the offence of having overstayed leave without permission/sanction from the competent authority, without sufficient cause under Section 10(m) of the CRPF Act, 1949 and having failed to join the duty. The Commandant as Judicial Magistrate First Class had imposed the sentence of "simple punishment till the rising of the court".*

2. *As a result of the imposition of the sentence of imprisonment, the Commandant had exercised jurisdiction under Section*

12(1) of the CRPF Act, 1949 read with Rule 27(a) of the CRPF Rules, 1955 directing that the petitioner be dismissed from service w.e.f. 30th May, 1994. The petitioner assailed this judgment by way of an appeal made to the Director General of Police (hereinafter referred to as `DIGP' for brevity) of the CRPF dated 24 th June, 1994 which was rejected by an order dated 29th August, 1994. The petitioner has challenged this order passed by the Director General of Police as well in the present petition.

―――――――――――――――――――――――――――――――――――――――

….Provisions of Section 12 of the Central Reserve Force Act, 1949 which reads as follows:-

"Place of imprisonment and liability to dismissal on imprisonment

12. (1) Every person sentenced under this Act to imprisonment may be dismissed from the force, and shall further be liable to forfeiture of pay, allowance and any other moneys due to him, as well as of any medals and decorations received by him.

(2) Every such person shall, if he is so dismissed, be imprisoned in the prescribed prison, but if he is not also dismissed from the force, he may, if the Court of the Commandant so directs, be confined in the quarterguard or such other place as the court or the Commandant may consider suitable."

Thereafter the Hon'ble Delhi High Court went on to observe as follows

"15.We have given our considered thought to the rival contention. The petitioner had undoubtedly sought leave on the ground of sickness of his wife. The respondents considered the same compassionately and granted him earned leave for a period of 33 days between 15th December, 1993 to 16th January, 1994. On the eve of the expiry of the said leave, the petitioner sent a telegram and a representation dated 12th January, 1994 to the respondents seeking extension of leave. The respondents expressed inability to grant the extension on ground of

deficiency in the available personnel. The petitioner has not assailed this position with regard to the personnel position with the respondents on any ground of arbitrariness, mala fide or illegality. In any case, faced with lack of adequate manpower, the respondents would have had no option but to reject the petitioner's request for extension of leave as was done.

16. We also find that in any case by the communication of 19th January, 1994, the respondents also asked the petitioner for proof of the wife's sickness including certification of the documentation by a doctor of a government hospital. The petitioner did not care to respond to these communications from the respondents and admittedly chose not to report for duty. He opted not to even acknowledge the respondents communications and sent no document let alone the required certification to support his stated ground for leave. Due service of the communications orders passed by the respondents is manifested from the fact that they have been annexed with the writ petition.

17. In this background, the respondents certainly had no option but to proceed in accordance with law. As noted hereinabove, warrants of arrest on 22nd March, 1994 issued to the petitioner were issued pursuant to the request made by the CRPF. It appears that it was only because of the issuance of these warrants that the petitioner was persuaded to report back to his unit. Interestingly, by this time, a period of almost 125 days since 17th January, 1994 when the petitioner's leave expired, have passed.

18. When the petitioner returned, he was taken into custody and tried for the offence of overstaying his leave without authority. The petitioner pleaded guilty and has not assailed the findings of guilt by the judicial magistrate before us. The only issue which has to be examined is as to whether the sentence of imprisonment till rising of the day by the order dated 30th May, 1994 and the consequent order of dismissal of the petitioner from service passed on the same day, is disproportionate to the seriousness of the allegations levelled against the petitioner.

19. It is trite that a challenge to a sentence on grounds of proportionality can be successfully laid only if the sentence of punishment is so disproportionate to the gravity of the allegations that it shocks the conscience of the court.

20. So far as the scope and manner of judicial review of disciplinary action raising an issue of proportionality of a sentence imposed upon a person is concerned, the principles are well settled.

21. Placing reliance on the enunciation of the applicable principles in several judgments of the Supreme Court, a division bench of this court of which one of us (Gita Mittal, J) was a member, had passed a judgment dated 27th January, 2010 in WP (C) No.12952/2009 entitled Ram Gopal Vs. Union of India &Ors., and rejected a similar challenge as raised by the petitioner. The statement of law was noted as follows:-

"The judgment of the Supreme Court in B.C. Chaturvedi Vs. Union of India &Ors. is an authority with regard to the principles which apply. In para 18 of the judgment, the Supreme Court laid down the law as follows:-

"18. ....The High Court/Tribunal, while exercising the power of judicial review, cannot normally substitute its own conclusion on penalty and impose some other penalty. If the punishment imposed by the disciplinary authority or the appellate authority shocks the conscience of the High Court/Tribunal, it would appropriately mould the relief, either directing the disciplinary/appellate authority to reconsider the penalty imposed, or to shorten the litigation, it may itself, in exceptional and rare cases, impose appropriate punishment with cogent reasons in support thereof."

19. In (2000) II LLJ 648 SC Union of India &Anr. Vs. G. Ganayutham (Dead) by LRs., the court summed up the legal position in para 31 which reads as follows:-

"31. In such a situation, unless the Court/ Tribunal opines in its secondary role, that the administrator was, on the material before him, irrational according to Wednesbury or CCSU norms, the punishment cannot be quashed. Even then, the matter has to be remitted back to the appropriate authority for reconsideration. It is only in very rare cases as pointed out in B. C. Chaturvedi's case AIR 1995 SCW 4374 that the Court might, - to shorten litigation - think of substituting its own view as to the quantum of punishment in the place of the punishment awarded by the competent authority. (In B. C. Chaturvedi and other cases referred to therein it has however been made clear that the power of this Court under Article 136 is different). For the reasons given above, the case cited for the respondent, namely. State of Maharashtra v. M. H. Mazumdar MANU/SC/0485/1988 : (1988)IILLJ62SC cannot be of any help.

32. For the aforesaid reasons, we set aside the order of the Tribunal which has interfered with the quantum of punishment and which has also substituted its own view of the punishment. The punishment awarded by the departmental authorities is restored. In the circumstances, there will be no order as to costs."

20. These decisions were examined and the principles reiterated by the court in the judgment reported at (2006) 6 SCC 794 Union of India Vs. K.G. Soni wherein the court stated as follows:-

"14. The common thread running through in all these decisions is that the Court should not interfere with the administrator's decision unless it was illogical or suffers from procedural impropriety or was shocking to the conscience of the Court, in the sense that it was in defiance of logic or moral standards. In view of what has been stated in the Wednesbury's case (supra) the Court would not go into the correctness of the choice made by the administrator open to him and the Court should not substitute its decision to that of the administrator. The scope of judicial review is limited to the deficiency in decision-making process and not the decision.

15. To put differently, unless the punishment imposed by the Disciplinary Authority or the Appellate Authority shocks the conscience of the Court/Tribunal, there is no scope for interference. Further to shorten litigations it may, in exceptional and rare cases, impose appropriate punishment by recording cogent reasons in support thereof. In a normal course if the punishment imposed is shockingly disproportionate, it would be appropriate to direct the Disciplinary Authority or the Appellate Authority to reconsider the penalty imposed."

21 In Ranjit Thakur Vs. Union of India &Ors., the court was considering the legality of punishment which was imposed upon the petitioner upon trial by a court martial. The court held that judicial review was directed against the decision making process while the choice of quantum of punishment was within the jurisdiction and discretion of court martial. It was held that the sentence must suit the offence and the offender, and should not be so disproportionate to the offence so as to shock the conscience of the court and amount to conclusive evidence of bias. On application of the doctrine of proportionality which has derived its shades from the Wednesbury test, it was observed that if the decision of the court martial as to sentence is outrageous defiance of logic, the sentence would not be immune from correction. Para 25 of the judgment deserves to be considered in extenso which reads as follows:-

"25. Judicial review generally speaking, is not directed against a decision, but is directed against the "decision making process". The question of the choice and quantum of punishment is within the jurisdiction and discretion of the

Court-Martial. But the sentence has to suit the offence and the offender. It should not be vindictive or unduly harsh. It should not be so disproportionate to the offence as to shock the conscience and amount in itself to conclusive evidence of bias. The doctrine of proportionality, as part of the concept of judicial review, would ensure that even on an aspect which is, otherwise, within the exclusive province of the Court-Martial, if the decision of the Court even as to sentence is an outrageous defiance of logic, then the sentence would not be immune from correction. Irrationality and perversity are recognised grounds of judicial review. In Council Of Civil Service Unions v. Minister For The Civil Service (1984) 3 W L R 1174 Lord Diplock said:

...Judicial Review has, I think, developed to a stage today when without re-iterating any analysis of the steps by which the development has come about, one can conveniently classify under three heads the grounds upon which administrative action is subject to control by judicial review. The first ground I would call 'illegality', the second 'irrationality' and the third 'procedural impropriety'. That is not to say that further development on a case by case basis may not in course of time add further grounds. I have in mind particularly the possible adoption in the future of the principle of 'proportionality' which is recognised in the administrative law of several of our fellow members of the European Economic Community..."

22. In the instant case, the petitioner has treated his service casually. He has shown dereliction and utmost contempt for the directions by the respondents to him to resume his duties. The petitioner has not even cared to support his request for extension of his leave on grounds of his wife's sickness with the medical record which has been sought from him.

23. Before this court, the petitioner has placed reliance on a medical certificate dated 13th May, 1994 to support his plea of his wife's sickness. This certificate has been issued by a private hospital and polyclinic in district Gohana which merely states that Smt. Kamla Devi wife of Suresh Chand was suffering from PIVD Lumba Spine and was under the treatment at hospital from 2nd January, 1994 to 13th May, 1994 as an OPD case. The stamp of doctor on this certificate reflects that it had been issued by a general physician and not by any specialist. No treatment card or medical prescriptions or bills which would manifest the petitioner's contention that his wife was genuinely sick

preventing him from resuming duties, has been placed before this court. This certificate on the other hand manifests that even if the petitioner's wife was ill, her sickness was not so serious and she did not require any hospitalisation.

24. The above discussion would show that the petitioner who was a member of the disciplined paramilitary force, has treated his service with utmost casualness which is completely intolerable. The petitioner was willfully absent from duty not for any short period but for a period of over four months. The excuse put forth by the petitioner as a reason for his absent is not supported by any credible documentation or medical record. The petitioner was aware of the fact that the respondents were having shortage of manpower and his services were urgently needed. Let alone resuming duties, the petitioner did not even care to respond to such requests from the respondents.

The para military and military forces certainly cannot brook indiscipline of this kind. Their personnel are expected to display discipline and sincerity in performance of duty of the highest order. The petitioner has displayed neither.

25. In support of his submission that the petitioner ought to have filed an appeal, reliance is placed on a decision dated 19th July, 2006 of the Gauhati High Court in Criminal Revision No.386/2003 entitled Shri Srikand Prasad Vs. Union of India and other connected cases, holding that in case of a conviction by the commandant in exercise of power under Section 12 of the CRPF Act, the same would be subject to the challenge which would lie by way of an appeal before the learned Sessions Judge in accordance with the provisions of the Code of Criminal Procedure. In view of our finding on the merits of the petitioner's challenge as well as the long pendency of the matter in this court since 1995, we are not inclined to divert the petitioner to a remedy of an appeal at this stage. Rejection of a writ petition on the ground of availability of an alternate remedy is a rule of convenience and not an absolute bar. In any case, the remedy of appeal would be neither available nor be efficacious in view of the statutory limitation after passage of fifteen years of filing of this writ petition. Such objection as and when raised, should be brought to the notice of the court and adjudication thereon sought at the earliest. Even otherwise, there is no absolute bar to the maintainability of a writ petition against orders of a magistrate. The parameters of such challenge though narrow, are well settled. Maintainability of the challenge will depend on the facts and circumstances and grounds of challenge in the case. We are not opining on this issue in the present case for the aforenoticed reasons.

26. In view of the above discussion, we are unable to hold that the punishment imposed upon the petitioner is disproportionate to the gravity of the charges of the allegations levelled against him.

13. ACCOMMODATION RULES IN CRPF

13.1 The Hon'ble Delhi High Court while dealing with the subject of Retention of Accommodation for Force Officers and Personnel on their transfer to LWE (Left Wing Extremist Region) NER (North East Region) and State of Jammu & Kashmir (as it was then) in the Writ Petition being WPC 1824 of 2015 titled Neeraj Kumar Singh Vs Union of India & Ors in its judgement dated 25.02.2015 had made certain critical observation on the illegal action of the Authorities in getting the quarters vacated from the family of such officers in the following manner "...*It is not in dispute that family accommodation is provided to the force personnel of CRPF as per the CRPF Family Accommodation Rules, 2008. Under the Rules, vide Rule 25, a family accommodation allotted can be retained for the prescribed period of five years. But the same i.e. five year period is not to be applied to the force personnel posted in the North Eastern region of the country and the State of Jammu & Kashmir.*

5. It is apparent that the policy has the underlying reasoning; of a force personnel being posted at a place for five years. For it would make a nonsense of the policy to post a person for more than five years at a place but restrict family accommodation being provided for only five years.

6. It appears that there was some problem in understanding the Rules, resulting in a circular being issued on April 28, 2009. It was clarified that CRPF personnel posted in the North Eastern region as well as in the State of Jammu & Kashmir would be allowed to retain the family quarter till their actual posting lasts in said areas. Meaning thereby, as per the family accommodation Rules read with the policy guidelines dated July 28, 2009, a force personnel posted in the State of Jammu & Kashmir or the North Eastern region was entitled to retain the family quarter till duration of posting in the State of Jammu & Kashmir or the North Eastern region.

7. On December 30, 2013, general guidelines were issued concerning family accommodation allotted to CRPF force personnel and as per para 7 thereof it was once again made clear that the period of allotment would be till posting lasts in the State of Jammu & Kashmir or the North Eastern region. However, it was indicated therein that separate instructions would be issued pertaining to the flats in Dwarka.

8. The separate instructions regarding allotment and right to retain the family accommodation in Dwarka has been issued on January 19, 2015, and this would be sufficient reason to quash the impugned order dated October 14, 2014 charging penal rent as also the eviction notice dated August 27, 2014 for the reason as of said dates the general pool accommodation Rules and the guidelines issued thereunder would govern the entitlement of the petitioner.

9. Concededly, being posted State of Jammu & Kashmir, the petitioner would be entitled to retain family accommodation allotted to him.

10. But we need to speak something more.

11. The policy dated January 19, 2015 requires that the maximum period of allotment would be four years inclusive of extension.

12. Now, there has to be a special reason to make separate guidelines for the family accommodation at Dwarka for the reason one cannot think of only a group of flats being subjected to a separate allotment and retention policy and the remainder under a general policy.

13. From the facts noted above it would be apparent that for family accommodation other than in Dwarka, a force personnel posted in the State of Jammu & Kashmir or the North Eastern region of the country would be entitled to retain the residential accommodation allotted in any city in India including Delhi before, till the officer completes the posting in the State of Jammu & Kashmir or the North Eastern region.

14. Though not expressly stated in the policy guidelines dated January 19, 2015, for the flats at Dwarka, a perusal thereof would evince that in Dwarka, CRPF has 816 quarters out of which 215 have specifically been earmarked for the 88th Mahila Battalion and 17 for the 135th Mahila Battalion and the 213th Mahila Battalion. 10 have been left in the discretionary quota of the Direction General for allotment on compassionate ground, 19 have been distributed for various prescribed purposes. 555 quarters have been reserved for allotment to CRPF officers on 'first-cum-first-serve' basis.

15. Though not stated in the policy, learned counsel for the respondents states that fixing maximum four years' duration period for retention of flats in Dwarka is that the Dwarka area in Delhi is isolated from the general city of Delhi and transport is made available to the officers to whom flats are allotted there. If a flat at Dwarka is retained by an officer not stationed at Delhi and he is allowed to retain the same for the benefit of his family, another force personnel would be required to be given a family accommodation elsewhere and this would create transport problem.

16. If this be so, the only way forward is to first allot a flat to a CRPF force personnel in a complex outside Dwarka where his family could shift till when the force personnel serves in the State of Jammu &

Kashmir or the North Eastern region of the country and thereupon call upon the officer to vacate the quarter allotted in Dwarka.

17. To our mind, it would be arbitrary to let a force personnel retain the family accommodation allotted if the same is not in Dwarka area of Delhi till the officer serves in the State of Jammu & Kashmir or the North Eastern region but to require the officer to vacate the accommodation if family accommodation allotted in Dwarka.

18. The fortuitous circumstances of the place where family accommodation is allotted coupled with the fortuitous circumstance of being attached at a particular office in Delhi resulting in a curtailment of the entitlement of the officer under the family accommodation Rules and general guidelines would be arbitrary.

19. We would commend to CRPF officers to issue a clarification removing the anomaly afore-noted. The best clarification would be that if a force personnel has been allotted residential accommodation in Dwarka when the force personnel was posted at Delhi, he would be entitled to retain the accommodation in Dwarka for his family on being posted in the State of Jammu & Kashmir or the North Eastern region of the country till alternative accommodation is made available for the family in Delhi. Once the alternative accommodation is made available the entitlement to retain the accommodation in Dwarka would automatically lapse.

20. Impugned order dated August 27, 2014 and October 14, 2014 are quashed.

21. It is declared that the petitioner would be entitled to retain the family accommodation at Dwarka at the normal license fee till he is serving in the State of Jammu & Kashmir, which period could be curtailed upon the petitioner being allotted a general pool accommodation by CRPF in any part of the city of Delhi."

14. RECOVERY WHEN IMPERMISSIBLE

14.1 Judgemet dated 01.10.2019 in WP(C) No. 3232/2019 Dilshad Ali Vs. UOI & Ors in Delhi High Court

1.This writ petition challenges an order dated 27th July, 2018, issued by the Deputy Inspector General of Police („DIGP"), Central Reserve Police Force („CRPF"), Hyderabad, inter alia, directing a deduction of a sum of Rs.2,80,275/- from the Petitioner.

2. The Petitioner also challenges the proposal dated 8th March, 2018, for revision of the Petitioner's pension consequent upon the recommendations of the Seventh Central Pay Commission („CPC"), which reflects the deductions of the aforementioned sum, while calculating the revised pension payable to the Petitioner. The Petitioner consequently prays for a mandamus to the Respondents to refund the aforementioned sum that has been deducted from his account.

3. The background facts are that the Petitioner was appointed as an Head Constable/General Duty („HC/GD") in the CRPF on 26th September, 1981. He was promoted as Sub Inspector („SI") on 1st April, 1988 and thereafter as Inspector in October, 1994. He was promoted as Assistant Commandant („AC") in October, 2003 and lastly as Deputy Commandant in November, 2008.

4. In 2011, the Petitioner was posted to the Group Centre („GC"), Hyderabad, during which time, for a brief period of around two months, he was given additional charge of Accounts Officer, since the incumbent had proceeded on leave. On 29th June, 2012, the Petitioner was posted with the 5th Battalion in New Delhi, which was his last leg posting.

5.On 19th August, 2013, while serving in the 5th Battalion, a Court of Inquiry („COI") was instituted to inquire into the circumstances under which dues pertaining to 21 personnel in the sum of Rs.53,78,627/- were deposited into an account of one Smt. U. Sarada at the State Bank of India („SBI"), Barkas Branch. The said Smt. U. Sarada was the wife of Ex. Constable (GD) U. Durga Prasad Rao of the Group Centre, Hyderabad.

6. The COI, in which the Petitioner did not participate, came to the conclusion that various final payment dues/TA/DA in the sum of Rs. 66,79,155/- received from Pay and Accounts Office for payment of 21 personnel of affiliated units of GC, who proceeded on voluntary retirement/superannuation and death cases, were fraudulently diverted into the aforementioned savings account of Smt. U. Sarada intentionally by Ex. Constable (GD) U. Durga Prasad Rao, who was attached with the Cash Section of the GC for assisting the cashier. The COI found Ex. Constable (GD) U. Durga Prasad Rao solely responsible for the misappropriation of the entire amount. It found no other staff or officer to be involved in the embezzlement.

7. On 29th December, 2015, based on the report of the COI, the Respondents issued an order that C. T. Venkatesh, DIG be issued an advisory letter and major penalty proceedings should be initiated against the five officers who had worked as Accounts Officer during the said relevant period.

8. The Petitioner superannuated on 30th June, 2016, and was paid all his retirement dues and pension.

9. After the Petitioner learnt of the aforementioned order dated 29th December, 2015, he made a representation dated 24th August, 2016, seeking recall of the order dated 29th December, 2015.

10. In the meanwhile, it appears that on 26th March, 2016, a show cause notice („SCN") was issued to the Petitioner, consequent upon the report of the COI and proposing recovery of the aforementioned sum of Rs.2,80,275/- from him. Enclosed with the counter affidavit of the Respondents in the present petition is a copy of the said SCN, and the Petitioner"s reply dated 16th April, 2016, as Annexure-R2. Inter alia, he pointed out in this reply that he had taken the charge of Additional Accounts Officer for a short period, and even during this

period, he had been graded as „very good/outstanding". He pointed out that recovery of such a huge sum at the fag end of his career, with his date of superannuation being 30th June, 2016, would affect him adversely.

11. It appears that on 25th January, 2017, the DIG, Range Office, CRPF, issued a direction to the IGP, Southern Sector, CRPF, suggesting how the aforementioned sum could be recovered. It was inter alia suggested that a gazetted officer from the 5th Battalion be sent to the house of the Petitioner as a representative to collect the balance amount to be deposited in the government treasury, and if that was not possible, then the officers/ personnel issuing „no dues certificate" should be investigated.

12. However, on 3rd February, 2017, an order was passed by the DG, CRPF, on the reply to the SCN submitted by the Petitioner, where inter alia in paragraph 3, it was ordered as under:

"3.Though the conduct on your part calls for stern disciplinary action, yet keeping in view your explanation during my personal interview on 15/01/2016 and considering your past record of service and length of service, I am inclined to take a lenient view and ADVISE you to be more careful while dealing with such sensitive cases."

13.Thus the order dated 3rd February, 2017 effectively brought to a close the SCN dated 26th March, 2016, which itself had been issued on the basis of the report of the COI dated 29th December, 2015.

14. It appears that ignoring the above facts, on 27 th July, 2018, another order was issued by the DIGP, CRPF at Hyderabad proposing the recovery of Rs. 2,80,275/- from the Petitioner. Strangely, this order makes no reference to the advisory dated 3rd February, 2017 issued by the DG. It noted how six of the eleven officers against whom such recoveries were contemplated, had approached the High Court of Andhra Pradesh and had an interim order in their favour staying such recovery.

15. The first time the Petitioner realized that there was a proposal for recovery was when pursuant to the 7th CPC"s recommendations, his pension was proposed to be revised, and an order was issued to that effect on 8th March, 2018. This order reflected the deduction of the aforementioned sum of Rs. 2,80,275/- from the Petitioner"s account.

16. The Court asked a pointed question to the learned counsel for the Respondents whether prior to such recovery of Rs. 2,80,275/- from the Petitioner"s account, any SCN was issued to the Petitioner. Apart from pointing out the SCN dated 26th March, 2016, which is annexed as R-1 to the counter affidavit, which came to an end with the issuance of the advisory to the Petitioner on 3rd February, 2017, no other document was shown to the Court to indicate that any SCN was issued to the Petitioner proposing a recovery of the above sum.

17. In effect, therefore, the above recovery was made without any notice to the Petitioner. The recovery also appears to be contrary to the law explained by the Supreme Court in *State of Punjab and Ors. v. Rafiq Masih (White Washer) and Ors.* (2015) 4 SCC 334, wherein the Supreme Court directed as under:

"18. It is not possible to postulate all situations of hardship, which would govern employees on the issue of recovery, where payments have mistakenly been made by the employer, in excess of their entitlement. Be that as it may, based on the decisions referred to herein above, we may, as a ready reference, summarise the following few situations, wherein recoveries by the employers, would be impermissible in law:

(i) Recovery from employees belonging to Class-III and Class-IV service (or Group 'C' and Group 'D' service).

(ii) Recovery from retired employees, or employees who are due to retire within one year, of the order of recovery.

(iii) Recovery from employees, when the excess payment has been made for a period in excess of five years, before the order of recovery is issued.

(iv) Recovery in cases where an employee has wrongfully been required to discharge duties of a higher post, and has been paid accordingly, even though he should have rightfully been required to work against an inferior post.

(v) In any other case, where the Court arrives at the conclusion, that recovery if made from the employee, would be iniquitous or harsh or arbitrary to such an extent, as would far outweigh the equitable balance of the employer's right to recover."

18. The documents that have been enclosed with the counter affidavit include the signals and messages sent by the Respondents, again without any notice to the Petitioner, on 6th August, 2018, 3rd October, 2018, and 10th October, 2018 to the Pay & Accounts Section, directing the recovery of the aforementioned amount from the Petitioner"s account.

19. In the circumstances explained hereinbefore, the Court finds that the recovery of the aforementioned sum from the Petitioner"s account was without following the due process of law and contrary to the law explained by the Supreme Court in <u>State of Punjab and Ors. v. Rafiq Masih (White Washer) and Ors.</u> *(supra).*

20. The Court accordingly sets aside the revised pension proposal dated 8 th March, 2018 to the extent that it has proposed the recovery of the aforementioned sum of Rs .2,80,275/- from the Petitioner"s account as well as the order dated 27th July, 2018 issued by the DIGP, CRPF, directing such recovery. The Court issues a mandamus to the Respondents to refund to the Petitioner the aforementioned sum of Rs. 2,80,275/- within a period of 4 weeks failing which simple interest at 6% per annum will be charged on the said sum for the period of delay.

21. The writ petition is allowed in the above terms. No costs.

15. ROLE OF PRESENTING OFFICER

15.1 Judgement dated 02.07.2018 in Civil Appeal No. 2608 of 2012 titled Union Of India vs Ram Lakhan Sharma AIR 2018 SUPREME COURT 4860

These appeals have been filed by the Union of India questioning the judgments of the Gauhati High Court by which writ petitions filed by the respondents challenging their orders of removal were allowed by setting aside the removal/dismissal orders and the respondents were directed to be reinstated. The High Court had allowed the writ petitions filed by the respondents on more or less similar grounds, hence, it shall be sufficient to notice the facts and pleadings in detail in Civil Appeal No.2608 of 2012 for deciding this batch of appeals.

2. The respondent- Ram Lakhan Sharma was appointed as constable in the Central Reserve Police Force (hereinafter referred to as "CRPF") on 10.04.1991. On 23.10.1999 while he was posted as constable 11 Bn., CRPF at Agartala, Tripura he went out from Guard duty at 09.00 a.m. and returned back at 09.50 a.m. In the afternoon, an allegation was made by one lady Smt. Gita Paul making allegation of rape against the respondent and First Information Report was registered on 23.10.1999 at the Police Station under Section 376 IPC.

3. On 23.10.1999 the appellant was placed under suspension. On 04.12.1999 chargesheet was issued to the respondent containing articles of charges I and II. First charge was that the appellant remained absent without proper permission of competent authority with consent of his Guard Commander from his duty on 23.10.1999 from 0900 hrs. to 0930 hrs. Second charge was that he while functioning as constable (Guard) has committed an act of misconduct in his capacity as a member of the force in that he tried to do sexual intercourse with a woman with mutual consent by giving money which amounts to indiscipline/moral turpitude.

4. The disciplinary authority appointed one Shri S.S. Bisht, Second-in-Command, 11 Bn CRPF as Inquiry Officer. The Inquiry Officer recorded the prosecution evidence. The Inquiry Report was submitted which was also supplied to the delinquent vide letter dated 07.02.2000 asking the respondent to submit reply within 15 days. The Commandant, 11 Bn passed an order on 19.03.2000 imposing penalty of removal from service w.e.f. 19.03.2000 under Section 11(1) of the Central Reserve Police Force Act, 1949 read with Rule 27 of the Central Reserve Police Force Rules, 1955.

5. On the basis of First Information Report registered against the respondent a chargesheet was submitted in the Court of Sessions Judge, Tripura, Agartala. Learned Sessions Judge after completing the trial on 20.09.2001 acquitted the respondent from charges levelled against him. After acquittal from criminal case the respondent filed a Writ Petition No.6778 of 2000 in the High Court of Allahabad challenging his order of removal. The High Court by order dated 20.05.2004 disposed of the writ petition giving liberty to the respondent to file an appeal under CRPF Rules, 1955 within two weeks. In pursuance of the order of the High Court an appeal was filed before D.I.G.R., CRPF, Patna. The Appellate Authority rejected the appeal by its order dated 22.07.2004 against which order a revision was filed before the Inspector General of Police, CRPF which too was rejected on 02.03.2005. Challenging the order of removal as well as orders passed in appeal and revision the respondent filed Writ Petition (C) No.14 of 2006. Learned Single Judge vide judgment dated 12.04.2010 allowed the writ petition by setting aside the removal order and directed for reinstatement of the respondent. The learned Single Judge also permitted the appellant to initiate the disciplinary inquiry afresh from the stage of appointing Presenting Officer. It was further directed that if the departmental proceeding is required to be started afresh, the respondent shall be placed under suspension and during the period of suspension, subsistence allowance should be paid. It was left to the wisdom of the authority to decide on arrear pay and allowances of the respondent.

6. Union of India filed an appeal against the judgment of the learned Single Judge being Writ Appeal No.25 of 2010. The Division Bench of the High Court by its judgment dated 10.01.2011 dismissed the writ appeal aggrieved by which order Civil Appeal No.2608 of 2012 has been filed by the Union of India.

7. The facts and pleadings in other civil appeals being more or less similar they need to be only briefly noted.

8. Union of India has filed this appeal challenging the judgment of the Division Bench dated 18.01.2013 by which Writ Appeal No.1 of 2013 filed by the Union of India questioning the judgment of the learned Single Judge was dismissed. The respondent, Shri T. Lupheng while posted at Manipur on 24.03.2008 sought permission from his senior during his duty hours for going to the Bank to withdraw his salary. He was allowed to go and directed to report back to his duties. On his return he was found under the influence of alcohol. On 07.04.2008 the personnel was suspended. On four articles of charges inquiry was held. The Inquiry Officer recorded the evidence of prosecution. The inquiry was completed and report was submitted on 19.06.2008. The disciplinary authority vide its order dated 05.07.2008 awarded the punishment of dismissal from service. An appeal was filed which was dismissed by DIG, CRPF on 07.11.2008. The revision was also dismissed by IGP-C/S, CRPF on 05.06.2009. Writ Petition No.556 of 2009 was filed in the Gauhati High Court which was allowed by the learned Single Judge by judgment dated 04.08.2012. A writ appeal was filed by the Union of India which was dismissed by the Division Bench on 18.01.2013 against which this appeal has been filed.

Civil Appeal Nos.9373-74 of 2013

9. These appeals have been filed by the Union of India against the Division Bench judgment dated 24.08.2012 by which the appeal filed by the Union of India questioning the judgment dated 08.02.2012 has been dismissed. The respondent was serving as constable in F/27 Bn CRPF. It was alleged that on 13.04.2000 he left lines without seeking

prior permission, consumed liquor and created nuisance in the market. The chargesheet was issued to the respondent containing two articles of charges. The Inquiry Officer was appointed. Inquiry Officer recorded the statement of 12 prosecution witnesses. By an order dated 30.08.2000 the respondent was dismissed from services. There were two other delinquents apart from the respondent who were proceeded with and dismissed by the common order. Learned Single Judge relying on an order of the High Court in Writ Petition (C) No.297 of 2002 (<u>Sri Mutum Shanti Kumar Singh vs. Union of India</u>) on 08.02.2012 set aside the order of the dismissal and directed reinstatement of the respondent. Union of India filed Writ Appeal No.32 of 2012 challenging the order of Learned Single Judge before the Gauhati High Court. The Division Bench of the High Court by order dated 24.08.2012 dismissed the writ appeal. Review petition was filed by the Union of India which too was dismissed on 18.01.2013. Consequently, these appeals have been filed by the Union of India.

10. This appeal has been filed by the Union of India against the Division Bench judgment of the High Court dated 29.05.2013 by which writ petition filed by the respondent challenging the disciplinary proceedings for dismissal of the respondent was allowed. The respondent while serving at Chothegaon, Bishnupur (Manipur) on 12.03.2007 deserted from line without permission of competent authority. Subsequently, an FIR was lodged on 12.03.2007. A warrant was issued to apprehend him on 29.07.2007 but he could not be apprehended. A Court of Inquiry was conducted and the respondent was declared "DESERTER" w.e.f. 12.03.2007 vide order dated 13.07.2007. A Departmental proceeding was initiated with articles of charges on 12.11.2007. Since, the respondent had not reported in the Unit, the inquiry proceeded ex parte. Charges levelled against the respondent were found proved. An order dated 20.05.2008 was passed awarding dismissal from service to the respondent. Thereafter, he submitted appeal before DIG, CRPF. A writ petition was filed by the respondent. The writ petition was disposed of on 29.05.2013 setting aside the dismissal order and directing for reinstatement. The appeal has been filed against the above said judgment.

11. The Gauhati High Court had allowed the writ petition filed by the respondents on the ground that in the disciplinary inquiry the principles of natural justice were violated. The High Court found that no Presenting Officer was appointed and the Inquiry Officer acted as prosecutor which violates the principles of natural justice and the entire inquiry was set aside on the aforesaid ground with liberty to the respondent to hold afresh inquiry from the stage of appointing of the Presenting Officer.

12. All the appeals filed by the Union of India raises almost similar question of law and facts and the learned counsel for the Union of India has also raised common submission in all the appeals.

13. Learned counsel for the appellant, Shri Vikramjit Banerjee, Addl. Solicitor General contends that the High Court committed error in setting aside the dismissal order on the ground of non-appointment of Presenting Officer. It is submitted that Rule 27 of CRPF Rules, 1955 which provides for holding of disciplinary inquiry does not provide for appointment of Presenting Officer. The appellants have followed the requirement of Rule 27 in holding disciplinary inquiry in consonance with principles of natural justice, hence, there was no occasion to set aside the dismissal order. It is submitted that the respondents were given full opportunity in the disciplinary inquiry including serving chargesheet, giving opportunity to cross-examine the witnesses, opportunity to lead evidence and submit a reply to the Inquiry Report.

14. Learned counsel for the appellant submits that Rule 27 does not mandate the appointment of Presenting Officer to hold disciplinary inquiry. It is further submitted that even if it is assumed that while non-appointment of Presenting Officer, principles of natural justice have been violated, respondents have to show what prejudice has been caused due to non-appointment of the Presenting Officer in the department enquiry. No prejudice having been caused to any of the

respondents, they were not entitled for grant of relief as has been granted by the High Court.

15. Learned counsel appearing for the respondents refuting the above submissions contends that the High Court has rightly set aside the dismissal/removal orders of the respondents. In the facts and circumstances of the present case, appointment of Presenting Officer was necessary to ensure compliance of principles of natural justice which having not been done the respondents have been seriously prejudiced. It is submitted that Inquiry Officer himself acted as prosecutor by putting questions to the prosecution witnesses. Inquiry Officer having become prosecutor with entire approach towards inquiry was tainted with bias and has rightly been interfered by the High Court. It is submitted that Inquiry Officer having acted as a prosecutor no further prejudice needs to be proved.

16. We have considered the submissions of the learned counsel for the parties and perused the records.

17. Before we proceed to consider the rival submissions of the learned counsel for the parties, it is relevant to look into the reasons given by the High Court for allowing the writ petitions filed by the respondents.

18. In Civil Appeal No.2608 of 2012(leading appeal) judgment of learned Single Judge allowing the writ petition is dated 12.04.2010 which is filed at Annexure P-7 to the appeal. After elaborately considering the facts of the case, the nature of charges and affidavit filed in the writ petition, learned Judge proceeded to decide the writ petition. Learned Single Judge had directed to make available the proceedings of the disciplinary inquiry and on perusal of the proceedings of the disciplinary inquiry Learned Single Judge came to the conclusion that no Presenting Officer was appointed in the said proceedings and the Enquiry Officer himself led the examination in chief of the prosecution witness by putting questions. The High Court further came to the conclusion that Enquiry Officer acted himself as prosecutor and Judge in the said disciplinary enquiry. It is useful to

extract paragraphs 9 and 10 of the judgment which are to the following effect:

"(9) This Court directed the learned Asstt. S.G. appearing for the respondents to make available the proceedings of the disciplinary enquiry against the petitioner. On perusal of the proceeding, it is crystal clear that no Presenting Officer was appointed in the said proceedings and the Enquiry Officer himself led the examination in chief of the prosecution witness by putting questions. This fact is not disputed by the learned Asstt. S.G. appearing for the respondents, but his only submission is that all opportunities were given to the writ petitioner to put up his defence case and also the writ petitioner had pleaded guilty for both the charges levelled against him.

(10) It is, therefore, crystal clear that the Enquiry Officer acted himself as Prosecutor and Judge in the said disciplinary enquiry against the writ petitioner. From this admitted fact, it may not be wrong to infer that there were no fair procedures in the disciplinary proceedings as a result of which principle of natural justice was undisputedly denied to the writ petitioner."

19. The Division Bench of the High Court in writ appeal against the aforesaid judgment also affirmed the aforesaid view of the learned Single Judge while dismissing the writ appeal.

20. As noted above there are two principal submissions raised by the learned counsel for the appellant, they are: (i) The disciplinary inquiry is required to be conducted under Rule 27 of 1955 Rules which does not contemplate appointment of a Presenting Officer. Hence, the inquiry proceedings are not vitiated by the non-appointment of Presenting Officer.

(ii) The disciplinary inquiry has been held against the respondents by complying with the principles of natural justice. No principle of natural justice is violated by non-appointment of Presenting Officer. No prejudice has been caused to the respondents by non-appointment of Presenting Officer.

21. Rule 27 sub-rule (c) of the CRPF Rules, 1955 provides for the procedure for conducting a departmental enquiry which is as follows:

"Rule 27(c) The procedure for conducting a departmental enquiry shall be as follows:-

(1) The substance of the accusation shall be reduced to the form of a written charge which should be as precise as possible. The charge shall be read out to the accused and a copy of it given to him at least 48 hrs. before the commencement of the enquiry.

(2) At the commencement of the enquiry the accused shall be asked to enter a plea of Guilty or Not Guilty after which evidence necessary to establish the charge shall be let in. The evidence shall be material to the charge and may either be oral or documentary, if oral:

(i) it shall be direct:

(ii) it shall be recorded by the Officer conducting, the enquiry himself in the presence of the accused:

(iii) the accused shall be allowed to cross examine the witnesses.

(3) When documents are relied upon in support of the charge, they shall be put in evidence as exhibits and the accused shall, before he is called upon to make his defence be allowed to inspect such exhibits.

(4) The accused shall then be examined and his statement recorded by the officer conducting the enquiry. If the accused has pleaded guilty and does not challenge the evidence on record, the proceedings shall be closed for orders. If he pleads "Not guilty", he shall be required to file a written statement and a list of such witnesses as he may wish to cite in his defence within such period, which shall in any case be not less than a fortnight, as the officer conducting enquiry may deem reasonable in the circumstances of the case. If he declines to file a written statement, he shall again be examined by the officer conducting the enquiry on the expiry of the period allowed.

(5) If the accused refuses to cite any witnesses or to produce any evidence in his defence, the proceedings shall be closed for orders. If he produces any evidence the officer conducting the enquiry shall proceed to record the evidence. If the officer conducting the enquiry considers that the evidence of any witness or any document which the accused wants to produce in his defence is not material to the issues involved in the case he may refuse to call such witness or to allow such document to be produced in evidence, but in all such cases he must briefly record his reasons for considering the evidence inadmissible. When all relevant evidence has been brought on record, the proceedings shall be closed for orders.

(6) If the Commandant has himself held the enquiry, he shall record his findings and pass orders where he has power to do so. If the enquiry has been held by any officer other than the Commandant, the officer conducting the enquiry shall forward his report together with the proceedings to the Commandant who shall record his findings and pass order where he has power to do so."

22. A perusal of the aforesaid Rule does not indicate that Rule contemplates appointment of Presenting Officer. Service conditions including punishment and appeal procedure of an employee are governed by statutory rules. The CRPF Act, 1949 has been enacted by the Parliament for the constitution and regulation of an armed Central Reserve Police Force. Section 18 of the Act empowers the Central Government to make rules for carrying out the purposes of this Act.

23. The disciplinary proceedings are quasi-judicial proceedings and Inquiry Officer is in the position of an independent adjudicator and is obliged to act fairly, impartially. The authority exercises quasi-judicial power has to act in good faith without bias, in a fair and impartial manner.

24. Rules of natural justice have been recognised and developed as principles of administrative law. Natural justice has many facets. Its all facets are steps to ensure justice and fair play. This Court in Suresh

Koshy George vs. University of Kerala and others, AIR 1969 SC 198 had occasion to consider the principles of natural justice in the context of a case where disciplinary action was taken against a student who was alleged to have adopted malpractice in the examination. In paragraph 7 this Court held that the question whether the requirements of natural justice have been met by the procedure adopted in a given case must depend to a great extent on the facts and circumstances of the case in point, the constitution of Tribunal and the rules under which it functions. Following was held in paragraphs 7 and 8:

"7....The rules of natural justice are not embodied rules. The question whether the requirements of natural justice have been met by the procedure adopted in a given case must depend to a great extent on the facts and circumstances of the case in point, the constitution of the Tribunal and the rules under which it functions.

8. In Russel v. Duke of Norfolk, Tucker, L. J. observed:

"There are, in my view, no words which are of universal application to every kind of inquiry and every kind of domestic tribunal. The requirements of natural justice must depend on the circumstances of the case, the nature of the inquiry, the rules under which the tribunal is acting, the subject matter that is being dealt with, and so forth. Accordingly, I do not derive much assistance from the definitions of natural justice which have been from time to time used, but, whatever standard is adopted, one essential is that the person concerned should have a reasonable opportunity of presenting his case."

25. A Constitution Bench of this Court has elaborately considered and explained the principles of natural justice in *A.K. Kraipak and others vs. Union of India and others*, AIR 1970 SC 150. This Court held that the aim of the rules of natural justice is to secure justice or to put it negatively to prevent miscarriage of justice. The concept of natural justice has undergone a great deal of change in recent years. Initially recognised as consisting of two principles that is no one shall be a judge in his own cause and no decision shall be given against a party

without affording him a reasonable hearing, various other facets have been recognised. In paragraph 20 following has been held:

"20. The aim of the rules of natural justice is to secure justice or to put it negatively to prevent miscarriage of justice. These rules can operate only in areas not covered by any law validly made. In other words they do not supplant the law of the land but supplement it. The concept of natural justice has undergone a great deal of change in recent years. In the past it was thought that it included just two rules namely (1) no one shall be a judge in his own case (Nemo debet esse judex propria causa) and (2) no decision shall be given against a party without affording him a reasonable hearing (audi alteram partem).Very soon thereafter a third rule was envisaged and that is that quasi-judicial enquiries must be held in good faith, without bias and not arbitrarily or unreasonably...."

26. In <u>State of Uttar Pradesh and others vs. Saroj Kumar Sinha</u>, 2010 (2) SCC 772, this Court had laid down that inquiry officer is a quasi-judicial authority, he has to act as independent adjudicator and he is not a representative of the department/disciplinary authority/ Government. In paragraphs 28 and 30 following has been held:

"28. An inquiry officer acting in a quasi-judicial authority is in the position of an independent adjudicator. He is not supposed to be a representative of the department/disciplinary authority/ Government. His function is to examine the evidence presented by the Department, even in the absence of the delinquent official to see as to whether the unrebutted evidence is sufficient to hold that the charges are proved. In the present case the aforesaid procedure has not been observed. Since no oral evidence has been examined the documents have not been proved, and could not have been taken into consideration to conclude that the charges have been proved against the respondents.

30. When a departmental enquiry is conducted against the government servant it cannot be treated as a casual exercise. The enquiry proceedings also cannot be conducted with a closed mind. The inquiry

officer has to be wholly unbiased. The rules of natural justice are required to be observed to ensure not only that justice is done but is manifestly seen to be done. The object of rules of natural justice is to ensure that a government servant is treated fairly in proceedings which may culminate in imposition of punishment including dismissal/removal from service."

27. When the statutory rule does not contemplate appointment of Presenting Officer whether non-appointment of Presenting Officer ipso facto vitiates the inquiry? We have noticed the statutory provision of Rule 27 which does not indicate that there is any statutory requirement of appointment of Presenting Officer in the disciplinary inquiry. It is thus clear that statutory provision does not mandate appointment of Presenting Officer. When the statutory provision does not require appointment of Presenting Officer whether there can be any circumstances where principles of natural justice can be held to be violated is the broad question which needs to be answered in this case. We have noticed above that the High Court found breach of principles of natural justice in Inquiry Officer acting as the prosecutor against the respondents. The Inquiry Officer who has to be independent and not representative of the disciplinary authority if starts acting in any other capacity and proceed to act in a manner as if he is interested in eliciting evidence to punish an employee, the principle of bias comes into place.

28. Justice M. Rama Jois of the Karnataka High Court had occasion to consider the above aspect in <u>Bharath Electronics Ltd. vs. K. Kasi, ILR</u> 1987 Karnataka 366. In <u>the above case</u> the order of domestic inquiry was challenged before the Labour and Industrial Tribunal. The grounds taken were, that inquiry is vitiated since Presenting Officer was not appointed and further Inquiry Officer played the role of prosecutor. This Court held that there is no legal compulsion that Presenting Officer should be appointed but if the Inquiry Officer plays the role of Presenting Officer, the inquiry would be invalid. Following was held in paragraphs 8 and 9:

"8. One other ground on which the domestic inquiry was held invalid was that Presenting Officer was not appointed. This view of the Tribunal is also patently untenable. There is no legal compulsion that Presenting Officer should be appointed. Therefore, the mere fact that the Presenting Officer was not appointed is no ground to set aside the inquiry See :

Gopalakrishna Reddy v. State of Karnataka (ILR 1980 Kar 575). It is true that in the absence of Presenting Officer if the Inquiring Authority plays the role of the Presenting Officer, the inquiry would be invalid and this aspect arises out of the next point raised for the petitioner, which I shall consider immediately hereafter.

9. The third ground on which the Industrial Tribunal held that the domestic inquiry was invalid was that the Inquiry Officer had played the role of the Presenting Officer.

The relevant part of the findings reads :

"The Learned Counsel for the workman further contended that the questions put by the Enquiry Officer to the Management's witnesses themselves suggest that he was biased and prejudiced against the workman. There has been no explanation as to why no Presenting Officer was appointed and as to why the Enquiry Officer took upon himself the burden of putting questions to the Management witnesses. The enquiry proceedings at Ext. A-6 disclose that after the cross-examination of the Management's witnesses by the defence, the Enquiry Officer has further put certain questions by way of explanation, but from their nature an inference arises that they are directed to fill in the lacuna. The Learned Counsel for the Management contended that the Enquiry Officer has followed the principles of natural justice and that the domestic enquiry is quite valid. I am of the view that the fact that the Enquiry Officer has himself taken up the role of the Presenting Officer for the management goes to the root of the matter and vitiates the enquiry,"

As far as position in law is concerned, it is common ground that if the Inquiring Authority plays the role of a Prosecutor and cross-examines defence witnesses or puts leading questions to the prosecution witnesses clearly exposing a biased state of mind, the inquiry would be opposed to principles of natural justice. But the question for consideration in this case is : Whether the Inquiry Officer did so ? It is also settled law that an Inquiring Authority is entitled to put questions to the witnesses for clarification wherever it becomes necessary and so long the delinquent employee is permitted to cross-examine the witnesses after the Inquiring Authority questions the witnesses, the inquiry proceedings cannot be impeached as unfair. See : Munchandani Electric and Radio Industries Ltd. v. Their Workman."

29. *This Court had occasion to observe in* <u>Workmen of Lambabari Tea Estate vs. Lambabari Tea Estate</u>, *1966 (2) LLJ 315, that if Inquiry Officer did not keep his function as Inquiry Officer but becomes prosecutor, the inquiry is vitiated. Following was observed:*

"The inquiry which was held by the management on the first charge was presided over by the manager himself. It was conducted in the presence of the assistant manager and two others. The enquiry was not correct in its procedure. The manager recorded the statements, cross-examined the labourers who were the offenders and made and recorded his own statements on facts and questioned the offending labourers about the truth of his own statements recorded by himself. The manager did not keep his function as the enquiring officer distinct but became witness, prosecutor and manager in turns. The record of the enquiry as a result is staccato and unsatisfactory."

30. *A Division Bench of the Madhya Pradesh High Court speaking through Justice R.V. Raveendran, CJ (as he then was) had occasion to consider the question of vitiation of the inquiry when the Inquiry Officer starts himself acting as prosecutor in Union of India and ors. vs. Mohd. Naseem Siddiqui, ILR (2004) MP*

821. In <u>the above case</u> *the Court considered Rule 9(9)*

(c) of the Railway Servants (Discipline & Appeal) Rules, 1968. The Division Bench while elaborating fundamental principles of natural justice enumerated the seven well recognised facets in paragraph 7 of the judgment which is to the following effect:

"7. One of the fundamental principles of natural justice is that no man shall be a judge in his own cause. This principle consists of seven well recognised facets:

(i) The adjudicator shall be impartial and free from bias, (ii) The adjudicator shall not be the prosecutor, (iii) The complainant shall not be an adjudicator,

(iv) A witness cannot be the Adjudicator,

(v) The Adjudicator must not import his personal knowledge of the facts of the case while inquiring into charges, (vi) The Adjudicator shall not decide on the dictates of his Superiors or others, (vii) The Adjudicator shall decide the issue with reference to material on record and not reference to extraneous material or on extraneous considerations. If any one of these fundamental rules is breached, the inquiry will be vitiated."

31. The Division <u>Bench further held</u> that where the Inquiry Officer acts as Presenting Officer, bias can be presumed. In paragraph 9 is as follows:

"9. A domestic inquiry must be held by an unbiased person who is unconnected with the incident so that he can be impartial and objective in deciding the subject matters of inquiry. He should have an open mind till the inquiry is completed and should neither act with bias nor give an impression of bias. Where the Inquiry Officer acts as the Presenting Officer, bias can be presumed. At all events, it clearly gives an impression of bias. An Inquiry Officer is in position of a Judge or Adjudicator. The Presenting Officer is in the position of a Prosecutor. If the Inquiry Officer acts as a Presenting Officer, then it would amount to Judge acting as the prosecutor. When the Inquiry Officer conducts

the examination-in-chief of the prosecution witnesses and leads them through the facts so as to present the case of the disciplinary authority against the employee or cross-examines the delinquent employee or his witnesses to establish the case of the employer/disciplinary authority evidently, the Inquiry Officer cannot be said to have an open mind. The very fact that he presents the case of the employer and supports the case of the employer is sufficient to hold that the Inquiry Officer does not have an open mind."

32. The Division Bench after elaborately considering the issue summarised the principles in paragraph 16 which is to the following effect:

"16. We may summarise the principles thus:

(i) The Inquiry Officer, who is in the position of a Judge shall not act as a Presenting Officer, who is in the position of a prosecutor.

(ii) It is not necessary for the Disciplinary Authority to appoint a Presenting Officer in each and every inquiry. Non-appointment of a Presenting Officer, by itself will not vitiate the inquiry.

(iii) The Inquiry Officer, with a view to arrive at the truth or to obtain clarifications, can put questions to the prosecution witnesses as also the defence witnesses. In the absence of a Presenting Officer, if the Inquiry Officer puts any questions to the prosecution witnesses to elicit the facts, he should thereafter permit the delinquent employee to cross-examine such witnesses on those clarifications.

(iv) If the Inquiry Officer conducts a regular examination-in-chief by leading the prosecution witnesses through the prosecution case, or puts leading questions to the departmental witnesses pregnant with answers, or cross-examines the defence witnesses or puts suggestive questions to establish the prosecution case employee, the Inquiry Officer acts as prosecutor thereby vitiating the inquiry.

(v) As absence of a Presenting Officer by itself will not vitiate the inquiry and it is recognised that the Inquiry Officer can put questions

to any or all witnesses to elicit the truth, the question whether an Inquiry Officer acted as a Presenting Officer, will have to be decided with reference to the manner in which the evidence is let in and recorded in the inquiry.

Whether an Inquiry Officer has merely acted only as an Inquiry Officer or has also acted as a Presenting Officer depends on the facts of each case. To avoid any allegations of bias and running the risk of inquiry being declared as illegal and vitiated, the present trend appears to be to invariably appoint Presenting Officers, except in simple cases. Be that as it may."

33. We fully endorse the principles as enumerated above, however, the principles have to be carefully applied in facts situation of a particular case. There is no requirement of appointment of Presenting Officer in each and every case, whether statutory rules enable the authorities to make an appointment or are silent. When the statutory rules are silent with regard to the applicability of any facet of principles of natural justice the applicability of principles of natural justice which are not specifically excluded in the statutory scheme are not prohibited. When there is no express exclusion of particular principle of natural justice, the said principle shall be applicable in a given case to advance the cause of justice. In this context reference is made of a case of this Court in <u>Punjab National Bank and others vs. Kunj Behari Misra</u>, 1998 (7) SCC 84. In <u>the above case</u>, this Court had occasion to consider the provisions of Punjab National Bank Officer Employees' (Discipline and Appeal) Regulations, 1977. <u>Regulation 7</u> provides for action on the enquiry report. <u>Regulation 7</u> as extracted in paragraph 10 of the judgment is as follows:

"7. Action on the enquiry report.—(1) The disciplinary authority, if it is not itself the enquiring authority, may, for reasons to be recorded by it in writing, remit the case to the enquiring authority for fresh or further enquiry and report and the enquiring authority shall thereupon proceed to hold the further enquiry according to the provisions of Regulation 6 as far as may be.

(2) The disciplinary authority shall, if it disagrees with the findings of the enquiring authority on any article of charge, record its reasons for such disagreement and record its own findings on such charge, if the evidence on record is sufficient for the purpose.

(3) If the disciplinary authority, having regard to its findings on all or any of the articles of charge, is of the opinion that any of the penalties specified in Regulation 4 should be imposed on the officer employee, it shall, notwithstanding anything contained in Regulation 8, make an order imposing such penalty.

(4) If the disciplinary authority having regard to its findings on all or any of the articles of charge, is of the opinion that no penalty is called for, it may pass an order exonerating the officer employee concerned."

34. The question which was debated before this Court was that since Regulation 7(2) does not contain any provision for giving an opportunity to the delinquent officer to represent before disciplinary authority who reverses the findings which were in favour of the delinquent employee, the rules of natural justice are not applicable. This Court held that principle of natural justice has to be read in Regulation 7(2) even though rule does not specifically require hearing of delinquent officer. In paragraph 19 following was held:

"19. The result of the aforesaid discussion would be that the principles of natural justice have to be read into Regulation 7(2). As a result thereof, whenever the disciplinary authority disagrees with the enquiry authority on any article of charge, then before it records its own findings on such charge, it must record its tentative reasons for such disagreement and give to the delinquent officer an opportunity to represent before it records its findings. The report of the enquiry officer containing its findings will have to be conveyed and the delinquent officer will have an opportunity to persuade the disciplinary authority to accept the favourable conclusion of the enquiry officer. The principles of natural justice, as we have already observed, require the authority which has to take a final decision and can impose a

penalty, to give an opportunity to the officer charged of misconduct to file a representation before the disciplinary authority records its findings on the charges framed against the officer."

35. Thus, the question as to whether Inquiry Officer who is supposed to act independently in an inquiry has acted as prosecutor or not is a question of fact which has to be decided on the facts and proceedings of particular case. In the present case we have noticed that the High Court had summoned the entire inquiry proceedings and after perusing the proceedings the High Court came to the conclusion that Inquiry Officer himself led the examination in chief of the prosecution witness by putting questions. The High Court further held that the Inquiry Officer acted himself as prosecutor and Judge in the said disciplinary enquiry. The above conclusion of the High Court has already been noticed from paragraphs 9 and 10 of the judgment of the High court giving rise to Civil Appeal No.2608 of 2012.

36. The High Court having come to the conclusion that Inquiry Officer has acted as prosecutor also, the capacity of independent adjudicator was lost which adversely affecting his independent role of adjudicator. In the circumstances, the principle of bias shall come into play and the High Court was right in setting aside the dismissal orders by giving liberty to the appellants to proceed with inquiry afresh. We make it clear that our observations as made above are in the facts of the present cases.

37. In result, all the appeals are dismissed subject to the liberty as granted by the High Court that it shall be open for the appellants to proceed with the inquiry afresh from the stage as directed by the High Court and it shall be open for the appellant to decide on arrear pay and allowances of the respondents

16 MEDICAL REQUIREMENTS IN RECRUITMENT PROCESS (Tattoo Mark)

16.1 Judgement dated 07.05.2024 in DB Spl Appl Writ No. 414/2024 titled Union of India vs Sanyogita (Rajasthan High Court)

This appeal is directed against the order dated 28.11.2023 passed by the learned Single Judge by which the respondent's petition has been allowed, declaring the decision of the appellants in rejecting the candidature of the respondent as illegal.

3. Learned Deputy Solicitor General of India referred to the provisions contained in sub-clause (3) of Clause 11 of the Uniform Guidelines for Recruitment Medical Examination for Recruitment of GOs and NGOs in CAPFs and AR dated 20.05.2015, in support of his submission by elaborating that tattoo marks are ordinarily attributes of medical unfitness unless they are found on permissible part of the body with permissible content and size. Learned counsel would argue that in disciplined force, the standard of medical fitness is higher than the medical fitness required in other services, because such issues have bearing on the performance and duties in a disciplined force. He would submit that the learned Single Judge while allowing the writ petition, ignored and failed to appreciate that the spirit of the provisions, referred to above, required the writ petitioner to be free from any kind of tattoo inscribe or scar of removed tattoo on the inner aspect of right forearm. He would further submit that the scar, which has a permanent imprint, would be a ground for medical unfitness. The decision taken by the body of experts including review medical board, in absence of there being any violation of the provisions of law or binding guidelines, could not be interfered with by the Court in exercise of its writ jurisdiction, as the scope of judicial review against the opinion of the medical board/medical expert is extremely limited and it is not permissible under the law to substitute the opinion through judicial process. He would further submit that the learned Single Judge also did not properly appreciate the facts and circumstances, distinguishing features of the case of Shridhar Mahadeo Pakhare Vs. Union of India & Ors *(Writ Petition No.10026 of 2017) decided by the Bombay High Court.*

4. On the other hand, learned counsel for the respondents, on advance copy, supporting the order passed by the learned Judge submits that the learned Single Judge, after taking into consideration that the scar mark of removed tattoo, by itself, could not be made a basis to hold a candidate medically unfit in terms of the qualifying provisions contained in sub-cause (3) of clause 11 of the Guidelines, allowed petition.

5. Having heard learned counsel for the parties any having gone through the impugned order of the learned Single Judge, we do not find any ground to interfere with the order of the learned Single Judge for the reasons which are stated infra.

6. Admittedly the only ground on which the respondent- petitioner was declared medically unfit is that she was having scar mark on the inner aspect of her right forearm.

7. The relevant provisions contained in the guidelines, which have been referred to by the appellants and also analyzed by the learned Single Judge and are relevant for our purposes in this case, read as below:

"3) Tattoo : The practice of engraving / tattooing in India is prevalent since time immemorial, but has been limited to depict the name or a religious figure, invariably on inner aspect of forearm and usually on left side. On the other hand the present young generation is considerably under the influence of western culture and thus the number of potential recruits bearing skin art had grown enormously over the years, which is not only distasteful but distract from good order and discipline in the force. Following criteria are to be used to determine permissibility of tattoo:

b) Content-being a secular country, the religious sentiments of our countrymen are to be respected and thus tattoos depicting religious symbol or figure and the name, as followed in Indian army, are to be permitted.

a) Location- tattoos marked on traditional sites of the body like inner aspect of forearm, but only LEFT forearm, being non saluting limb or dorsum of the hands are to be allowed.

b) Size- size must be less than ¼ of the particular part (Elbow or Hand) of the body."

8. A bare perusal of the aforesaid provision would reveal that what could be made a ground for disqualification of a candidate would be existence of tattoo mark. The background in which the tattoo mark has been treated to be a ground for medical unfitness has been stated in the first part of the provisions. It is stated that such tattoo marks are not only distasteful but also distract from good order and discipline in the force. However, there is no absolute prohibition in having a tattoo mark. The provisions carve out exception that a candidate despite having tattoo mark, would not be held to be medically unfit.

9. Firstly, the tattoo depicting religious symbol or figure and the name are to be permitted. This is being allowed in the CRPF consistent with the practice which has been followed in the Indian Army. This fact has been clearly stated in the provisions itself. Thus there is no absolute prohibition in having tattoo mark.

10. Secondly, other provisions deal with location and size, which may render a candidate medically unfit. The tattoo marked on traditional sites of the body like inner aspect of forearm but only left forearm, being non saluting limb or dorsum of the hands, are permissible. Further it has been stated that the size must be less than 1/4 of the particular part (elbow or hand) of the body. Therefore, tattoo inscribe is a ground of medical unfitness only in certain conditions. In all other cases, it is not a ground to declare a candidate medically unfit.

11. We would thus find that mere existence of tattoo by itself is not a disqualification on the ground of medical fitness but the size and the place of the body where it is inscribed is relevant for deciding whether it is a case of medical unfitness or not. In any case if the tattoo mark has already been removed leaving behind a scar, in our opinion, it will not be within the teeth of the disqualification clause, as referred to hereinabove. Merely because the scar happens to be on the inner right forearm, that by itself cannot be treated to be a case of medical unfitness for the simple reason that existence of scar as such is not a ground for medical unfitness. In other words, the scar of removed tattoo and the scar for any other reason like injury etc. cannot be treated differently. In the absence of there being any ground of medical unfitness only on the ground of there being scar on the inner aspect of right forearm, disqualifying a candidate on the ground of there being by a scar of removed tattoo, will result in hostile discrimination as classification is not based on any rational integra and such discrimination would render it unconstitutional being violative of Articles 14 and 16 of the Constitution of India.

12. Therefore, for the reasons stated by the learned Single Judge as also the additional reasons which are stated by us, we are of the view that the action of the appellants in rejecting the candidature of the respondent on the ground of medical unfitness suffers from the vice of arbitrariness and has rightly been struck down by the learned Single Judge by the impugned order.

13. The appeal has no merit and the same is dismissed.

17 REQUIREMENT OF MANDATORY FIELD SERVICE FOR PROMOTION

17.1 Judgement dated 21.08.2015 in WP (C) 3778/2014 titled Commandant Rakesh Sethi vs Union Of India And Anr. (Delhi High Court)

1. This is a writ petition filed by the petitioner who is aggrieved by the actions of the respondents in refusing him promotion to the rank of Deputy Inspector General (DIG) and consequent emoluments and benefits by letters dated 13.12.2013 and 10.02.2014. The Central

Reserve Police Force ("CRPF"), which is the Petitioner's parent organization, was of the view that he did not fulfill the criteria for Mandatory Field Service (hereafter "MFS"), as required by the CRPF Group 'A' General Duty Officers Recruitment Rules, 2001 and as interpreted by a letter issued by the Ministry of Home Affairs, MHA UO No. I.45024/10/2003.Pers.II dated 17.06.2003 and subsequently communicated by DG, CRPF on 24.06.2003 read with letter dated 04.07.2012 and letter dated 19.09.2012.

2. The Petitioner is a Commandant in the CRPF, which he joined in 26.09.1992 as an Asst. Commandant. He was later promoted to the rank of Commandant on 29.09.07. The Petitioner applied and was successful in clearing the interview for the position of Joint Director (Technical), Lok Sabha. After 3 months of Field Service he was posted on deputation as Joint Director (Technical), Lok Sabha (subsequently the post was changed to Additional Director) under same pay scale and grade -`14,300 -18,300- for a period of 3 years i.e. from 31.01.2008 to 21.01.2011. Subsequently, the tenure of deputation was extended for a period of 12 months at the behest of Additional Secretary (Security), Lok Sabha from 31.01.2011 to 23.12.2011.

It was again, further extended to 23.12.2012. In this manner, 3 more extensions (of 2 months, 6 months, and 4 months respectively) were sought to extend his deputation till 23.12.2013 on account of a lack of substitutes available to fill his vacancy.

3. During the pendency of his deputation the petitioner sent a letter dated 20.10.2011 requesting consideration of his deputation posting, as an "operational post" on account of the job profile including security and collaboration with the CRPF"s battalions. The Additional Secretary (Security), Lok Sabha forwarded the said letter to DG, CRPF, with a comment stating that the „request of the officer seemed genuine" and the same job profile was viewed as an operational post in other branches of Government Service as well. The CRPF, in this regard stated in its letter dated 24.01.2012 that "Further, with regard to notify the post being held by the above officer at present in LS (Sectt) as operational post in view of the duties being performed by him, we have no objection." to the same and communicated this to the Central Government (first respondent herein). Later on 26.12.2012 a request was made by the Lok Sabha Secretariat to the CRPF to again extend the petitioner"s period of deputation, since no nomination for his substitute had been received. This was approved by the CRPF on 7.01.2013, by a letter. A consequential order was issued on 05.04.2013 extending the petitioner"s deputation tenure till 23 rd June, 2013.

4. Subsequently, the petitioner was considered for promotion and promoted by Presidential Order dated 16.06.2013 and Signal dated 18.5.2013. A letter requesting intimation of such promotion to the Petitioner and subsequent release from deputation to enable him to receive his rank and consequential posting, unless „deemed necessary to extend", was sent to the Lok Sabha by letter dated 22.05.2013. In the interregnum, the petitioner's period of deputation was extended till it ultimately ended in December, 2013. By letter dated 23.12.2013, CRPF clarified to the first respondent with respect to the petitioner's promotion:

"Certain clarifications have been sought by MHA with reference to the promotion of Shri Rakesh Sethi , Commandant (IRLA:3382) of CRPF to the rank of DIG. In this regard, it is intimated that promotion of the said officer is kept in abeyance till the issue is resolved."

5. The Petitioner represented against this on three occasions, i.e. by letters dated 23.12.2013, 06.01.2014, and 23.01.2014. In reply to these representations, the CRPF by its letter, dated 23.01.2014 informed the Petitioner that his representations were rejected and that the Central Government, Ministry of Home Affairs had referred the question of his promotion to a DPC. The petitioner is aggrieved by this and terms the impugned action of the respondents as unjustified withdrawal of promotion.

6. Ms. Jyoti Singh, learned senior counsel for the Petitioner argues that the Respondents have acted in an arbitrary and fanciful manner by revoking his promotion subsequently given that his deputation was sanctioned by CRPF itself. She states that considering the deputation was extended with the Respondents" permission, the petitioner cannot be denied the benefit of relaxation of the MFS criterion to his detriment. She also contended that the deputation entailed an operational character akin to Field Service and that the CRPF issued a „no objection" with respect to his request dated 20.10.2011. She argues that in summarily dismissing his representations without affording him an opportunity to be heard is a violation of natural justice and such administrative action revoking his promotion must be set aside.

7. Learned senior counsel also argued that the petitioner's period of deputation was extended due to exigencies of service and with the concurrence of both the Lok Sabha Secretariat and CRPF. Such being the case, the CRPF should not have resiled on its earlier commitment or no objection to treat the period of deputation as having been spent on operational duties. She underscored the fact further by stating that being involved with the overall security detail for the whole Lok Sabha establishment was no less onerous than being detailed on field or operational duty. Keeping in mind these factors, she argued that the CRPF had conveyed no objection to the Lok Sabha's request to treat the duties in its establishment as having spent on field duties. It was argued that besides, the DPC which considered the petitioner's claim did so after taking into consideration that he was on deputation in the Lok Sabha. He was declared fit and selected for promotion. In the conspectus of these circumstances, the letter of 23.12.2013 was wholly untenable; the determination by the DPC as to the petitioner"s suitability and merit to hold the post of DIG was conclusive. It was also argued that the requirement of having to undergo MFS cannot be insisted upon as a precondition for granting promotion. The Petitioner relied on the decisions in <u>Ashok Kumar v. UOI & Ors</u> W.P. (C) No.21900/2005, decided on 27.10.09 and Devender Singh Sandhu v. Union of India W.P.(C) No.2405/2013, decided on 29.05.13.

8. *The CRPF contends that the Petitioner showed unwillingness to undergo MFS; rather, he willingly sought extensions to his deputation knowing fully well that service conditions required him to complete two years of MFS and he had only completed 3 months. It relies on letters written by the Petitioner to his superior officials in the Lok Sabha requesting extensions on account of his daughter's exams and aged parents till December 2012. For subsequent dates we have no evidence of any requests. It is submitted that the Petitioner could not have assumed that the post he was holding was declared to be an operational one. The Ministry"s rejection letter, refusing finally, the proposal to declare certain posts (i.e. the Director (Security) and Jt. Director (Security)) in the Rajya Sabha Secretariat as operational, was dated 13.05.2013. In these circumstances, the Petitioner's promotion, made later, was in ignorance of the Central Government's order, disapproving the proposal for declaring the post held by him to be an operational one. It was argued that in the facts of this case, in the absence of MFS, the Petitioner could not claim entitlement to promotion as DIG on the basis of the June, 2013 order.*

9. *The Central Government's stated position is that promotion was granted on the information that the Petitioner had completed MFS requirements for promotion and subsequent clarification from the CRPF resulted in reconsideration of promotion subject to DPC. It was stressed by Mr. Kirtiman Singh, learned counsel, that the requirement to possess MFS has never been relaxed or set aside. Consequently, in the absence of a declaration that the post held by the petitioner was equivalent to a field or operationally functioning post, he was ineligible for promotion as he lacked an essential condition to hold the post of DIG. It was argued by counsel that the CRPF"s "no objection" to treat the deputation posting of the Petitioner as equivalent to "operational duty" was not absolute and conditional upon the Central Government's approval. The counsel relied on the Central Government's decision conveyed in this regard on 13.05.2013 and submitted that consequently, the Petitioner's selection through the*

DPC, held on 18.05.2013 was a mistake because this development had not been noticed by it.

10. The first question which has to be decided in this case is if the willingness showed by the petitioner to continue on deputation in any manner disentitled him to promotion on the ground that he had to undergo the MFS. The second is whether the decision of the Central Government to not treat the deputation posting as "operational duty" justified the CRPF"s action to revoke the promotion given to the Petitioner.

11. The Central Government's policy that an officer should undergo an MFS is embodied in its letter dated 03.02.2003. The policy of not promoting an officer unless he had undergone the field posting was questioned and in several decisions of this court, it was held that the CRPF could not deny promotion for something which was not within his control, i.e. posting. These decisions also directed that the CRPF should exercise its discretion and relax the condition requiring mandatory posting in such cases where the officer did not have any MFS. The judgments in turn led to a clarification, dated 04.07.2012 by the Central Government. Relying upon the CRPF Group "A" (General Duty) Officers Recruitment Rules, 2001, the Central Government's letter dated 03.02.2003 recites minimum two years" MFS to become eligible for the post of DIG. Relevant portions of the letter are reproduced below:

"..under mentioned eligibility criteria to be met for consideration for next rank promotion in various ranks of Group „A" officers:

Commandant to Addl. DIG

(i) ..

(ii) Two years Command as Commandant in Duty Bn.

(iii) ..

(iv) .."

(v) The rank of Additional DIG was done away with subsequently and promotion directly occurs to rank of DIG. The policy of the Union Ministry of Home Affairs, contained in its U.O. No. P-VII-10/2012 dated 04.07.2012

- to the extent it is relevant is extracted below:

"Therefore, based on guidelines received from MHA, the following instructions are hereby issued for compliance/ implementation:

a) ..

b) In ordinary course, no person should be posted to an establishment where duty is not counted as a service in a field Unit till he completes required service in a field unit. However in exceptional circumstances where services of a person are essentially required in the interest of work for the force or due to other technical reasons / grounds in an establishment where duty is not counted towards service in a field unit, approval of IG (Pers) DTE or Sector IsGP may be obtained. ...

c) In case such a person becomes due for his next promotion before completion of required field service, his case may be submitted to this DTE with full justification under circumstances he was allowed to continue in such static establishment duly supported by copy of approval accorded by IG (Pers) DTE or Sector IsGP. The promotion of such person will be released after obtaining such relaxation or waiver....

d) The personnel who do not complete required MFS owing to their own request for posting in static establishment where duty is not counted towards MFS or wherever such personnel have expressed their unwillingness for posting to a field unit and get posting/ attachment on their own request to static establishment, their cases will not be considered for granting relaxation in MFS."

12. A subsequent letter dated 19.09.2012 amended the list of deputation terms to be counted towards MFS. The relevant portion is quoted:

"(i) In existing paragraph 2f (vi) Parliament Duty Group (PDG) may also be inserted besides SDG."

13. Whilst there is an eligibility criterion of 2 years MFS in order to be promoted to the rank of DIG, the power to relax the same has been granted to the CRPF under Section 6 of the Central Reserve Police Force Act, and this is to be exercised according to the above policy especially in light of exigent circumstances resulting in postings to "static" posts. Besides, in the present circumstances, given that there was a lack of clarity on behalf of the CRPF itself as to whether the concerned deputation is a 'static' post or a field posting, the CRPF should have first ensured that a non-static posting was offered to an officer on the threshold of promotion, or at least warned him before that if he accepted the deputation he would lose his chance of promotion. The request for treating his posting in the Lok Sabha as one on "operational duty", was accepted by way of a 'no-objection' on 24-01-2012.

14. The second point which has to be highlighted is that the CRPF declared this policy (rather, an exception by way of additional disqualification for eligible officers) after the Petitioner's deputation tenure had been approved. The declaration of the policy later, on 04.07.2012, was well after this particular extension of his tenure. By then the Petitioner was sanguine in his belief that the deputation posting tenure given him was an operational duty post. It is accepted that the CRPF owes no duty of relaxation to officers who show an unwillingness to perform field duties; since the Petitioner had been told categorically that his deputation posting itself was being treated as operational (hence, counting towards MFS) the question of his seeking a separate MFS did not then arise. It is only by letter dated 13.05.2013 that the Central Government seems to have indicated that posting to the Rajya Sabha secretariat could not be considered as a field or operational posting. In this Court's opinion, that letter would make no difference to the Petitioner's entitlement for consideration-which took place shortly afterwards, on 18th May, 2013. The letter of

13.05.2013 pertained to treatment to deputation posting in Rajya Sabha, not Lok Sabha. The Petitioner was deputed to Lok Sabha security detail. More importantly, the Petitioner's deputation tenure had been extended and approval communicated over a year earlier- on 24.01.2012, stating that experience/posting in Lok Sabha in the post held by him was operational/field posting. Therefore, the Central Government's view - expressed later, could not have impacted his case. The most salient aspect of this case, in the Court's opinion is the complete opacity of the CRPF and its silence in not alerting the Petitioner at any time, whenever his deputation tenure had to be extended (for which he had sought and was granted after due consideration by CRPF- in some instances, only because there was no replacement in sight) that if he were not to return, his case for promotion to DIG would not be considered.

15. The CRPF"s subsequent letter dated 23.08.2013 revoked the relaxation of MFS criteria for promotions of candidates on deputations to various organisations considered in clause (f) i.e. (of the O.M. of 04.07.2012 read with amendment vide letter dated 19.09.2012), the result being that deputations to RAW, CBI, IB, NIA etc. were no longer considered as valid periods of service counting as MFS on grounds that deputationists are 'having an easy time'. The CRPF's plea that the Petitioner showed willingness to extend static deputation, for which MFS relaxation is not accorded, is untenable as there would no longer exist any accepted deputations where service would count towards MFS. The removal of the substance of OM dated 04.07.2012, has resulted in a return to the earlier legal position in _Ashok Kumar and Ors. v. Union of India and Anr_ [supra] and allied judgments. So, requests made for extension of deputation by the Petitioner could not have been considered to his detriment. Thus, the first question is decided in favour of the Petitioner.

16. Now, to consider the second question. The Respondents had urged that the Petitioner's promotion was granted on a mistaken belief that the deputation had been considered as an operational post. It cannot

be said that such promotion was given in absence of material facts as both the deputation and the request by the Petitioner for consideration of his deputation as operational were a matter of record. In addition the Additional Secretary for Security, Lok Sabha has given a comment stating that other organisations view such deputations as operational posts. The delay in intimating rejection of his request was clearly detrimental to the Petitioner as he had laboured under the assumption that CRPF had no objections. Hence, even if being aware of his apparent lack of field service was the Petitioner's liability, he was not given adequate time to act upon it considering he was first informed of such infirmity on 23.12.2013.

17. *This Court's judgment in* Ashok Kumar and Ors. v. Union of India and Anr *[W.P. (C) No. 21900 of 2005] and subsequent judgments (i.e.* Shri Virendra Singh Rajput v. Union of India and Ors *[W.P. (C) No. 2427/2010],* S. Arul Raj v. Union of India and Ors *[W.P. (C) No. 2266/2011],* Ram Naresh Pratap Singh v. Union of India & Ors *[W.P. (C) No. 82/2012] , Ghamman Singh v. Union of India [W.P. (C) No. 8046/2011] and Devender Singh Sandhu v. Union of India [W.P. (C) No. 2405/2013]) which have followed it, is an authority for the proposition that MFS conditions cannot be invoked to deny promotion if the officer never was posted to any of those field battalions, or given field postings and that the Force should invoke the power of exempting its personnel in such eventualities. Those judgments hold the field even today.*

18. Ashok Kumar *(supra) observed inter alia, that:*

"36. *We may note that with the increase in posts in the year 2004 and knowing fully well that the continued requirement of two years" service in a duty battalion would hamper the promotional career of the officers, the respondents have themselves, put on track mode, the identification of its officers in various non-duty posts because the respondents know and recognize that transfer/posting is not in the hands of the officers but is a prerogative of the department and the department has to ensure that it affords an opportunity to all its officers to become qualified by serving in duty battalions. This also highlights the fact that the sudden change in situation in the year 2004, being unexpected, required a proper administrative redressal.*

37. We accordingly quash the decision of the Central Government declining to relax the eligibility condition of two years" service in a duty battalion for promotion to the post of Inspector and 2 IC under BSF as also the post of Inspector under CRPF.

38. A mandamus is issued to the Central Government to re- consider the issue pertaining to the promotions to the posts of 2 IC and Inspector under BSF and the post of Inspector under CRPF; the issue being exercising the power of relaxation vested under the Rules, to be exercised by the Central Government. While reconsidering the matter, the questions framed by us would be kept in mind while deciding the issue and the backdrop circumstances would be kept in mind while deciding the issue. Needless to state the decision of the Central Government would be a reasoned decision evidencing the application of mind with reference to the questions and the backdrop circumstances. The decision would be taken within a period of 8 weeks from date of receipt of this decision in the Ministry of Home Affairs i.e. the Nodal Ministry of the Central Government. We further mandate that if the decision taken is in favour of the petitioners, they would be promoted with effect from the date, persons junior to the petitioners were promoted and in said eventuality, the petitioners would be entitled to all consequential benefits such as seniority, pay fixation and arrears of pay."

19. This Court's reasoning in Ashok Kumar (supra) is supported by authority- i.e. the judgment of the Supreme Court in State Bank of India v Kashinath Kher 1996 (7) SCC 470. Discussing the efficacy of one such mandatory requirement of a Bank employee previously having to function in rural areas, it was observed that:

"It would thus be seen that it is not a case of ineligible persons made eligible, but a case of giving opportunities to those officers, who for no *fault of theirs, were not made eligible to be considered and given opportunity to be considered for promotion and after consideration, on fulfillment of the service of line assignment and rural/semi-urban service for a minimum of two years were promoted to the MMGS-III. Thus, we hold that the policy adopted by the Board is not violative of Article 14 of the Constitution. But it must be remembered that in considering whether the candidate has completed the line of assignment or rural/semi-urban service for the required period, a clear demarcation be drawn between the officers who either due to volitions refusal to serve and those on account of inaction or deliberate omission on the part of the controlling authority did not have an opportunity as the case may be, to get the required service qualifications. Therefore, an exercise requires to be done by the appellant to identify this grouping and consider all those candidates who have otherwise become eligible but did not get opportunity, for no fault of theirs', to secure the service qualification but should be denied to those who volunteered not to go for line assignment or rural or semi-urban service as the case may be, and then to consider according to the criteria prescribed under the rules or the circulates issued from time to time."*

20. In the present case, the facts do not anywhere indicate the Petitioner's unwillingness to shoulder responsibilities in a field posting; the CRPF never told him that the period of deputation spent by him would be treated as his unwillingness for being given field posting; it is not on record stating that any such field posting had been offered. In these circumstances, the respondents are hereby directed to exercise the power of exemption, and ensure that he is fixed in the rank and pay of DIG from the date he became entitled to it, after his name was cleared by the DPC and in terms of the Presidential order dated 16.06.2013. Notional pay fixation in the said grade shall be granted from that date, and his increments worked out on that basis; actual pay and arrears shall be calculated and disbursed to him, from the day he rejoined the CRPF after completion of his deputation tenure with the Lok Sabha. It is also declared that he is entitled to all consequential

benefits such as seniority, etc. The relevant orders shall be issued and consequent disbursements made, within eight weeks from today.

21. The writ petition is allowed in the above terms without any order as to costs.

18 REQUIREMENT OF HEADQUARTER FOR ENTITLEMENT OF HRA TO OFFICERS IN CRPF

18.1 Judgement dated 10.01.2023 in WP(C) 243/2020 titled J S Chauhan vs the Union of India (MANIPUR HIGH COURT)

The prayer in W.P.(C) No.243 of 2020 is as follows:

"Admit the Writ petition and issue Rule Nisi calling upon the respondents to show cause as to why a Writ/order/directive(s) should not be issued for quashing and setting aside the stoppage of HRA given to the Petitioner with effect from 16.2.2019, as it was done without due process of law and without issuing any order and violation of Principle of Natural Justice and stoppage is against the OM issued by the Ministry of Finance, in the facts and circumstances;

To show cause as to why a Writ in the nature of Mandamus or any other appropriate writ/order/directive(s) should not be issued directing the Respondents to pay the HRA in terms of the Sanction order dated 21.2.2019 issued by the Commandant - 32 Bn CRPF, Loktak, Manipur and also directed the respondents to pay the illegal recovery amount of Rs.27,827/ to the petitioner;

Make the Rule absolute;

To pass any appropriate order or direction(s) which may be appropriate to be passed under such facts and circumstance of the instant case, for the ends of justice."

2. The prayer in W.P.(C) No.508 of 2020 is as follows:

"To admit the Writ Petition, call for the records of the case and issue rule nisi calling upon the Respondents to show cause as to why the

prayer prayed for by the Petitioner should not be granted. And, after hearing them your Lordships may make the rule absolute;

To issue a writ in the nature of mandamus/certiorari or any other appropriate writ thereby quashing the letter dated 27.2.2020 and to direct the concerned respondents to release the HRA entitled to the petitioner with effect from 13.8.2019 in terms of the Sanction order dated 3.9.2019 issued by the Commandant 109 Bn., CRPF, Mongsangai, Imphal West, Manipur;

To direct the concerned respondents to release the HRA entitled to the petitioner w.e.f. 13.8.2019 along with 6% interest per annum;

To direct the concerned respondents to refund the amounts deducted from the salary of the petitioner without giving any reason/clarification;

To direct the concerned respondents to consider the letter dated 6.3.2020 submitted by the petitioner to the IGP(ADM) DTE, CRPF (through proper channel) within a stipulated timeframe by issuing necessary speaking order;

To pass any other appropriate order(s) or direction(s) that this Hon'ble Court deem fit and proper; and To award cost of the Petition to the Petitioner."

3. Since the grounds raised and relief sought in the writ petitions are similar, both the writ petitions were heard together and are being disposed of by this common order.

4. The case of the petitioner in W.P.(C) No.243 of 2020 is that he was remained posted in 103 Bn RAF/CRPF, New Delhi by drawing HRA with his pay and after completing his tenure period of posting at 103 Bn, the petitioner was transferred to 32 Bn CRPF, Loktak, Churchandpur District, Manipur. Pursuant to the transfer order dated 29.1.2019, he reported duty at 32 Bn and the Commandant, 32 Bn had also taken him in the strength of the unit with effect from 15.2.2019. Vide order of the Commandant, 32 Bn, a sanction was accorded for his

entitlement of HRA and was also drawing his HRA with his pay regularly with effect from 15.2.2019 without any interruption till March, 2020. However, in the month of April, 2020, the respondent authority without giving any opportunity of hearing and without issuing any recovery order, recovered a sum of Rs.27,827/- from the petitioner's pay and also stopped the HRA of Rs.22,584/-. After knowing the stoppage of HRA and recovery of Rs.27,827/-, the petitioner has submitted a representation on 25.4.2020 to the competent authority. Despite the receipt of the said representation, the same has not been considered till date. Hence, the writ petition.

5. Resisting the writ petition, the respondents filed affidavit-in-opposition stating that on checking of dues being drawn by officers, it was found that many officers whose Notional HQ (i.e. Group Centre) is not situated in North Eastern region (for short, "NE region") are also drawing HRA at the rates applicable to their previous headquarters. Accordingly, all HRA drawal cases were reviewed and all those officers, whose detachment headquarter is in NE region but their notional headquarter is away from NE region, were stopped and recovery of irregular HRA was scheduled in equal instalments. It is stated that the HRA case of the petitioner Chauhan was of similar nature as his notional headquarter is GC CRPF Kathgodam (Uttrakhand) and detachment headquarter is in NE region and, therefore, his HRA was found irregular and stopped from month of April 2020 and recovery of irregular HRA already drawn for period from 16.2.2019 to 31.3.2020 amounting to Rs.2,78,263/- was booked in 10 equal instalments for recovery @ Rs.27,827/- per month from the pay of April 2020. It is stated that the representation of the petitioner has been examined by the DIG (Adm) Dte. General vide their signal dated 12.5.2020 and passed an order to recover the HRA amount in 20 equal instalments instead of 10 instalments and the same has been conveyed to the petitioner through Commandant 32 Bn.

6. The case of the petitioner in W.P.(C) No.508 of 2020 is that after completing his tenure period of posting at DG, CGO, Lodhi Road, New

Delhi, the petitioner was transferred on 25.7.2019 to 109 Bn. located at Imphal and upon report, the petitioner has been taken into 109 Bn. with effect from 13.8.2019. According to the petitioner, while posted at DG, Headquarters, Delhi as Deputy Commandant (CR&VIG) from January, 2014 to August 2019, he was allotted Government quarters from 16.10.2014 to 12.6.2019. The petitioner vacated the Government accommodation and shifted his family members to a rented accommodation at Delhi-85. Vide order dated 3.7.2019, the DIG (Adm) Dte issued sanction order according for drawing HRA with effect from 13.6.2019. Although the sanction order was issued, the petitioner has failed to receive the HRA since September 2019 and he was informed deduction of Rs.26,807/- from the salary of September, 2019 without disclosing any reason. The stoppage of HRA with effect from September 2019 is against the Office Memorandum and the same is illegal, arbitrary and unreasonable. Hence, the writ petition.

7. The respondents 1 to 6 filed affidavit-in-opposition stating that on his reporting, the petitioner has been sanctioned HRA at 24% with effect from 13.8.2019 vide 109 Bn. sanction order dated 3.9.2019 for residing his family at House No.60-61, Third Floor, BLK, a-Pkt-3 Sector-16, Rohini City, Delhi-85. It is stated that the officer/personnel who are posted to NE region from outside of NE region but kept their family at the last place of posting are entitled to HRA of the old duty station. However, officer/personnel posted in a unit deployed in NE region, the notional Headquarter i.e. GC of which is situated outside of NE region are not entitled for grant of HRA at the last place of posting. It is stated that no such order exists to grant HRA to those personnel who is posted in a unit deployed in NE region but kept their family at the last place of posting without linking his notional Headquarter i.e. GC. Therefore, on receipt of 109 Bn. sanction order dated 3.9.2019, the office of DIG (Amn) has not drawn the sanctioned HRA to the petitioner in the light of clarification/direction and the same has been intimated to 109 Bn. on 27.2.2020 which has further been communicated to the petitioner through Commandant, 109 Bn. vide endorsement dated 20.03.2020. It is stated that the personnel

posted in those Units which are deployed in NE region but their notional Headquarter i.e. GC are situated outside of NE region, are not entitled for grant of HRA at the last place of posting. No order has so far been received from the Government of India to grant of HRA to the personnel posted in unit deployed in NE region and kept their family at last place posting without linking his notional Headquarter. Further, the petitioner prior to his posting as Deputy Commandant (Legal) M&N Sector Headquarter, Imphal was posted in 109 Bn. as Deputy Commandant.

8. Assailing the impugned stoppage of HRA and recovery of Rs.27,827/-, Mr. A. Mohendro, the learned counsel for the petitioner in W.P.(C) No.243 of 2020 submitted that the petitioner was drawing HRA as per the sanction order dated 21.2.2019 till March 2020 without any interruption, as the petitioner has been posted at NE region. He would submit that HRA was being drawn to the officer as per the admissibility by PAO of Government of India, but after taken over of entitlement section by CRPF, point of notional HQ (GC) raised at their own which is nowhere mentioned in the order of the Government of India.

9. The learned counsel further submitted that the petitioner came to know from his pay slip for the month of April 2020 that his HRA was stopped and recovery of total amount of Rs.2,78,263/- was made and recovery instalment of a sum of Rs.27,827/- per month for 10 instalments started without any recovery order to the petitioner or did not cancel the sanction order dated 21.2.2019 issued by the Commandant, 32 Bn. The said act is illegal and malafide and violation of Office Memorandum of the Ministry of Finance, Department of Expenditure for granting benefit to the Central Government employees employed in the NE region, whereas the petitioner is now posted at 32 Bn., which is under the NE region and therefore, the petitioner is entitled for the benefit of HRA.

10. The learned counsel for the petitioner urged that the petitioner has been transferred from 103 Bn. to 32 Bn. and is still keeping his family

at the last place of posting i.e. Delhi. Hence, the stoppage of HRA and recovery ordered to be made is illegal.

11. The learned counsel for the petitioner then submitted that the respondents are twisting the issue and misinterpreting the rules/orders of the Government at their whims and do not try to understand the spirit of granting NE concession extended under the Government policy. The learned counsel added that most of the CRPF battalions whose Group Centres are located in NE region are deployed outside the region. But these battalions are not allowed NE concessions though its affiliated GC are located in NE region and that it is clear that presence in the NE region of an employee is mandatory for granting NE region benefits.

12. The learned counsel appearing for the petitioner in W.P.(C) No.508 of 2020 submitted that as per the Office Memorandum dated 22.1.2019, HRA is entitled to the CRPF personnel on their transfer to non-family location viz., North Eastern Region, Sikkim, Andaman & Nicobar Island, Lakshadeep island, J&K and left wing extremist area and there cannot be a classification whether the headquarters are within the NE region or not. The petitioner who is posted at non-family location at NE region is very much entitled to HRA in terms of Office Memorandum dated 22.1.2019.

13. The learned counsel further submitted that the petitioner Vinod Sawant has been again transferred vide signal dated 13.7.2021 from 109 Bn. to M&N Sector Headquarters with effect from 13.9.2021 and the petitioner has been taken on the strength of Manipur and Nagaland Sector Headquarters vide signal dated 20.9.2021. He would submit that on 27.9.2021, the petitioner submitted an application to the office of M&N Sector Headquarters for sanction of HRA for his last place of posting i.e. Delhi mentioning that headquarter of the petitioner is now situated in North East only and hence, he is entitled for HRA of last place of posting. However, vide letter dated 21.10.2021, the petitioner has been informed that he was not drawing HRA at old station.

14. Mr. S. Vijayanand Sharma, the learned Sr.PCCG for the respondents submitted that HRA is a headquarter based allowance and that the petitioners are posted at the duty Bn. whose notional headquarters are situated outside the present place of posting. As such, the petitioners are not entitled for HRA. Further, the HRA is given to an employee in case Government Provided Residential Accommodation is not available to him. Since the petitioners are given GPRA, they are not entitled to claim HRA in the present place of posting. The petitioners could only avail the allowance under additional HRA scheme and not regular HRA.

15. The learned counsel for the respondents further submitted that the petitioner in W.P.(C) No.508 of 2020 vacated his GPRA on his own on 12.6.2019 whereas vide signal dated 6.5.2029, he has been transferred from Dte. General to 109 Bn. Since the petitioner in W.P.(C) N.508 of 2020 vacated his GPRA within the retention period of three years, he is not eligible to claim for the benefit of additional HRA. Similarly, the petitioner in W.P.(C) No.243 of 2020 was transferred from 103 Bn. to 32 Bn. vide signal dated 25.7.2018 and that the petitioner applied for HRA while being posted in 32 Bn. for his previous place of posting and sanction order was passed vide order dated 21.2.2019. Since the said sanction order is not in consonance with the rules, it was stopped by the respondent authority. Further, the petitioner in W.P.(C) No.243 of 2020 has applied for the additional HRA before completion of the retention period of three years as stipulated in the rules.

16. The learned counsel for the respondent urged that since both the petitioners are posted at duty battalion whose notional headquarters are situated outside the State of Manipur and HRA being a headquarter based allowance, the petitioners are not entitled to claim for HRA.

17. This Court considered the rival submissions and also perused the materials available on record.

18. The grievance of the petitioner in W.P.(C) No.243 of 2020 is that he is a second in command and after completion of his tenure period he was transferred from 102 Bn. New Delhi to 32 Bn at Loktak, Manipur and after relieving from 103 Bn., the petitioner joined his new posting at 32 Bn. on 15.2.2019 and at 32 Bn., he was sanctioned HRA vide order dated 21.2.2019 and was enjoying till March, 2020. However, the respondent authorities without giving any opportunity to the petitioner, stopped payment of HRA and also started recovery in 10 instalments with effect from 16.2.2019 to March, 2020 at the rate of Rs.27,827/-. However, pursuant to the interim order of this Court, the recovery was not effected. Thus, a prayer has been made to direct the respondents to pay the HRA with effect from April, 2020 and also to refund the recovery amount, if any, to the petitioner.

19. Similar is the grievance made by the petitioner in W.P.(C) No.508 of 2020, who contended that he was posted at the Directorate General, CGO Complex as Deputy Commandant (CR & VIG) from January, 2014 to August, 2019 and after completing his tenure period of posting at DG, CGO, New Delhi, vide transfer order dated 25.7.2019, he was transferred to 109 Bn. at Mongsangai, Manipur. According to the petitioner, while he was at DG, New Delhi, the GPRA quarters allotted to him was vacated and shifted his family to a rented accommodation at Delhi and also the DIG (Adm) Dte. had issued sanction order dated 3.7.2019 for drawing HRA with effect from 13.6.2019. According to the petitioner, on reporting at the new station, the petitioner requested the authority for sanction of HRA of his last place of posting and the Commandant, 109 Bn. had also issued sanction order dated 3.9.2019 for drawing HRA. When the order copy was forwarded to the Director Accounts, PAO, CRPF, New Delhi for needful action for drawal of HRA, his claim was returned stating that no such order received from the Government of India to grant HRA to the personnel posted in unit deployed in NE region and kept their family at last place of posting without linking his notional headquarter i.e. Group Centre. Thus, a prayer has been made to quash the letter dated 27.2.2020 and to release the HRA entitled to the petitioner with effect from 13.8.2019 in terms of the sanction order dated 3.9.2019 and to refund the amount, if any, deducted from the salary of the petitioner.

20. On the other hand, it is the say of the respondents that in the case of the petitioner in W.P.(C) No.243 of 2020, he was transferred from 103 Bn. to 32 Bn., Manipur. While the petitioner was posted at 32 Bn., he had applied for HRA for his previous place of posting and sanction order was issued on 21.2.2019. After finding that the said sanction order was not in consonance with the rules, it was stopped by the respondent authorities. As far as the petitioner in W.P.(C) No.508 of 2020 is concerned, it is the say of the respondents that the petitioner had vacated his GPRA on his own on 12.6.2019, whereas vide signal dated 6.5.2019, he has been transferred from Dte. CG to 109 Bn. Since the petitioner had vacated his GPRA within the retention period of three years, he is not eligible to claim HRA.

21. The respondents urged that since the petitioners are posted at duty battalion whose notional headquarters are situated outside the State of Manipur and HRA being headquarter based allowance, the petitioners are not entitled to claim for HRA. Even if the argument of the petitioners qua claim of HRA is considered on the ground of being posted at non- family station i.e. Manipur, since both the petitioners are provided with GPRA, they are not entitled to claim HRA at the present place of posting. Further, even if the petitioners are entitled to claim for HRA or additional HRA for their previous place of posting, they ought to have claimed the HRA or additional HRA within the retention period of three years and, as such, violated the eligibility criteria to claim HRA or additional HRA.

22. As could be seen from the records, in the case of the petitioner in W.P.(C) No.508 of 2020, a sanction order was issued by the DIG (Adm) Dte according sanction to the petitioner for drawal of HRA at the rate applicable in X Class cities i.e. 24% of basic pay with effect from 13.6.2019. On a perusal of the pleadings, it is clear that pending writ petition, the petitioner was again transferred to M&N Sector headquarters from 109 Bn. vide order dated 13.7.2021 with effect from 13.9.2021 and he has been taken on the strength of Manipur and Nagaland Sector headquarters. On 27.9.2021, the petitioner in

W.P.(C) No.508 of 2020 had also submitted his application for sanction of HRA for his last place of posting i.e. Delhi mentioning that the headquarter is now situated in NE only and, therefore, he is entitled for HRA of last place of posting. This has not been refuted by the respondents. In fact, as could be seen from the records, vide letter dated 21.10.2021, the petitioner in W.P.(C) No.508 of 20202 has been informed that he was not drawing HRA at old station. Hence, the last station HRA amount is not known and, therefore, the fixed amount of HRA of last station under NE provisions could not be sanctioned to him. It was also informed that when his HRA at last place of posting i.e. 109 Bn. is drawn, he may submit his claim for drawing old station headquarter HRA in this headquarter for sanction.

23. At this juncture, it is pertinent to note that the respondent authorities adopted two yardsticks for drawing the entitled HRA in the case of the petitioner in W.P.(C) No.508 of 2020. Earlier, the department had refused the HRA of the petitioner on the ground that the headquarter of him is situated outside NE. Now the petitioner has been posted to M&N Sector headquarter which is located in NE, the M&N Sector has raised an objection that only on drawal of HRA at 109 Bn., his subsequent drawal will be considered. The aforesaid objection raised by the respondent authorities is arbitrary in nature for the simple reason that the respondent authorities without applying their mind have come to such conclusion.

24. As far as the claim of the petitioner in W.P.(C) No.508 of 2020 for sanction and drawal of HRA at 109 Bn. is concerned, while the petitioner was posted at DG, CGO, New Delhi, a Government quarters was allotted to him where he resided from 16.10.2014 to 12.6.2019 and had vacated the said quarters on transfer to 109 Bn. and shifted his family to a rented accommodation at Delhi. Accordingly, he was issued with sanction order vide order dated 3.7.2019 for drawing HRA with effect from 13.6.2019. On reporting at 109 Bn., when the petitioner requested for sanction of HRA of his last place of posting, the Commandant, 109 Bn. had also issued sanction order on 3.9.2019 for

drawing HRA and a copy of the sanction order forwarded to DG, CGO for drawal of arrear HRA. However, vide impugned letter dated 27.2.2020, the DG, CRPF, New Delhi returned the claim by stating as under:

"A clarification on the subject was sought from DIG (Adm) Dte., in reply, DIG (Adm) Dte, vide their ION No.H.III.1/2019-20/DA- IV dated 12/1/2020 has intimated that no such orders so far received from GoI/MHA to grant of HRA to the personnel posted in unit deployed in NE region and kept their family at last place of posting without linking his notional headquarter i.e. Group Centre. As and when it has been received from GoI/MHA, the same will be provided. Copy of this letter is enclosed herewith for your further needful. Hence, HRA sanction order in respect of Shri Vinod Sawant, D/C (IRLA-7171) of your unit is returned herewith. Officer may be informed accordingly."

25. The Office Memorandum dated 22.1.2019 issued by the Ministry of Home Affairs, Government of India, provides as under:

"The undersigned is directed to say that a proposal for grant of HRA of Old Station/Selected Place of Residence, in addition to the HRA admissible at the new place of posting, to CAPF personnel on their transfer to non-family locations, viz., North Eastern Region, Sikkim, Andaman & Nicobar Islands, Lakshadweep Islands, State of Jammu & Kashmir and Left Wing Extremist (LWE) areas, in the event of their vacation of Government accommodation retained by them after three years, as per Ministry of Housing & Urban Affairs OM No.12035/4/2015-Pol.II dated 14.11.2017 and 01.08.2018, till they remain posted in such non-family stations, was examined in this Ministry in consultation with Ministry of Finance (Department of Expenditure), and it has agreed to:-

(i) allow HRA, on vacation of the Government accommodation by families of CAPF personnel after 3 years retention period, who are posted in non-family stations/locations (as defined by M/o Housing &

Urban Affairs in their OM dated 01/08/2018), in addition to the HRA admissible at the new place of posting.

(ii) relax the mandatory provision of keeping families of CAPF personnel at last place of posting for allowing HRA at the rate of Selected Place of Residence.

2. This issues with the approval of Ministry of Finance (Department of Expenditure), vide their ID No.28/2/2018-E.II(B) dated 18.01.2019 and as vetted by integrated Finance Division of this Ministry vide their Dy No.3437419 dated 22.01.2019."

26. The petitioner in W.P.(C) No.508 of 2020 contended that the Government quarters was allotted to him while he was at DG, CGO and he and his family members resided in the said quarters from 16.10.2014 to 12.06.2019 and thereafter, vacated the said quarters and shifted his family to a rented house at Delhi. Thus, as per the Office Memorandum dated 22.1.2019, the petitioner in W.P.(C) No.508 of 2020 is entitled to receive HRA along with additional HRA, as he has been transferred to North Eastern region from DG, CGO, New Delhi to 109 Bn., Manipur and also he had vacated the Government quarters after three years retention in compliance to the Office Memorandum dated 22.1.2019.

27. Coming to the case of the petitioner in W.P.(C) No.243 of 2020, the only contention of the respondents is that the petitioner being posted in battalion in NE region is treated as on tour and not eligible for NE concession as headquarter of the battalion is Group Centre, Kathgodam which is located outside NE region. The aforesaid contention of the respondents cannot be appreciated for the reason that while granting the concession the only criteria laid down by the Government is posting of a person in NE region. The purpose to attract and retain services of the person in NE region and the issue of headquarter of a person is nowhere mentioned in the Office Memorandum/Government Order.

28. *Admittedly, the petitioner in W.P.(C) No.243 of 2020 is not on tour as he was posted to 32 Bn., Lokatak, Manipur on transfer from 103 Bn., New Delhi. The CRPF personnel are posted in a battalion for years and minimum tenure has been laid down in the transfer policy. Therefore, there is no question of treating such long tenure as on tour.*

29. *The Commandant, 32 Bn. issued a sanction order dated 21.2.2019 for the entitlement of the petitioner for drawal of HRA and as per the sanction order dated 21.2.2019 and the petitioner was drawing his HRA with his pay regularly with effect from 15.2.2019 without any interruption till the month of March, 2020. However, in the month of April, 2020, the respondent authorities without giving any prior notice or opportunity of hearing cancelled the sanction order dated 21.2.2019 and directed to recover a sum of Rs.27,827/- from the petitioner's pay and also ordered to stop HRA amount of Rs.22,584/-. After knowing the stoppage of HRA and recovery, on 25.4.2020, the petitioner has submitted a representation to the respondent authorities and, admittedly, the said representation has not been considered till date.*

30. *It is apposite to mention that the Ministry of Finance, Department of Expenditure, issued an Office Memorandum dated 14.8.2018 for grant of additional HRA to the civilian employees of the Central Government serving in the States of NE region, Andaman & Nicobar Island, Lakshadweep Islands and Ladakh, which provides as under:*

"(i) In case of civilian employees of Central Government transferred to and posted from a date prior to 01.07.2017 who leave their families behind at the old duty station, the HRA of the old duty station will be calculated on the revised pay drawn on 01.07.2017 with percentage rates of HRA effective on 01.07.2017 as per O.M. No.2/5/2017-E.II(B) dated 07.07.2017.

(ii) In case of civilian employees of Central Government transferred to an posted from a date on or after 01.07.2017 who leave their families behind at the old duty station, the HRA of the old duty station will be

calculated on the revised pay drawn on the date of transfer with the percentage rates of HRA effective on the date of transfer."

31. Thus, as per the aforesaid Office Memorandum, the petitioner in W.P.(C) No.243 of 2020 is entitled to receive the HRA along with additional HRA, as he has been transferred to NE region from 103 Bn. Therefore, the stoppage of HRA to the petitioner and recovery of HRA being paid to him from 16.2.2019 to March, 2020 is not appreciable and without opportunity of hearing to the petitioner.

32. Drawal of two HRAs by a Central Government employee would be admissible even if the employee keeps their family in the previous station on the own or rented house after vacating the Government quarters due to transfer to NE region.

33. It is not the case of the respondents that the petitioners herein are still occupying the Government quarters at the previous place of posting. The essential requirement for applicability of the benefit of HRA to the employee is that the family members of the employee must be residing with the employee at the previous place of transfer before being sent to NE region. It is not the case of the respondent authorities that the family members of the petitioners have not resided with the petitioners at the previous place of transfer before they have been transferred to NE region. The specific case of the petitioners is that before the transfer, they resided with their family members at the previous place.

34. The rationale behind grant of double HRA to employees, who are posted to NE region or at Andaman and Nicobar Islands is that on their posting to those difficult stations, they are not expected to take their families along with them. That is the reason why posting to these places is called difficult posting, as it is not normally feasible to keep the families along while working at such stations. In order to ensure that such employees join these difficult stations, the benefit of HRA is extended to their families as well, who are allowed to remain at the last station of posting.

35. It is not in dispute that the petitioners otherwise fulfilled the conditions for grant of HRA. As stated supra and also the circumstances in which the petitioners' families could not be expected to be at 32 Bn., Loktak, Manipur and 109 Bn., Imphal respectively, the petitioners are entitled to the benefit of HRA.

36. There is no dispute that most of the CRPF battalions whose Group Centres are located in NE region are deployed outside region. However, they are not allowed to NE concessions though its affiliated Group Centres are located in NE region. As rightly argued by learned counsel for the petitioners, hundreds of thousands of CRPF personnel serving in difficult areas leaving their family behind are deprived of the concession granted by the Government only because of the whimsical attitude and misinterpreting of the rules/orders of the Government.

37. It is settled law that grant of HRA under special concession to NE region should also be treated on the same line without restriction of the location of the headquarter.

38. In W.P.(C) No.11083 of 2019 (*Praveen Yadav and others v. Union of India and others*) with W.P.(C) No.3370 of 2020 (*Gaurav Singh and others v. Union of India and others*), decided on 16.12.2022, a Division Bench of the Delhi High Court held as under:

"16. *The afore-noted commendation of the Seventh Pay Commission acknowledging the services of uniformed services regarding HRA is highly appreciated. We are also in consent with the view that they are required to stay in the fields, far off from all necessary amenities while leaving their families behind. We, while holding the Chair as the Judges of this Court as well as normal civilians, respect their will power to stay away from their families. Interestingly though the competent authority of Seventh Pay Commission also recognized the lack of proper compensation and need of paying HRA to these employees, we fail to understand why the Commission only thought of giving parity to the PBORs of CAPF at par with PBORs of Defence*

Forces; while leaving behind the proposal of extending the same benefit to the Coy Commanders (officers of the level of Assistant Commandants/ Deputy Commandants) under examination. It is a strange anomaly which is sought to be corrected in this petition.

17. Even in the counter affidavit filed on behalf of respondents and during the course of arguments, no such submission was made by learned CGSC appearing on behalf of respondents that the proposal of extending the same benefit to the Coy Commanders/ Officers of Group A was under consideration. To the contrary, the stand of respondents is that the impugned Signal has been passed in compliance of the recommendations of the Seventh Pay Commission. We are unable to find any reason as to why officers belonging to the rank of Officers / Coy Commanders or PBROs, should not be granted similar benefit more so as the factum of their serving at far off locations has been recognized and it cannot be differentiated on cadre basis. We fail to understand why such policy decisions discriminating within the force should be permitted to continue, especially to the officers of the force who spend their lives serving the nation.

18. We have gone through the decision in Supreme Court in Prem Chand (Supra) relied upon by the petitioners and find that the said case relates to benefits of flexibilities in imports given to Export Houses and though the facts of the case are distinguishable and not applicable to the present case, however, there is no dispute qua the settled position that the right to equality guaranteed under Article 14 ensures equality amongst equals and its aim is to protect persons- similarly placed against discriminatory treatment. We have also gone through the decision of this Court in Govind Kumar Srivastava (Supra) relied upon by the petitioners, which pertains to grant of pro-rata pension only to the Commissioned Officers of the Defence Services and not to non-Commissioned Officers/ PBORs and this Court held that such denial of pro-rata pension to them is violative of Article 14 of the Constitution. In Dev Sharma (Supra) this Court while dealing with the case of retirement age of members of the Central and Allied Forces

held that element of discrimination of retirement age must be done away with.

19. Applying the ratio of law settled in various decisions to these petitions, we find that respondents cannot be permitted to take discriminatory view for personnel of different forces deployed in common areas for grant of HRA. Accordingly, the Signal dated 15.03.2018 and letter 22.03.2018, rejecting petitioners' request for grant of HRA, are hereby set aside. The impugned Office Memorandum No. II-270 12/35/CF-

3396486/20 17-PF-I dated 31.07.2017 issued by the Government of India, Ministry of Home Affair, Police-II Division (PF-I Desk) and the Signal No. P.I-1I2017 dated 08.09.2017 in respect of Seventh Pay Commission issued by the DIG (Adm) Dte.

CRPF, are hereby partly set aside with direction to the respondents that the benefit of HRA shall not be confined to only PBORs but shall be extended to all the personnel of the Forces irrespective of their rank, as per their entitlement. Further, respondents are directed to take necessary steps within six weeks of this judgment, in consultation with the Ministry of Home Affairs as well as Ministry of Finance, to grant benefit of HRA to the petitioners and similarly situate personnel w.e.f. passing of this judgment.

20. In view of the above, these petitions are accordingly disposed of."

39. The ratio propounded by the Division Bench of the Delhi High Court squarely applies to the case on hand. The benefit of HRA is for the welfare of the families of the employees who are posted in the difficult stations like NE region etc. Those Central Government employees, particularly the civilians, who on their transfer to the notified region keep their families at the previous place of posting in a rented or own accommodation after vacating the Government quarters which they were occupying and had to vacate after transfer shall be entitled to the benefit of the HRA/additional HRA.

40. The purpose and object of granting the benefit of HRA is to reward the persons who are posted in the NE region. When the basis for granting HRA to the employees posted in NE region is provided, this Court fails to understand why the respondents are denying the benefit of HRA to the petitioners, who were posted in NE region.

41. In <u>Director General, CRPF and others v. Janardan Singh and others</u>, (2018) 7 SCC 656, the Hon'ble Supreme Court held:

"23. The classification as made in the Government Order dated 31.3.21987 does not pass the twin test as noted above. The Government having itself realised the error has corrected the same by the Government Order dated 3.8.2005 permitted the special (duty) allowance to all who are posted and serving in North-East region irrespective of the facts as whether their headquarters are within the North-Eastern Region or outside the North-Eastern region."

42. Thus, it is clear from <u>the above decision</u> of the Hon'ble Supreme Court that there is no intelligible differentia between two classes of employees posted and serving in the NE region. The policy of law as is clear from the Government notification is that the Government came with a scheme of special (duty) allowance with the object and purpose of encouraging, attracting and retaining the services of the officers in the NE region. The two categories, namely (i) whose headquarters are within NE region and (ii) whose headquarters are outside the NE region clearly indicate that classification is not founded on any intelligible differentia.

43. Nowhere in Chapter-XV of FR-SR Part-IV it is mentioned that HRA is a headquarter based allowance. While issuing the impugned order, the respondent authorities have not stated anything about the specific rule that HRA is a headquarter based allowance. Further, there is no such detachment of headquarter or notional headquarter in any rules or Government Orders granting HRA to Government servants posted in NE region.

44. For the foregoing discussions, this Court is of the considered view that the petitioners have established their case and also the petitioners are still keeping their families at the last places of posting and since they were posted in NE region, the petitioners are entitled to HRA of last place of posting. However, without applying the mind and affording any opportunity of hearing before stopping the payment of HRA, the respondent authorities have issued the impugned orders, which are arbitrary and, therefore, the same are liable to be set aside.

45. In the result,

(i) W.P.(C) No.243 of 2020 and W.P.(C) No.508 of 2020 are allowed.

(ii) The order dated 27.2.2020 issued by the respondent authorities in W.P.(C) No.508 of 2020 and the stoppage of HRA granted to the petitioner in W.P.(C) No.243 of 2020 are set aside.

(iii) The respondent authorities are directed to release the entitled HRA to the petitioner in W.P.(C) No.508 of 2020 with effect from 13.8.2019 in terms of sanction order dated 3.9.2019 issued by the Commandant, 109 Bn., CRPF, Mongsangai, Imphal West, Manipur.

(iv) Similarly, the respondent authorities are directed to release the HRA to the petitioner in W.P.(C) No.243 of 2020 in terms of the sanction order dated 21.2.2019 issued by the Commandant, 32 Bn., CRPF, Loktak, Manipur with effect from April, 2020.

(v) The respondent authorities are directed to refund the recovery of HRA, if any made, to the petitioners within a period of four weeks from the date of receipt of a copy of this order.

CHAPTER III

INDO – TIBETAN BORDER POLICE- LAW INCLUDING LEADING CASE LAWS

1. REQUIREMENT OF CONSULTATION WITH UPSC

1.1 The Delhi High Court vide Judgment dated 25.5.2015 in Writ Petition (C) No. 7545/2011 in the matter of Saurabh Dubey & Ors. vs Union Of India &Ors. and other connected matters held as under:

"These batch of writ petitions have impugned the Office Memorandum dated 26.11.2010 issued by the respondents whereby the officers of Minor Cadres have been merged with that of the GD Cadre and a combined seniority list of the General Duty Cadre Group A officers (hereafter referred to as the " GD Cadre") have been notified along with Minor Cadres officers. Furthermore, the seniority of the officers has been fixed on the basis of their respective date of appointment, as a result whereof the petitioners have been placed below the private respondents (in these writ petitions) in the seniority list. ....

48. Most importantly, the non-consultation of the UPSC is fatal to the entire process of decision-making. Furthermore, it is noticed that the notification of the Ministry of Home Affairs dated 30.4.2003 amending the ITBP General Duty Cadre Group „A" Recruitment Rules, 1999, in particular mentions in the Schedule thereto that: "(g) in column 14 for the entry, the following entry shall be substituted, namely:- "Exempted from the purview of the Union Public Service Commission but consultation with Union Public Service Commission shall be necessary for direct recruitment."

55. The contention of the respondents that a larger number of officers likely to be affected by the impugned notification have already agreed to the new arrangement, hence these petitions by a handful of employees ought to be dismissed, is untenable because change of the Recruitment Rules effecting service conditions is not a democratic process where the will of the majority prevails; nor can there be any place for ex post facto justification for an action which is fundamentally flawed in law and procedure. The actions of the Government have to be governed by law and must have the flavour of equity. The Recruitment Rules can be changed only by the procedure prescribed in law, which is spelt out in the Conduct of Business Rules as well as the in extant Recruitment Rules themselves. The letter of August 1969, upon which the respondents rely, for according exclusion to the BSF, CRPF, ITBP and CISF from the purview of the UPSC need to examined. The letter observed that "the posts in the Forces mentioned above are not a charge on the Defence Services Estimates, though it should be argued that some of them involve duties "connected with defence". The Commission are, therefore, unable to accept the view that the posts in any of these Forces should not be treated as civil posts for purposes of Article 320 of the Constitution of India. However, having regard to the nature of duties to be performed by the Central Reserve Police Force, the Indo-Tibetan Border Force and the Border Security Force, and the special conditions of service of persons belonging to these Forces, the Commission agree that the posts in the above Forces may be excluded from their purview on a permanent basis under Regulation 2 of the Union Public Service Commission (Exemption from Consultation) Regulations, 1958. I am accordingly to request that formal amendments to the Schedule to the Regulations may kindly be notified in due course." Evidently, the requisite amendment has not been effected till date. Therefore, till such time that the amendment comes about, the extant Schedule would be applicable. The opinion of the UPSC was for a situation in futuro and would come into effect only upon the notification of the due amendments. It is another matter though that such amendments may well entail

challenges in law. The advise of the Ministry of Law was brushed aside on the ground that the ITBP had already been exempted from the purview of the UPSC because the recruitment into the merged cadre was to be conducted through the UPSC itself, but oddly enough another very pertinent objection of the Ministry of Law that the proposal of the SSB regarding merger of technical posts which is also akin to the present proposal, had not been decided due to objection of the UPSC, was not even addressed or responded to by the MHA.

56. As held in S.L. Dutta & Ors. (supra), judges and lawyers can hardly be expected to have much knowledge by reason of their training and experience about the highly technical and scientific nature concerning the discharge of duties by the personnel of the five cadres of ITBPF sought to be merged. Therefore, a technical body such as the UPSC would have best examined it or there ought to have been, at least, some discussion on record in this regard. The respondents have not shown any discussion or application of mind in this regard, in the original file. The procedure laid down in the conduct of business rules has not been followed nor have the RRs themselves been followed. Therefore, the action of the Government cannot be sustained.

....

59. From the preceding discussion, it is evident that the impugned Notification dated 26.11.2010 is premature, violative of the prescribed procedure for due consultation and in the face of the extant Recruitment Rules. The Notification is without the approval of the Ministry of Finance as well as of the UPSC. The approval of the Ministry of Law was upon the condition that the approval of the UPSC too would be sought in this regard. The latter was never sought. Therefore the approval of the Ministry of Law cannot be said to have come into effect. In the circumstances, the impugned Office Memorandum dated 26.11.2010 cannot be sustained and hence, it is quashed. Should the respondents desire to pursue the matter, it would always be open to them to have the proposal examined by the Ministry of Finance as well as by the UPSC before any fresh Notification is issued purporting to amend the Recruitment Rules."

2. REGARDING PRE-PROMOTIONAL TRAINING FOR PROMOTION

2.1 The Allahabad High Court vide Judgment dated 8.1.2019 in Writ A No. 31182 of 2014 in the matter of Force No. 937040966 Ram Charan Singh vs. Union of India vs. Ors. held as under:

"By the order dated 19.07.2012 passed by the respondent No.4, the claim of the petitioner for seniority benefits, promotion to the post of Inspector GD from the date his immediate junior was promoted and grant of backwages/salary of the promotional post in the relevant period has been rejected. The same reasons for invalidating the claim of the seniority and promotion made by the petitioner have been reiterated in the order dated 28.07.2012.

The petitioner thus aggrieved, has assailed the order dated 19.07.2012 passed by the respondent No.4 and the consequential order dated 28.07.2012 passed by the respondent No.6 declining the prayer of the petitioner for the benefits of the seniority, promotion from the date of his immediate junior was promoted to the post of Inspector GD and grant of backwages/salary for the promotional post in the relevant period in this writ petition. The petitioner has sought further relief for grant of promotion to the post of Inspector GD with effect from 04.07.2008, i.e., the date when his immediate junior in the seniority list was promoted to the post of Inspector in the respondent-Indo-Tibetan Border Police (ITBP). The prayer for all consequential service benefits including backwages/salary for the post of Inspector GD for the period such salary was denied is also made in the instant writ petition......

......After receiving the said orders the petitioner made a representation to the competent authority to permit him to join SO TAC course, which was 6 already underway. The request of the petitioner was not acceded to. Consequently, juniors to the petitioner in the seniority list were promoted over the petitioner. Such juniors

permanently stole a march over the petitioner in the year 2008. Later on, the petitioner was provided an opportunity to attend the SO TAC course in the year 2010-11 which he duly availed. The petitioner was promoted to the rank of Inspector GD in 2011. However, the loss of seniority and denial service benefits inflicted on him in 2008 is a recurring loss with cascading effects. The petitioner continues to suffer the adverse consequences. A promotional avenue creates an opportunity of self advancement for an employee. Existence of prospects of promotion creates a quest of excellence and self fulfillment in the employees. This in turn ensures highest levels of efficiency and a better morale of the employees. On the other hand, absence of avenue of promotions creates stagnation. Such stagnation leads to a self reinforcing downward spiral of low morale and decreasing efficiency among the employees. Over the years employers have looked at the promotion policies in the above perspective. Employers have endeavoured to create opportunities of promotion and avoid possibilities of stagnation, even when promotional posts are not available. The concept of grant of time bound promotional pay scale has been introduced by many employers. Methodology is different but the larger purpose remains the same. The right of an employee to be promoted has to be considered in the above said perspective by any employer. Service law jurisprudence has also analyzed the concept of promotion and the nature of the right to promotion. While adverting to the nature and scope of the right to promotion in the case of Union of India Vs. **Sangram Keshari Nayak, reported in (2007) 6 SCC 704,** *the Hon'ble Supreme Court opined that the right to be considered for promotion would be meaningful, if it brings within its purview and effective, purposeful and meaningful consideration. The Hon'ble Supreme Court laid down the law in the case of Sangram Keshari Nayak (supra) in the following terms:*

"*Promotion is not a fundamental right. Right to be considered for promotion, however, is a fundamental right. Such a right brings within its purview an effective, purposeful and meaningful consideration. Suitability or otherwise of the 8 candidate concerned, however, must be left at the hands of the DPC, but the same has to be determined in terms of the rules applicable therefore. Indisputably, the DPC recommended the case of the respondent for promotion. On the day on which, it is accepted at the bar, the DPC held its meeting, no vigilance enquiry was pending. No decision was also taken by the employer that a departmental proceeding should be initiated against him."*

In the light of the law laid down by Hon'ble the Supreme Court, the petitioner clearly has right to be considered for promotion in the correct light of the standing order No.01/92 dated 22.07.1992. The right to be considered for promotion would have no meaning in case the consideration of the claim for promotion is not made with the correct understanding of the standing order No.01/92. This is of paramount importance. Considering the strenuous nature of conditions of service in the force, the Director General of ITBP issued a standing order No.01/92 dated 22.7.1992 to protect the seniority and promotional prospects from any adverse consequences due to exigencies of service. This applies to individuals who are unable to attend promotional courses due to such exigencies. ....

..The exigency of service delineated in Clause 2(घ) in standing order No.01/92 contemplates grant of protection of benefits of seniority and promotional prospects to personnel who are appointed or deployed in foreign missions. The interpretation of the aforesaid clause has to be made in the context of the purpose the provision seeks to serve. In case the promotional prospects of personnel made to suffer for honouring commitments in the line of duty or on account of definite exigencies of service or their deployment in difficult areas, it would have a debilitating effect on the morale of the force. Moreover, even on a plain reading of clause 2(घ), the petitioner is clearly entitled for the protection and the benefits which the standing order seeks to provide to the eligible and category of personnel. The petitioner was deployed as part of the Indian contingent to Afghanistan. The word 'deployment'

or 'appointment' in the standing order No.01/92 dated 22.07.1992 does not mean physical deployment in Afghanistan. The deployment in terms of clause (ब) of standing order No.01/92 is complete when the personnel are ordered to report to the camp for pre-training for the purposes of deployment in a foreign mission. Such personnel who are struck off the strength of their parent unit and are borne on the strength of the contingent which is undergoing training for deployment, come within the ambit of the beneficial provisions of standing order No.01/92 dated 22.07.1992. In the facts of the case, once the petitioner was struck off the strength of his parent Battalion & he reported to and was borne on the rolls of the Tigri Camp for pre-training for deployment in Afghanistan, his deployment in a foreign mission was complete in terms of the standing order No.01/92 dated 22.07.1992. The petitioner is held entitled to the benefits of protection seniority and promotional avenues under the standing order No.1/92 dated 22.07.1992.

Judicial approach to interpretation of service regulations of an armed or a paramilitary force has to be nuanced. Peculiar service conditions of the armed forces and paramilitary forces have to be borne in mind. ***In certain matters a distinction has to be drawn from other departments of the government, and a departure has to be made from the usual rule of interpretation of service regulations.*** *As distinct from other departments of government, the armed & the paramilitary forces are called upon to execute tasks or assigned to hazardous duties at the peril of their lives, in the service of the nation. While on such hazardous missions or perilous assignments the service prospects of such personnel cannot be made to suffer. Similarly, on such occasions pecuniary benefits which these personnel would have otherwise gained have to be protected. At all times it has to be ensured that service conditions do not operate to the detriment of and adverse service consequences do not visit the personnel when they answer the call of duty by going on such dangerous missions. The clause for denial of back-wages in the standing order does not subserve the object sought* *to be achieved by the provision as a whole. The pre-determination made by the offending clause in the standing order No.01/92 dated 22.07.1992 of denial of back-wages, disincentives the personnel who have opted for or sent to a tour of duty at the peril of their own lives. This clause would thus provoke the adverse effects on the morale of the members of the force, which the standing order seeks to prevent.*

*I am fortified in taking above view by the law laid down by the Hon'ble Supreme Court in case of **Major General H.M. Singh, VSM Vs. Union of India** and another, reported at **(2014) 3 SCC 670**. The Hon'ble Court in the case of **Major General H.M. Singh, VSM (supra)** had the occasion to consider the nature of relief to be granted when promotion has been denied on arbitrary grounds. The Hon'ble Supreme Court in the case of Major General H.M. Singh, VSM (supra) while granting all monitoring benefits to the petitioner which would have been due to him but for the arbitrary denial of such promotion, held thus:*

"33. Insofar as the present controversy is concerned, there is no doubt whatsoever, that a clear vacancy against the rank of Lieutenant General became available with effect from 1.1.2007. At that juncture, the Appellant had 14 months of service remaining. It is not as if the vacancy came into existence after the Appellant had reached the age of retirement on superannuation. The present case is therefore, not covered by the technical plea canvassed at the hands of the learned senior Counsel for the Respondents. The denial of promotion to the Appellant mainly for the reason, that the Appellant was on extension in service, to our mind, is unsustainable besides being arbitrary, specially in the light of the fact, that the vacancy for which the Appellant was clamouring consideration, became available, well before the date of his retirement on superannuation. We have, therefore, no hesitation in rejecting the basis on which the claim of the Appellant for onward promotion to the rank of Lieutenant General was declined, by the Appointments Committee of the Cabinet.

34. In view of the fact, that we have found the order of rejection of the Appellant's claim for promotion to the rank of Lieutenant General, on the ground that he was on extended service to be invalid, we hereby set aside the operative part of the order of the Appointments Committee of the Cabinet. It is also apparent, that the Selection Board had recommended the promotion of the Appellant on the basis of his record of service, past performance, qualities of leadership, as well as, vision, out of a panel of four names. In its deliberations the Appointments Committee of the Cabinet, did not record any reason to negate the aforesaid interference, relating to the merit and suitability of the Appellant. We are therefore of the view, that the Appellant deserves promotion to the rank of Lieutenant General, from the date due to him. Ordered accordingly. On account of his promotion to the post of Lieutenant General, the Appellant would also be entitled to continuation in service till the age of retirement on superannuation stipulated for Lieutenant Generals, i.e., till his having attained the age of 60 years. As such, the Appellant shall be deemed to have been in service against the rank of Lieutenant General till 28.2.2009. Needless to mention, that the Appellant would be entitled to all monetary benefits which would have been due to him, on account of his promotion to the rank of Lieutenant General till his retirement on superannuation, as also, to 14 revised retiral benefits which would have accrued to him on account of such promotion. The above monetary benefits shall be released to the Appellant within three months from the date a certified copy of this order becomes available with the Respondents."

This Court takes notice of the fact that the assignment to Afghanistan was fraught with danger. The petitioner had volunteered to continue with his tour of duty/assignment in Afghanistan, which involved a peril to his life. He opted out of a more secure assignment of attending a promotional course, to face the hazards of a dangerous assignment in the service of the nation. The Court cannot award any medal for such acts of commitment to duty, but can certainly commend such acts which are in plain sight. The petitioner certainly cannot be visited by any adverse consequences financial or otherwise for performing his duties in an exemplary fashion. This more so when the law provides for *protection of service benefits of the petitioner in such situations. Contrary provisions denying such benefits in the standing order no.01/1992 are read down to that extent and held not applicable to the cases like that of the petitioner.*

The petitioner has clearly made out a claim for back-wages/salary for the post of Inspector GD from the date his immediate junior was so promoted till the petitioner was promoted to the rank of Inspector GD in the year 2011 and the prayer in that regard has to be granted.

In the light of the aforesaid legal narrative and the facts found in the earlier part of the judgement, the impugned order dated 19.07.2012 is evidently in the teeth of the Standing Order No. 1/92 dated 22.07.1992. The denial of seniority and promotional benefits to the petitioner by the order dated 19.07.2012 and the order dated 28.07.2012 is arbitrary and illegal. The impugned orders dated 19.07.2012 and 28.07.2012 cannot stand. The impugned order dated 19.07.2012 passed by the respondent No.4 and consequential order dated 28.07.2012 passed by the respondent No.6 (Annexure 12 to the writ petition) are quashed. The matter is remitted back to the respondent No.4-Deputy Inspector of General (Administration), East Frontier I.T.B.P Force. A writ of mandamus is issued commanding the respondent no.4-Deputy Inspector of General (Administration), East Frontier I.T.B.P Force to reconsider the claim of the petitioner for grant of seniority and promotion and backwages with effect from the date of immediate junior was promoted to the rank of Inspector G.D. consistent with the observations made in this judgment and in the light of the Standing Order No.1/92 dated 22.07.1992. The petitioner shall be given the promotion, seniority, back-wages, and all consequential benefits for the post of Inspector GD from the date of his immediate junior, who was promoted to the post of Inspector GD, i.e., with effect from 04.07.2008 till the date the petitioner was promoted to the rank of Inspector GD in the year 2011. The above directions shall be executed within a period of two months from the date of receipt of a certified copy of this order. The writ petition is allowed."

3. RELEVANT JUDGEMENTS INTERPRETING ITBP ACT

3.1 S.KANNAN v. THE DIRECTOR GENERAL (Madras High Court, 2024)

"*2. The case of the petitioner is that he joined the Indo-Tibetan Border Police Force (Respondent) in 1988 as Constable and has served in the service for more than 23 years with an amicable record and the petitioner was awarded on several occasions by the respondents for his exemplary duty. The petitioner had also had the honour of serving the country even during the Kargil war during which time he was stationed in Jammu and Kashmir executing his duty courageously. In fact the petitioner after putting in 20 years of service has an option of voluntary retirement for his sustenance/aid. The petitioner rather than retiring from service had decided to continue in the service has he was physically fit and wanted to continue serving for the country. In February 2010, the petitioner applied permission to go on leave in order to attend his hailing father who was staying at Kodavasal, Tiruvarur District. Accordingly, the respondent granted permission to the petitioner to go on leave starting from 07.10.2010 till 14.04.2010. Subsequently in lieu of the deteriorating health of his father, the petitioner sought for extension of leave period. The 2nd Respondent was also pleased to extend the leave period till 20.05.2010.*"

7. Section 20 of the Act refers to a "Deserter" as a person who intentionally acts in order to return/report to duty. The order of the respondent deeming the petitioner as a Deserter suffers from non-application of mind as the petitioner has made it clear that he has not intentions of avoiding is duty and to return to his post. Learned counsel would further submit that the petitioner has even acquired the necessary medical service to show the reasons for his absenting from service. In such circumstances, an opportunitymay be given to the person to work efficiently and proof his excellence. It is also understood by the petitioner that similar personnel who had been held 'Deserters' had been accorded a second opportunity and had allowed to rejoin duty and the same benefit may be extended to the petitioner in the light of his long service to the country. Learned appearing for the petitioner would also drew the attention of this Court in regard to the death certificate of the petitioner's father K.Saminatha Thevar who died on 20.08.2010 and date of death certificate issued by the Revenue Department, Government of Tamilnadu vide Na.Ma.No.1377/2017/A7 dated 30.11.2017.

14. Heard both sides and perused the materials available on records.

15. In this case, the petitioner was granted 60 days earned leave with effect from 07.02.2010 till 14.04.2010 and the petitioner failed to report back to duty on the due date and the same was not communicated to the respondents. On 24.04.2010, he sent telegram request for extension of 45 days of earned leave stating that his father was serious and that father was admitted in the hospital. Though the petitioner had not stated any formal letter seeking extension of leave enclosing therewith documents to substantiate his claim for extension of leave. His leave was extended for further period of 30 days and the same was communicated to the petitioner by express telegram and it was also specifically intimated that he should report back for duty on 14.05.2010. Thereafter, he did not report back to duty on 14.05.2010 neither there was any communication sent by him seeking extension of leave or explaining the reasons why he was unable to join duty to the respondents. The reason given by the petitioner for overstaying beyond the leave granted up to 14.05.2010 is that his father died and his brother met with an accident and he himself met with an accident. But no documents were filed to substantiate or to prove the same before the respondents before this Court.

16. Learned counsel appearing for the petitioner has filed the death certificate of the petitioner's father namely K. Swaminatha Thevar issued by the Revenue Department, Government of Tamil Nadu vide Na.Ma.1377/2017/A7 dated 13.11.2017 and it is pertinent to note that the date of the death of his father was mentioned as 20.08.2010. Hence the first reason given by the petitioner for overstaying beyond 14.05.2010 that is due to the death of his father is false and the same

baseless for the simple reasons in the death certificate, the date of the death of his father is mentioned is 20.08.2010. In regard to the second reason that his brother met with an accident as contended by the respondent in their counter affidavit, no FIR copy was filed to substantiate or to prove the same.

17. It is also pertinent to observe or note from the discharge summary issued by Vinodhagan Memorial Hospital (P) Ltd, Tanjore in which it is mentioned as follows:-

i) Date of admission - 10.04.2010

ii) Date of surgery - 11.04.2010

iii) Date of discharge - 15.04.2010 And the same is within the leave which has been extended by the respondents upto 14.05.2010. Hence, the second reason given by the petitioner is also not true.

18. In regard to the third reason that the petitioner he himself met with an accident, the medical certificate is dated 09.07.2011 given by one Dr.P.Rajagopal, Retd. Senior Civil Surgeon, Government Hospital, Mannargudi in which he had stated that the petitioner has undergone treatment for severe acute disk prolapse from 05.05.2010 to 09.07.2011 and the same is not believable for the reason the treatment period is for nearly 14 months and medical certificate is not supported by any medical prescription, admission in hospital or what is the treatment given to the petitioner. All these vital informations are missing in the above medical certificate and the genuineness of the medical certificate itself is doubtful.

19. The above three documents in regard to the death of the petitioner's father, accident of the petitioner's brother and the accident of the petitioner himself has been filed before this Court by the learned counsel appearing for the petitioner by way of additional type set of papers dated 23.02.2020 after duly serving the same to the learned Senior Central Government Standing Counsel appearing for the respondents. It is also pertinent to note as contended by the respondents that the two letters dated 22.05.2010 and 13.06.22010, there is no postal receipts or acknowledgment card to prove that the same has been sent or dispatched to the respondent. The letter dated 01.10.2010 written by the petitioner's wife to the second respondent and delivered on 19.10.2010 that her husband is staying along at Iruppalai Village, Edapadi Taluk, Salem District, Tamil Nadu State and not to take severe action against her husband considering the plight that her children undergoing School Education at a School situated in Namakkal District.

20. *In order to give one more opportunity to the petitioner, he was directed to report to duty on 14.05.2010 immediately under Telegram No.3943 dated 18.05.2010 and Memo No.4339 dated 31.05.2010 addressed to the petitioner's address near amman Koil, Eruppali Post, Edappadi Taluk, Salem District, Tamilnadu Statewhich is the address given by the petitioner that he will be staying during the leave period and the same was also stated in the letter written by the wife of the petitioner dated 01.10.2010 address to the second respondent. The Superintendent of Police, Salem District was requested to apprehend and hand over the petitioner to the second respondent under letter dated 11.06.2010 and he in turn vide letter dated 13.09.2010 intimated the second respondent that the petitioner had informed him that he is on medical leave as his brother met with motor accident and also enclosed a statement to that effect said to have been given by the petitioner. This also goes to prove beyond doubt that the petitioner is always making false statement before the respondent authorities as well as to the police authorities. The petitioner has committed the same misconduct even previously which is evident from the counter affidavit filed by the respondent and the same is extracted here under:-*

"He was granted 60 days Earned leave with effect from 11.12.1999 to 08.02.2000. But he overstayed the leave for 36 days of absence was treated as dies none vide 21st Bn Force Order No.26/2000 dated 24.05.2000. He was sent to CBI on deputation while was service in 21st Bn, ITB Police. But he was sent back to his parent battalion by the CBI

charging that he got a cooking Gas connection by practicing fraud. The petitioner was warned that he shall not repeat such type of misdeeds vide TPT Bn order No.12195-97 dated 15.07.1999. These will go to show that the petitioner indulges in habitual misdeeds and repeatedly overstayed leave without any just causes or reasons."

21. Indo-Tibetan Border Police Force is a Central Armed Police force of the Union of India. No doubt a very high standard of discipline is expected of and is required by the Police personnel.The respondents have followed the procedures as contemplated in Indo-Tibetan Border Police Force Act, 1992 and Indo-Tibetan Border Police Force Rules of 1994. The order of the competent authority duly conducted court of inquiry declared the petitioner as "Deserter" from 11.05.2010 (AN) by order vide 31st Bn No.5400-25 dated 01.07.2010. There was no response from the petitioner for the repeated requests/ reminders/ directions, the Competent Authority/Commandant of 31st Bn was forced to consider this case in accordance with Section 10 of Indo-Tibetan Border Police Force Act, 1992 read with Rules 17 & 25 of Indo-Tibetan Border Police Force Rules, 1994 and after taking into consideration his past conduct and service records, had passed the impugned order No.1837-50 dated 04.10.2010 and there is no violation of principles of natural justice nor any procedural irregularity or illegality or infirmity in the above order.

22. In view of the above factual matrix of the case, this Court is of the considered view that the order passed by the second respondent in 31st Battalion/Indo Tibetan Border Police/Place-02/Bhagauda(Head Constable/Driver S. Kannan) 10-8137-50,dated 04.10.2010 does not warrant any interference by this court and the same is confirmed.

23. In the result, the writ petition stands dismissed. There shall be no order as to costs in this writ petition.

3.2 Judgement Dated 29.05.2023 in SWP No. 2449/2012 Titled Bharosi Lal Vs Union Of India & Ors - High Court Of Jammu & Kashmir And Ladakh At Jammu

> *...Petitioner was tried under ITBP Force Act and was dismissed from his services on 06-10-2000 by an order issued by an Order issued by Respondent No. 4.*
>
> *8. Sh. R.K. Bhatia Ld. Counsel for petitioner, has sought quashing of proceedings of Summary Court Force coupled with order of dismissal of service of the petitioner dated 06-10-2000 issued by respondent No.4 & order dated 22-042001 issued by respondent No.3, by vehemently canvassing arguments, that Rule 45 of ITBP Rules has been violated by respondent No.4 as prior to recording of evidence respondent No.4 (Commandant of the petitioner) was required to hear the petitioner on charge; as per Rule 50(3) of ITBP Rules petitioner was required to be cautioned before making statement but there is nothing on record to show that any such warning was ever give to petitioner, moreso, there is nothing on record to indicate that petitioner was granted any opportunity to lead defence evidence during the recording of evidence; Rule50(9) of ITBP Rules has been violated as no certificate has been issued by the officer who recorded the evidence regarding correctness of "recording of evidence". It is argued, that Rule 142 of ITBP Rules has been violated as the certificate at the bottom of proceedings of Summary Force Court does not show that anyone has explained to the petitioner the general effect of plea of guilty; Rule 143(2) of ITBP Rules has been violated by respondent No.4 because it is nowhere mentioned in the proceedings of SFC that petitioner was ever advised to withdraw or not plead guilty. It is moreso argued, that if an accused person pleads "guilty" that plea shall be recorded as finding of the court, but before it is recorded, the court shall ascertain that the accused understands the nature of charge to*

*which he has pleaded guilty and shall inform him of general effect of that plead and in particular of the meaning of the charge to which he has pleaded guilty and shall advise him to withdraw the plea if it appears from the summary of evidence (if any) or otherwise that the accused ought to plead not guilty. <u>It is argued,</u> that pleading of guilty means an admission of an accused having committed offence for which he is charged, the <u>plea shall be recorded as the finding of the court in the words used by accused or nearly as possible in the words used by accused,</u> such a recording will enable the party seeking justice to know whether higher authorities or the confirming authority to determine whether the plea recorded really amount to admission of guilt, <u>the requirement of recording a plea as stated above is mandatory and violation thereof vitiates the trial.</u> To support his arguments, Ld. Counsel for petitioner has relied upon the judgments reported in, **(i) 1991 KLJ 513** [Union of India & Ors **Vs** Ex Havildar Clerk Prithal Singh &Ors], **(ii) 1992 (1) GauLR 445** [Sadacharan K and 18 Others—Petitioners **Versus** Union of India and Others—Respondents] &**(iii) RLW 1997(2) Raj 1209** [Ex-Sepoy Chander Singh—Appellants **Vs.***

Union of India(UOI) and Ors—Respondents .

<u>9. Ld. Counsel for respondents</u> has supported the proceedings of Summary Force Court and order of dismissal of petitioner dated 06-10-2000 by strenuously portraying arguments, that petitioner has not come to the court with clean hands, has misstated and misrepresented the facts, there is a delay of 12 years in filing the petition, allegations against petitioner are in regard to molestation of women namely Ms. Naseema for which petitioner was tried by SFC on the charges for offences u/ss 26 r/w 43 of ITBPF Rules wherein petitioner pleaded guilty, moreso, Rule 143 of ITBP Rules has been compiled with as petitioner has been held guilty to the charges and was accordingly punished which led to his dismissal from services on 06-10-2001.

11. It will be my endeavor to appreciate the judgments relied upon by Ld. Counsel for petitioner to ascertain the procedure for recording "plea of guilty of accused" and whether such proceedings of rule position is mandatory in nature or not?

In 1991 KLJ 513 *[Union of India &OrsVs Ex-Havildar Clerk Prithpal Singh &Ors] relied by Ld. Counsel for petitioner, J&K High Court while quashing the proceeding of Summary Court Marshal and appreciating Rule 115(2) of Army Rules whereby respondent Ex-Havildar Clerk Prithpal Singh of J&K Light Infantry Regiment at Srinagar was tried on 3 charges, reduced in rank and was dismissed from services on May 2, 1983 and observing that Rule 115 (2) of Army Rules dealing with procedure for recording plea of guilty of accused is mandatory in nature, in head note of the case law and in para 8 of the judgment held as under:-*

Army Rules—*Rule 115(2)—Procedure for recording „plea of guilt of the accused.*

Whether mandatory in nature or not? Held—Mandatory in nature.

At the time of recording the „plea of guilt" of the accused in Summary Trial as well as the accused should be necessarily informed of the nature of charges leveled against him and the court should ascertain that the accused has understood the nature of the charge to which he pleaded guilty and shall inform him of the general effect of that plea and in particular of the meaning of the charge to which he pleads guilty. The court should further require to advise the accused to withdraw that plea if it appears from summary of evidence or otherwise that the accused ought to the plead not guilty.—Non fulfillment of such a procedure violates and said rule and vitiates the trial as the rule is mandatory in nature.

8. The other point which has been made basis for quashing the sentence awarded to respondent-accused relates to clause (2) of rule 115. **Under this mandatory provision the court is required to ascertain before it records plea of guilt of the accused, as to whether the** *accused understands the nature of charge to which he has pleaded guilty and shall inform him of the general effect of that plea and in particular of the meaning of charge to which he has pleaded guilty.* The court is further required under the provision of law to advise the accused to withdraw that plea if it appears from summary of evidence or otherwise that the accused ought to plead not guilty. How to follow this procedure is the main crux of the question involved in this case. Rule 125 provides that the court shall date and sign the sentence and such signatures shall authenticate whole of the proceedings. It comes out from this rule that the signing of the proceedings by the court shall amount to authentication of the same. We may take it that the signatures of the accused are not required even after recording plea of guilt but as a matter of caution same should be taken. But in order to come to a finding as to whether compliance of Sub-Rule 2 of Rule 125 has been made **there should have been some certificate of the court to the effect or at least some minutes pointing out that fulfillment of the procedure**. Nothing is coming out from record in this effect. It is certainly a violation of the above said rule. Respondent accused is clamoring from the very beginning regarding holding of a fair trial in his case and he has also taken a specific stand that he never pleaded guilty. He addressed so many communications to the court as well as to the authorities for providing him friend of the accused of his choice and other facilities for the trial and in such circumstances recording of plea of guilty by the court without strictly following rule 115 is to be viewed with suspicion. However on record there are signatures of the respondent-accused showing that he willingly pleaded guilty.

In 1992 (1) GauLR 445 *[Sadacharan K and 18 Others—Petitioners Versus* Union of India and Others—Respondents*] relied by Ld. Counsel for petitioner, Division Bench of Gauhati High Court while appreciating Rule 115 of Army Rules 1984 and observing that the Army Court is required to record the plea of guilt of accused in the words or as nearly as possible in the words used by accused which Rule is mandatory in nature and violation thereof vitiates the trial, conviction and penalty, in paras 6, 8,9,11 of the judgment held as under:-*

(6.) Under sub-rule (1) of rule 115 of the Army Rules, 1984, for short, 'the Rules' provides: **"The accused person's plea-'Guilty' or 'Not guilty'** *(or if he refused to plead, or does not plead intelligibly either one or the other, a plea of 'Not guilty')-**shall be recorded on each charge"***. *(emphasis added), Sub rule (2) of rule 115 provides, inter alia, that, if an accused person pleads 'Guilty', that plea shall be recorded as the finding of the Court.*

(8.) Pleading of 'guilty' means an admission of an accused having committed the offence with which he is charged. Under section 115(2) the plea of guilty shall be recorded as the finding of the Court. The use of expression 'does not plead intelligibly' in rule 115(1) indicates that the plea must be clear and unambiguous. Whether the plea is clear and unambiguous, or, whether the accused pleads or does not plead intelligibly, will depend on the words used by the accused. **A mere entering or recording the word 'guilty' may mean Court's own conclusion or interpretation**. *Therefore, the clause "if the accused pleads guilty, the plea shall be recorded as the finding of the Court" means that the* **Court shall record the plea in the words used by the accused, or, the Court shall record the plea as nearly as possible in the words used by the accused.** *Such a recording will enable the party seeking justice to know as well as the higher authority or the confirming authority to determine whether the plea recorded really amounts to an admission of guilt. (9.) Coming to the cases on hand, it appears that the accused persons pleaded guilty, but the* **Court has not recorded the plea in the words, or, as nearly as possible in the words, used by the accused. Therefore, there was procedural impropriety. The requirement of recording of the plea as stated above is mandatory & the violation of it will vitiate the trial, conviction or penalty**. *The view taken by us finds support from a decision of the Supreme Court in Mahanta Kaushalya Das Vs. State of Madras, AIR 1966 SC 22 .*

(11.) For the forgoing reasons, the trial, conviction and sentences are set aside. The cases are sent back to the summary court martial for

disposal of the matter afresh in the light of the observations made above.

In **RLW 1997(2) Raj 1209** *[Ex-Sepoy Chander Singh—Appellants* **Vs.** *Union of India(UOI) and Ors—Respondents] relied by Ld. Counsel for petitioner, High Court of Rajasthan while observing that Army Rules 34,36 &115(2) are mandatory in nature and non-observance thereof vitiates the trial in paras 14,18,25 of the judgment held as under:-*

14. From the above narration of facts, the first question which arises for determination is whether under Rule 4(1) of the Army Rules, the mandatory requirement of warning of holding the trial after a notice of 96 hours had been complied with or not or whether any notification had been issued under Section 9 of the Army Act for declaring this unit to be a unit "On Active Service".

18. The provisions of this Rule have salutary effect. **The accused is to be told the consequence of the fact if he pleads "guilty".** *It is mandatory on the part of Commanding Officer before he records the plea of "guilty" to ascertain that accused understands the nature of the charge to which he pleaded guilty and it is also obligatory on the part of Commanding Officer/Court to inform him of the general effect of that plea and in particular of the meaning of the charge to which he has pleaded guilty and of the difference in procedure which will be made by his pleading of guilty and* **shall advise him to withdraw that plea if it appears from the summary of evidence or otherwise that the accused ought to plead not guilty***. To support the proposition, counsel for the petitioner relies on 1989 (3) SLR, 405 (Uma Shanker Pathak v. Union of India(All.)) wherein the Division Bench had held as under:*

10. The provision embodies a wholesome provision which is clearly designed to ensure that an accused person should be fully forewarned about the implications of the charge and the effect of pleading guilty. The procedure prescribed for the trial of the cases where the accused pleads guilty is radically different from that prescribed for trial of cases where the accused pleads "not guilty". The procedure in cases where the plea is of "not guilty" is far more elaborate than in cases where the accused pleads "guilty". This is apparent from a comparison of the procedure laid down for these two classes of cases. It is in order to save simple, unsuspecting and ignorant accused person from the effect of pleading guilty to the charge without being fully conscious of the nature thereof and the implications and general effect of that plea, that the framers of the rule have insisted that the court must ascertain that the accused fully under stands the nature of the charge and the implications of pleadings guilty to the same."

12. The proceedings extracted above do not, in our opinion, fulfil the requirement of the law. **A bald certificate by the Commanding Officer that "the provisions Army Rule 115(2) are here complied with" is not enough.** As the note quoted above and underlined by us would bear what is expected of the court where the accused pleads guilty to any charge is that the record of proceedings itself must explicitly state that the court had fully explained to the accused the nature and the meaning of the charge arid made him aware of the difference in procedure. The instructions to the court printed on the proforma quoted in Annex. 1 (copy of the impugned order stating that "question to the accused and his answers both will be recorded verbatim as far as possible "make this amply clear.

25. For the reasons and in view of the above discussion, **that a definite prejudice had been caused in non-observing the mandatory provisions of the Army Rules which were of mandatory nature.** For the reasons mentioned, as the writ petition is to be allowed, therefore, there is no necessity to go into the other grounds of attack made by the petitioner in writ petition, writ petition is allowed and the impugned order of punishment and proceedings of summary court martial trial dated 17.9.90 (Annex. 4) punishing the petitioner for 6 months rigorous imprisonment and dismissing him from service is set aside. The petitioner has already suffered the imprisonment for six months for which no monetary compensation shall be adequate. However, in the circumstances, he is entitled to costs of petition which is assessed as

Rs. 10,000/-. The petitioner who was working as a cook, shall be entitled to all benefits including reinstatement in service, which shall be made to him within 2 months from the date of receipt of certified copy of this order. The writ petition is allowed as observed above.

Ratios of the judgments of **"Prithpal Singh"**, **"Sadacharan K"** & **"Chander Singh's"** cases(Supra) relied by Ld. Counsel for petitioner, make the legal proposition manifestly clear, "<u>that Army Rules are mandatory in nature, Army Court shall record the plea in the words used by the accused or nearly as possible in the words used by the accused, the requirement of recording of the plea is mandatory and violation of it will vitiate the trial, conviction or penalty, the accused is to be told the consequence of the fact if he pleads "guilty", court shall advise the accused to withdraw that plea if it appears from the summary of evidence or otherwise that the accused ought to plead not guilty</u>". While applying the ratios of the judgments (Supra) to the facts of the case in hand, the foresaid Army Rules when read in conjunction with the ITBP Rules aforesaid, it can be safely held, that the ITBP Rules viz; Rule 45, Rule 50(3), Rule 50(9), Rule 142 & 143 etc. are also mandatory in nature and violation thereof vitiate the trial, conviction and penalty imposed upon the accused/employee. **Annexure-A** to the petition in the case in hand, is copy of the statement of petitioner wherein nowhere the petitioner has pleaded guilty. **Annexure-B** to the petition is the copy of office memorandum which show that on 30-09-2000 petitioner was informed by respondent No.4 Sh. J.V.S. Choudhary Commandant 22nd BN. ITBPF THQ c/o 56 APO about the framing of charge when petitioner was posted at duty at Shishmehal Post (Qazigund) and he molested a civil women, and Summary Force Court proceedings were initiated against the petitioner who was asked to give the list of witnesses in his defense. It is apt to mention here, that on 29-09-2000 petitioner was charged for on two counts viz;

<u>Charge-1</u> .... ITBP Act 1992 r/w Section 26, that on 28.09.2000 petitioner while on ROP duty with L.M.G. at Shishmehal (Glass House)

molested a civil women namely Naseema which act of petitioner amounted to unbecoming conduct being member of force and <u>Charge-2</u>... *ITPB Act 1992 R/w Section 43 regarding violation of good order and discipline.* **Annexure-D** *(pages 19 to 23) of the petition are copies of the proceedings conducted by Summary Force Court (SFC) wherein at page 20 the plea of guilt of petitioner/accused has been recorded and it has been shown that petitioner has pleaded guilty to the charges u/s 26 and 43 of ITBPF Act 1992.* <u>Rule 45 of ITBPF Rules</u> *has been violated by respondent No.4 as prior to recording of evidence respondent No.4 has not heard the petitioner on the charge.* <u>Rule 50(3) ITBPF Rules</u> *has also been violated as there is nothing on record to show that petitioner was cautioned before making the statement or any warning was given to him.* <u>Rule 50(9) of ITBPF Rules</u> *has been violated as no certificate has been issued by the officer who recorded the evidence regarding the correctness of recording of evidence. It is apt to reiterate here, that record reveals that there is no certificate appended at the bottom of proceedings of Summary Force Court (SFC) that anyone has explained to the petitioner the general effect of plea of guilty.* <u>Vide Rule 143(2) of ITBPF Rules,</u> *the Court of respondent No.4 was further required under this provision of law to advise petitioner/accused to withdraw that plea of guilt if it had appeared to respondent No.4 from summary of evidence recorded that petitioner/accused ought to plead not guilty. Page 21 of the petition relates to the proceedings of plea of guilty.* <u>Rule 143 of ITBPF Rule</u> *relates to plea of*

"Guilty "or "Not Guilty". Sub-Rule 2 of Rule 143 mandates that the court shall ascertain that accused understands the nature of charge to which he has pleaded guilty and shall also inform him effect of that plea and meaning of the charge. In the case in hand, nothing has been placed on record that court of respondent no.4 has ascertained from petitioner/accused that whether he understands the nature of charge to which he has pleaded guilty and even the petitioner has not been informed regarding the effect of such plea of guilty and meaning of the charge. Moreso, record further demonstrates, that respondent No.4

has not advised the petitioner that he ought not to have pleaded guilty. Furthermore, it has not come on record that the plea of guilty of petitioner/accused has been recorded by respondent No.4 in the words used by the petitioner or as nearly as possible in the words used by him. Therefore, there has been procedural impropriety. The requirement of recording of the plea of guilt as stated above is mandatory in nature and violation of it has vitiated the trial and penalty imposed by respondent No.4 upon petitioner/accused. It is unambiguously reiterated here, that petitioner/accused who was facing criminal charges in the court of Ld. Pr. Session Judge Kulgam in aforesaid FIR No. 156/2000 of Police Station Qazigund for alleged commission of offences u/ss 376/354/511 RPC registered by the complainant namely Naseema Akhter for which petitioner was charged u/s 26 & 43 of ITBP Act 1992 and dismissed from services on 06-10-2000, has been acquitted of the charges by the trial court vide its judgment dated 17.06.2014 r/w order dated 13-10-2014.

For the foregoing reasons, and in view of the above discussion, a definite prejudice has been caused to the petitioner and the conclusion is therefore inevitable, that since there has been no compliance of the mandatory provisions of ITBPF Rules aforesaid, the trial of petitioner alongwith the whole proceedings of Summary Force Court (SFC) conducted by respondent No.4 stand vitiated. For the reasons aforesaid, writ petition stands allowed. Accordingly, by a writ of certiorari the proceedings of Summary Force Court (SFC) as well as order of dismissal of the petitioner from services dated 06-102000 issued by respondent No.4 and order dated 22-04-2001 issued by respondent No.3 stand quashed. Further by a writ of mandamus, the respondents are commanded to reinstate the petitioner into service forthwith on providing copy of the judgment. Petitioner shall be entitled notional benefits to his service from the date of his dismissal from services till his acquittal dated 17-06-2014 (r/w order dated 13-10-2014), and thereafter, shall also be entitled to all the consequential monetary and service benefits.

4. GENERAL SECURITY FORCE COURT UNDER ITBP ACT

4.1 Judgement dated Commandant/Gd Rajesh Kumar Tomar vs Union Of India & Ors. AIRONLINE 2021 DEL 1106

"1 *The petitioner, a Commandant (GD) in the respondents Indo-Tibetan Border Police (ITBP) and against whom, on 28th October, 2020 a General Security Force Court (GSFC) has been convened, has filed this petition, (i) impugning the order dated 12th April, 2021 of the Director General, ITBP and the order dated 16th February, 2021 of the Convening Authority of the GSFC; and, (ii) for declaration, that the proceedings conducted against the petitioner in pursuance to the convening order dated 28 th October, 2020 of the Convening Authority, are unlawful for all practical purposes.*

---

4. We have heard the counsel for the petitioner.

5. The counsel for the petitioner has argued, that (i) the GSFC was constituted vide order dated 28th October, 2020 and assembled on 18th November, 2020; (ii) as per Section 80 of the ITBP Act, 1992, GSFC has to have minimum five members and as constituted, had five members; (iii) the trial of the petitioner before the GSFC commenced with effect from 2nd December, 2020; (iv) the petitioner was "arraigned" under Rule 73, on 30 th December, 2020; (v) the petitioner, before pleading to the charge, elected to submit statutory plea of jurisdiction under Rule 74 of the ITBP Rules, 1994, that GSFC had no jurisdiction to try the petitioner; (vi) the GSFC recorded evidence of the petitioner on the said plea of the petitioner and the prosecutor also adduced evidence in reply; (vii) thus, the trial continued post "arraignment" of the petitioner; (viii) on 11th February, 2021, GSFC found that one of its five members was disqualified from being a member of the GSFC; with such disqualification, GSFC fell short of the stipulated coram of five, under

Section 80 of the ITBP Act; (ix) GSFC, on 11th February, 2021, wrote to the Convening Authority that one of the members of the GSFC suffered from disqualification to be a member of the GSFC and without him, the GSFC had fallen short of the coram stipulated in Section 80 of the ITBP Act; the GSFC thus, on 11st February, 2021 adjourned the proceedings sine die and referred the matter to the Convening Authority for passing appropriate orders; (x) the Convening Authority, vide impugned order dated 16th February, 2021, inter alia ordered:-

" Whereas, Court assembled on dated 18.11.2020 and the trial commenced on dated 02.12.2020.☐

Whereas, charge sheet was read over to the accused and he was asked to make a plea as per Rule 73 of ITBP Rules 1994.☐

And whereas, accused before pleading guilty or not guilty to the charges made a special plea to the jurisdiction under Rule☐74.

And whereas, the PO of GFC vide letter No-02 dated- 11.02.2021 has conveyed that by virtue of signing of affidavit before Hon'ble High Court J☐ And whereas, when the GFC trial procedure was at the stage of Rule 74, it came to the notice of Court as referred to undersigned vide letter No-02 dated 11.02.2021. ☐& And whereas, as per the provision contained in Rule 116(2) An officer shall not be added to a☐K at Jammu in WP(C) No- 890/2020 titled Rajesh Kumar Tomar V/s Union of India and others, by Sh. Davinder Singh, DIG, SHQ(SNR) is disqualified. Hence the court fallen short of quorum stipulated U/S 80. Court after the accused has been arraigned. In the instant case since the accused has not yet pleaded guilty or not guilty to the charges and as such he has not yet been arraigned, as per the definition of arraignment given in the Rule 73 ITBPF Rules 1994.

And whereas, the undersigned has considered view since the accused has not yet been arraigned, if fresh member are added to the court, the quorum stipulated U/s-80 of the ITBPF Act 1992 is met and the trial can proceed further. Now therefore following members are hereby *detained under Rule 68(11) of ITBPF Rules, 1994 as member to serve on the said court, that has been convened vide convening order dated 28.10.2020.*☐

Sh. Gambhir Singh Chauhan, DIG, Central Ftr Bhopal. Sh. Mandhir Ekka, DIG, Northern Ftr, Dehradun.

As this addendum to the convening order supra is hereby issued under my hand and seal. ";

and, (xi) the petitioner, being aggrieved from the aforesaid order, represented to the Director General, under Section 131 of the ITBP Act and who has vide impugned order dated 12th April, 2021, rejected the representation of the petitioner, reasoning as under:-

"3. Whereas, the accused vide his petition dated 10.03.2021 under section 131 (1) has raised an issue that under section 83 of the ITBP Act, no member can be added and thus present GFC trial should have been dissolved.

4. As per scheme of the ITBP Act and the Rules made thereunder, once order convening the court is issued, Force Court assembles and satisfies itself as per Rule 67. Thereafter, Court is opened and the trial commences. At this stage, the order convening the Court and names of officers appointed to try the accused are read in the hearing of the accused and he is given an opportunity to object to any of the members, if he so wishes. In this case, the accused did not object to any members. Thereafter, members of the Court were sworn /affirmed, as the case may be.

5. The stage of arraignment came where the charges were read over to the accused and he was asked to plead to the charges. At this stage, the accused did not tender his plea to the charges and instead raised a plea to jurisdiction of the Court as per Rule 74 of ITBPF Rules, 1994.

6. During the course of scrutiny of the documents for replying to the plea to jurisdiction, the prosecution found out that Sh. Davinder Singh. DIG, Member III had filed an affidavit on behalf of the Department in the writ petition filed by the accused. Matter was raised before the Court and thereafter the Court keeping in view absolute fairness and transparency to the cause of justice decided to refer the matter to the Convening Authority with its recommendation.

The Convening Authority replaced Sh. Davinder Singh, DIG, Member-III by a suitable member namely Sh. G.S. Chauhan, DIG. Sh. G.S. Chauhan, DIG was accordingly drafted in the Court in place of Sh. Davinder Singh, DIG, Member-III. The Court thereafter again gave an opportunity to the accused to object to Sh. G.S. Chauhan, DIG which the accused availed and thereafter Sh. G.S. Chauhan was affirmed and the Court, after duly substitution, proceeded in the matter.

7. The plea of the accused that after disqualification of Sh. Davinder Singh, DIG, Court ought to have been dissolved as per Section 83 of the ITBPF Act, 1992 does not appear to be correct. Section 83 supposes a stage where trial has commenced that means the stage of arraignment is also complete whereupon a member cannot be added to the trial and, thus, Court is to be dissolved if it is reduced below minimum.

8. Arraignment is provided under Rule 73 of ITBPF Rules, 1994 which is reproduced as under:-

"73. Arraignment-

(1) When the Court and the Judge Attorney(if any) have been sworn, the charge will be read to the accused and he shall be asked whether he pleads guilty or not guilty to the charge or charges.

(2) If there is more than one charge against the accused he shall be required to plead separately to each charge.

(3) If there is more than one charge-sheet against the accused before the Court, the Court shall proceed with the charges in the first of such charge-sheets and shall announce its finding hereon and if the accused has pleaded guilty, comply with rule 80, before it arraigns him upon the charges in any subsequent charge-sheet."

9. "Arraignment" consists of (a) calling upon the accused by his number, rank, name and description as given in the charge-sheet and asking him "Is that your number, rank, name and unit (or description)?" (b) reading the charge to him; and (c) asking him whether he is guilty or not guilty.

10. As already noted, the issue which was raised by the Court for consideration of the Convening Authority was whether a member can be added at the GFC to fill up the vacancy created after disqualification of a member of the Court namely Sh. Davinder Singh, Member-III. Since the arraignment was not yet complete as the accused had not pleaded to the charges, as provided under Rule 73 of ITBPF Rules, the Convening Authority, in the interest of justice, decided to fill up the vacancy created by disqualification of Sh. Davinder Singh, DIG. Such action on the part of the Convening Authority is absolutely fair and in the interest of justice. Besides, accused has not been prejudiced in any manner as all the members of the Court were sworn/affirmed, as the case may be, after the accused was given an opportunity to object to their presence at the GFG. Fact of the matter is that the accused did not raise any objection to any member of the Court, on both the occasions.

11. Matter has been examined in detail. DG, ITBP, being the competent authority, has come to the conclusion that after disqualification of Sh. Davinder Singh, DIG, Member No.3, inclusion of Sh. G.S. Chauhan, as member of the Court to complete the quorum did not infringe any of the legal provision as process of arraignment was not yet complete and thus Rule 116(2) is not applicable in the case. DG, ITBP has thus, rejected the petition dated 10.03.2021."

6. The argument of the counsel for the petitioner is, that upon the officer, who was a part of the GSFC and who on 11th February, 2021 was found to be disqualified from being a member of the GSFC, ceasing to be a member of the GSFC, the Convening Authority could not have substituted the said officer by another officer, since the

petitioner already stood "arraigned". It is argued, that per Rule 116(2) of the ITBP Rules as under:-

"(2) An officer shall not be added to a Court after accused has been arraigned.", and the impugned orders, adding an officer to the GSFC, are violative of the said Rule 116(2).

7. On enquiry, whether "arraigned" is defined in the ITBP Act or in the ITBP Rules, attention is invited to Rule 73 (as already reproduced in the order of the Director General set out hereinabove).

8. The question for consideration is, whether the impugned orders, substituting an earlier member of the GSFC who was discovered to be disqualified, with another, is violative of Rule 116(2) supra. The answer to the said question, in turn depends on the question, when can an ITBP personnel facing a GSFC, be said to have been "arraigned".

9. We have examined the scheme of the Rules aforesaid qua the proceedings before the GSFC, with

(i) Rule 67 providing for Assembly and swearing of the Court;

(ii) Rule 68 as under:

"68. Commencement of Trial-(1) The order convening the Court and the names of the officers appointed to try the accused shall be read in the hearing of the accused who shall be given an opportunity to object to any of those officers in accordance with the provisions of section 96.

(2) When a Court is to try more than one accused whether separately or jointly, each accused shall be given an opportunity to object to any officer on the Court in accordance with sub rule (1) and shall be asked separately whether he has any such objection.

(3) An accused shall state the names of all the officers to whom he objects before any objection is disposed of.

(4) If more than one officer is objected to, the objection to each officer shall be disposed of separately and the objection to the lowest in rank shall be disposed of first.

(5) An accused may make a statement and call any person to make a statement in support of his objection.

(6) An officer to whom the accused has objected may state in open Court any thing relevant to the objection of the accused whether in support or in rebuttal thereof.

(7) An objection to any officer shall be considered in closed Court by all the other officers on the Court and the officer objected to shall not be present at that time.

(8) When an objection to an officer is allowed under subsection (3) of section 96 that officer shall forthwith retire and take no further part in the proceedings.

(9) When an officer objected to retires and there is duly qualified waiting member in attendance, the presiding officer shall immediately appoint him to take the place of the officer who has retired.

(10) The Court shall satisfy itself that a waiting member who takes the place of a member of the Court is of the required rank and not disqualified under the Act and shall give the accused an opportunity to object to him and shall deal with any such objection in accordance with the Act and these rules.

(11) If as the result of the allowing of an objection to a member there are insufficient officers available to form a Court in compliance with the provisions of the Act, the Court shall report to the convening officer without proceeding further with the trial and the convening officer may either appoint an officer as a member to fill the vacancy or convene a fresh Court to try the accused." ;

(iii) Rule 69 providing for Swearing or affirming of members of the GSFC;

(iv) Rule 70 providing for Swearing or affirmation of Judge Attorney and other officers;

(v) Rule 71 providing for Objection to Interpreter or Shorthand Writer;

(vi) Rule 72 providing for Objection to Judge Attorney and Prosecutor;

(vii) Rule 73 titled "Arraignment" being as reproduced above;

(viii) Rule 74 as under:-

"74. Plea to Jurisdiction.-(1) The accused, before pleading to the charge, may After a plea regarding the jurisdiction of the Court, and in such a case

(a) the accused may adduce evidence in support of the plea and the prosecutor may adduce evidence in answer thereto: and

(b) the prosecutor may address the Court in answer to the plea and the accused may reply to the prosecutor's address. (2) If the Court allows the plea it shall adjourn and report to the convening officer.

(3) When the Court reports to the convening officer under this rule, the convening officer shall :

(a) if he approves the decision of the Court to allow the plea, dissolve the Court;

(b) if he disapproves the decision of the Court; either :-

(i) refer the matter back to the Court and direct them to proceed with the trial; or

(ii) convene a fresh Court to try the accused.";

(ix) Rule 75 permitting an accused to, before pleading, object to the charge framed against him;

(x) Rule 76 permitting an accused to, before pleading to the charge, offer a plea that the trial is barred under Sections 87 or 88 of the Act;

(xi) Rule 77 providing for two or more accused to apply for separate trials, again before pleading to the charge;

(xii) Rule 78 providing for the accused to apply for trial on separate charges;

(xiii) Rule 79 providing as under:-

"79. Pleading to the charge.-(1) After any plea under rules 74 and 76, any objection under rule 75 and any applications under rules 77 and 78 have been dealt with, the accused shall be required subject to sub-rule (2) to plead either guilty or not guilty to each charge an which he is arraigned.

(2) Where a Court is empowered by section 105 to find an accused guilty or an offence ether than that charged or guilty of committing the offence in circumstances involving a less degree of punishment or where it could After hearing the evidence, make a special finding of guilty, subject to exceptions or variations in accordance with rule 100, the accused may plead guilty to such other offence or to the offence charged as having been committed in circumstances involving a less degree of punishment or to the offence charged subject to such exceptions and variations.";

(xiv) Rule 80 providing for the procedure when the accused pleads guilty;

(xv) Rule 81 providing for alternative charges;

(xvi) Rule 82 providing for more than one charge;

(xvii) Rule 83 providing for "change of plea"; and, (xviii) Rules 84 to 97 providing for procedure, on the accused pleading not guilty, including for examination of witnesses on the charge.

10. The counsel for the petitioner has argued, (a) that Rule 116(2) bars adding an officer to the GSFC after the accused has been "arraigned" and "arraignment", as per Section 73, is only asking the accused, whether he pleads guilty or not guilty; and, (b) the petitioner, prior to taking the objection under Rule 74, had already been "arraigned" within the meaning of Rule 116(2) read with Rule 73 and no officer could thus have been added to the GSFC, as has been done vide impugned orders dated 12 th April, 2021 and 16th February, 2021.

11. We are unable to agree. The scheme aforesaid noticed permits the accused to, after the charge has been read out to him and before he pleads guilty, to take the objections as to jurisdiction, charge etc., as provided in Rules 74 to 78. Needless to state, that if no such objection is taken, the accused would immediately, after the charge is read out to him, plead guilty or not guilty thereto. However if an objection is taken, the pleading of guilty or not guilty by the accused is deferred till the decision on the said objection.

12. The objections under Rules 74 to 78 are in the nature of preliminary objections, though qua some, recording of evidence is also permitted. However such recording of evidence is confined to the objection and not on the charge, inasmuch as till then, the accused has not even pleaded guilty or not guilty.

13. If the said objection fails, the accused, under Rule 79 aforesaid is required to plead either guilty or not guilty. However if the objection succeeds, under Rule 74, the GSFC has to report to the Convening Authority and the Convening Authority, if approves of the decision of the GSFC on the objections, required to dissolve the Court and / or to convene a fresh Court to try the accused.

14. The admitted position is, that though the charge has been read out to the petitioner by the GSFC and he has been asked whether he pleads guilty or not guilty to the charge, the petitioner has not yet pleaded guilty or not guilty. The GSFC, when one of its members was discovered to be disqualified, was still at the stage of recording evidence on the objection of the petitioner to the jurisdiction of GSFC. Such disqualification, though not on an objection of the petitioner within the meaning of Rule 68(3), is nevertheless a disqualification within the meaning of Rule 68(8), and Rule 68(9) itself provides for

substitution of the disqualified member by a member in waiting. Since in the present case there was no "waiting member in attendance" within the meaning of Rule 68(9), Rule 68(11) was followed and a report submitted to the Convening Authority. Rule 68(11) empowered the Convening Authority to appoint an officer as member to fill the vacancy or to convene a fresh Court to try the accused. The Convening Authority is thus found to have acted in accordance with Rule 68(11) and the Director General, ITBP is found to have rightly dismissed the petition of the petitioner under Section 131(2) of the ITBP Act.

15. Rule 68, though titled "Commencement of Trial" does not in its body provide therefor. The provisions for trial are contained in the Rules following Rule 79, after the accused has pleaded guilty or not guilty. The Rules immediately following Rule 68, on the contrary provide merely for swearing in of members and for disposal of preliminary objections permitted to the accused.

16. The purport of Rule 116(2) prohibiting addition of an officer to the GSFC after the accused has been arraigned, is to ensure that the officers before whom trial on the charges against the accused is recorded, are the officers who decide on the said charge. This, even otherwise forms the fulcrum of adjudication/quasi adjudication process, with the decision being required to be given only by a judicial officer/authority who has heard the parties. It has been held in <u>Gullapalli Nageswara Rao Vs. Andhra Pradesh State Road Transport Corporation</u> AIR 1959 SC 308, Rasid Javed Vs. State of U.P. <u>(2010) 7 SCC 781, Automative Tyre Manufacturers Association Vs. Designated Authority</u> (2011) 2 SCC 258 and Union of India Vs. <u>Shiv Raj</u> (2014) 6 SCC 564, that where the decision is rendered by an officer/authority other than the officer who has heard the party, whether in compliance of principles of natural justice or in compliance of a Rule, such a decision is a nullity. The principle of law is, that if one person hears and the other decides, then the personal hearing becomes an empty formality.

17. Merely because, on the objection of the petitioner under Rule 74, to the jurisdiction of the GSFC, testimonies of some witnesses of the petitioner as well as the prosecutor may have been recorded, under the Rules, is not a bar to the substitution of a disqualified member of the GSFC. It is significant, that Rule 116(2) also bars addition to the GSFC after the accused has been arraigned and not after recording of evidence on objections under Rule 74 has commenced. The reason is obvious. The objections under Rules 74 to 78, as aforesaid are in the nature of preliminary objections, evidence whereon is recorded and which objections are decided before the accused has even pleaded guilty or not guilty. The trial on the charges commences after the accused has pleaded not guilty. The Scheme of the ITBP Rules prohibits change in constitution of the GSFC only at that stage and rather, vide Rule 68(11) expressly permits such change at earlier stages. There is no challenge in this petition to any of the Rules. All the Rules aforesaid have to be read harmoniously and if the construction thereof, as contended by the counsel for the petitioner, is accepted, the same will render otiose Rule 68(11).

18. We have also enquired from the counsel for the petitioner, the prejudice suffered by the petitioner from the impugned orders.

19. The counsel for the petitioner has contended that the Rules aforesaid being mandatory in nature, have to be complied with, irrespective of whether cause any prejudice or not. Reliance in this regard is placed on <u>Union of India Vs. A.K. Pandey</u> (2009) 10 SCC 552.

20. We have perused <u>the said judgment</u> and find the same to be concerned with Rule 34 of the Army Rules, 1954 prescribing minimum 96 hours interval between the accused being informed of charge for which he is to be tried and his arraignment. The said provision was held to be mandatory, considering the purpose behind the same. It was held that the purpose is that the accused be given adequate time to give a cool thought to the charge for which he is to be tried, decide about his defence and ask the authorities, if necessary, to take reasonable

steps in procuring the attendance of his witnesses. It was further held that merely because the accused *in that case* pleaded guilty, was of no avail since he was required to be given minimum 96 hours to take *the said decision* also. It was in these facts that it was held that the mandatory provision had been breached. However in the facts of the present case, the petitioner has neither pleaded nor has the counsel for the petitioner, inspite of query, informed, the prejudice suffered by the petitioner.

21. Rather, the judgment cited by the counsel for the petitioner, on the aspect of "arraignment", appears to be against the petitioner and indicates that the arraignment, in the context of ITBP Rules, is complete not merely when, in accordance with Rule 73 the charge is read out to the accused and the accused is asked whether he pleads guilty or not guilty to the charge, but when the accused, under Rule 79 pleads either guilty or not guilty to the charge "on which he is arraigned". If in the interregnum between Rule 73 and Rule 79, any objections under Rules 74 to 78 are dealt with by the GSFC, arraignment remains incomplete and the accused cannot be said to have been "arraigned" within the meaning of Rule 116(2) of the ITBP Rules. "Arraignment", in our view, comprises of both, Rule 73 and Rule 79 and merely on the charge being read to the accused and the accused being asked whether he pleads guilty or not guilty to the charge and before the accused has answered thereto, the accused cannot be said to have been arraigned.

22. In the facts and circumstances aforesaid, Rule 74, mandating the Convening Authority to, if agreeing with the decision of the GSFC on an objection under Rule 74 of the accused, dissolve the Court and convene a fresh Court to try accused, to which also attention was drawn, has no application. It is not the case of the petitioner that the GSFC has rendered any decision on the objection of the petitioner under Rule 74 or that *the said decision* has been accepted by the Convening Authority.

23. It cannot be lost sight of, that if proceedings such as of GSFC in the Armed Forces are delayed indefinitely, the same can play havoc on the discipline which is necessary for effective performance of the duties of the Armed Forces. The petitioner, on an earlier occasion also had approached this Court by way of W.P.(C) No. 6227/2021, which was disposed of vide order dated 8th July, 2021. Filing of this petition, without disclosing the prejudice if any suffered by the petitioner, is found to be yet another step to delay the GSFC proceedings. It cannot be lost sight of that the GSFC proceedings, with several officers forming part thereof, are a drain on the activities of the Armed Forces and unusual delay in the same is injurious to the functioning of the Armed Forces.

24. We are thus unable to find any error in the impugned orders dated 12th April, 2021 and 16th February, 2021 or any merit in the petition, which is dismissed."

CHAPTER IV

BORDER SECURITY FORCE -LAW INCLUDING LEADING CASE LAWS

1. CASE LAWS RELATED TO SECURITY FORCE COURTS

1.1 The Supreme Court vide Judgment dated 13.4.2023 in Criminal Appeal No. 1890 OF 2014 in the matter of B. S. Hari Commandant Versus Union of India & Ors. held as under:

"2. The present criminal appeal is directed against the Final Judgment and Order dated 19.02.2010 (hereinafter referred to as the "Impugned Judgment") [2010 SCC OnLine P&H 2558] rendered by the High Court of Punjab and Haryana at Chandigarh dismissing Criminal Writ Petition No. 03 of 1997 (hereinafter referred to as the "High Court") preferred by the appellant (original writ petitioner). Leave was granted vide Order dated 29.08.2014.

THE FACTUAL PRISM:

3. The appellant joined the Indian Army on 09.02.1964. He was absorbed as an Assistant Commandant in the Border Security Force (hereinafter referred to as the "Force") on 04.06.1969. Thereafter, he was promoted to the post of Commandant in the Force as well as granted selection grade in the rank of Commandant. He was also awarded various medals, including the Police Medal in 1994 by Hon'ble the President of India for rendering about 30 years of unblemished service. Later, he was transferred to Punjab as Commandant of the 1956 Battalion (BN) (BSF) with Headquarters at Mamdot, Punjab.

4. On 05.04.1995, the local police conducted a search and a few Jerrycans of Acetic Anhydride, a controlled substance under Section 9A of the Narcotic Drugs and Psychotropic Substances Act, 1985 (hereinafter referred to as the "NDPS Act"), were stated to be located in Pakistani territory and in the fields owned by Indian civilians adjoining the 2 border, for which First Information Report No. 92 dated 05.04.1995 i.e., on the same day, was lodged in Police Station Ferozepur, Punjab by the local police naming two persons viz. Lakhwinder Singh and Surjit Singh @ pahalwan as the accused showing them to be smugglers. 5. On 07.04.1995, the appellant was directed to hand over charge and move to the STC, the Force, Kharkan, where he was placed under arrest. However, search of the appellant's house did not lead to any recovery of any incriminating material(s).

6. On 09.04.1995, a one-man Staff Court of Inquiry was ordered into the incident headed by one Mr. V.K. Sharma. In the said Inquiry, Inspector Didar Singh, who was in actual and physical command and control of the area in the vicinity of which the alleged Jerrycans were recovered, is said to have made a statement that he was involved in the incident at the behest of the appellant.

7. On the basis of the Inquiry Report, the appellant was issued charge sheet dated 04.07.1995 under Sections 40 & 46 of the Border Security Force Act, 1968 (hereinafter referred to as the "BSF Act"). However, the charges, as laid aforesaid, were dropped.

8. Thereafter, the appellant superannuated on 31.08.1995 after rendering service in the Force for 31 years, 6 months and 22 days.

9. On 20.10.1995, a fresh charge sheet containing three charges was served on the appellant. Two charges were under Section 46 of the BSF Act for Civil offence committed in contravention of Section 25 of the NDPS Act and one charge under Section 40 of the BSF Act. Trial against the appellant commenced on 30.10.1995 by convening a General Security Force Court (hereinafter referred to as the "GSFC").

10. The appellant, invoking Article 226 of the Constitution of India (hereinafter referred to as the "Constitution"), filed Writ Petition No. 16008 of 1995 before the High Court, against the rejection of his application questioning jurisdiction of the GSFC, which was dismissed on 18.01.1996.

11. Meanwhile, one accused alleged smuggler in FIR No. 92 dated 05.04.1995 (described supra), namely Surjit Singh @ Pahalwan, moved the High Court, by way of Criminal Miscellaneous No. 10562-M of 1996, seeking quashing of the FIR against him. The ground urged was that, on the date of alleged incident, Surjit Singh @ Pahalwan was lodged in the Central Jail, Amritsar and could not have been involved in 4 the crime. The said petition was allowed vide order dated 01.11.1996.

12. On 10.04.1996, the GSFC gave its verdict, finding the appellant not guilty of the first charge but guilty of the second and third charges. It sentenced him to 10 years' Rigorous Imprisonment; imposed fine of Rs. 1,00,000/-, and; dismissed him from service. This was confirmed by the Confirming Officers.

13. Statutory petition against his conviction and sentence was then filed by the appellant on 15.05.1996. As the same was not being decided by the concerned authority, the appellant moved the High Court vide Civil Writ Petition No. 13020 of 1996, which was disposed of by order dated 28.08.1996, directing the respondent-Authority to dispose of the statutory petition within a period of two months.

14. Pursuant thereto, the respondent-Authority rejected the appellant's statutory petition on 02.11.1996. In this light, the appellant filed Criminal Writ Petition No. 3 of 1997 before the High Court for quashing his trial and the impugned order therein, as also seeking directions to quash all consequential orders and to release the pensionary and other benefits to the appellant.

15. On 19.09.1997 [1997 SCC OnLine P&H 1176], the appellant was granted bail by the High Court and he remained on bail w.e.f., 19.09.1997 till 19.02.2010.

16. In the meantime, the other co-accused viz. Lakhwinder Singh was discharged by the learned Trial Court in the absence of any evidence.

17. The High Court dismissed Criminal Writ Petition No. 3 of 1997 on 19.02.2010, which is the Impugned Judgment.

SUBMISSIONS BY THE APPELLANT:

18. Learned counsel for the appellant submitted that as far as Charge No.1 was concerned, i.e., of knowingly having permitted Lakhwinder Singh, on the intervening night of 9/10th March, 1995, to take out 30 Jerrycans of 40 litres each of Acetic Anhydride from India to Pakistan through border fencing gate No. 205 of BOP Barrake under his control, the same was not proved against the appellant.

19. However, the learned counsel for the appellant submitted that Charge No. 2, which was identical though the date(s) were 4/5th April, 1995, of having knowingly permitted the two smugglers to take out 44 Jerrycans of 40 litres each of Acetic Anhydride from India to Pakistan from Border fencing gate No. 205 of BOP Barake, under his control has been held to be 6 proved by the GSFC, is clearly unsustainable as one accused Surjit Singh @ Pahalwan was given relief by the High Court by quashing the FIR against him on the ground that he was lodged in Central Jail, Amritsar on the said date(s), and the other co-accused Lakhwinder Singh was also discharged by the trial court itself in the absence of any evidence. Thus, according to learned counsel, two persons, stated to have taken away the Jerrycans having themselves been let off, the case against the appellant automatically fails. As far as Charge No. 3, of knowingly acting prejudicial to good order and discipline of the Force during his tenure as Commandant at Mamdot between November, 1994 and April, 1995 of the 67 Battalion of the Force and having improperly influenced Subedar Didar Singh of his unit to facilitate the alleged smuggling of contraband goods from

India, is clearly not established for the reason that it was on the statement of the said Didar Singh (who was his subordinate and the actual in-charge of the area where the said activity is alleged to have occurred) has, clearly, made a statement to save himself from the obvious and severe consequences, which would have entailed. Learned counsel submitted that this may even have been at the behest of the superior officers of the appellant, inasmuch as there was genuine apprehension of the same, for the appellant had stoutly refused to oblige his Controlling Officer, on an earlier occasion. It was contended that the trial itself was a nullity as the BSF Act does not envisage the GSFC trying offence(s) under the NDPS Act and it also did not obtain the requisite sanction from the Central Government for initiating trial against the appellant as required under and in terms of Section 59(3) of the NDPS Act. It was further contended that Rule 102 of the BSF Rules, 1969 (hereinafter referred to as "the Rules") provides that only one sentence shall be awarded in respect of all the offences of which the accused is found guilty. However, in the present case three punishments were given, which contravenes Rule 102 of the Rules read with Section 48 of the BSF Act.

20. It was the submission of learned counsel that the sentence of dismissal from service is also illegal as the appellant retired on 31.08.1995, even before the issuance of the charge sheet in question and thus there cannot be any sentence of dismissal from service, which is made clear from Rule 166 of the Rules, which stipulate that the sentence of dismissal shall take effect from the date of promulgation of such sentence or from any subsequent date as may be specified at the time of promulgation, which in the present case is much after the superannuation of the appellant from service. Likewise, it was contended that once the first charge sheet dated 04.07.1995 was dropped, apparently for insufficient evidence, the appellant was required to be discharged under Rule 59(1)(i) of the Rules and thus, the second charge sheet dated 20.10.1995 is illegal more so since Chapter VIII of the Rules do not contemplate the issuance of any second charge sheet under the BSF Act and the Rules. It was submitted that the Rules specifically provide for amendment of the charge sheet i.e., addition, omission or alteration in the charge by the GSFC; whereas in the instant case, an entirely new charge sheet had been issued by the Additional DIG which tantamounted to, in effect, a second trial which is prohibited under Section 75 of the BSF Act.

21. On the point of withholding the appellant's pension, gratuity and other benefits, it was submitted that having already superannuated on 31.08.1995, there was no authority vested in the Force to withhold the same and due to such arrogant and arbitrary action, the appellant, now aged about 82 years and having superannuated about almost 28 years back, is in a very poor financial condition and is unable to sustain himself, having no means for his daily needs and medical expenses.

22. Learned counsel submitted that neither the BSF Act nor the Rules envision withholding pension, gratuity, leave encashment and other dues/benefits of any retiree, after retirement without there being a 9 specific order under Section 48(1)(k) & 48(1)(l) of the BSF Act, which in the present case has admittedly, not been passed. Even otherwise it was contended that withholding pension is violative of Rule 9 of the Central Civil Services (Pension) Rules, 1972 (hereinafter referred to as "the Pension Rules") which provide that only Hon'ble the President of India can withhold pension of an employee.

23. In support of such contention, reliance was placed on the decisions of this Court in State of Jharkhand v Jitendra Kumar Srivastava, (2013) 12 SCC 210, the relevant being at Paragraph No. 16 holding that a person cannot be deprived of his pension without the authority of law, which is the constitutional mandate enshrined in Article 300A of the Constitution of India, and further, in Veena Pandey v Union of India, (2022) 2 SCC 379, the relevant being at Paragraph No. 10 where it was held that pension is the deferred portion of compensation for rendering long years of service and is a hardearned benefit accruing to an employee and has been held to be in the nature of property. We note that the appellant had addressed representations to different authorities seeking release of his dues or a copy of the order

by which the same have been withheld, filed alongwith the application seeking 10 early hearing i.e. Crl. M.P. No. 74756/2021 at Pages 16-17.

24. It was also submitted that as far as Acetic Anhydride is concerned, it is neither a narcotic drug nor a psychotropic substance, but only a controlled substance under Section 9A of the NDPS Act, punishable under Section 25A of the NDPS Act.

25. Summing up, it was submitted by learned counsel for the appellant that there have also been violations of other statutory provisions of the BSF Act and the Rules and the principles of natural justice were not conformed to during trial.

SUBMISSIONS OF THE RESPONDENTS:

26. Per contra, learned senior counsel for the respondents supported the Judgment under challenge. It was submitted that there was no infirmity in the appellant being tried separately as he was charged under the NDPS Act and under Sections 40 & 46 of the BSF Act read with Section 25 of the NDPS Act.

27. It was urged that Subedar Didar Singh was tried and convicted by GSFC and sentence of forfeiture of ten years of service for the purpose of pension and severe reprimand were handed out; Sub. N. K. Satpal was tried by GSFC and inflicted with reduction to the rank of Lance Naik (L/NK), and Constable Keshav Singh 11 was tried by the GSFC and awarded sentence of rigorous imprisonment for 45 days in force custody. It was contended that the appellant cannot derive benefit from the discharge of the two purported smugglers as they were charged with the offence of placing the contraband substance on the spot from where it was recovered, while the appellant was charged under Section 25 of the NDPS Act. It was submitted that the contraband items could not have been taken outside the area controlled by the Force, which was under the overall control of the appellant, to the Pakistani side without it having passed through the gates which were manned by the personnel of the Force. Further, it was submitted that Surjit Singh @

Pahalwan was given relief by quashing the FIR concerned, as he was able to establish his incarceration in jail on the date of the incident.

28. Learned counsel submitted that as per the secret information received by the appellant, the Jerrycans of Acetic Anhydride were placed near the international borders by the two smugglers with the help of the officials of the Force and even if the said two persons were the lead perpetrators, the role of the appellant and other officers/personnel of the Force, in aiding such movement was clearly established. It was submitted that the appellant was in overall command of the area and is, hence, responsible for the incidents narrated hereinbefore.

29. On the question of pension, gratuity and other retiral benefits being withheld, learned counsel for the respondents submitted that the appellant had been paid GPF and CGEIS. Further, it was stated at the Bar that he had also been paid provisional pension under Rule 69 of the Pension Rules, and only later on, the same was stopped, taking recourse to Rule 24 of the Pension Rules, as dismissal from service entails forfeiture of past service.

ANALYSIS, REASONING AND CONCLUSION:

30. Having perused the materials on record and surveyed the relevant judicial pronouncements, upon an overall examination, this Court is unable to uphold the view taken by the learned Single Bench of the High Court.

31. Procedural deficiencies in the process and/or trial, canvassed by learned counsel for the appellant, have purposely not been dealt with. Expressing no opinion thereon, we leave those question(s) of law open for adjudication in a more appropriate case, as we are interfering on merits.

32. In Council of Civil Service Unions v Minister for the Civil Service, [1984] 3 WLR 1174 (HL), the House of Lords, speaking through Lord Diplock, stated: 13 "... Judicial review has I think developed to a stage

today when, without reiterating any analysis of the steps by which the development has come about, one can conveniently classify under three heads the grounds on which administrative action is subject to control by judicial review. The first ground I would call 'illegality', the second 'irrationality' and the third 'procedural impropriety'. That is not to say that further development on a case by case basis may not in course of time add further grounds. I have in mind particularly the possible adoption in the future of the principle of 'proportionality' which is recognised in the administrative law of several of our fellow members of the European Economic Community; ..." (emphasis supplied)

33. In Bhagat Ram v State of Himachal Pradesh, (1983) 2 SCC 442, it was opined: *"15. ... It is equally true that the penalty imposed must be commensurate with the gravity of the misconduct, and that any penalty disproportionate to the gravity of the misconduct would be violative of Article 14 of the Constitution. ... " (emphasis supplied)*

34. In Ranjit Thakur v Union of India, (1987) 4 SCC 611, this Court, in the circumstances therein, commented, at paragraph no. 27, that: *"... the punishment is so strikingly disproportionate as to call for and justify interference. It cannot be allowed to remain uncorrected in judicial review.".*

35. *In Andhra Pradesh Industrial Infrastructure Corporation Limited v S N Raj Kumar, (2018) 6 SCC 410, this Court exposited:*

"20.... In the realm of Administrative Law "proportionality" is a principle where the court is concerned with the process, method or manner in which the decision-maker has ordered his priorities and reached a conclusion or arrived at a decision. The very essence of decision-making consists in the attribution of relative importance to the factors and considerations in the case. The doctrine of proportionality thus steps in focus true nature of exercise — the elaboration of a rule of permissible priorities [Union of India v. G. Ganayutham, (1997) 7 SCC 463: 1997 SCC (L&S) 1806]. De Smith

[Judicial Review of Administrative Action (1995), para 13.085, pp. 601-605; see also, Wade: Administrative Law (2009), pp. 157-158, 306-308.] also states that "proportionality" involves "balancing test" and "necessity test". The "balancing test" permits scrutiny of excessive onerous penalties or infringement of rights or interests and a manifest imbalance of relevant considerations." (emphasis supplied)

36. We are quite conscious that in the armed forces of the Union, including the paramilitary forces, utmost discipline, unity of command after all is the sine qua non. That said, the doctrine of proportionality still holds the field.

37. In the absence of direct and cogent evidence against the appellant, even if the GSFC was convinced of the appellant's guilt, the punishment handed out was too harsh, paying heed that the appellant would, even then, be a first-time delinquent, and not a habitual offender. Arguendo, that there be some semblance of truth in the allegations, the punishment meted out, in our considered view, was disproportionate.

38. Another factor which has nudged this Court to introspect vis-à-vis proportionality herein, is that the appellant has served the country for over 31 ½ years without blame or blemish, and has received various awards, inter alia, including medal from Hon'ble the President of India. The appellant's track record is otherwise unquestionable.

39. There is no quarrel with the propositions enunciated in Jitendra Kumar Srivastava (supra) and Veena Pandey (supra). The need to restate the settled position of law in, inter alia, D S Nakara v Union of India, (1983) 1 SCC 305; State of West Bengal v Haresh C Banerjee, (2006) 7 SCC 651, and; Dr Hira Lal v State of Bihar, (2020) 4 SCC 346, is obviated – this Court has taken the consistent view that a person cannot be deprived of pension dehors the authority of law.

40. If things stood only thus, we may have considered remanding the matter back to the GSFC. But, given the long period of time elapsed, the age of the appellant, and our finding below on the evidentiary aspect, we refrain from adopting that course of action.

41. On the alleged criminality, the undisputed and uncontroverted fact remains that the appellant was commanding the Force operating over a large area, including from where the Jerrycans allegedly moved from the Indian side to the Pakistani side. However, it is equally not in dispute that the actual manning of the area is by the subordinate personnel of the Force. In the present instance, the subordinate personnel have been adjudged guilty, indicating their active involvement. Being the persons on the spot, it was their primary responsibility to ensure that no crimes/offences/questionable incidents took place on their watch. Moreover, there is no direct evidence against the appellant.

42. Illustratively, it would not be out of place to draw an analogy from a situation where a crime occurs under the jurisdiction of the Superintendent of Police and in the criminal proceedings emanating therefrom, some police personnel are held guilty, and thereafter, a criminal case as also departmental proceedings, based on such acts of commissions or omissions, is opened against the said Superintendent of Police, on the premise that such incident transpired under his overall watch and control. This would be an extreme and absurd extension of the principle of dereliction of duty and/or active connivance, in the absence of overwhelming material establishing guilt, or at the very least, negating the probability of his innocence.

43. This Court would hasten to add that it should not be construed that the appellant, being the Commandant, had no responsibility/duty to prevent such incident, but to stretch it to the extent to label him an active partner and/or facilitator of such crime is wholly unjustified, having regard to the present factual matrix. Notably, solely on the strength of the statement of Subedar Didar Singh – who is said to have confessed to his involvement in the incident but goes on to add that it was at the behest of and upon the direction of the appellant – the appellant was subjected to punishment.

44. In *Mohd. Jamiludin Nasir v State of West Bengal*, (2014) 7 SCC 443, examining Sections 10 and 30 of the Evidence Act, 1872, it was held:

"144. Going by the above provisions, the relevance, efficacy and reliability of the confessional statement of appellant Nasir when examined on the touchstone of Sections 10 and 30 of the Evidence Act, it will have to be stated that the confession of a co-accused cannot be treated as substantive evidence to convict other than the person who made the confession on the evidentiary value of it. It is, however, well established and reiterated in several decisions of this Court that based on the consideration of other evidence on record and if such evidence sufficiently supports the case of the prosecution and if it requires further support, the confession of a co-accused can be pressed into service and reliance can be placed upon it. In other words if there are sufficient materials to reasonably believe that there was concert and connection between the persons charged with the commission of an offence based on a conspiracy, it is immaterial even if they were strangers to each other and were ignorant of the actual role played by them of such acts which they committed by joint effort. Going by Section 30 of the Evidence 18 Act, when more than one person are being tried jointly for the same offence and a confession made by one of such persons is found to affect the maker as well as the co-accused and it stands sufficiently proved, the Court can take into consideration such confession as against other persons and also against the person who made such confession from the above proposition, we can make reference to the decisions of this Court in *Natwarlal Sakarlal Mody v. State of Bombay* [(1963) 65 Bom LR 660 (SC)] and *Govt. (NCT of Delhi) v. Jaspal Singh* [(2003) 10 SCC 586 : 2004 SCC (Cri) 933]."
(emphasis supplied)

45. As emphasised hereinbefore, save and except Subedar Didar Singh's statement, roping in the appellant, there is no material against him. Hence, ceteris paribus, without other material(s) incriminating

the appellant or pointing to his guilt, the statement of a single person alone, ought not to have, in this instance, resulted in his conviction.

46. This Court is mindful that at the proximate time, the search of the appellant's house, did not result in recovery of any incriminating documents/articles. Such non-recovery would obviously enure to the appellant's benefit.

47. While declining to consider the plea raised of insufficiency of evidence, the learned Single Bench, at page 13 (of 19) of the Impugned Judgment, has commented: 19 "The finding by a Security Force Court on the basis of appreciation of evidence would be beyond the purview of a writ Court as has been consistently held by various Courts including the Hon'ble Supreme Court."

48. The High Court ought to have been cognizant that, considering the seriousness of the issue(s) raised, it was not denuded of the power to sift through the evidence, even in a criminal writ petition. This Court in Nawab Shaqafath Ali Khan v Nawab Imdad Jah Bahadur, (2009) 5 SCC 162, held:

"48. If the High Court had the jurisdiction to entertain either an appeal or a revision application or a writ petition under Articles 226 and 227 of the Constitution of India, in a given case it, subject to fulfilment of other conditions, could even convert a revision application or a writ petition into an appeal or vice versa in exercise of its inherent power. Indisputably, however, for the said purpose, an appropriate case for exercise of such jurisdiction must be made out." (emphasis supplied)

49. In respectful agreement with the above statement of law, we reiterate that High Courts, under Articles 226 and/or 227, are to exercise their discretion "... solely by the dictates of judicial conscience enriched by judicial experience and practical wisdom of the judge.", as highlighted in Surya Dev Rai v Ram Chander Rai, (2003) 6 SCC 675. This guiding principle still governs the field, and the 3-Judge Bench in Radhey Shyam v Chhabi Nath, (2015) 5 SCC 423 had only 20 partly overruled Surya Dev Rai (supra) in terms below:

"29.1. Judicial orders of the civil court are not amenable to writ jurisdiction under Article 226 of the Constitution. 29.2. Jurisdiction under Article 227 is distinct from jurisdiction under Article 226. 29.3. Contrary view in Surya Dev Rai [Surya Dev Rai v. Ram Chander Rai, (2003) 6 SCC 675] is overruled."

50. Article 226 of the Constitution is a succour to remedy injustice, and any limit on exercise of such power, is only self-imposed. Gainful reference can be made to, amongst others, A V Venkateswaran v Ramchand Sobhraj Wadhwani, (1962) 1 SCR 573 and U P State Sugar Corporation Ltd. v Kamal Swaroop Tandon, (2008) 2 SCC 41. The High Courts, under the Constitutional scheme, are endowed with the ability to issue prerogative writs to safeguard rights of citizens. For exactly this reason, this Court has never laid down any strait-jacket principles that can be said to have "cribbed, cabined and confined" [to borrow the term employed by the Hon. Bhagwati, J. (as he then was) in E P Royappa v State of Tamil Nadu, AIR 1974 SC 555] the extraordinary powers vested under Articles 226 or 227 of the Constitution. Adjudged on the anvil of Nawab Shaqafath Ali Khan (supra), this was a fit case for the High Court to have examined 21 the matter threadbare, more so, when it did not involve navigating a factual minefield.

51. For reasons aforenoted, this criminal appeal succeeds and stands allowed. Consequently, (a) the Impugned Judgement is quashed and set aside, and; (b) the conviction and sentence awarded by the GSFC dated 10.04.1996 is also set aside. The appellant is held entitled to full retiral benefits from the date of his superannuation till date. All payments due to him be processed and made within twelve weeks from today, albeit after adjusting amount(s), if any, already paid.

52. Costs made easy.

ADDITIONAL DIRECTIONS:

53. The Impugned Judgment annexed in the paperbook is a certified copy obtained from the High Court. However, it is not numbered paragraph-wise.

54. In Shakuntala Shukla v State of Uttar Pradesh, 2021 SCC OnLine SC 672, this Court had the occasion to observe: "35. ... A judgement should be coherent, systematic and logically organised ...". 55. Likewise, in State Bank of India v Ajay Kumar Sood, 2022 SCC OnLine SC 1067, this Court opined: 22 "21. It is also useful for all judgments to carry paragraph numbers as it allows for ease of reference and enhances the structure, improving the readability and accessibility of the judgments. A Table of Contents in a longer version assists access to the reader." (emphasis supplied)

56. It is desirable that all Courts and Tribunals, as a matter of practice, number paragraphs in all Orders and Judgments in seriatim, factoring in the judgments afore-extracted.

57. The learned Secretary-General shall circulate this judgement to the learned Registrars General of all High Courts, to place the same before Hon'ble the Chief Justices, to consider adoption of a uniform format for Judgments and Orders, including paragraphing. The learned Chief Justices may direct the Courts and Tribunals subordinate to their High Courts accordingly as well."

1.2 **JUDGEMENT DATED 05.07.2016 IN CIVIL APPEAL NO. 8360 OF 2010 TITLED UNION OF INDIA Vs L/NK VISHAV PRIYA SINGH (SUPREME COURT)**

In the aforesaid judgement the Supreme Court of India, addressed several civil appeals challenging the correctness of decisions made by the High Courts of Delhi and Rajasthan regarding the convening and conduct of Summary Courts Martial (SCM) under the Army Act, 1950. The primary issues before the court were whether SCMs can be convened and completed by a Commanding Officer (CO) of a unit to which the accused did not belong and the circumstances under which an SCM can be convened instead of a General Court Martial (GCM),

District Court Martial (DCM), or Summary General Court Martial (SGCM).

The High Court of Delhi had held that an SCM should be convened only in exceptional cases where immediate action is necessary and that the CO of the unit to which the accused belongs is the only one empowered to convene an SCM, except in cases of deserters where the CO of the unit to which the accused is attached can convene the SCM. The Supreme Court, however, disagreed with the High Court's finding that the CO of the accused's unit is the only competent authority to convene an SCM. The court held that the CO of the unit to which the accused is attached or sent for trial is also competent to convene, constitute, and complete an SCM, provided the requirements of Section 120(2) of the Army Act are met.

The Supreme Court emphasized that the convening of an SCM should be the exception rather than the rule and should be justified by articulated reasons or supported by the record. The court also noted that the Army Act and Rules do not require the CO of the accused's unit to be the one to convene the SCM and that Regulation 9 of the Defence Service Regulations provides a broad definition of a CO, which can include the CO of a unit to which the accused is attached.

The Supreme Court set aside the High Court of Delhi's view on the competence of the CO to convene an SCM and remitted the matters back to the High Court for consideration on merits. The court affirmed the High Court of Rajasthan's view on the competence of the CO and dismissed the appeals from that court, as well as appeals where the major offences were not proved on facts.

In conclusion, the Supreme Court clarified that the CO of a unit to which the accused is attached can convene an SCM, provided there is a grave reason for immediate action and the procedural requirements are met. The court also underscored the need for caution in convening SCMs and suggested that the provision may be reviewed in the future to align with constitutional norms and the aspirations of judiciousness. The observation can is as under

"...The Committee recommends that the environment may be sensitized that the provision of SCM should be used sparingly and exceptionally and preferably only in operational areas where resort to a regular trial is not practicable or when summary/administrative action would not meet the requirements of discipline. It may be emphasized that SCM is an exception and not the rule and was not even originally meant to be a peace-time provision or regular recourse. In the times to come, the desirability of even having such a provision on the statute book may be examined with the suitability of a replacement by a more robust system meeting the aspirations of judiciousness and Constitutional norms."

1.3 JUDGEMENT DATED 05.09.2023 IN CIVIL APPEAL 8629 OF 2014 TITLED UNION OF INDIA & OTHERS Versus JOGESHWAR SWAIN (SUPREME COURT)

The case of Union of India vs. Jogeshwar Swain, decided on September 5, 2023, by the Supreme Court of India, involved an appeal by the Union of India and the Border Security Force (BSF) against the High Court of Delhi's judgment setting aside the dismissal of Jogeshwar Swain, a constable in the BSF, and granting him consequential benefits except for 50% of his salary. Swain was accused of taking photographs of a lady doctor while she was bathing, an act prejudicial to the good order and discipline of the BSF under Section 40 of the BSF Act, 1968.

The Supreme Court, in its judgment, examined the procedural aspects of the case and the evidence presented. It found that the Summary Security Force Court (SSFC) proceedings, which led to Swain's dismissal based on his alleged guilty plea, were flawed. The Commandant of Swain's unit, who was also the presiding officer of the SSFC, had initiated the proceedings and ordered the preparation of the record of evidence, which included a confession by Swain that was later disputed.

The High Court had found procedural infirmities in the trial, including the Commandant's dual role, the lack of evidence against Swain, and the dubious nature of the confession. The Supreme Court agreed with the High Court's findings, noting that the SSFC proceedings did not comply with the procedural safeguards laid down in the BSF Rules, 1969, particularly with regard to the acceptance of Swain's guilty plea. The Court emphasized the importance of ensuring that a guilty plea is made voluntarily and with full understanding of the consequences, which was not the case here.

The Supreme Court also pointed out that the minutes of the SSFC proceedings did not bear Swain's signature, and there was no evidence to support the ownership of the camera or the photographs in question. The Court concluded that the High Court was justified in setting aside Swain's dismissal due to the lack of credible evidence and procedural irregularities.

In light of these findings, the Supreme Court dismissed the appeals by the Union of India and the BSF, upholding the High Court's decision. The Court's judgment underscores the importance of adhering to procedural fairness and ensuring that confessions are voluntary and informed, especially in cases involving members of disciplined forces. The observations of the Supreme Court are as under:-

1. These appeals are directed against the judgment and order of the High Court of Delhi ... dated 21.02.2013, by which W.P. (C) No. 17430 of 2006 filed by the respondent (the original petitioner) was allowed, the punishment of dismissal imposed upon the original petitioner was set aside ...

FACTS

2. The original petitioner/accused ... was a Constable (General Duty) in the Border Security Force (in short "BSF"). The case against him was that while he was posted as a security aide to a lady doctor, on 17.06.2005, ... he clicked pictures of that lady doctor while she was taking her bath.

FINDINGS OF THE HIGH COURT

6. *Before the High Court, the orders impugned in the writ petition were questioned on two grounds: (a) that there were procedural infirmities in conducting the proceedings and recording of evidence; and (b) that the evidence recorded did not inculpate him.*

DISCUSSION

17. *We have considered the submissions and have perused the record. ... It would thus be useful to have a glimpse of the relevant provisions of the BSF Act, 1968 and the BSF Rules, 1969 concerning a "Security Force Court" and proceedings before it.*

28. *In our view, there appears substance in the aforesaid submission of the learned counsel for the original petitioner. Moreover, in the instant case after preparing the record of evidence, the Commandant ... remanded the original petitioner for trial by an SSFC.*

35. *Before acting on the plea of guilty, compliance of the procedural safeguards laid down in sub-rule (2) of Rule 142 is important as it serves a dual purpose. ... That apart, even if the accused pleads guilty, if it appears from the record or abstract of evidence or otherwise that the accused ought to plead not guilty, the SSFC is required to advise him to withdraw that plea.*

37. *... The minutes of the proceedings of the SSFC dated 23.07.2005 do not indicate as to what advise was rendered to the accused with regard to the general effect of the plea of guilty taken by him. ... Therefore, we are of the view that the appellants cannot draw benefit from the minutes of the proceedings as to canvass that the plea of guilty was accepted after due compliance of the requirements of sub-rule (2) of Rule 142 of the BSF Rules, 1969.*

38. *... In these circumstances, where was the occasion for the original petitioner to make confession of his guilt when there was hardly any evidence against him. ... The High Court was therefore justified in*

looking at the evidence to find out whether punishment solely on the basis of confession (i.e., plea of guilty) was justified.

39. In light of the discussion above and also taking into account that the minutes of the proceedings recording the plea of guilty did not bear the signature of the original petitioner, in our considered view, the High Court was justified in finding the dismissal of the original petitioner on the basis of the plea of guilty unwarranted and liable to be set aside in exercise of powers under Article 226 of the Constitution of India.

40. For all the reasons above, we do not find it a fit case for interference in exercise of our jurisdiction under Article 136 of the Constitution of India. The appeals are dismissed. Parties to bear their own costs.

1.4 JUDGEMENT DATED 12.02.2007 IN THE MATTER OF DIRECTOR GENERAL, BORDER SECURITY FORCE VS IBOTON SINGH (KH) 2007(1)GLT903

In the aforesaid Writ Petition the Gauhati High Court further delved into the issue of Roles Powers and duties of Law Officer in a General Security Force Court proceedings. The High Court observed as follows

1. The respondent herein, namely, Kh. Iboton Singh, while working as a constable in 95 Bn. of the Border Security Force (in short, 'the BSF'), was arrested, on 15-12-84, by police in connection with Moreh Police Station Case No. 65 (12/1984) under Section 302 IPC on the allegation that he had stabbed to death constable Gharbaran Ram of 95 Bn. of BSF, the FIR against the accused having been lodged by the Coy. Commander, Moreh Coy. The BSF authorities exercised their discretion, under Section 80 of the Border Security Force Act, 1968 (in short, 'BSF Act'), to institute a General Security Force Court (in short, 'GSFC'). A GSFC was accordingly convened and the respondent herein faced the trial on the charge of having intentionally caused death of constable Gharbaran Ram, on 14-12-94, by stabbing him with a knife, and committing thereby the civil offence of murder punishable under [Section 302](#) IPC, the case of the prosecution being, in brief, thus: On 14-12-84, while Barbar Keshab Thakur of 95 Bn. BSF was cooking chicken in the kitchen-room of Coy HQ, the accused-respondent was also present there along with constable Ghabaran Ram (since deceased). At that time, CQMH Mazumder came there and enquired as to why so many children were , dining in the kitchen-room daily. Constable Ghabaran Ram replied by saying that the children had been dining there since long. Reacting to what constable Gharbaran Ram had said, the accused remarked by replying that his child had taken food in the kitchen only once and he (the accused) would make payment for the same. Ghabaran Ram retorted by saying as to who he (the accused) was to make the payment. Following exchange of words between the accused and the deceased, a scuffle took place between them and both of them hurled abuses on each other. The deceased, then, left for the barrack, but the accused remained inside the kitchen-room. Shortly thereafter, Ghabaran Ram was heard shouting, "Iboton sale aoo; main batata hun." It was quite a dark night and as the deceased shouted exhorting the accused to come out of the kitchen- room, the accused also replied by saying, "Sale mareko mat bulao, accha nahi hoga." Barbar Keshab Thakur, in the meanwhile, went to fetch water and the accused went out of the kitchen-room. Moments thereafter, Barbar Keshab Thakur heard HC Lal Bahadur and constable Choubay Singh uttering, "Ghabaran Ram ko marker Iboton bhag gaya" or words to that effect. The other witnesses had also heard the deceased exhorting the accused to come out and the accused uttering to the effect that he was coming out and, two or three minutes thereafter, the deceased was seen coming back towards the door of the kitchen with injuries on his person and a knife in his right hand, the deceased holding the grip of the knife pointing towards himself and blade towards the opposite direction. Looking at the condition of injured Ghabaran Ram, HC Lal Bahadur Chetri asked the injured as to what had happened to him and the injured replied by saying, "Iboton ne maar diya" or words to that effect. The injured was, then, taken to

Moreh hospital and while undergoing treatment there, the injured succumbed to his injuries. The accused disappeared in the darkness and remained untraceable. Pursuant to an FIR lodged by Coy. Commander, a case was registered, as mentioned above, against the accused. Thereafter, the accused was arrested and put on trial as indicated hereinabove.

2. In support of their case, the prosecution examined as many as 13 witnesses. The statement of the accused was, then, recorded. The accused also adduced evidence by examining himself as a witness, his case being, briefly stated, thus: An altercation had taken place between him and the deceased inside the kitchen-room. HC Nirmalaya Mazumder got them separated and sent the deceased towards his living barrack; whereas the accused stayed back inside the kitchen-room. While leaving the kitchen-room, the deceased abused the accused. Thereafter, the deceased called the accused repeatedly by saying, "Iboton aoo" whereupon the accused too retorted by saying "main araha hun"; but barely after taking about 10 steps towards the living barrack, the accused felt scared, because of the darkness and thought that he might be harmed by the deceased in the darkness. The accused, therefore, walked towards the market instead of proceeding towards their living barrack. On the way to the market, the accused fell down and sustained injury, whereupon he went to a dispensary in the market, but, having found the same closed, he went to the quarter of constable driver, Shekhar Singh, of Moreh Police Station, because the said driver was known to the accused. As the said driver was not present in his residential quarter, the accused waited for the driver for quite sometime. However, when the driver arrived, he asked the accused by saying, "Tum ne apne BSF camp ka ek admi mar diya, woh hospital me mar giya; BSF ka admi rifle le kar turn ko mardene ke lie dhund raha hai." The accused felt stunned, because he had not injured or killed anyone and he was completely innocent. As the accused felt frightened, he left the residential quarter of the said driver and proceeded towards Moreh police station; but he did not go inside the police station and

stayed in his deserted hut for the night and, on the following day, in the morning, he was arrested by the police from the said hut.

3. After the prosecution and the defence delivered their respective closing addresses, the Law Officer summed up the case and the Members of the Court returned the verdict of 'guilty' against the accused. On the basis of the finding of guilt reached against the accused, the accused, on 30-7-88, was sentenced to imprisonment for life and also dismissal from service. The finding and sentence, so rendered, were confirmed by appropriate authority on 4-11-88. The accused, then, made an application seeking review of the finding reached against him by the GSFC and the sentence awarded to him. As this application did not yield any favourable result, the accused moved this High Court with an application under Article 226 of the Constitution of India challenging the finding of guilt reached by the GSFC and the sentence passed against him. This writ application gave rise to Civil Rule No. 444/1989. The learned Single Judge found, amongst others, that the case against the accused was based on circumstantial evidence, but the circumstantial evidence was not of conclusive nature. The learned Single Judge also found, as regards the oral dying declaration, which the deceased had allegedly made, that there was a qualitative difference as regard the words, which were said to have been used by the deceased, while describing the accused as his assailant. The learned Single Judge noted that the blood-stained knife had not been sent for chemical examination and nobody had proved that the knife, in question, was ever used. The learned Single Judge also noted that the summing up of the Law Officer was not legal and proper inasmuch as the Members of the Court had not been adequately told the difference between 'culpable homicide amounting to murder' and 'culpable homicide not amounting to murder', though the GSFC, in the facts and circumstances of the case, ought to have been told by the Law Officer that it is their duty to examine if the acts already done by the accused constituted offence of 'murder' or 'culpable homicide not amounting to murder'. The learned Single Judge took the view that there was no sufficient evidence of conclusive nature, which could make a prudent person reach verdict of 'guilty' against the accused. The learned Single Judge further took the view that even if the law and facts had been properly explained and summed up by the Law Officer, it was not possible to predicate that the accused could have been legally found 'guilty'. For the reasons, so assigned, the learned Single Judge held that the finding of guilt reached by the GSFC was not sustainable. The finding of guilt reached by the GSFC and the sentence awarded to him were accordingly set aside by the impugned judgment and order, dated 20-6-97. Aggrieved by the outcome of the writ petition, the BSF authorities have preferred the present appeal.

4. We have heard Mr. C. Komal, learned Asst. Solicitor General, for the appellants, and Mr. A. Nilamani Singh, learned Sr. counsel appearing on behalf of the accused-respondent.

5. Appearing on behalf of the appellants, the learned Asst. Solicitor General has submitted that in the present case, the learned Single Judge has re-appreciated the entire evidence as if he was entertaining an appeal against the conviction. Such is, according to the learned Asst. Solicitor General, not the scope of judicial review under Article 226 against the findings of a Security Force Court (in short, 'SFC'). This apart, contends Mr. Komal, the evidence on record convincingly proves that it was the accused, who had intentionally killed the said deceased and, in these circumstances, when the GSFC had concluded that the accused was 'guilty' of the charge, this finding could not have been legally substituted by a finding of 'not guilty' as has been done, in the present case, by the learned Single Judge. It is further submitted by Mr. Komal that even if the learned Single Judge had noticed some infraction, in either following the procedure prescribed under the BSF Act and the Border Security Force Rules (in short, 'the BSF Rules') framed thereunder or even if the learned Single Judge had found that the summing up by the Law Officer was not entirely in conformity with the relevant provisions of law, the remedy really lied in setting aside the finding and remanding the case, with necessary directions to the BSF authorities and not in setting aside the verdict of 'guilty' reached

against the accused, the sentence passed against him and letting him off completely free.

6. Resisting the submissions made on behalf of the appellant, Mr. A. Nilamani Singh, learned Senior counsel, appearing on behalf of the accused-respondent, has submitted that this appeal is only an appeal in principle and unless there is patent illegality or wrong committed by the learned Single Judge, this Court should not interfere with the direction given by the learned Single Judge. Further points out Mr. Singh that when two views of a case is possible and the learned Single Judge has accepted one of such views, a Division Bench should not substitute its views in place of the views of the learned Single Judge merely on the ground that the other view is more plausible and acceptable. In the case at hand, the learned Single Judge, submits Mr. Singh, reached conclusions in accordance with law and, in the face of such irrefutable conclusions reached by the learned Single Judge, the penultimate directions given by the learned Single Judge were in consonance with the law contained in that behalf and the impugned order, therefore, does not call for interference in appeal.

7. Resisting further the present appeal, Mr. Nilamani Singh further submits that the learned Single Judge has correctly held that there was no evidence to found conviction of the accused thereon and when the learned Single Judge has, on arriving at this definite conclusion, set aside the verdict of 'guilty' and the sentence passed against the accused, the order may not be interfered with.

8. Before we enter into the merit of the rival submissions made before us on behalf of the parties, and before we determine the correctness or otherwise of the ultimate directions given by the learned Single Judge, it is apposite to ascertain the scope of judicial review under Article 226 against the finding reached by a SFC.

9. While considering the ambit of the exercise of the power of judicial review by the High Court under Article 226, it may be borne in mind that the proceedings of a SFC (Security Force Court) stand on the same

footing as do the proceedings of a Court Martial. Hence, the judicial pronouncements, which have been rendered on the scope of juridical review of the findings of the General Court Martial, would apply with equal vigour to the proceedings of a General Security Force Court (GSFC), inasmuch as the procedure prescribed for trial of an accused by a General Court Martial and the GFC are quite akin to each other.

10. While considering the scope of judicial review of the findings of a SFC, it also needs to be borne in mind that a SFC is not subject to power of superintendence of the High Court under Article 227 of the Constitution of India. Though the proceedings of the SFC fall outside the purview of Article 227, these proceedings are nonetheless subject to the, overall, power of judicial review by the High Court under Article 226 of the Constitution. If a SFC has been properly convened, there is no challenge to its constitution and if the procedure, which it followed, was in accordance with the procedure prescribed by the BSF Act and the BSF Rules, the High Court would not interfere with the findings of such a Court unless the findings reached by it are perverse, that is, when the finding reached is wholly without any supporting evidence or wholly against the evidence. The proceedings of a SFC are not to be compared with the proceedings of a trial, in the ordinary criminal courts, under the Code of Criminal Procedure. A SFC remains, to a great degree, an integral and specialized part of the overall mechanism by which discipline is maintained in a 'force', such as, BSF. It is for the special needs of such a 'force' that instead of ordinary criminal court, the offenders are tried by SFC even when the offence is punishable by Indian Penal Code. At the same time, what cannot be ignored is that a SFC functions as a Court to which the provisions of the Evidence Act are applicable. The concept of relevance of admissibility of evidence, the burden of proof, and the standard of proof, as envisaged in the Evidence Act, are applicable, without exception, to the trial of an accused by SFC. Viewed thus, it is clear that a SFC has the same responsibility, as any other criminal court, to protect the rights of an accused arraigned before it and, therefore, follow the procedural safeguards given to an accused in order to ensure that he has a fair trial.

11. When the provisions contained in the BSF Act and the BSF Rules are analysed, in the light of the various administrative instructions, which have been issued from time to time, it becomes manifestly clear that the procedure prescribed is a fair procedure for trial and it is for this reason that the High Court does not, ordinarily, interfere with the proceedings of a trial held by a SFC. When there is sufficient evidence to sustain conviction, the SFC had the jurisdiction over the subject-matter, the SFC followed the prescribed procedure and the punishment awarded was also within its powers, the High Court would not allow challenge to the validity of the conviction and sentence. The High Court, while considering a challenge posed to the findings of guilt reached against an accused or the sentence passed against him, would not function as a Court of appeal. The role of the High Court, under Article 226, in such a case, would, ordinarily, be to review the decision-making process and not the decision as such. If the decisionmaking process suffers from non-consideration of relevant factors or consideration of irrelevant factors, the High Court may interfere with the decision, so reached, if the High Court is of the view that such a decision-making process has caused failure of justice. The merit of the decision of a SFC can be looked into by the High Court only when it is challenged on grounds of perversity. If two views on the basis of the materials on record are possible to be formed, the High Court would not substitute its views in place of the decision of the SFC merely because of the fact that the High Court is of the opinion that the view taken by it is more plausible and reasonable.

12. Referring to the scheme of the proceedings of a Court Martial, as conceived under the Army Act and the Rules made thereunder, a two Judge Bench of the Apex Court, in Union of India and Ors. v. Major A. Hussain , while holding that the procedure for trial prescribed by a Court Martial, is fair, observed and held as follows:

22. We find the proceedings of the General Court-Martial to be quite immaculate where trial was fair and every possible opportunity was afforded to the respondent to defend his case. Rather it would appear that the respondent made all efforts to delay the proceedings of the court-martial. Thrice he sought the intervention of the High Court. Withdrawal of the defence counsel in the midst of the proceedings was perhaps also a part of his plan to delay the proceedings and to make that a ground if the respondent was ultimately convicted and sentenced. Services of qualified defending officer were made available to the respondent to defend his case, but he had rejected their services without valid reasons. He was repeatedly asked to give the names of the defending officers of his choice but he declined to do so. The court-martial had been conducted in accordance with the Act and Rules and it is difficult to find any fault in the proceedings. The Division Bench said that the learned Single Judge minutely examined the record of the court-martial proceedings and after that came to the conclusion that the respondent was denied reasonable opportunity to defend himself. We think this was a fundamental mistake committed by the High Court. It was not necessary for the High Court to minutely examine the record of the General Court-Martial as if it was sitting in appeal. We find that on merit, the High Court has not said that there was no case against the respondent to hold him guilty of the offence charged.

23. Though court-martial proceedings are subject to judicial review by the High Court under Article 226 of the Constitution, the court-martial is not subject to the superintendence of the High Court under Article 227 of the Constitution. If a court-martial has been properly convened and there is no challenge to its composition and the proceedings are in accordance with the procedure prescribed, the High Court or for that matter any court must stay its hands. Proceedings of a court-martial are not to be compared with the proceedings in a criminal court under the Code of Criminal Procedure where adjournments have become a matter of routine though that is also against the provisions of law. It has been rightly said that court-martial remains to a significant degree, a specialised part of overall mechanism by which the military

discipline is preserved. It is for the special need for the armed forces that a person subject to Army Act is tried by court-martial for an act which is an offence under the Act. Court-martial discharges judicial function and to a great extent is a court where provisions of Evidence Act are applicable. A court-martial has also the same responsibility as any court to protect the rights of the accused charged before it and to follow the procedural safeguards. If one looks at the provisions of law relating to court-martial in the Army Act, the Army Rules, Defence Service Regulations and other Administrative Instructions of the Army, it is manifestly clear that the procedure prescribed is perhaps equally fair if not more than a criminal trial provides to the accused. When there is sufficient evidence to sustain conviction, it is unnecessary to examine if pre-trial investigation was adequate or not. Requirement of proper and adequate investigation is not jurisdictional and any violation thereof does not invalidate the court-martial unless it is shown that the accused has been prejudiced or a mandatory provision has been violated. One may usefully refer to Rule 149 quoted above. The High Court should not allow the challenge to the validity of conviction and sentence of the accused when evidence is sufficient, court-martial has jurisdiction over the subject-matter and has followed the prescribed procedure and is within its powers to award punishment.

13. Since the entire procedure of a trial by SFC is provided in the BSF Act and the Rules made thereunder and since the provisions contained therein require that the findings reached, and the sentence passed, against and accused by a SFC, be considered by a competent authority for the purpose of confirmation thereof, such confirmation of the findings and sentence by such an authority shall be final and shall not be, ordinarily, interfered with by invoking the power of judicial review under Article 226. Though it is true that notwithstanding the finality attached to the proceedings of a SFC, which stands confirmed by a competent authority, the High Court shall not, ordinarily, exercise its power of judicial review by invoking Article 226, the fact remains that constitutionally, there is no limitation, on the power of the High Court, to examine, under Article 226, if there has been any infraction of the provisions of the relevant enactments resulting into miscarriage of justice. Thus, for the limited purpose of determining if the proceedings of a SFC have been conducted in accordance with the requirements of the law, the High Court's power, under Article 226, would always remain available. The power, under Article 226, will also be available to find out if there has been violation of the principles of natural justice, while conducting the trial and whether such violation has vitiated the entire proceedings. The power of judicial review, so exercisable, does not, however, empower the High Court, if one can point out, to sit on the findings of a SFC or on the proceedings of a SFC as an appellate authority and re-appreciate the findings for the purpose of determining if the evidence were sufficient for the conclusion reached. However, when the findings reached are found to be perverse and/or contrary to, or in violation of, the provisions of the law relevant thereto and if such infraction has resulted, in the opinion of the High Court, failure of justice, it becomes the duty of the High Court to step in under Article 226 and undo the wrong. If the High Court sits over the findings of a SFC as if it is sitting as an appellate authority, then, such an approach of the High Court would amount to overstepping its jurisdiction. Pointing out these aspects of law, the Supreme Court, in Union of India v. Himmat Singh Chahar, , observed:

"4. Since the entire procedure is provided in the Act itself and the Act also provides for a further consideration by the Chief of the Naval Staff and then by the Union Government then ordinarily there should be a finality to the findings arrived at by the competent authority in the court-martial proceedings. It is of course true that notwithstanding the finality attached to the orders of the competent authority in the court-martial proceedings the High Court is entitled to exercise its power of judicial review by invoking jurisdiction under Article 226 but that would be for a limited purpose of finding out whether there has been infraction of any mandatory provisions of the Act prescribing the procedure which has caused gross miscarriage of justice or for finding out that whether there has been; violation of the principles of natural *justice which vitiates the entire proceedings or that the authority exercising the jurisdiction had not been vested with jurisdiction under the Act. The said power of judicial review cannot be a power of an appellate authority permitting the High-Court to reappreciate the evidence and in coming to a conclusion that the evidence is insufficient for the conclusion arrived at by the competent authorities in court-martial proceedings. At any rate it cannot be higher than the jurisdiction of the High Court exercised under Article 227 against an order of an inferior tribunal. This being the parameter for exercise of power of judicial review against the findings of a competent authority in court-martial proceedings, and applying the same to the impugned judgment of the High Court we have no hesitation to come to the conclusion that the High Court overstepped its jurisdiction in trying to reappreciate the evidence of Mrs Nirmala Sharma and in coming to the conclusion that her evidence is not credible enough to give a finding of guilt against the respondent of a charge under Section 354. We have also perused the statement of Mrs Nirmala Sharma and the conclusion becomes inescapable on the basis of the said statement of Mrs Nirmala Sharma that the respondent has been rightly found to have committed offence under Section 354 by the authorities in the court-martial proceedings."*

14. *While considering the scope of judicial review by the High Court in matters of the proceedings of a trial by a SFC, what is also pertinent to note is that Article 33 of the Constitution has conferred, on Parliament, the power to abridge the fundamental rights of not only armed forces, but also of the forces entrusted with the maintenance of public order. This, however, does not mean that merely because of the fact that a person belongs to an armed force or a force entrusted with the maintenance of public order, he is denuded of the constitutional guarantees given to him by Article 21 of the Constitution, which ensures to every person a fair trial in accordance with law. Viewed from this angle, it is clear that when the procedures prescribed are followed as a mere formality by a SFC and not in substance or in its true spirit, the accused may, in an appropriate case, be held to have*

been denied a fair trial and such a proceeding may warrant interference by the High Court in exercise of its extra-ordinary jurisdiction under Article 226. The procedure prescribed adopted for trial by a SFC has to be tested on the touchstone of Article 21 and if the procedural safeguards given to a person from the Border Security Force, under the BSF Act and/or the BSF Rules, are violated, violation thereof would, in substance, be denial of the right to a fair trial. A person, even when he comes from the BSF, is as much a citizen as any other citizen of India and he is entitled to all such protections as have been given to him by making various laws in conformity with the provisions of Article 21. The Constitution-makers were conscious of the fact that no more restriction should be placed than what are necessary and indispensable for ensuring maintenance of discipline and proper discharge" of duties by the armed forces and the forces entrusted-with the maintenance of public order. Hence, when an Indian citizen, being a member of any such forces, is tried under its own established mechanism, such as, SFC, on a charge of having committed the civil offence of 'murder' punishable under Section 320 IPC, it is the duty of the High Court to examine, when such a person approaches the High Court with an application under Article 226, to determine if, while holding the trial, the provisions of the BSF Act and the Rules made thereunder, which provide protection to the accused, have been adhered to or not and whether, for the purpose of reaching its findings, the SFC has kept itself informed of all the relevant provisions of the Evidence Act and the Indian Penal Code.

15. It is for the reasons indicated above that in Union of India v. LT Ballam Singh , the Apex Court has pointed out that even an army personnel is entitled to the protection, which the Narcotic Drugs and Psychotropic Substances Act (in short, 'the NDPS Act') gives to any other person. In other words, the protection available, in the form of Sections 42 and 50 of the NDPS Act, shall be applicable to the case of even an army personnel, for, there is nothing, in the law, that the protection, given in the NDPS Act, are not applicable to the members of the armed forces. Logically, therefore, when the Evidence Act is

applicable to the proceedings of a trial by a SFC, it is but natural to interfere, and, in fact, we have no hesitation in holding, that if the provisions of the Evidence Act are ignored or are not taken into account by a SGFC and/or when the provisions of the Indian Penal Code are not properly applied, such noncompliance may, in an appropriate case, compel the writ Court to interfere, in exercise of its powers under Article 266, with the findings, which may have been reached by either ignoring, or in ignorance of, the relevant provisions of law, particularly, when such non-compliance results in gross miscarriage of justice. This apart, and as already indicated above, the procedural safeguards, which the BSF Act and the Rules themselves provide, cannot be ignored, for, ignoring them may amount to, in a given case, denial of a fair procedure to a person accused of having committed offence under the Indian Penal Code.

16. We may also point out that the power of judicial review aims at ensuring that public bodies and adjudicatory authorities exercise powers within their own parameters. Not only that an erroneous exercise of power may, in a given case, be amenable to the power of judicial review, but even refusal or failure by such an authority may make the High Court interfere in exercise of its power of judicial review. The High Courts, under Article 226, are obliged to ensure that the adjudicatory authorities exercise the powers vested in them in the manner prescribed by law and that such exercise of power is within their limits; it is equally important for the High Court to ensure that the power, which belongs to an adjudicatory authority, is not left without being exercised and/or when it is exercised, such exercise is in conformity with the power conferred on it by the legislature. The judicial review is basically one of the facets and an adjunct of 'parliamentary sovereignty' so as to ensure that the will of the legislature is aciduously observed by the concerned authority. The judicial review is, therefore, concerned with the legality of the decision and not necessarily with the merit of the decision. It is for this reason that it is the decisions-making process, which becomes the subject of judicial review, and, rarely, the decision itself. If, while reaching a decision, an adjudicatory authority does not take into account the relevant fact or relevant aspect of law, its action would be bad in law and can be interfered with by the High Court in exercise of its power of judicial review. Similarly, when an adjudicating authority takes into account a fact or a provision of law, which is irrelevant, the decision rendered would be bad in law and open to judicial review. According to Prof. Hilarie Barnett, what the courts essectially seek by judicial review to ensure are:

(i) that Acts of Parliament have been correctly interpreted,

(i) that discretion conferred by statutes has been lawfully exercised; and

(ii) that the decision-maker has acted fairly

17. What is, however, important to bear in mind is that while exercising power under Article 226 of the Constitution, the High Court cannot act as an appellate Court. The judicial review, if one can borrow the words of Lord Brightman, in Chief Constable of the North Wales Police v. Evans (1982) 1 WLR 1155 (1174), "is not an appeal from a decision, but a review of the manner in which the decision was made'. When an authority, executive or adjudicatory, while exercising its power and discretion, takes into consideration irrelevant and extraneous matters or overlooks the relevant materials, such a decision cannot be said to be a lawful decision.

18. In the present case, in exercise of power of judicial review, though it was not possible to re-appreciate the evidence for the purpose of determining if there were sufficient evidence warranting conviction of the accused-respondent or as to whether the accused-respondent ought to have been given benefit of doubt, it was nevertheless the duty of the learned Single Judge, while exercising the power under Article 226, and, it is, now, our duty too, to ascertain if the GSFC was conducted accordingly to law. The determination of the question as to whether, while conducting the trial, the procedures, prescribed by the BSF Act and the BSF Rules as well as the other provision of law relevant thereto, were followed by the GSFC and if the GSFC had not followed the relevant provisions of law, whether such omission had prejudiced the accused-respondent are questions, which come within the ambit of Article 226. *If there were no evidence to come to a finding of 'guilty', there is nothing in law, which could stop a High Court, under* Article 226, *from interfering with the conviction. For instance, if an accused faces a charge of murder and without even an iota of evidence to support such a charge, he is convicted by GSFC, he would be entitled to challenge his conviction before the High Court and the High Court would not be able to shirk its responsibility to determine if the finding of 'guilty' reached against the accused is supported by any evidence at all.*

19. Bearing in mind, as indicated above, the scope of judicial review of the decisions reached by adjudicatory authorities, we, now, revert to the case at hand. In this regard, it is noteworthy that the procedures for trial by SFCs are prescribed in Chapter-VII of the BSF Act *and the procedures, so prescribed, are similar as those contained in* Sections 128 *to* 152 *of the Army Act, which prescribe the procedure for trial by court-martials. There are three different kinds of Security Force Courts as conceived in* Chapter-VI of the BSF Act. *These three Courts, according to* Section 64, *are General Security Force Courts (GSFC), Petty Security Force Courts (PSFC) and Summary Security Force Courts (SSFC). In the present case, the Court convened for trial of the accused-respondent was a General Security Forc Court which, according to* Section 68, *shall consist of not less than five officers, each of whom has held the post of Deputy Superintendent of Police for not less than three whole years and of whom not less than four are of a rank not below that of a confirmed Deputy Superintendent of Police.*

20. The present one is a case of 'murder' and, hence, it is necessary to determine as to what role the Law Officer in such a case shall play. We may point out that the Law Officer, under the BSF Act, *performs the same function as does a Judge Advocate in the proceedings of a court martial.* Section 82 *makes it clear that the senior-most member of the*

GSFC shall be the Presiding Officer. While the act of taking decision rests with the Presiding Officer and members of the Court, it is the Law Officer, who plays a pivotal role at the trial, for, it is on him that the burden pests to guide the member of the Court, who may not be acquainted with law, to come to a decision in accordance with law.

21. Section 83 makes it clear that every GSFC shall be attended by a Law Officer and if no such officer is available, then, an officer approved by the General Law Officer, or a Law Officer. While Rule 66 vests in the accused a right to object to a person, who has been appointed as a member of the Court, from functioning as a member of the Court, Rule 70 of the BSF Rules disentitles such an accused from objecting to a person acting as a Law Officer. The Law Officer is, however, administered oath and is, therefore, expected to be above board and not align himself either with the prosecution or with the defence. Rule 89 makes it clear that the Presiding Officer, the Law Officer and any Member of the Court may put questions to a witness. Rule 97 further makes it clear that after examination of their respective witnesses, the prosecution and the defence shall deliver their closing addresses and after their closing addresses are over, the Law Officer shall, according to Rule 97, sum up, in the open Court, the evidence and 'advise' the Court on the law relating to the case.

22. Coupled with the above, it is also worth noticing that the 'summing up' of the 'evidence' and the 'law', relevant to a case, by a Law Officer, as indicated by Rule 97, is not an idle requirement or an empty formality; it is, rather, a solemn act, for, it is this summing up by the Law Officer, which helps the Court to come to a decision - correct or incorrect. Since the members of the Court may not be knowledgeable persons in law, it is incumbent, upon the Law Officer, to advise the Court on every aspect of law, which may be relevant to a case. It is equally important that the Law Officer shall not merely recite as to what witnesses have deposed, but he must marshall the evidence adduced by the parties to the trial and help the Court to come, in accordance with the law relevant thereto, to a correct and lawful

decision. Since a Court must take into account all material aspects of 'evidence' and 'law' in order to reach a lawful decision, it is the onerous task of the Law Officer to not only marshall the evidence to help the Court, but also advise the Court on all such aspects of law, which may have a bearing on the trial of an accused.

23. The question, now, is as to what are the legal consequences of a 'summing up', which is inadequate or incorrect either in fact or in law. For the purpose of correctly understanding the legal effect of an incorrect or inadequate 'summing up', one has to ascertain not only the role of a Law Officer in a SFC, but also the importance thereof. Since a Law Officer, in a SFC, stands on the same footing as does a Judge Advocate, in a Court Martial, the judicial precedents describing the role and importance of a Judge Advocate would, therefore, apply, with equal force, to the case of a Law Officer also.

24. On the role of the Judge Advocate in a court-martial, the Apex Court has pointed out, in S.N. Mukherjee v. Union of India, that the Judge Advocate plays an important role during the course of trial at the General Court Martial and he is enjoined to maintain an impartial position. It is also pointed, in S.N. Mukherjee (supra), that the Court Martial records its findings after the Judge Advocate has summed up the evidence and has given his opinion upon the legal bearing of the case and that the members of the court have to express their opinion as to the finding, by word of mouth, on each charge separately, and the finding on each charge is to be recorded simply as a finding of "guilty" or of "not guilty".

25. In the case of Cheranjit S. Gill (supra), it was contended before the Supreme Court that in effect and in practice, the Judge Advocate is the court and the court martial is the 'jury' for all practical purposes so far as the trial of an accused is concerned. Responding to this submission, the Apex Court observed that the Judge Advocate plays an important role during the course of trial at a General Court Martial and he is enjoined to maintain an impartial position. The Court Martial records its findings after the Judge Advocate has 'summed up' the evidence and

has given his opinion upon the legal bearing of the case. The Members of the Court have to express their opinion as to the finding by word of mouth on each charge separately and the finding on each charge is to be recorded simply as a finding of 'guilty' or of 'not guilty'.

26. Emphasizing that a Judge Advocate must be free from such disqualification, which disentitles an officer to be a member of the Court Martial, the Apex Court in <u>Cheranjit S. Gill</u> (supra), emphasized that the Judge Advocate forms an integral part of the trial by Court Martial. The observations made by the Supreme Court, in <u>Cheranjit S. Gill</u> (supra), have crucial bearing on the present appeal; hence, the relevant observations, made in <u>Cheranjit S. Gill</u> (supra), are quoted herein below:

Referring to various provisions of the Act and the Rules as noticed earlier, the learned Counsel appearing for Respondent 1 has argued that in effect and practice the Judge Advocate is the "Court" and the "Court Martial" is the jury for all practical purposes so far as the trial of the accused is concerned. The argument may be an exaggerated version of the reality but is not totally without substance inasmuch as the powers exercised by the Judge Advocate indicate that though not forming part of the Court Martial, he is an integral part thereof particularly in Courts Martial which cannot be conducted in his absence. It cannot be denied that the justice dispensation system in the Army is based upon the system prevalent in Great Britain. The position of the Judge Advocate is by no means less than that of a Judge Advocate associated with a Court Martial in that country. The importance of the role of the Judge Advocate in U.K. was noticed and considered in R. v. Linzee (1956) 3 All ER 980.

It is true that a Judge Advocate theoretically performs no function as a Judge but it is equally true that he is an effective officer of the Court conducting the case against the accused under the Act. It is his duty to inform the Court of any defect or irregularity in the charge and in the constitution of the Court or in the proceedings. The quality of the advice tendered by the Judge Advocate is very crucial in a trial conducted under the Act. With the role assigned to him a Judge Advocate is in a position to sway the minds of the Members of the Court Martial as his advice or verdict cannot be taken lightly by the persons composing the Court who are admittedly not law-knowing persons. It is to be remembered that the Courts Martial are not part of the judicial system in the country and are not permanent courts.

27. From the observations, made in <u>Charanjit S. Gill</u> (supra), it is clear that to describe a 'court-martial' as a 'jury trial' may be an exaggeration, but not wholly without substance. Though a court-martial may differ from a 'jury trial' and though a Judge Advocate does not form part of a court-martial, for, he is distinct from, and independent of, the members, who constitute a court-martial, and though a Judge Advocate does not theoretically perform the function of a Judge, in a jury' trial, the fact remains that a Judge Advocate is an effective officer of the court conducting the case against the accused and the quality of advice, tendered by him, to the members of the court-martial, has a very crucial bearing on the trial and that with the kind of role, which a Judge Advocate has been assigned to perform, he is in a position to sway the minds of the members of the court-martial inasmuch as his advice or verdict cannot be taken lightly by the persons constituting the court, for, the members are admittedly, not law-knowing persons. It is, therefore, the duty of the Judge Advocate to inform the members of the court of such facts and law as may be relevant to a case tried by a court-martial.

28. Coupled with the above, it is also worth pointing out that Rule 110 of the BSF Rules provides that a court shall, where it is so directed by these rules, and may, in any other case, on any deliberation amongst the members, sit in closed Court and that no person shall be present in closed Court except the members of the Court, the Law Officer (if any) and any officers under instruction.

29. The provisions of Rule 110 show that whenever a SFC is required, by the rules or otherwise, to deliberate in 'closed" Court, none other than members of the Court shall be present unless someone is

instructed by the Court to be present. The Law Officer shall, however, as a matter of rule, remain present in the 'closed" Court. Obviously, there is an intent and purpose for making the presence of the Law Officer mandatory in the 'closed" Court, for, on the Law Officer rests the responsibility of advising the Court on the questions of law and fact or to give such advice as may be sought for. For example, while deliberating in 'closed" Court, if the members of the Court seek to rely on a piece of evidence, which is inadmissible in law, the Law Officer would be, within his powers, to point out that the evidence, sought to be relied upon, is inadmissible in law. No wonder, therefore, as indicated in <u>Charanjit S. Gill</u> (supra), that the powers that the Judge Advocate possesses and the role that he performs, he (as a Judge Advocate or a Law Officer) may sway the minds of the Court.

30. *A Judge Advocate, in the court-martial in India, points out the Supreme Court, in <u>Charanjit S. Gill</u> (supra), holds the same place and position as a Judge Advocate does in a court-martial in the United Kingdom. The Supreme Court further points out, in <u>Charanjit S. Gill</u> (supra), that the importance of the role of the Judge Advocates, in the United Kingdom, was noticed and considered in R.V. Linzee (1956) 3 All E.R. 980.*

31. *Bearing in mind what has been pointed out above, if one turns to Linzee's case (supra), it will be seen that though a court-martial is, to some degree, analogous to a 'jury' trial, it is not same as a 'jury' trial. Making this aspect clear, the Court, speaking through Lord Goddard, C.J., observed: "We have had some rather interesting discussions about the position of the court-martial, and how far it is analogous to a jury. I do not think it is analogous to a jury, and there is no true analogy between a court-martial - martial, a jury or a bench of magistrates. It is a court which is sui generis."*

32. *Notwithstanding, however, that the Court, in Linzee's case (supra), held that a court-martial is not analogous to a 'jury' trial, the Court still observed:*

We have had read to us various passages from the summing-up, a summing-up, which we have all read with care ourselves, and the court cannot find misdirection of any sort or kind. We think that the judge-advocate gave a summing-up which is quite impeccable.

33. From the above observations made in Linzee's case (supra), it becomes clear that the Court, in Linzee's case (supra), had to read the 'summing-up' by the Judge Advocate, at the court-martial, for the purpose of determining if there was 'misdirection' and, upon such examination, held that there was no 'misdirection' and that the 'summing-up' was impeccable. The question, therefore, is as to what does a 'misdirection' mean, convey or signify?

34. 'Misdirection', it needs to be noted, is a concept developed in the realm of 'jury' trial. While considering the concept of 'misdirection' in a trial, it is pertinent to recall that under the Criminal Procedure Code, 1898, the Judge was required to sum up the evidence in terms of Section 297 thereof for the benefit of the 'jury' and the High Court, under Sub-section (3) of Section 307, could interfere with the verdict of the 'jury' if there was 'misdirection' or 'non-direction' by the Judge to the 'jury'. A 'non-direction' by the Judge to the 'jury' means that the Judge has not correctly advised and guided the 'jury' by pointing out to them the relevant pieces of evidence, the legality thereof and other relevant provisions of law. A 'misdirection' indicates that the Judge has failed to bring to the notice of the 'jury' a relevant piece of evidence or a relevant provision of law or the Judge has put to the 'jury' the evidence in such a manner, which was improper and could have misled the 'jury' or the Judge has, while putting to the 'jury' an aspect of law, though relevant, did not put the proposition of law correctly or in its entirety. The verdict of the 'jury', in such circumstances, was liable to be set aside if it occasioned the failure of justice. 'Misdirection' is something, which a Judge, in his charge to the 'jury', tells the 'jury', which is either wrong or in a manner, which is wrong and may tend to mislead the 'jury'. Even an omission, on the part of the Judge, to point out to the 'jury' such matters, which are essential for proper

appreciation of the case of the prosecution or of the defence, and help thereby the 'jury' to reach a correct verdict, may amount to a 'misdirection'. However, each and every misdirection or non-direction cannot be a ground for setting aside a verdict in the absence of failure of justice.

35. In K. M. Nanavati (supra), the Supreme Court has described 'misdirection' thus:

Misdirection' is something which a judge in his charge tells the jury and is wrong or in a wrong manner tending to mislead them. Even an omission to mention matters which are essential to the prosecution or the defence case in order to help the jury to come to a correct verdict may also in certain circumstances amount to a misdirection. But, in either case, every misdirection or non-direction is not in itself sufficient to set aside a verdict, but it must be such that it has occasioned a failure of justice.

36. Though there is a difference between 'non-direction' and 'misdirection', no real distinction, in some cases, can be drawn between 'non-direction' and 'misdirection'. For the purpose of ascertaining if there is 'mis-direction' or 'non-direction', the summing up by the judge, as a whole, needs to be looked into and examined [See <u>Fakira Appaya v. Emperor</u> AIR 1915 Bom 249]. In Reg. v. Fattechand Vastachand (1868-69) 5 B.H.C.R. 85 Cr, Sargent, J (as his Lordship then was), took the same view of the responsibilities of a judge, in a summing up to the jury, when his Lordship observed, "The summing up contemplated by this section cannot mean any statement of the evidence which a judge may, in his caprice, think proper to make to the jury, but a proper' summing 'up, by which is to be understood a full and distinct statement of the evidence on both sides, with such advice as to the legal bearing of that evidence, and the weight which properly attaches to the several parts of it, as a sound judicial discretion would suggest." In another passage, his Lordship observed, "I think, therefore, that the Judge committed an error in confining himself to so

very brief a summary of the evidence, and in not giving a more careful analysis of that evidence".

37. *'Non-direction' is a case, wherein the Judge fails to give to the Jury help and guidance, which they are entitled to expect from a Judge and which it is his duty to give. A summing up, having long rambling repetition of the evidence, without any attempt to marshall the facts under appropriate heads or to assist the Jury to sift and weigh the evidence, so that they will be in a position to understand, which are the really important parts of the evidence and which are of secondary importance, constitutes 'misdirection'. [See <u>Nabi Khan v. Emperor</u> AIR 1936 Calcutta 186]. No wonder, therefore, that observed by Henderson, J, in Mahasara Khatim and Anr. v. Emperor AIR 1939 Cal 610, thus, It is the duty of a Judge to place the case before the jury in such a way as to enable them to come to a reasonable and fair conclusion. The Judge's charge to the jury, in this case, is so confusing that I am sure that the jury received no assistance from it whatsoever. In fact, I think that the jury must have been confused by the charge of the learned Judge. In no part of the charge can one find a connected account of what the case for the prosecution is or what the defense case is. The learned Judge has mixed up the arguments of the defense with the statement of the case for the prosecution. The whole charge is muddled. Speaking for myself, the charge left me quite unable to form a clear idea of what the respective cases of the parties were. Apart from the other illegalities in this case, I am of opinion that this unsatisfactory feature of the charge to the jury by itself would be a sufficient ground for setting aside the verdict of the jury.*

38. When a common man's perception of an offence is, generally, different from the legal concept of an offence, it becomes the duty of the Judge to explain to the 'jury' the ingredients of such an offence. For example, a common man's understanding of an offence of cheating is different from what legally constitutes cheating. Similarly, it is too much to expect a common man to know the distinction between 'culpable homicide not amounting to murder' and 'culpable homicide

amounting to murder'. It is in this context that observed, Blacker, J. in *Arnold Monteath Mathews v. Emperor* AIR 1940 Lahore 87, thus, Coming to the first question, the point taken by counsel is that in order to comply with S.297, Criminal P.C., the Judge should concisely, but lucidly explain to the jury the ingredients of the Section under which the accused is being charged and should also explain the meanings of any terms in the Section, which are not likely to be immediately understood by a layman. There is plenty of authority in support of the view put forward by counsel for the appellant. I think that in the present case, it was clearly the duty of the Judge to explain to the jury the necessary ingredients, which the prosecution had to prove before the charges could be held to be established. This is, particularly, necessary in a case like the present, where that main charges are of cheating. The criminal definition of cheating is not exactly what an ordinary layman in the ordinary use of the English language would understand by the term. In a case of this sort, it is clearly necessary to point out to the jury the difference between a promise, which is not intended to be kept at the time it is made, and a promise, which is intended to be kept at the time it is made, but is subsequently broken

39. Even in <u>Nga Muga v. Emperor</u> AIR 1916 LOWER BOURMA 114, the Court held that when the facts appearing in a case may constitute a border line case, which may fall either under Section 302 or under <u>Section 304</u> IPC, the judge is bound to explain to the jury not only as to what constitutes the offence of murder but also as to when a case of killing may become a culpable homicide not amounting to murder.

40. In fact, even, in Linzee's case (supra), while holding that a court-martial is not analogous to a 'jury' trial, the Court nevertheless held, Then, if any question of law arose, we have to see whether or not the law has been correctly laid down by the judge-advocate.

X x x x x x x x "We have to see that the summing-up was adequate."x x x x x x "The summing-up must be taken as a whole and it must be seen that there is no misstatement of law; that is the first thing."x x x x x x x

"The judge-advocate's duty is to advise the court-martial on questions of law." x x x x x x x "A judge directs an acquittal if there is no evidence, and so would a judge-advocate. He would say: "There is no evidence on which you can convict."

41. What surfaces from the above discussion is that if, in his 'summing up', the Law Officer does not bring to the notice of the Court any relevant piece of evidence or a relevant provision of law, such an omission really amounts to 'misdirection' or 'non-direction' to a 'jury' by a Judge and the findings reached, with such deficient summing up, may, in a given case, warrant interference by the court, in exercise of its power under Article 226, if such an omission, on the part of the Law Officer, has caused prejudice to the accused. Similarly, if in his summing up, the Law Officer summarizes the evidence in a manner, which conveys to the Court, some conjecture or surmises, which are not tenable in law, or when the Law Officer puts to the Court a provision of law, which is not relevant for the trial or a proposition of law, which is not correct, and thereby causes prejudice to the case of the defence, it will be the bounden duty of the High Court to step in and remedy the wrong, done to the accused, by invoking its extra-ordinary jurisdiction under Article 226.

42. We may, at this stage, pause here to point out that though a writ Court, while exercising jurisdiction under Article 226, would not re-appreciate evidence for the purpose of determining sufficiency or otherwise of the evidence, which formed the basis of conviction of an accused tried by a court martial or SFC, the fact remains that, the High Court may, in a given case, examine the record of the proceedings of the trial, to determine if, in the light of the evidence on record, the Judge Advocate or the Law Officer, as the case may be, has summed up the case not only adequately, but in such a manner that the members of the Court stood informed of all the relevant aspects of the case including such provisions of law, which were applicable to the facts of the given case. Such examination of the evidence by the High Court for the purposes, indicated hereinbefore, would not amount to re-appreciation of evidence.

43. Though in Linzee's case (supra), the Court dealt with the appeal against the order of conviction by the court martial, what is important to note is that if in a court-martial, the Judge Advocate does not sum up the case in accordance with law and the lapse committed by him constitutes misdirection, it may justify interference by the High Court in exercise of its power under Article 226, if such misdirection is found to have caused prejudice to the accused. Thus, for the purpose of determining if there was misdirection by the Law Officer, while summing up the case in the present case, and if such misdirection had caused prejudice to the accused-respondent, the High Court was free to examine the evidence on record and interfere, in exercise of its power under Article 226, if it was satisfied that there was misdirection and that such misdirection had caused prejudice to the accused warranting interference by the writ Court.

44. In the case at hand, it is the admitted position that there was no eye witness to the occurrence of assault on, or stabbing of, the deceased. The prosecution rested its case on circumstantial evidence and oral dying declaration. What we notice is that the Law Officer, while summing up the case to the Court, did tell the Court as to what would, generally, constitute offence of 'murder' punishable under Section 302 IPC, he has spoken not even a word to let the members of the Court know as to when an act, though an act of 'killing', may not necessarily amount to the offence of 'murder' and fall in the category of those offences, which are described as 'culpable homicide not amounting to murder' and covered by Section 304 IPC.

45. While considering the above aspect of the case, it is also important to bear in mind that an accused need not specifically plead that his case comes under any of the Exceptions to Section 300 IPC so as to bring the offence, even if committed by him, under Section 304 IPC and not one under Section 302 IPC. Under Exception 1 to Section 300 of

the Indian Penal Code, 'culpable homicide' is not 'murder' if the following conditions are satisfied:

(i) The deceased must have given provocation to the accused;

(ii) The provocation must have been grave;

(iii) The provocation must have been sudden;

(iv) The offender, by reason of such provocation, shall have been deprived of his power of self-control;

(v) The offender should have killed the deceased during the period, when he remained deprived of the power of self-control; and

(vi) The offender must have caused the death of the person, who gave the provocation or that of any other person, by mistake or accident.

46. When, in a given case, the accused does not take specific defence that his act falls under Exception I to Section 300 IPC, it does not relieve the Court of its duty to ascertain if the facts of the given case are such, which attract Exception I to Section 300 IPC or not; and if the Court finds that the deceased had provoked the accused, the provocation was not only grave but also sudden and that the accused, because of such provocation, had been deprived of his power of self-control and killed the deceased during the continuance of the deprivation of his power of self-control, it becomes the duty of the Court to resort to Exception I to Section 300 IPC and, in such a case, the Court shall, instead of holding the accused 'guilty' of the offence of 'murder', hold him 'guilty' under Section 304 IPC.

47. In Mancini v. Director of Public Prosecutions 1942 AC 1 atpg. 9, Viscount Simon, L.C., defined the scope of the doctrine of 'provocation' in the following words:

It is not all provocation that will reduce the crime of murder to manslaughter. Provocation, to have that result, must be such as temporarily deprives the person provoked of the power of self-control, as a result of which he commits the unlawful act, which causes death....

48. One must, however, bear in mind that the 'provocation', referred to in Section 300 IPC, is provocation of a reasonable man and not of an unusually excitable or pugnacious individual. While under the English Law, words and gestures were not, at one point of time, taken into account for the purpose of determining if there was provocation, the fact remains that words and gestures, in India, may, under certain circumstances, be treated to have caused 'grave and sudden provocation' to an accused so as to deprive him of his power of self-control and bring his act of killing within the first Exception to Section 300 IPC. The mental condition, which the 'previous act' of the victim might have caused to the accused, needs to be taken into account, while ascertaining if the 'subsequent act' of the deceased caused 'grave and sudden provocation'. What is, however, of immense importance to note is that a 'reasonable man' will differ from another according to social background and various other imponderables, such as, customs and traditions prevailing in his society, level of emotion etc. Describing the meaning and explaining the standard of 'reasonable man', the Supreme Court, in K.M. Nanavati v. State of Maharashtra AIR 1062 SC 605, observed as follows:

Is there any standard of a reasonable man for the application of the doctrine of "grave and sudden" provocation? No abstract standard of reasonableness can be laid down. What a reasonable man will do in certain circumstances depends upon the customs, manners, way of life, traditional values etc.; in short, the cultural, social and emotional background of the society to which an accused belongs. In our vast country there are social groups ranging from the lowest to the highest state of civilization. It is neither possible nor desirable to lay down any standard with precision: it is for the court to decide in each case, having regard to the relevant circumstances.

49. A crucial factor, in the defence of 'provocation' from earliest times, has been the relationship between the gravity of provocation and the way in which the accused retaliated, both being judged by the social standards of the day. As the law, in India, permits words being treated

as provocation, even though unaccompanied by any other act, the gravity of verbal provocation may well depend on the characteristics or circumstances of the person to whom a taunt or insult is addressed. To taunt a person, because of his race, his physical infirmities or some shameful incident in his past, may well be considered by the 'jury' to be offensive to the person addressed. (See Lord Diplock's observations in DPP v. Camplin (1978) 2 All E.R. 168). In fact, in Beddar v. DPP (1954) 2 All E.R. 801, the House of Lords had rejected as irrelevant the fact that the defendant had been taunted with impotence and, on having been so taunted, he had killed the deceased. Subsequent decision by the Privy Council, in Luc Thief Thuan V.R. 19962 All E.R. 1033, showed that the conclusion reached by the House of Lords in Beddar's case (supra) was not good law.

50. Laying down as to what constitutes 'grave and sudden' provocation and the tests therefor, the Supreme Court, in K.M. Nanavati (supra), held thus:

The Indian law, relevant to the present enquiry, may be stated thus: (1) The test of "grave and sudden" provocation is whether a reasonable man, belonging to the same class of society as the accused, placed in the situation in which the accused was placed would be so provoked as to lose his self-control. (2) In India, words and gestures may also, under certain circumstances, cause grave and sudden provocation to an accused so as to bring his act within the first Exception to Section 300 of the Indian Penal Code. (3) The mental background created by the previous act of the victim may be taken into consideration in ascertaining whether the subsequent act caused grave and sudden provocation for committing the offence. (4) The fatal blow should be clearly traced to the influence of passion arising from that provocation and not after the passion had cooled down by lapse of time, or otherwise giving room and scope for premeditation and calculation.

51. While considering the present writ appeal, it is worth pointing out that to a common man, killing of a man amounts to murder, though 'murder' is a well defined offence and every killing does not amount to 'murder'. To put it differently, there is really no difference to an ordinary man between the act of 'killing' and 'murder ', though the reality remains that every act of 'killing' may not amount to 'murder '. It is for this reason that Rule 78 of the BSF Rules provides that when an accused pleads 'guilty' to a charge, GSFC shall not, under Clause (c) of Sub-rule (2) of Rule 78, accept the plea of guilt of the accused if the accused is liable, on his conviction, to be sentenced to death. In other words, since a person, found 'guilty' of an offence of murder, can be sentenced to death, the GSFC is not permitted to accept the plea of guilt of an accused to the charge of murder and Rule 78 makes it mandatory for the GSFC, in such a case, to record the plea of guilt as 'not guilty" and proceed with the trial. These provisions have been made for the purpose of ensuring that a person, who is arraigned on a charge of murder under Section 302 IPC, is not convicted of such an offence if the offence does not really fall under Section 302 IPC in accordance with law, for, i t is possible that even though an accused has killed a person and has, in his opinion and in the opinion of common man, committed thereby the offence of 'murder', the act of killing may not, in law, amount to an, offence under Section 302 IPC, but an offence under Section 304 IPC.

52. In the case at hand, while the accused-respondent denied the charge and denied the fact that he had killed the deceased, what cannot be ignored is that the accused-respondent admitted that he had altercation with the deceased in the kitchen and following the altercation, which he so had with the deceased, the deceased had called him and challenged him and in order to meet this challenge, he did go out of the kitchen-room. What the accused-respondent, however, denied was that he was the one, who had killed the deceased; rather, his defence was that he, on going out of the kitchen-room, felt frightened and, therefore, went away; but while so going away, he fell down and sustained injury on his person. Notwithstanding this defence version, which may not have been believed by the GSFC, the fact remains that if there were any material to show that either the accused had acted in 'self-defence' or if there were any material to show that

the accused had acted under 'grave and sudden provocation', then, the act of the accused could not have fallen under Section 302 IPC, but under 304 IPC irrespective of the fact as to whether the accused had taken a specific plea of 'self-defence' or of his having acted under 'grave and sudden provocation' or not. So long as the evidence on record disclosed materials, which could attract an act of 'self-defence ' or of the accused having acted under 'grave and sudden provocation', it was the bounden duty of the Law Officer to have told the members of the GSFC, while summing up the case, that there is something called 'culpable homicide not amounting to murder', what this concept of 'culpable homicide not amounting to murder' is, and when an act of an accused becomes an act of 'culpable homicide not amounting to murder'.

53. The Law Officer, in the present case, as we notice, has not, while 'summing up' the case, brought to the notice of the members of the Court that they may consider if the case at hand was a case, which fell within the first Exception to Section 300 IPC. Though the case, as already indicated above, was, to a large extent, based on circumstantial evidence and the Law Officer, we find, had told the members of the Court as to what 'circumstantial evidence', in general, is, he did not tell the members of the Court as to when circumstantial evidence may be taken as proof of the killing of an accused and/or as to when a false explanation given by an accused can be used as an additional link. The Supreme Court, in Gambhir v. State of Maharastra , succinctly described as to when 'circumstantial evidence' can furnish basis for conviction of an accused. The observations of the Supreme Court, in Gambhir case (supra), run thus:

The law regarding circumstantial evidence is well-settled. When a case rests upon the circumstantial evidence, such evidence must satisfy three tests (1) the circumstances from which an inference of guilt is sought to be drawn, must be cogently and firmly established (2) those circumstances should be of a definite tendency unerringly pointing towards guilt of the accused; (3) the circumstances, taken cumulatively; should form a chain so complete that there is no escape from the conclusion that within all human probability the crime was committed by the accused and none else. The circumstantial evidence in order to sustain conviction must be complete and incapable of explanation of any other hypothesis than that of the guilt of the accused. The circumstantial evidence should not only be consistent with the guilt of the accused but should be inconsistent with his innocence.

54. In *Sharad Birdhichand Sarda v. State of Maharashtra*, the Apex Court has made it clear that the following conditions must be fulfilled before a case against an accused, based on circumstantial evidence, can be said to be fully satisfied:

(1) the circumstances from which the conclusion of guilt is to be drawn should be fully established, (2) the facts so established should be consistent only with the hypothesis of the guilt of the accused, that is to say, they should not be explainable on any other hypothesis except that the accused is guilty, (3) the circumstances should be of a conclusive nature and tendency.

(4) they should exclude every possible hypothesis except the one to be proved, and (5) there must be a chain of evidence so complete as not to leave any reasonable ground for the conclusion consistent with the innocence of the accused and must show that in all human probability the act must have been done by the accused.

55. The Law Officer, we notice, advised the members of the Court thus, "In the definition of the term "proved", no distinction is drawn between circumstantial evidence and direct evidence. In certain cases, circumstantial evidence is superior to direct evidence, for, it has become proverb that, "Facts cannot lie, whilst witnesses may". On the other hand, gentleman, it may also be borne in mind that, "If facts cannot lie, they may often deceive." Therefore, before judging an accused guilty on circumstantial evidence, the Court must be satisfied not only that circumstances are consistent with the accused having

committed the act, but also that they are inconsistent with any other rational conclusion."

56. From the above advice tendered by the Law Officer, it is apparent that while the Law officer did tell the members of the Court that the circumstances must be consistent with the guilt of the accused and must be inconsistent with his innocence, he did not tell them that before 'circumstantial evidence' is acted upon as basis for conviction of an accused, the 'circumstantial evidence' must not only be consistent with the guilt of the accused and inconsistent with his innocence, but that every reasonable hypothesis of innocence of the accused needs to be excluded. In the present case, since it was an admitted case of the parties that the occurrence took place in pitch darkness of the night, the Law Officer ought to have pointed out that it is the duty of the members of the Court to exclude the possibility of the accused having acted in his 'self-defence', for, the person of the accused bore injuries, he had not carried any knife or dagger, while going out of the kitchen, and, hence, he might have acted in his self-defence, though, while acting in his self-defence, he might have exceeded the right of his self-defence. The Law Officer also did not tell the members of the Court that it is their duty, in the facts and circumstances of the present case, to consider if the accused had been provoked by the words, acts and/or gesture of the deceased and the 'provocation' was so 'grave and sudden' that it could have deprived a person, placed in the situation in which the accused was found placed, of his power of self-control leading him to cause stab wounds on the person of the deceased.

57. We also cannot ignore the fact that the Law Officer has not advised the members of the Court as regards the 'standard of proof' expected from an accused in a case of present nature. The Law Officer ought to have told the Court that the accused need not discharge his burden beyond reasonable doubt and that it was enough, if the accused probablised his plea, either by adducing evidence or on the basis of the evidence already present on record, that he (accused) had acted in 'self defence' or under 'grave and sudden provocation'. The Law Officer ought to have explained, in terms of Section 3 of the Evidence Act, that a fact is said to be 'proved' when, after considering the matter before it, the Court either believes it to exist or consider its non-existence so probable that a prudent man ought, under the circumstances of the particular case, to act upon the supposition that it exists.

58. The Law Officer, we find, did not explain to the members of the Court as to what the evidentiary value of a statement recorded, at the time of preparation of the 'record of evidence', is. A 'record of evidence ', it needs to be borne in mind, is a misnomer, for, it is not evidence as explained in Section 3 of the Evidence Act. A record of evidence is prepared at the stage of investigation. Though it is called the 'record of evidence', the fact remains that what is stated, at the stage of investigation, is not really evidence. A statement, which is recorded at the stage of investigation, is not on oath and such a statement, though called record of evidence, stands on the same footing as does a previous statement of a witness recorded by police during investigation under Section 161 CrPC. Such a previous statement of a witness is not substantive evidence and can be used by the prosecution, with the leave of the Court, to contradict the testimony of the witness at the trial, and the defence can use such a statement, as a matter of right, for the purpose of contradicting the witness. No reliance can be placed on the previous statement of a witness or of an accused nor can a conviction be founded on such previous statements.

59. Sub-sections (6) and (7) of Section 97 of the BSF Act make it clear that a person may be held guilty of a lesser offence meaning thereby that though a person may have been charged with an offence under Section 302 IPC, he may be found guilty and convicted accordingly under Section 304 IPC. The Law Officer, in the present case, did not tell the members of the Court that if the acts of the accused did not amount to the offence of 'murder', the Court must consider if the accused had killed the deceased and whether his act of 'killing' fell under Section 304 IPC. The members of the Court were not told at all as to what offence, if any, a person commits if he, under 'grave and

sudden provocation', loses power of self-control and kills a person: This aspect of the law was not at all told to the members of the Court.

60. It is also of immense importance to note that in the present case, the medical evidence on record shows that on conducting post-mortem on the dead body of Constable Charbaran Ram, the doctor found the following three injuries:

(i) Cut injury on the left side of the neck 1" x below the (L) Ear 2" x 1/2"

(ii) Cut injury (3"x 1/2 ") on the (L) Temporal region.

(iii) Cut injury 2" x 1/2 "on the (L) Chest wall below the (L) Nipple In mid clavicular line.

61. It is in the evidence of the doctor that these type of injuries could be caused by some sharp edged weapon. In the opinion of the doctor, the cause of death was due to excessive bleeding from the cut injury of left carotid artery leading to shock and cardio-respiratory failure, the age of injuries being around 15 to 17 hrs and that the injuries were ante-mortem in nature.

62. In his cross-examination, the doctor has clarified that a layman cannot recognize carotid artery, but if he happens to cut it or cause injury on it, it might be by chance or by accident.

63. The medical evidence on record clearly shows that the fatal injury sustained by the deceased might not have been necessarily intentional, but even accidental. When the oral evidence on record is considered, in the light of the medical evidence on record, it clearly follows that even if the deceased had sustained injuries at the hands of the accused, the fact remains that there is no evidence on record to show that the accused went out of the kitchen- room with a knife or any weapon in his hand or that the weapon (which was used as the weapon of assault) was a weapon carried to the place of occurrence by the accused nor is there any evidence to show that the accused could have seen as to where he was stabbing even if one were to believe the prosecution's

case that the accused was the assailant; rather, the evidence on record speaks loud and clear that the place of occurrence was under pitch darkness. In such circumstances, it was the bounden duty of the Law Officer to tell the members of the Court the law with regard to 'self-defence' and also with regard to 'grave and sudden provocation' so that the members of the Court could have determined for themselves if the accused had intentionally killed the deceased or he had killed him in his self-defence, though he might have exceeded the right of self-defence. The Law Officer did not tell the members of the Court to determine if the deceased had provoked the accused and if so, the provocation was so grave and sudden that it could have deprived a person, placed in the circumstances in which was placed the accused, of his power of self-control. The members of the Court ought to have been told by the Law Officer that, while considering this aspect of the case, it is necessary for the Court to bear in mind the social background and standard of the accused, for, two persons, coming from two different social background, may not act or react similarly. The standard of the society to which an accused belongs and the standard of the society to which a judge belongs may well be different. It is, therefore, necessary, as observed in K.M. Nanavati (supra), that a Judge must place himself in the position of the accused and decide, in the backdrop of the social background of the accused, if the accused could have been provoked to such a level that his act falls within the ambit of Exception I to Section 300 IPC.

64. What crystallizes from the above discussion is that the summing up of the case at hand by the Law Officer was highly unsatisfactory and full of legal infirmities. In the face of such serious legal infirmities, one has no option, but to hold that the trial held was not in accordance with law and the procedural safeguards given to the accused was, most improperly, denied to him. We are wholly satisfied that in the present case, the accused did not receive a 'fair trial' and that there was serious failure of justice in the present case.

65. The question, now, is as to whether the High Court could have interfered with the conviction of the accused in exercise of its power under Article 226 and if so, what ought to have been the directions by the Court.

66. While considering the above aspect of the case, it may be pointed out that though the High Court cannot sit as a court of appeal on the verdict of the GSFC, it is the duty of the High Court to ascertain, when the finding and sentence of a GSFC are challenged before it, if the decision making process suffers from any such legal infirmity, which can be treated to have caused prejudice to the accused. Since the judicial review is not directed against the decision, but against the decision making-process, it logically follows that the High Court will not look into the merit of the decision, but only determine if the decision has been reached by complying with the relevant provisions of law and in accordance with the procedure prescribed for the trial.

67. In the case at hand, the relevant provisions of law, as indicated above, were not taken into account or adhered to and this has resulted into failure of justice. But the present one is not a case, we are satisfied, which can be said to be a case of no evidence. Having considered the evidence on record, we do not find that one can say that there was no incriminating evidence against the accused-respondent. In such circumstances, the remedy lied in remanding the case for trial by the learned Court below with direction to the Law Officer to sum up the case in accordance with law. Instead of doing so, the learned Single Judge, we find, set aside the conviction and sentence passed against the accused-respondent and set him at liberty completely.

68. The fall-out of the above discussion is that while the conviction of the accused-respondent and the sentence passed against him cannot be sustained, the impugned order, dated 20.06.1997, passed in Civil Rule No. 444/89, can also not survive.

69. In the result, and for the reason discussed above, this appeal partly succeeds. While the order of the learned Single Judge setting aside the

finding and sentence is not interfered with, the case is remanded to the Inspector General of Border Security Force for convening a General Security Force Court and proceed with the trial from the stage of summing up of the case by the Law Officer. In view of the fact that it is possible that some members of the Court or even the Law Officer may have retired, the respondent authority shall remain at liberty to convene a General Security Force Court with such new members and Law Officer, as may be necessary in order to hold the trial from the stage as indicated hereinabove.

2. GSFC- FINDING, CONVICTION AND SENTENCE AWARDED BY GSFC MODIFIED BY SUPREME COURT

2.1 JUDGEMENT DATED 14.06.2022 IN CIVIL APPEAL NO 2606 OF 2012 TITLED EX. CT. MAHADEV vs THE DIRECTOR GENERAL BSF

"1. The appellant is aggrieved by the judgement dated 3 rd March, 2011 passed by the Division Bench of the High Court of Delhi dismissing a writ petition filed by him, registered as WP(C)No.6709/2008, wherein he had challenged the order dated 19th March, 2008 passed by the respondent No.4 herein convicting him to life imprisonment for an offence committed under Section 46 of the Border Security Force Act, 1968 1 , that is to say for murder punishable under Section 302 of the Indian Penal Code, 1860 2. By the impugned order, the Division Bench has upheld the order passed by the respondent No.2 - Appellate Authority, whereby the statutory appeal filed by the appellant was 1 for short 'BSF Act' 2 for short 'IPC' dismissed and the order dated 10th March, 2007 passed by the General Security Force Court was upheld.

…………………………………………………….

4. For arriving at the aforesaid conclusion, the High Court has primarily relied on the testimony of Dr. Ranjit Kumar Das (PW-10), who had conducted the postmortem on the body of the deceased and deposed that he had died due to firearm injuries and two bullets had pierced his body. It was noticed that PW-10 had deposed that having regard to the nature and place of the injuries, the position of the firer as against that of the deceased was such that the one who would have fired the shot, must have been on an elevated position compared to the victim since the direction of the bullets were from above the chest, going downwards and backward. Going by the said testimony read along with the testimony of SI Shanti Bhushan Bhuiya (PW-13), who had deposed that when he saw the dead body, both the legs were in a folded position, the High Court arrived at the conclusion that the appellant had made the deceased to crouch down and thereafter, had fired two shots at him.

5. Mr. Lalit Kumar, learned counsel for the appellant argued that the High Court has erred in concurring with the findings of the GSFC and discarding the defence taken by the appellant that he was compelled to exercise his right of private defence to save his life when suddenly confronted with intruders who were armed with weapons and had 'gheraoed' him. He alluded to the topography of the Rubber plantation where the incident had taken place, which was admittedly uneven with depressions and undulations, to urge that merely because the deceased was found with his legs in a folded position, could not be a ground to indict the appellant having regard to the fact that even as per the version of CT H. Vijay Kumar (PW-1), the eye-witness who was patrolling in the area along with the appellant, the latter was positioned at a higher level vis-à-vis the deceased and therefore, it was but natural that on his firing from his rifle, the bullets would have hit the deceased on the upper part of his body as he was positioned at a lower level. It is in this manner that learned counsel for the appellant has sought to explain the path of the bullets that had pierced the body of the deceased and indicated that the shots were fired by the appellant taking a downward angle and not face on face.

6. Learned counsel for the appellant also referred to the testimony of Sapan Das (PW-2) and other prosecution witnesses to submit that villagers in the area being close to the border of Bangladesh, used to

regularly indulge in smuggling activities and even the deceased used to do so. He pointed out that this fact had not only been deposed by PW-1, but also by SI (M) Suresh Kumar Dagar (PW-17), who during his cross- examination, had stated in so many words that since the deployment of 131 Battalion, BSF and prior to the incident in question, trans-border criminals had attacked BSF personnel seven times and most of the times, they had to use force by opening fire in self-defence and the defence of property. In fact, the deceased had been apprehended for indulging in smuggling activities and his name features in the list of smugglers maintained by the BSF. He also adverted to the fact that currency worth 24,700 Bangladeshi Takas was recovered from the shirt pocket of the deceased along with a 'Dah' that was found lying at the spot next his body. The point sought to be made was that in the above backdrop, the High Court ought not to have discarded the testimony of PW-1 and PW-17 to arrive at a conclusion that this was a case of cold-blooded murder committed by the appellant whereas he had acted in the heat of the moment, purely in his self defence.

7. Per contra, Ms. Aishwarya Bhati, learned Additional Solicitor General, appearing for the respondents – Union of India, has stoutly defended the findings returned by the GSFC and upheld the High Court. She submitted that the High Court cannot be faulted for disbelieving the testimony of PW-1, an eye-witness to the incident who was on duty at the Rubber plantation along with the appellant on the fateful day. It is her contention that the findings of the GSFC are sound and reliance has rightly been placed on the testimonies of the local villagers, namely, Sapan Das (PW-2), another witness by the name of Sapan Das (PW-3), Tapan Das (PW-4) and Sunil Das (PW-5), who had stated that the appellant had summoned the deceased and then shot at him twice without any provocation. She submitted that the testimony of the doctor (PW-10) was a clincher and left no manner of doubt that the appellant had made the deceased to kneel down and thereafter fired two shots directly at him, causing his death.

....

18. The situation in which the plea of a right to private defence would be available to the accused was discussed by this Court in Bhanwar Singh and Others v. State of Madhya Pradesh14 and it was held thus :

"50. The plea of private defence has been brought up by the appellants. For this plea to succeed in totality, it must be proved that there existed a right to private defence in favour of the accused, and that this right ex - tended to causing death. Hence, if the court were to reject this plea, there are two possible ways in which this may be done. On one hand, it may be held that there existed a right to private defence of the body. However, more harm than necessary was caused or, alternatively, this right did not extend to causing death. Such a ruling may result in the application of Section 300 Exception 2, which states that culpable homicide is not mur- der if the offender, in the exercise in good faith of the right of private de - fence of person or property, exceeds the power given to him by law and 14 (2008) 16 SCC 657 causes the death of the person against whom he is exercising such right of defence without premeditation, and without any intention of doing more harm than is necessary for the purpose of such defence. The other situa -

tion is where, on appreciation of facts, the right of private defence is held not to exist at all.

xxx

"60. To put it pithily, the right of private defence is a defence right. It is nei- ther a right of aggression or of reprisal. There is no right of private defence where there is no apprehension of danger. The right of private defence is available only to one who is suddenly confronted with the necessity of averting an impending danger not of self-creation. Necessity must be present, real or apparent."

19. The principles underlying the doctrine of right to private defence have been neatly summed up in the captioned case in the following words :-

"61. The basic principle underlying the doctrine of the right of private de- fence is that when an individual or his property is faced with a danger and immediate aid from the State machinery is not readily available, that indi- vidual is entitled to protect himself and his property. That being so, the necessary corollary is that the violence which the citizen defending himself or his property is entitled to use must not be unduly disproportionate to the injury which is sought to be averted or which is reasonably apprehended and should not exceed its legitimate purpose. We may, however, hasten to add that the means and the force a threatened person adopts on the spur of the moment to ward off the danger and to save himself or his property cannot be weighed in golden scales. It is neither possible nor prudent to lay down abstract parameters which can be applied to determine as to whether the means and force adopted by the threatened person was proper or not. Answer to such a question depends upon a host of factors like the prevailing circumstances at the spot, his feelings at the relevant time; the confusion and the excitement depending on the nature of assault on him, etc. Nonetheless, the exercise of the right of private defence can never be vindictive or malicious. It would be repugnant to the very concept of private defence. (See Dharam v. State of Haryana15)" 15 (2007) 15 SCC 241

20. In Raj Singh v. State of Haryana and Others 16, supplementing the view of Justice R. Banumathi, who had authored the decision on behalf of a three Judges Bench, Justice T.S. Thakur had the following to state on the application of the provisions of Exception 2 to Section 300 IPC where an accused sets up the right to private defence :

"32. A conjoint reading of the provisions of Sections 96 to 103 and Exception 2 to Section 300 IPC leaves no manner of doubt that culpable homicide is not murder if the offender, in the exercise in good faith of the right of private defence of person or property, exceeds the power given to him by law and causes the death of the person against whom he is exercising such right of defence, provided that such right is exercised without premeditation and without any intention of doing

more harm than is necessary for the purpose of such defence. A fortiori in cases where an accused sets up right of private defence, the first and the foremost question that would fall for determination by the court would be whether the accused had the right of private defence in the situation in which death or other harm was caused by him. If the answer to that question is in the negative, Exception 2 to Section 300 IPC would be of no assistance. Exception 2 presupposes that the offender had the right of private defence of person or property but he had exceeded such right by causing death. It is only in case answer to the first question is in the affirmative viz. that the offender had the right of defence of person or property, that the next question viz. whether he had exercised that right in good faith and without premeditation and without any intention of doing more harm than was necessary for the purpose of such defence would arise. Should answer to any one of these questions be in the negative, the offender will not be entitled to the benefit of Exception 2 to Section 300 IPC.

33. Absence of good faith in the exercise of the right of private defence, premeditation for the exercise of such right and acts done with the intention of causing more harm than is necessary for the purpose of such defence would deny to the offender the benefit of Exception 2 to Section 300 IPC. The legal position on the subject is fairly well settled by a long line of decisions of this Court to which copious reference has been made 16 (2015) 6 SCC 268 by Banumathi, J. No useful purpose would, therefore, be served by referring to them over again. All that need be said is that whether or not a right of private defence of person or property was available to the offender is the very first question that must be addressed in a case of the present kind while determining the nature of the offence committed by the accused, whether or not a right of private defence was available to an offender is, in turn, a question of fact or at least a mixed question of law and fact to be determined in the facts and circumstances of each individual case that may come up before the court."

21. To sum up, the right of private defence is necessarily a defensive right which is available only when the circumstances so justify it. The circumstances are those that have been elaborated in the IPC. Such a right would be available to the accused when he or his property is faced with a danger and there is little scope of the State machinery coming to his aid. At the same time, the courts must keep in mind that the extent of the violence used by the accused for defending himself or his property should be in proportion to the injury apprehended. This is not to say that a step to step analysis of the injury that was apprehended and the violence used is required to be undertaken by the Court; nor is it feasible to prescribe specific parameters for determining whether the steps taken by the accused to invoke private self-defence and the extent of force used by him was proper or not. The Court's assessment would be guided by several circumstances including the position on the spot at the relevant point in time, the nature of apprehension in the mind of the accused, the kind of situation that the accused was seeking to ward off, the confusion created by the situation that had suddenly cropped up resulting the in knee jerk reaction of the accused, the nature of the overt acts of the party who had threatened the accused resulting in his resorting to immediate defensive action, etc. The underlying factor should be that such an act of private defence should have been done in good faith and without malice.

22. Being mindful of the afore-stated parameters, we may examine the plea of self- defence raised by the appellant in the attending facts and circumstances of the case. The factum of rampant smuggling in the area has not been disputed by either side. The records reveal that border fencing in the area in question had been erected just a few months before the incident had taken place. Prior to that, many villagers used to freely indulge in smuggling activities by crossing over to the Bangladesh side and vice versa. A couple of months after the fencing had been fixed along the International border with Bangladesh, there was an incident where smugglers had assaulted one of the members of the Battalion when he was trying to prevent them from crossing the border. That the deceased used to indulge in smuggling activities and his name was mentioned in the list of smugglers maintained by the BSF, is also a matter of record.

23. Viewed in the above setting, we may proceed to examine the statement by way of defence made by the appellant which has been extracted at some length in the impugned judgment. He has stated at the relevant time, that he was posted at BOP Bamutia, Tripura, which is adjoining to the border of Bangladesh. While on patrolling duty in the early hours of 5 th June, 2004, he admitted to have fired from his rifle at one Nandan Deb, who died as a result of the firearm injuries. The version of the appellant was that when he was patrolling along with CT H. Vijay Kumar (PW-1), in the Rubber plantation, an area with depressions and undulations on the ground surface, he had noticed 6-7 persons crossing over from Bangladesh by cutting across the International border. They had tried to 'gherao' him and PW-1. They were armed with weapons like "Bhala', 'Dah' and 'Lathi'. Seeing himself cornered, the appellant started to retreat. But the intruders kept closing him and were in or at a distance of ten yards. Faced with such a precarious situation where the appellant gathered an impression that the intruders were going to attack him any minute, fearing for his life, the appellant fired two rounds in the air. This did not deter the intruders who kept on inching closer to the appellant. When one of the intruders, namely, Nandan Deb came as close as 3-4 yards from him and tried to attack him by raising his 'Dah', apprehending an imminent and perceptible threat to his life, the appellant fired at him due to which he fell on the ground. While, the other miscreants fled away to Bangladesh, Nandan Deb collapsed at the spot and was declared dead.

25. On a broad conspectus of the events as they had unfolded, we are of the opinion that the right of private self defence would be available to the appellant keeping in mind preponderance of probabilities that leans in favour of the appellant. In a fact situation where he was suddenly confronted by a group of intruders, who had come menacingly close to him, were armed with weapons and ready to launch an assault on him, he was left with no other option but to save his life by firing at them from his rifle and in the process two of the shots had pierced through the deceased, causing his death. We are therefore of the opinion that the appellant ought not to have been convicted for having committed the murder of the deceased. Rather, the offence made out is of culpable homicide not amounting to murder under Exception 2 to Section 300 IPC, thereby attracting the provisions of Section 304 IPC.

26. In view of the aforesaid discussion, the appeal is partly allowed and the impugned judgment is modified to the extent that the appellant is held guilty for the offence of culpable homicide, not amounting to murder as contemplated under Exception 2 to Section 300 IPC. Records reveal that by the time the appellant was granted bail by this Court on 4 th July, 2016, he had already suffered incarceration for a period of over eleven years, which given the peculiar facts and circumstances of the present case, is considered sufficient punishment for the offence. The appellant is accordingly set free for the period already undergone and the bail bonds stand discharged.

2.2 Judgement dated 18 October, 2005 in Civil Appeal 4792 of 1999 titled Union of India & Ors vs Ashok Kumar & Ors

"2. Both these appeals have matrix in a judgment rendered by a Division Bench of the Jammu & Kashmir High Court in a Letters Patent Appeal filed by Ashok Kumar, the respondent in Civil Appeal No. 4792 of 1999 and the appellant in the connected appeal. For the sake of convenience said Ashok Kumar is described hereinafter as the 'delinquent officer'. By the impugned judgment the High Court held that the removal of the delinquent officer from service was in violation of the provisions contained in Section 10 of the Border Security Force Act, 1968 (in short 'the Act') read with Rule 20 of the Border Security Force Rules, 1969 (in short 'the Rules'). The appeal filed by the delinquent officer was allowed upsetting the judgment of the learned Single Judge who had dismissed the writ petition filed by the delinquent officer.

3. *Factual position, filtering out unnecessary details, is as follows :*

There was a raid in the house of militants on 23rd and 24th March, 1992. The delinquent officer being Deputy Inspector General in Command was having Supervisory power over the Commandant who raided the hideout of militants. On the night intervening 23rd and 24th March 1992 house of one Mohd. Maqbool Dhar in Bemina Colony of Srinagar was raided by 23 men of the force. During the raid two militants described as 'dreaded militants' namely Javed Ahmed Shalla and Mohd. Siddiqui Soffi were apprehended. According to the authorities huge quantity of arms, ammunitions and explosives and household articles including gold ornaments were recovered. The recovery of arms, ammunition and explosives and gold ornaments were not reflected in the seizure report sent to higher authorities. Respondent was not present at the spot and he indicated is presence at the scene of operation with a view to claim undue credit of achievements of the operation. Full quantity of seized articles was not reflected in the report. 31 major weapons were recovered but only 22 were shown. Two pistols, five AK-56 rifles, one rocket launcher and one Telescopic Rifle were not shown in the list of ammunition. Out of 31 gold ornaments 25 pieces were not shown in the list of seized articles. Second situation Report was also sent, but the same also did not reflect recovery of complete articles. To cover up these lapses another encounter was shown to have taken place and a report regarding fake encounter was sent vide No. 0-7209 which indicated the recovery of some gold ornaments. Another report was also sent from office of delinquent officer declaring goods which were not declared earlier. It was admitted that recovery of some weapons was not reflected in earlier report. Therefore, a Staff Court of Inquiry was ordered to be held on 16th May, 1992 and the delinquent officer was found responsible for following act of omission and commission :

(a) Falsely showing his presence at the scene of operation and search.

(b) Failure to make any observations regarding serious omissions and discrepancies in the unit site report and detailed report.

(c) Suppression of information regarding seizure of six weapons out of nine which were not declared by the Commandant.

(d) Suppression of information regarding seizure of household items.

(e) Suppression of information regarding seizure of a substantial quantity of gold ornaments.

(f) Failure in supervisory duties by not giving expected directions to the Commandant in regard to accounting and disposal of seized items.

4. On 18.9.1992 Director-General recorded his satisfaction that the material witnesses connected with case will not be available and as such the trial of the delinquent officer before Security Force Court was inexpedient and impracticable and opined that further retention of the delinquent officer in service was undesirable.

..

13. The High Court is plainly in error in holding that it is only the Central Government which is competent to act in terms of sub-rule (2). Expression "as the case may be" is otherwise rendered superfluous. Both the authorities can act in terms of sub-rule (2). High Court overlooked the salient factor that any other interpretation would render reference to the Director-General meaningless.

14. A bare reading of Rule 20 makes the position clear that both the Director-General and the Central Government can act in different situations and consideration by the Director-General is not ruled out. Sub-rule (3) makes the position clear that the explanation is to be considered by the Director-General and only when it is directed by the Central Government, the matter shall be submitted to the Central Government with the officer's defence and the recommendations of the Director-General. When Director-General finds the explanation unsatisfactory he recommends for action. There may be cases where the Central Government directs the Director-General to submit the case. There can be a case where the Central Government finds that the explanation is unsatisfactory. In that case the Central Government may direct the case to be submitted to it. At the first stage the consideration is by the Director-General. When he finds the explanation unsatisfactory, he recommends action by the Central Government. But even if he finds explanation to be satisfactory, yet the Central Government can direct the case to be submitted to it. Recommendations in terms of sub-rule (4) are made by the Director-General and the final order under Rule 20(5) is passed by the Central Government. The expression "as the case may be" is used in sub-rule (2) and sub-rule (5). It obviously means either of the two. It is to be further noted that the order in terms of sub-rule (5) is passed by the Central Government. But the enquiry can be either by the Central Government or the Director-General, as the case may be. There is another way of looking at sub-rule (2). Where report of the officer's misconduct is made by the Director- General, the matter is to be placed before the Central Government and in all other cases the consideration is by the Director-General.

15. The words "as the case may be" means "whichever the case may be" or "as the situation may be". (See Shri Balaganesan Metals v. M.N. Shanmugham Chetty and Ors., 1987(2) SCC 707). The expression means that one out of the various alternatives would apply to one out of the various situations and not otherwise.

16. Therefore, the High Court's conclusions that Central Government is the only authority to consider the matter whether holding of trial is inexpedient or impracticable is clearly indefensible.

17. Coming to the conclusion whether there was application of mind, the High Court had perused the concerned file and come to the conclusion that there was independent application of mind in passing the order of removal. Though in the appeal filed by the delinquent officer the order of removal is assailed on the ground that only the Desk Officer's opinion was endorsed without application of mind, we do not find the situation to be so. Copies of the entire file were produced before us. It is clearly indicative of the fact that though the Desk Officer's opinion was noted, there was independent application of mind and, therefore, the plea of the delinquent officer that the order suffers from the vice of non-application of mind is clearly untenable. Similarly, we find the plea of mala-fides does not appear to have been pressed before the High Court, and grievance related to other respondents and the personal allegations of mala-fides do not appear to have been urged.

18. Doubtless, he who seeks to invalidate or nullify any act or order must establish the charge of bad faith, an abuse or a misuse by the authority of its powers. While the indirect motive or purpose, or bad faith or personal ill-will is not to be held established except on clear proof thereof, it is obviously difficult to establish the state of a man's mind, for that is what the employee has to establish in this case, though this may sometimes be done. The difficulty is not lessened when one has to establish that a person apparently acting on the legitimate exercise of power has, in fact, been acting mala fide in the sense of pursuing an illegitimate aim. It is not the law that mala fide in the sense of improper motive should be established only by direct evidence. But it must be discernible from the order impugned or must be shown from the established surrounding factors which preceded the order. If bad faith would vitiate the order, the same can, in our opinion, be deduced as a reasonable and inescapable inference from proved facts. (S. Pratap Singh v. State of Punjab, AIR 1964 Supreme Court 72). It cannot be overlooked that burden of establishing mala fides is very heavy on the person who alleges it. The allegations of mala fides are often more easily made than proved, and the very seriousness of such allegations demand proof of a high order of credibility. As noted by this Court in E.P. Royappa v. State of Tamil Nadu and Another, (AIR 1974 Supreme Court 555), Courts would be slow to draw dubious inferences from incomplete facts placed before it by a party, particularly when the imputations are grave and they are made against the holder of an office which has a high responsibility in the administration. (See Indian Railway Construction Co. Ltd. v. Ajay

Kumar, 2003(2) SCT 291 (SC) : 2003(4) SCC 579). As observed by this Court in Gulam Mustafa and Ors. v. The State of Maharashtra and Ors., (1976(1) SCC 800) mala fide is the last refuge of a losing litigant. That being so, the delinquent officer's appeal is sans merit.

19. The inevitable conclusion is that the appeal filed by the Union of India deserves to be allowed. The judgment of the Division Bench taking the view contrary to that of learned Single Judge in its analysis of Rule 20 deserves to be set aside, which we direct. Similarly, the other appeal filed by the delinquent officer lacks merit and is dismissed. In the peculiar circumstances of the case, parties are directed to bear their respective costs.

Appeal dismissed.

3. NON COMPLIANCE OF RULE 45 B OF BSF RULES

3.1 Union Of India (Uoi) And Ors. vs B.N. Jha on 7 March, 2003 AIR 2003 SC 1416

1. *The Border Security Force (BSF) has a Training center and School (TCS) in the District of Hazaribagh. The said training center is one of the units of the BSF. It has several wings, namely, Admn. Wing, BTC (Basic Training center), STS (Specialist Training School) and STC (Subsidiary Training center) etc. All the wings of TCS are said to be located in the same premises.*
2. *The respondent herein was a Deputy Commandant in the TCS. The Unit Commandant of TCS happened to be one Mr. B.S. Garcha. In or about July, 1990 the respondent was accused of having received gratification from two persons, namely, B.K. Jha and Santosh Jha for procuring their recruitment as constables in the BSF which was discovered in the following circumstances.*
3. *On 17.7.1990 a sum of Rs. 1700/- was said to have been stolen from the said B.K. Jha. Allegedly,he gave out that the respondent had accepted a sum of Rs. 5,000/- for his recruitment. On 16.7.1990 one Mr. Raj Singh, Deputy Commandant reported to the Commandant, Mr. J.S. Bakshi that the said B.K. Jha had stated in presence of one*

Mr. G.S. Rana that he had brought out a sum of Rs. 8,500/from his house out of which he was, as per instruction of his father, to pay a sum of Rs. 7,000/- for his recruitment but he in fact paid a sum of Rs. 5,000/- to the respondent a week prior to the date of offence. One Constable of the Administrative Wing had allegedly came to him to collect money for the respondent and he had paid a further sum of Rs. 1,000/-. Mr. J.S. Bakshi at about 0930 hours on 17.7.1990 informed Mr. Garcha that the respondent came to his office and apologized for having taken the money. Mr. Garcha asked Mr. Bakshi to inquire into the matter further who thereupon submitted his report by way of a letter.

4. *Mr. Garcha allegedly examined the said two persons as also the respondent. An alleged confessionabout the commission of the office is said to have been made before him by the respondent herein. He was thereafter posted in BTC.*

....

13. Mr. Ranjit Kumar, the learned senior counsel appearing on behalf of the appellant had taken us through the Border Security force Act and the Rules framed thereunder and contended that in terms of the scheme of the Act sufficient procedural safeguards are provided to the delinquent. A finding on the guilt of the accused is reached after three different stages of filtration which an independent of each other. In each of the aforementioned stage, Mr. Ranjit Kumar would submit, the accused gets an opportunity to cross-examine the witnesses and the authority on the basis of the materials brought on record at each of the stage, may drop the proceedings against him. The learned counsel would contend that the learned Single Judge committed a manifest error in reappreciating the evidence which was not within the domain of the High Court exercising its jurisdiction under Article 226 of the Constitution of India having regard to the settled principle of law that it does not exercise any power of superintendence over the Courts constituted under the Army Act, BSF Act and in that view of the matter it could not have reappreciated the evidence. The learned counsel would contend that admittedly Mr. M.S. Arya was a Commandant of

BTC which being a unit to which the respondent was attached he was entitled to direct recording of evidence in terms of the Act and the Rules. According to the learned counsel. Mr. Garcha being a Deputy Inspector General of Police could have further asked the Commandant of a Unit to take disciplinary measures against the respondent both in terms of Rule 46 as also Rule 16(7) of the Rules.

14. Mr. Sharma, the learned counsel appearing on behalf of the respondent, on the other hand, would submit that admittedly Mr. Garcha was biased against the respondent. He was a witness in the trial and in fact he examined himself as PW 13. In that view of the matter the learned counsel would contend, in fairness he ought to have referred the matter to the Headquarters for attaching the respondent to another Unit. BTC being not a unit but merely a wing of TCS, Mr. Sharma would urge, Mr. M.S. Arya had no jurisdiction in the matter as a consequence whereof all proceedings subsequent thereto were rendered invalid.

15. Before embarking upon the rival contentions of the parties, we may notice the following provisions of the Border Security Force Act.

"2(1)(f) "Commandant", when used in any provision of this Act with reference to any unit of the Force, means the officer whose duty it is under the rules to discharge with respect to that unit, the functions of a Commandant in regard to matters of the description referred to in that provision;

2(1)(h) "Deputy Inspector-General" means a Deputy Inspector-General of the Force appointed under Section 5;

2(1)(n) "Inspector-General" means the Inspector-General of the Force appointed under Section 5;

5. Control, direction etc. (1) The general superintendence, direction and control of the Force shall vest in, and be exercised by, the Central Government and subject thereto and to the provisions of this Act and the rules, the command and supervision of the Force shall vest in an officer to be appointed by the Central Government as the Director-General of the Force.

(2) The Director-General shall, in the discharge of his duties under this Act, be assisted by such number of Inspector-General, Deputy Inspectors-General, Commandants and other officers as may be prescribed by the Central Government.

41. Miscellaneous offences--Any person subject to this Act who commits any of the following offences, that is to say-

(a) ...

(b) ...

(c) ...

(d) ...

(e) directly or indirectly accepts or obtains, or agrees to accept, or attempts to obtain, for himself or for any other preson, any gratification as a motive or reward for procuring the enrolment of any person, or leave of absence, promotion or any other advantage or indulgence for any person in the service; or

(f) ...

shall, on conviction by a Security Force Court, be liable to suffer imprisonment for a term which may extend to seven years or such less punishment as is in this Act mentioned.

48. Punishments awardable by Security Force Courts: (1) Punishments may be inflicted in respect of offences committed by persons subject to this Act and convicted by Security Force Courts according to the scale following, that is to say-

1(c) dismissal from the service;

44. Charge Sheet--Where it is alleged that an officer or a Subordinate Officer has committed an offence punishable under the Act, the allegation shall be reduced to writing in the form set out in Appendix VI.

45B. Hearing of charge against an officer and a subordinate officer:-

(1)(a) The charge against an officer or subordinate officer shall be heard by his Commandant: Provided that charge against a Commandant, a Deputy Inspector-General or an Inspector-General may be heard either by an officer commanding a Unit or Headquarters to which the accused may be posted or attached or by his Deputy Inspector-General, or his Inspector-General or, as the case may be, the Director-General.

(b) The charge sheet and statements of witnesses if recorded and relevant documents, if any shall be read over to the accused: Provided that where written statements of witnesses are not available the officer hearing the charge shall hear as many witnesses as he may consider essential to enable him to know about the case.

(c) The accused shall be given an opportunity to make a statement in his defence.

(2) After hearing the charge under Sub-rule (1), the officer who heard the charge may-

(i) dismiss the charge; or

(ii) remand the accused, for preparation of a record of evidence or preparation of abstract of evidence against the accused;

Provided that he shall dismiss the charge if in his opinion the charge is not proved or may dismiss it if he considers that because of the previous character of the accused and the nature of the charge against him, it is not advisable to proceed further with it;

Provided further that in case of all offences punishable with death, a record of evidence shall be prepared.

46. Attachment to another unit--The Commandant shall not deal with any case-

(i) where the offence with which the accused is charged is against the Commandant himself; or

(ii) where the Commandant it himself a witness in the case against the accused; or

(iii) where the Commandant is otherwise personally interested in the case and the accused shall be attached to another battalion or unit for disposal of the case under the order of the Deputy Inspector General:

Provided that a Commandant shall not be disqualified from hearing a charge merely because the offence was committed against the property of a Force Mess, band or institution of which the Commandant is a member or trustee or because of offence is one of disobedience of such Commandant's orders."

17. The scheme of the Act and the Rules leading to holding of a trial by the General Security Force Court leaves no manner of doubt that the basic principles of natural justice have been codified therein. The provisions of the Act and the Rules in no uncertain terms envisage protection from bias against an officer. We may notice that the Act which was enacted in the year 1968 even sought to fill up the gaps occurring in other Acts like Army Act, Navy Act or Armed Forces Act in this behalf so as to protect a person from personal bias or a real likelihood of bias. Rule 46 was made with a view to achieve the said purpose. It is not in dispute having regard to the phraseology used in Rule 45 B of the Rules that an accused at the first instance is bound to the tried by his Commandant. Necessarily, the question which arises for consideration would be as to who was the Commandant of the respondent at the relevant point of time. Concededly Mr. Garcha was the Commandant of the Respondent till 17.7.90. A question which is to be posed and answered is as to whether the BTC is a Unit to TCS. The appellant herein in their counter-affidavit before the High Court stated "that the respondent was posted to BSF. TC&S Hazaribagh and was

further posted to Basic Training center of the TC&S Hazaribagh on 19.7.1990 by the DIG, BSF TC&S Hazaribagh. The BSF Training center & School Hazaribagh is a Training Institution composing of the following wings:-

(a) Basic Training center

(b) Specialised Training center & School

(c) Administrative Wing"

18. *Having regard to the provisions of the Act and the Rules, as noticed hereinbefore, we are of the opinion that only because in a Unit or Battalion a Commandant is posted, existence of a Unit would not be presumed. Once it is held that Basic Training center or Specialised Training center and School or Administrative Wing are wings of the BSF, Training center & School; each wing being a component thereof the same cannot be treated to be a separate unit for the purpose of Rule 45B of the Rules.* Section 2(1)(f) *of the Border Security Force Act defines Commandant with reference to a unit and not Commandant as a holder of post.*

19. *Rule 46 is a proviso or an exception to Rule 45 B of the Rules. It seeks to protect an accused from bias or real likelihood of bias of a Commandant and in the event, the Commandant himself is a witness or is otherwise personally interested in the matter, he is to place the matter before a competent authority to see that the accused is attached to a different unit.*

20. *For the purpose of this case we need not go into the correctness or otherwise of the contention of Mr. Sharma to the effect that the principles of purposive construction should be adopted by us so as to hold that in a case of this nature the power under Rule 46 could not have been exercised by Mr. Garcha despite the fact that he was a Deputy Inspector General. However, we may notice that from the records it appears that all actions have been taken by Mr. Garcha as a Commandant and not as a Deputy Inspector General. He, having*

regard to the hierarchy of the officers, is higher in rank than the Commandant. In a case of this nature, however, we are of the considered opinion that keeping in view of the personal interest shown by Mr. Garcha he should not have exercised his purported statutory power under Rule 46 by attaching the respondent to a wing of the own unit. Exercise of a statutory power may, although not be invalidated on the ground of inherent lack of jurisdiction on his post but the order of attachment passed by Mr. Garcha having regard to the facts and circumstances of the case must be held to be illegal.

21. Submission of Mr. Ranjit Kumar to the effect that Mr. Garcha could delegate his power to Mr. Arya cannot be accepted. A power under Rule 16(7) of the Rules can be exercised in a general manner and not in a particular far less in a matter where Rule 46 will be applicable. The principles of special a generaliabus non derogant shall apply in such a case.

22. In the instant case, Mr. Garcha in his letter to Mr. M.S. Arya described himself as Commandant, BTC, TC&S which itself is a pointer to show that BTC is not a unit totally independent to TC&S. It is further not in dispute that Mr. Arya was an officer subordinate to him. His letter dated 4th September, 1990 in no uncertain terms points out that he had for all intent and purpose directed Mr. Arya to initiate a disciplinary action against the respondent. The said action was to be taken on the basis of the materials disclosed therein. Such a procedure is unknown in law. An authority who is higher than the Commandant, in exercise of his power conferred upon him under Rule 46 could not have directed the Commandant of a wing of his own unit to initiate departmental proceedings. In law it was the disciplinary authority alone who was required to apply his independent mind to the materials on record so as to enable him to arrive at the conclusion as to whether a disciplinary action is contemplated or not. He cannot do so at the instance of a higher authority who had not only no role to play in the matter but also admittedly was biased. [See Commissioner of Police, Bombay v. Gordhandas Bhanji and Union of India and Ors. v. Harish

Chandra Goswami]. *Bias against the respondent on the part of Mr. Garcha is undisputed*

....

39. Rule 45B confers a discretionary power upon the Commandant of the accused to discharge not only on the ground that there does not exist any material on record to proceed against him but also on the ground that having regard to the previous character of the accused and the nature of charges against him it was not advisable to proceed further in the matter.

40. Rule 45B of the Rules, therefore, having regard to the extent and nature of the power of the disciplinary authority, leaves no manner of doubt that the Commandant of the accused is required to apply his mind on the materials on record as to enable him to arrive at a finding in favour or against the officer. The manner in which the chargesheet has been drawn leads to only one conclusion that Mr. Arya did so only on the command of Mr. Garcha. On a query made by us, Mr. Ranjit Kumar stated that no record is available with him to show that the respondent was supplied with any material as is mandatorily required under Rule 45B. There is nothing on record also to show that at least the materials which were referred to in Shri Garcha's letter 4th September, 1990 were brought to the notice of the respondent and he has been given an opportunity to make a statement in his defence. There is also nothing on record to show that even the materials in possession of Mr. Bakshi were requisitioned by Mr. Arya and he applied his own independent mind thereupon for directing preparation of record of evidence. From the tenor of the charge sheet dated 7.9.1990, it only appears that he merely heard the officer as to whether he pleads guilty thereto or not. The learned Single Judge of the High Court has considered materials on record and came to the conclusion that valuable rights of the respondent had been breached. The Division Bench went through the entire records and arrived at the same finding. The findings of the learned Single Judge or the Division Bench cannot be said to be perverse or contrary to law.

41. We are, therefore, of the opinion that no case has been made out for interfering with the impugned judgment in exercise of our jurisdiction under Article 136 of the Constitution of India.

42. This appeal is, therefore, dismissed. But in the facts and circumstances of the case, there shall be no order as to costs.

3. DEFINITION OF ACTIVE DUTY UNDER THE BSF ACT AND RULES

3.1 STATE OF J&K VS LAKHWINDER KUMAR & ORS ON 25 APRIL, 2013 CRIMINAL APPEAL NO. 624 OF 2013 (SPECIAL LEAVE PETITION (CRL.) NO. 5910 OF 2012) (SUPREME COURT)

Background:

Incident Date: February 5, 2010

Location: Boulevard Road, Srinagar

Victim: Zahid Farooq Sheikh, a Kashmiri teenager

Accused: Lakhwinder Kumar (Border Security Force Constable) and R.K. Birdi (Commandant, 68th Battalion, BSF)

Event: Lakhwinder Kumar allegedly shot Zahid Farooq Sheikh at the instigation of R.K. Birdi during a traffic jam altercation.

Legal Proceedings:

FIR Registration: FIR No. 4 of 2010 at Police Station, Nishat.

Investigation: Conducted by local police, leading to the arrest of both accused.

Charges: Filed under Sections 302 (Murder), 109 (Abetment), and 201 (Causing disappearance of evidence) of the Ranbir Penal Code.

Jurisdiction Dispute:

BSF Claim: The BSF sought to try the accused in a Security Force Court as per Section 80 of the BSF Act, 1968, arguing they were on "active duty."

State's Opposition: The State of J & K and the victim's uncle, Ghulam Mohammad Sheikh, opposed this, preferring trial in a criminal court.

Court Decisions:

Chief Judicial Magistrate's Order (Nov 25, 2010): Approved BSF's request to transfer the case to a Security Force Court.

High Court's Order (Oct 21, 2011): Dismissed the appeals against the Magistrate's order.

Supreme Court Analysis:

Definition of Active Duty: As per Section 2(1)(a) of the BSF Act, active duty includes operations against enemies or duties along the borders. The Central Government's notification extended this definition to all BSF personnel in J&K from July 1, 2007, to June 30, 2010.

Jurisdiction: Despite being on active duty, the accused can be tried either by a Security Force Court or a criminal court. The discretion lies with BSF officials as per Section 80 of the BSF Act.

Conclusion:

Supreme Court's Decision: The Court held that the accused were on active duty during the incident, thus the Security Force Court had jurisdiction. However, it emphasized that the trial could still occur in a criminal court based on discretion under Section 80 of the BSF Act.

Final Outcome: The Supreme Court validated the discretion of BSF officials to decide the trial venue and upheld the provisions of the BSF Act and relevant rules.

This case highlights the complexity of jurisdictional issues when military personnel are involved in criminal activities during periods classified as "active duty," and the balance between para-military and civilian judicial processes.

RELEVANT PARAGRPAHS OF THE JUDGEMENT INCLUDE

Incident and Initial Investigation:

"The allegation in the case is very distressing. A Kashmiri teenager lost his life by the bullet of Lakhwinder Kumar, a constable of the Border Security Force (hereinafter referred to as 'the Force') at the Boulevard Road, Srinagar. He allegedly fired at the instigation of R.K. Birdi, Commandant of the 68th Battalion of the Force... Zahid died of the fire arm injury instantaneously. The aforesaid incident led to registration of FIR No. 4 of 2010 at Police Station, Nishat."

Jurisdictional Dispute:

"The Commandant of the Force by his letter dated 10.02.2010 handed over the investigation to the police... the police submitted the charge-sheet on 05th of April, 2010 against both the accused for commission of offence under Section 302, 109 and 201 of the Ranbir Penal Code before the Chief Judicial Magistrate, Srinagar, whereupon an application was filed on behalf of the Force seeking time to exercise option for trial of the accused by Security Force Court... The Chief Judicial Magistrate by his order dated 25th of November, 2010 allowed the application filed by the Commandant and handed over the accused together with the charge-sheet and other materials collected by the investigating agency for trying the accused by the Security Force Court."

High Court and Supreme Court Analysis:

"Aggrieved by the aforesaid order Ghulam Mohammad Sheikh and the State of Jammu & Kashmir filed separate revision applications before the High Court... According to the appellants, accused persons were not engaged in the duty of the nature specified above pursuant to any lawful command, therefore, they cannot be said to be on active duty so as to give jurisdiction to the Force to try them before Security Force

Court... In view of the aforesaid, there is no escape from the conclusion that the accused persons were on active duty at the time of commission of the offence."

Conclusion:

"The natural corollary of what we have found above is that the bar of trial by the Security Force Court provided in Section 47 of the Act would not operate... In a given case, there may not be a bar of trial by a Security Force Court, but still an accused can be tried by a Criminal Court. In other words, in such a situation, the choice of trial is between the Criminal Court and the Security Force Court."

Final Decision:

"We must answer here an ancillary submission. It is pointed out that the Rules made to give effect to the provisions of the Act has to be consistent with it and if a rule goes beyond what the Act contemplates or is in conflict thereof, the rule must yield to the Act... In the present case, the Criminal Court and the Security Force Court each have jurisdiction for trial of the offence which the accused persons are alleged to have committed. In such a contingency Section 80 of the Act has conferred discretion on the Director General or the Inspector General or the Deputy Inspector General of the Force within whose Command the accused person is serving, to decide before which court the proceeding shall be instituted."

4. SUMMARY SECURITY FORCE COURT

4.1 Judgement dated 03.12.2021 in Civil Appeal 6859 of 2021 titled Union of India and Ors. vs Mudrika Singh

Detailed Analysis of the Judgement: Union of India and Ors. vs Mudrika Singh

Background of the Case:

The Union of India and officials of the Border Security Force (BSF) appealed against a Division Bench judgment of the Calcutta High

Court dated 18 December 2018. The High Court quashed disciplinary proceedings against the respondent, Mudrika Singh, reinstating him to his initial position in the BSF.

At the time of the alleged misconduct in April 2006, Mudrika Singh was a Head Constable in the BSF, deployed to the Seventy-second Battalion.

Allegation:

Nature of the Allegation:

On 2 May 2006, the Commandant directed the Deputy Commandant to prepare a record of evidence (RoE) against Mudrika Singh for an offence constituting "disgraceful conduct" under Section 24(a) of the Border Security Force Act 1968. The specific allegation was that he committed sodomy against a fellow Constable during Naka duty between 02:00 and 06:00 hours on 16 April 2006.

Incident Description:

The incident allegedly took place on the night of 16-17 April 2006. The complainant, a Constable in the BSF, submitted a written complaint on 19 April 2006, detailing the alleged sexual assault.

Disciplinary Proceedings:

Initial RoE and Additional RoE:

The Deputy Commandant prepared the RoE and submitted it to the Commandant. On reviewing the RoE, the Commandant found inconsistencies in the witnesses' statements regarding the date of the incident. Consequently, on 10 June 2006, the Commandant called for the preparation of an additional RoE to clarify these discrepancies.

Summary Security Force Court (SSFC):

On 7 August 2006, the SSFC convened at the Headquarters of the seventy-second Battalion of the BSF to inquire into the charge under Section 24(a) of the BSF Act 1968. Mudrika Singh pleaded not guilty.

Four prosecution witnesses were examined, and the respondent was given the chance to cross-examine them and call for defense witnesses. The SSFC found him guilty and demoted him to the rank of Constable.

Statutory Petition:

On 6 September 2006, Mudrika Singh filed a statutory petition under Section 117 of the BSF Act 1968 before the Director-General of the BSF. The appellate authority found the charge established but commuted the punishment due to Singh's over 22 years of unblemished service. The commutation included forfeiting 5 years of service for promotion and 7 years of service for pension, along with a severe reprimand.

High Court Proceedings:

High Court Appeal:

Singh moved the High Court at Calcutta under Article 226 of the Constitution. The Single Judge set aside the order of punishment on grounds that (i) the original RoE was insufficient to prove the charge, and (ii) the Commandant's order for an additional RoE was beyond jurisdiction.

Division Bench Judgment:

The Division Bench upheld the Single Judge's decision, emphasizing that (i) the Commandant lacked jurisdiction to direct the preparation of an additional RoE under the then-existing Rule 51 of the BSF Rules 1969, and (ii) neither the SSFC nor the Appellate Authority furnished reasons for holding Singh guilty.

Legal Analysis:

Union of India's Submissions:

The Union argued that the High Court took a hyper-technical view and failed to appreciate the robustness of the BSF Act and Rules. It contended that the Commandant's directive for an additional RoE was to clarify a minor inaccuracy regarding the incident date, which did not amount to insufficient evidence under Rule 59. The Union also argued that Rule 6 of the BSF Rules provided sufficient authority for the Commandant's actions.

Respondent's Submissions:

The respondent countered that Rule 51 specifically delineates the Commandant's powers, which did not include ordering additional RoEs at the material time. Only a superior authority could order additional evidence under Rule 59. The respondent also highlighted the lack of reasons provided by the SSFC and the appellate authority for the guilty finding.

Detailed Legal Points:

Clarification of Active Duty:

The additional RoE was deemed necessary to rectify the date inconsistency and not due to insufficient evidence. The Commandant's directive was seen as clarificatory rather than an overreach of authority.

Jurisdiction of the Commandant:

Pre-2011, Rule 51 did not explicitly grant the Commandant the power to order additional evidence. The 2011 amendment, which allowed for such power, was argued to be clarificatory, indicating that the power was inherent even before the amendment. However, the High Court had interpreted the lack of explicit authority as a jurisdictional overreach by the Commandant.

Requirement for Reasons:

The court scrutinized whether the SSFC and the appellate authority were required to provide reasons for their decisions. The Union cited precedent suggesting that detailed reasons were not mandated under Rule 149 or Section 117(2) of the BSF Act, while the respondent argued that reasons were necessary to meet the standards of fairness and justice under Article 14 of the Constitution.

Conclusion:

Supreme Court's Decision:

The Supreme Court addressed whether the Commandant had the jurisdiction to order an additional RoE and whether the lack of reasons in the SSFC's guilty finding and the appellate authority's decision constituted a legal infirmity.

This detailed analysis highlights the procedural and substantive legal issues at play in the case, particularly focusing on jurisdictional authority and the requirement for reasoned decisions in disciplinary proceedings.

Relevant Paragraphs

Introduction:

"2….The Union of India and officials of the Border Security Force are in appeal against a judgment of a Division Bench of the Calcutta High Court dated 18 December 2018 which quashed disciplinary proceedings against the respondent and reinstated him to his initial position in the BSF."

"In April 2006, at the time of the alleged misconduct, the respondent was a Head Constable in the BSF and was deployed to the Seventy-second Battalion."

Allegation and Initial Proceedings:

"3. The incident in question is alleged to have taken place on the night intervening 16 and 17 April 2006. The complainant ... was on Naka duty between 02:00 to 06:00 hours when the respondent is alleged to have committed an act of sexual assault on him. The complainant submitted a written complaint on 19 April 2006."

"4. The RoE was prepared by the Deputy Commandant and submitted to the Commandant. On 10 June 2006, the Commandant noted that on a scrutiny of the RoE proceedings, it was found that there was an inconsistency in the statements of the witnesses as regards the date on which the incident had occurred. Hence, on 10 June 2006, the Commandant called for the preparation of an additional RoE."

Summary Security Force Court (SSFC):

"5. On 7 August 2006, the SSFC convened ... the respondent pleaded not guilty to the charge. Four prosecution witnesses were examined and the respondent was furnished with an opportunity to cross-examine them and to call for defense witnesses. The SSFC found the respondent guilty of the charge and demoted him to the rank of a Constable as a punishment."

Appeal and High Court Decision:

"7. The respondent moved the High Court at Calcutta under Article 226 of the Constitution. A Single Judge of the High Court, by an order dated 7 May 2009, set aside the order of punishment on the ground that: (i) The original RoE was insufficient to prove the charge; and (ii) The order of the Commandant for preparing an additional RoE was beyond jurisdiction."

"8. The judgment of the Single Judge has been upheld by the impugned judgment of the Division Bench of the High Court on 18 October 2018 on the ground that: (i) The Commandant did not have jurisdiction to direct the preparation of an additional RoE under Rule 51 of the Border Security Force Rules 1969 as it stood at the relevant time; and (ii) No reasons were furnished by the SSFC or the Appellate Authority - Director General of BSF - for holding the respondent guilty."

Analysis:

"12. Essentially, down to its core, the controversy in the present case turns upon two aspects: firstly, whether the Commandant prior to the amendment of Rule 51 in 2011 had jurisdiction to direct the preparation of an additional RoE; and secondly, whether the finding of guilt which has been recorded by the SSFC stands vitiated in the absence of reasons."

"15. In this backdrop, it becomes necessary to emphasize that the additional RoE which was ordered by the Commandant was essentially in the nature of a clarification having regard to the discrepancy about the date of the incident namely, whether it was on 16 or 17 April 2006."

Jurisdiction of the Commandant:

"16. The unamended Rule 51 of the BSF Rules 1969 provided as follows: ... (2) The Commandant may, after going through the record or abstract of evidence including additional evidence: (i) Dismiss the charge, or (ii) rehear the charge and award one of the summary punishments; or (iii) try the accused by a Summary Security Force Court where he is empowered so to do, or (iv) apply to a competent officer or authority to convene a Court for the trial of the accused."

Conclusion:

"18. Rule 48 of the BSF Rules 1969 provides for the preparation of a record of evidence: ... The officer ordering the record of evidence may either prepare the record of evidence himself or detail another officer to do so. The witnesses shall give their evidence in the presence of the accused and the accused shall have right to cross-examine all witnesses who give evidence against him."

These paragraphs capture the essential elements of the case, from the background and allegations to the legal arguments and the court's conclusions.

5 RELEVANT JUDGEMENTS UNDER THE BSF ACT

5.1 **JUDGEMENT DATED 05.07.2018 IN WPC 25431 OF 2015 EX-BSF PERSONNEL WELFARE ASSOCIATION v. UNION OF INDIA (Kerala High Court, 2018)**

"Ex.BSF Personnel Welfare Association has filed this writ petition aggrieved by Ext.P1 office memorandum by which the Director (Personnel) has informed that Ministry of Home Affairs has decided to adopt a uniform nomenclature of Central Armed Police Force (CAPF)

while referring to Boarder Security Force (BSF), Central Reserve Police Force (CRPF), Central Industrial Security Force (CISF), Indo-Tibetan Border Police (ITBP) and Sashastra Seema Bal (SSB). It is stated that reference of these Forces as Armed Forces of the Union creates an incorrect perception about these Forces and expectations from the Force become unrealistic. Even in the international references such incorrect nomenclature cause confusion regarding the role of such Forces, especially during elections, maintaining law and order etc.

2. The petitioner Association represents personnel from BSF who retired from the BSF on various dates. It is their case that the Border Security Force Act, 1968 provides for the Constitution of the Force under section 4, according to which there shall be an armed force of the Union called the Border Security Force for ensuring the security of the borders of India. Therefore it is stated that unless the provisions under the Act are amended the nomenclature cannot be changed and the BSF cannot be described as a police force. It is also their case that BSF which has been entrusted with the duties of protecting the borders of the nation, cannot be compared with CISF, CRPF etc. which does not have any such duties while CISF deals with the industrial security and CRPF deals with reserve police. It is also pointed out that ITBP which is also grouped along with BSF is already described as police force and the statutes governing them do not provide for constitution of an Armed Force as contained in section 4 of the BSF Act. According to them Ext.P1 order is in violation of the BSF Act. While Armed Forces of the Union is a subject coming under entry 2 of List I, Police is coming in entry 2 in List II. Entry 2 in List I is "Naval, para-military and air forces; any other armed forces of the Union". Entry 2 in List II is "Police (including railway and village police) subject to the provisions of entry 2A of List I". Entry 2A in List I provides for deployment of any armed force of the Union or any other force subject to the control of the Union or any contingent or unit thereof in any State in aid of the civil power; powers, jurisdiction, privileges and liabilities of the members of such forces while on such

deployment. According to the petitioner while describing the BSF as Police Force the Government of India has in effect amended the statute by an executive order even in the absence of a policy decision of Government of India. They also pointed out that the Government of Kerala had rejected their representation for extending the benefit available to the ex-servicemen of the Armed Force saying that in the event of granting such benefits demands would be raised by Motor Vehicles Department, State Police Department etc.

3. Respondents 1 and 2 have filed separate counter affidavits. According to the 1st respondent, the Ministry of Home Affairs had as

per its memorandum dated 23.11.2012 intimated that Cabinet Committee on Security had approved the proposal to declare retired Central Armed Police Force Personnel from Central Reserve Police Force (CRPF), Border Security Force (BSF), Central Industrial Security Force (CISF) Indo-Tibetan Border Police (ITBP) and Sashastra Seema Bal (SSB) as Ex-Central Armed Police Force Personnel and requested to extend suitable benefits to Ex-CAPF personnel on the lines of the benefits extended by the State/UT Government to the Ex-Servicemen of Defense Forces. But the Government of Kerala expressed its inability for extending the benefits and it is stated that the writ petition is filed by the Association because of that. It is stated that the terms like Central Police Organisation (CPOs), Central Para Military Forces (CPMFs), Para Military Forces (PMFs), Central Police Forces (CPFs) etc have been interchangeably used while referring to the Central Police Force and it was stated that use of the term "Military" for central forces was not appropriate and therefore it was decided to adopt a uniform nomenclature of Central Armed Police Force while referring to BSF, CRPF, CISF, ITBP etc in the year 2011.

4. The petitioners had raised a claim that Assam Rifles & National Security Guard have not been included in CAPF. It is stated that Assam

Rifles is under operational control of Indian Army and National Security Guard is established on 100% deputation basis, in which CAPF personnel are also deployed and hence those two forces were not included in CAPF. It is further stated that none of the benefits available to BSF personnel is reduced or affected by way of nomenclature. It is only for administrative purpose that Ext.P1 order is issued.

5. In the counter affidavit filed on behalf of the 2nd respondent, the Director General of BSF, it is stated that under Article 246 of the Constitution of India read with entry no.2 of List I (Union list) of seventh schedule, the BSF was raised as an Armed Force of the Union. The Central Government cannot raise a police force as Police is a State subject as listed at entry 2 of list II (State list). The Boarder Security Force Act received the assent of President of India and it is modeled on the lines of Army Act and it comes under the Other Armed Forces of the union in entry no.2 along with Naval, Military and Airforces. It is stated that under the Constitution of India, status of BSF is that of an Armed Force of the Union and not as Police Force. It is further stated that the name of BSF has not been changed and Ext.P1 is issued without making any amendment to the BSF Act and therefore by

referring BSF along with other forces as CAPF does not change the nature of BSF and it remains as Armed force of the Union of India and

its nomenclature continues to be BSF. It is also stated that retired personnel of BSF continues to have the same status i.e as retired members of Armed Force of the Union. In effect it is stated that the status of the BSF personnel as well as ex-BSF personnel continues to

be the same despite Ext.P1.

I heard the learned Counsel appearing on both sides. The learned counsel for the petitioner submitted that Ext.P1 is resulted on the basis of an article published at the instance of an Army Officer. In the light of the averments in the counter affidavit that none of the benefits or even the status of BSF personnel are altered and that it is only for the purpose of correspondence that the nomenclature has been adopted in Ext.P1, petitioner cannot have any grievance over

Ext.P1. Even otherwise grievance of the petitioner is that it has affected their reputation by the issuance of Ext.P1 order by the Government of India; there is nothing to suggest that reputation of BSF personnel has been reduced. As pointed out by the the 2nd respondent, who is the head of BSF, the status of BSF as well as ex- BSF personnel continues to be the same. The BSF continues to be an Armed Force as long as the Act is not amended. Provisions under section 4 are also not seen amended. In the above circumstances, I find that no interference is required in this case.

The writ petition is dismissed as above."

CHAPTER V

SASHASTRA SEEMA BAL (SSB) -LAW INCLUDING LEADING CASE LAWS

1. SENIORITY DISPUTE DIRECT RECRUITS vis-à-vis PROMOTEES

1.1 Detailed Analysis of the Judgement dated 27.11.2015 in WP (C) 7939/2012 titled B.S. Jaswal And Ors. vs Union Of India & Ors. (DELHI HIGH COURT)

Introduction:

Background of the Case:

The petitioners challenged the seniority list of Assistant Commandants in the Sashastra Seema Bal (SSB), issued on 25.11.2011. The SSB, initially known as the Special Service Bureau, was set up in 1963 and came under the administrative control of the Ministry of Home Affairs (MHA) in January 2001.

The recruitment and promotion within SSB were governed by the Central Reserve Police Force (CRPF) Rules, 1955, which were applicable to SSB since its inception. The post of Assistant Commandant was filled by direct recruitment, promotion, and deputation without a fixed percentage until 1986, when fixed percentages were introduced.

Allegation:

Dispute Over Seniority:

The dispute arose over the inter se seniority between direct recruits and promotees. The petitioners, who joined SSB as direct recruits, argued that the seniority list published in 2011 was arbitrary and incorrect as it showed them junior to their batchmates who were previously shown as juniors in the seniority lists of 1995 and 2000.

Disciplinary Proceedings:

Initial Recruitment and Training:

The petitioners joined SSB as Assistant Commandants in 1993 and underwent training at the Central Industrial Security Force (CISF) academy in Hyderabad. Their seniority was initially determined based on their performance in the UPSC recruitment process.

Change in Seniority Criteria:

An office memorandum (OM) dated 30.09.2002, and subsequent clarifications, introduced a new method for determining seniority by giving weightage to marks obtained in the recruitment test, foundation course, and basic professional courses. This was further amended in 2010 to give equal weightage to marks obtained in the UPSC selection and the foundational course.

Promotions Based on Initial Seniority:

The petitioners were promoted to Deputy Commandant in 2004, Second in Command (2IC) in 2007, and Commandant in 2009 based on their initial seniority. They argued that the revision of seniority after 18 years was unjust and arbitrary.

High Court Proceedings:

Petitioners' Arguments:

The petitioners contended that the new criteria for seniority introduced in 2002 could not have retrospective effect. They also argued that the seniority lists of 1995 and 2000, which were based on their UPSC performance, had attained finality and could not be revised after 15 years. The petitioners cited legal precedents to support their argument that settled seniority should not be disturbed after a reasonable period.

Respondents' Arguments:

The respondents, including other directly recruited Assistant Commandants, argued that the seniority list published in 2011 was in compliance with the CRPF Rules, which required weightage to be given to performance during training. They argued that wrongful placement in a seniority list never confers any right if the placement is contrary to rules.

Legal Analysis:

Rule Position and Interpretation:

The seniority of directly recruited Assistant Commandants in the CRPF (and by extension, SSB) was regulated by Rule 8(b) of the CRPF Rules, which required equal weightage to marks obtained in the UPSC selection and performance during training. The seniority lists of 1995 and 2000 did not follow this rule, leading to the revision in 2011.

Impact of Revision on Promotions:

The revision of seniority in 2011 affected the petitioners' promotions, which were based on their initial seniority. The court noted that the contesting respondents did not object to their seniority positions at the time of their promotions.

Delay and Equity Considerations:

The court considered the delay in challenging the seniority and the principle that equity does not favor disturbing settled seniority after a significant lapse of time. The court also noted that the SSB did not interpret the norms to require consideration of training performance until 2010.

Conclusion:

Court's Decision:

The court held that the revision of the seniority list in 2011 was not justified given the lapse of 18 years and the promotions that had taken place based on the initial seniority. The court emphasized that settled seniority should not be disturbed after a reasonable period, especially when the contesting respondents did not object to their positions earlier.

Final Judgment:

The court set aside the revised seniority list of 2011 and upheld the seniority lists of 1995 and 2000, thereby reinstating the petitioners to their original seniority positions. The court also directed that any promotions or benefits granted based on the revised seniority list should be re-evaluated in light of the restored seniority.

This detailed analysis highlights the key legal arguments, the court's reasoning, and the final decision regarding the dispute over seniority in the SSB. The judgment underscores the importance of adhering to established rules and the principle of not disturbing settled seniority after a significant period.

RELEVANT PARAGRAPHS

B.S. Jaswal And Ors. vs Union Of India & Ors. which address the main points, arguments, and conclusions:

Introduction:

"1. In the present writ petition, the seniority list of Assistant Commandants in the Sashastra Seema Bal (the respondent), issued on 25.11.2011 has been challenged."

"2. The Special Service Bureau [now Sashastra Seema Bal or 'SSB'] was set up in the year 1963 under the Cabinet Secretariat. In January 2001, the Administrative Control of the Force was transferred from the Cabinet Secretariat, to the Union Ministry of Home Affairs (MHA)."

Dispute Over Seniority:

"3. All the petitioners joined the SSB after successfully competing for the post of Asst. Commandant, in the direct recruitment quota; they

reported for training after having been required to do so, before 30th November, 1993."

".....It is stated that, later, on 25.11.2002, the Central Government clarified that all CRPF Rules would be made applicable to the combatized units of the SSB. On 10.06.2003, Rules regulating the method of recruitment to the post of Assistant Commandant Group 'A' (GD) in the Special Service Bureau were brought in force."

Initial Recruitment and Training:

".....The petitioners were subsequently promoted as Dy. Commandants (in 2004) and as Second in Command (2IC) on 01.04.2007. They were subsequently promoted to the cadre of Commandants, in November, 2009."

Change in Seniority Criteria:

"4........An office memorandum (OM) dated 30.09.2002, which is in turn referred to by three other memoranda. These clarified that while fixing inter se seniority of direct recruits in SSB, the marks obtained by them in the direct recruitment test, the foundation course and basic professional courses had to be given weightage of 50%; 10% and 40% respectively."

"This basis was later changed (on 23.07.2010) whereby equal weightage (50% each, by way of 100 marks each) was to be given for marks obtained in the UPSC selection and the basic foundational course, to work out the criteria for fixing direct recruits' inter se seniority."

Promotions Based on Initial Seniority:

"The petitioners impugn this because for the first time in 18 years, they have been shown in positions junior to their colleagues and batch mates. The said batch-mates (subsequently added as Respondent Nos. 6-11) were shown as junior to the petitioners at all relevant times, i.e.

in the previous seniority lists published on 30.03.1995 and 17.04.2000, in the cadre of Asst. Commandants."

Petitioners' Arguments:

"6. Ms. Rekha Palli, learned senior counsel for the petitioners, mainly advanced three arguments. It was submitted firstly that the question of including performance during training, for direct recruits, as a determinative criteria, to fix inter se seniority had not arisen till 30.9.2002, when the office memorandum was issued......."

"7. Learned counsel relied on the decisions reported as Shiba Shankar Mohapatra & Ors. v State Of Orissa & Ors AIR 2010 SC 706 and urged that though the context of the decision was where a direction to redraw seniority was rejected, the principle that any direction which seeks to disturb the vested rights of other persons regarding seniority, rank and promotion which have accrued to them during the intervening period should not be given, was emphasized."

Respondents' Arguments:

"10.......Mr. Abhay Prakash Sahay, learned counsel, submits that in 2008, a promotee, Neeraj Chand, promoted as Dy. Commandant (and appointed as Asst. Commandant in 2001) filed a writ petition before the Himachal Pradesh High Court questioning the seniority list of Dy. Commandant. The writ petition was disposed of on 22.02.2010, with direction to prepare the final seniority list within six months."

"Relying on the averments in the counter affidavit, Mr. Abhay Prakash Sahay, learned counsel, submits that in 2008, a promotee, Neeraj Chand, promoted as Dy. Commandant (and appointed as Asst. Commandant in 2001) filed a writ petition before the Himachal Pradesh High Court questioning the seniority list of Dy. Commandant."

Legal Analysis:

"15. In this case, all officers - the petitioners and the contesting respondents, i.e. the fourth to the eleventh respondents, were directly recruited as Asst. Commandant, by the SSB. That public employer did not have its independent rules; those of the CRPF were made applicable."

"SSB- and for that matter, the case of the private respondents is that in 2010, Mr. Slaria, a 1998 direct recruit, for the first time, urged that his performance in the training period had not been factored in while finalizing the seniority."

Conclusion:

"17. During the course of hearing, the SSB had produced the file to show that the petitioners' fresh seniority positions were determined after taking into account their performance and giving due weightage to the marks obtained in the training period. These materials were in the form of tabular compilation of the results obtained from the CISF Academy."

"18. All the above facts, in the opinion of the court clearly establish that whatever be the rule position about the determination of seniority, SSB never interpreted the norms to mean that the performance of direct recruit Asst. Commandants during the training period had to be taken into consideration and given due weightage; possibly this was because the SSB never had its own recruitment and promotion rules and had merely adopted those of the CRPF."

The court held that the revision of the seniority list in 2011 was not justified given the lapse of 18 years and the promotions that had taken place based on the initial seniority. The court emphasized that settled seniority should not be disturbed after a reasonable period, especially when the contesting respondents did not object to their positions earlier.

2. REQUEST FOR RESIGNATION

2.1 JUDGEMENT DATED 06.03.2024 IN W.P.(C) NO 8500/2021 TITLED RAKESH KUMAR BHARTIYA versus UNION OF INDIA, THROUGH ITS SECRETARY, MINISTRY OF HOME AFFAIRS & ANR. (DELHI HIGH COURT)

Rakesh Kumar Bhartiya vs Union Of India & Anr.

Issue: The core issue was whether an employer can process a resignation request that it initially declined to process.

Background of the Case:

The petitioner, Rakesh Kumar Bhartiya, filed a writ petition challenging the acceptance of his resignation by the Sashastra Seema Bal (SSB) and sought reinstatement along with consequential benefits.

The core issue was whether an employer can process a resignation request that it initially declined to process.

Factual Background:

Petitioner's Service and Circumstances:

The petitioner joined SSB on 15.07.2008 as an Assistant Commandant/Medical Officer. His wife was also a Medical Officer in SSB.

They had a specially-abled child requiring constant supervision. The petitioner's requests for posting both him and his wife at the same command center were not always granted.

Initial Resignation and Subsequent Developments:

On 04.11.2020, the petitioner tendered his resignation due to personal difficulties and repeated rejections of leave applications.

The respondents asked him to submit a fresh resignation application specifying the date from which he intended to resign and to ensure it reached them at least 30 days before the intended resignation date.

Petitioner's Decision to Continue Service:

After receiving the communication from the respondents on 21.12.2020, the petitioner decided not to resign and instead requested a personal interview with the Director General (DG), SSB, through an email dated 26.12.2020.

The petitioner also requested a transfer to a family-station on compassionate grounds via a letter dated 13.01.2021.

Respondents' Actions:

Despite the petitioner not submitting a fresh resignation application, the respondents processed his initial resignation application and informed him on 04.02.2021 that it had been accepted, relieving him of his duties effective from the same date.

The petitioner's request to recall the resignation acceptance was denied on 26.03.2021.

Legal Issues:

Contention of the Petitioner:

The petitioner argued that his initial resignation request was not processed and that he was asked to submit a fresh application. He claimed that the respondents' action to process his initial resignation was arbitrary and unlawful.

Contention of the Respondents:

The respondents argued that the petitioner should have formally withdrawn his resignation request. They claimed there was no prohibition on processing the initial resignation application since the petitioner did not submit a withdrawal request.

Court's Analysis:

Review of Resignation Request and Respondents' Communication:

The court reviewed the resignation request dated 04.11.2020 and the respondents' subsequent communication dated 12.12.2020, which asked the petitioner to submit a fresh application with specific particulars.

Interpretation of Respondents' Actions:

The court found that the respondents had, in no uncertain terms, declined to process the initial resignation request. The respondents' communication clearly indicated that a fresh application was required.

Central Civil Services (Pension) Rules, 1972:

The court noted that Rule 26 of the Central Civil Services (Pension) Rules, 1972, allows for the withdrawal of resignation even after acceptance under certain conditions. However, in this case, the initial resignation request was effectively declined, making it a 'deemed refusal.'

Sashastra Seema Bal Act, 2007 and Rules:

As per Section 8 of the Sashastra Seema Bal Act, 2007, and Rule 28 of the Sashastra Seema Bal Rules, no member of the force can resign at will. The Central Government must consider and accept the resignation request based on special circumstances.

Petitioner's Decision Not to Submit a Fresh Application:

The court noted that the petitioner did not submit a fresh resignation application and instead sought to continue in service by requesting a personal hearing and a transfer.

Conclusion:

Final Decision:

The court concluded that the respondents were estopped from processing the initial resignation application after directing the petitioner to submit a fresh one. The respondents' action to process the initial application, which had become stale and non-est, was impermissible.

Setting Aside the Resignation Acceptance:

The court set aside the order dated 04.02.2021, which accepted the petitioner's resignation. The petitioner was deemed to be in service and entitled to all consequential benefits.

Order and Relief:

The writ petition was allowed, and the petitioner was reinstated with all consequential benefits.

Relevant Paragraphs:

Paragraphs 3-5:

3. When the petitioner was posted as Second-In-Command (Medical) in 28th Battalion, SSB at Antagarh, Chhattisgarh, on account of the difficulties being faced by him and repeated rejection of his leave applications, he tendered resignation on 04.11.2020.

4. Respondents, however, asked him to submit application afresh asking him to specify therein specific date from which he intended to proceed on resignation and also directed him to submit such application, at least, 30 days before the intended date of resignation. Such communication was duly conveyed to the petitioner and he was directed to submit application afresh in the aforesaid terms. Such letter was received by him on 21.12.2020.

5. Petitioner, after due deliberation with his family members, decided to continue with his job and not to submit any fresh application. He, instead, in order to apprise Director General (DG), SSB about his grievances sent an e-mail dated 26.12.2020 requesting for a personal interview with him. Such email was duly received and acknowledged but petitioner did not receive any communication from the respondents. Since he was asked to submit application afresh, he remained under the impression that his previous request had become redundant.

Paragraphs 6-7:

6. Petitioner also sent one letter dated 13.01.2021 requesting respondents to transfer him to any family-station on compassionate grounds.

7. However, to his utter shock, he received a letter from respondents on 04.02.2021 informing him that his earlier application submitting resignation (letter dated 04.11.2020) had been accepted and that he stood relieved of his duties with effect from 04.02.2021.

Paragraph 12:

12. The factual aspects are not disputed by the respondents but according to them, if at all petitioner wanted to withdraw the request of resignation, he should have rather moved a proper specific application and since he never submitted any application seeking withdrawal of his resignation, there was no embargo and prohibition in processing the application already received by them. It is also claimed that the petitioner has no locus poenitentiae to withdraw an offer of resignation which had already been accepted. According to respondents, his application was acted upon and was forwarded to Ministry of Home Affairs, in terms of Rule 28 of the SSB Rules, 2009 for acceptance by the competent authority and MHA accepted the resignation and, therefore, there was no merit or substance in the present writ petition.

Paragraphs 17-18:

17. If one goes through the contents of letter dated 12.12.2020, issued by the respondents, it would become as plain as day that the respondents had declined to process the same. They wanted the petitioner to submit a fresh application of resignation with specific date from which he intended to proceed on resignation, asking further that such application should reach their office 30 days before the intended date of resignation so that it could be processed with MHA in time.

18. The only conclusion which one can draw from the contents of the aforesaid letter is that the respondents had, in no uncertain terms, refused to process such application as according to them it was lacking in some material particulars. The manner in which the aforesaid communication dated 12.12.2020 is worded leaves no element of ambiguity or vagueness and is clearly suggestive of the fact that such request of resignation was declined to be processed. Therefore, logically speaking and as an inevitable conclusion, there was no reason or occasion for them to have re-entertained the same. Respondents were fully aware that the petitioner had requested for a personal hearing and had even sought transfer to a family station and that he had not submitted any application afresh and therefore, it was in teeth of their own order to have picked up the previous application which they had declined to process and to have accepted the same, out of the blue.

.Paragraphs 20-21:

20. Firstly, as per Central Civil Services (Pension) Rules, 1972, there is no absolute bar on any employer in even permitting withdrawal of resignation after its acceptance. Rule 26 envisages certain situations wherein withdrawal of resignation can be permitted even after it had been accepted and had become effective. Here, as already noticed above, what to say of acceptance, the respondent had rather declined to process the resignation request which tantamount to 'deemed refusal'.

21. Secondly, in context of the Force in question i.e. Sashastra Seema Bal, no member of the force is at liberty to resign during the term of engagement. This is apparent from Section 8 of Sashastra Seema Bal Act, 2007. As per Rule 28 of Sashastra Seema Bal Rules, the Central Government may, having regard to the special circumstances of any case, permit any officer of the Forces to resign before the completion of the term of engagement and it may accept the resignation w.e.f. the date as it may consider expedient.

Paragraphs 24-25:

24. As noted already, the petitioner did not choose to submit any application afresh. He rather decided to continue in service and made twin request i.e. personal hearing from DG, Sashastra Seema Bal, and also transfer on compassionate grounds.

25. In such a peculiar backdrop, the respondents were estopped from taking any further action, unless they had received a fresh request. Thus, they had no reason/cause to process his previous application which had, obviously, become stale and non-est. Such action of respondents is, therefore, totally impermissible in the eyes of law.

Paragraph 28:

28. In view of our foregoing discussion, we hereby set aside order dated 04.02.2021. The petitioner would be, therefore, deemed to be in service and would be fully entitled to all consequential benefits.

CHAPTER VI

ASSAM RIFLES -LAW INCLUDING LEADING CASE LAWS

1. TRIAL FOR OFFENCES UNDER THE PC ACT, 1988 MAY BE UNDERTAKEN BY THE ASSAM RIFLES COURT UNDER THE ASSAM RIFLES ACT, 2006

1.1 JUDGEMENT DATED 01.07.2019 IN CIVIL APPEAL NO. 5136 OF 2019 TITLED UNION OF INDIA, REPRESENTED BY THE SECRETARY, MINISTRY OF HOME AFFAIRS & ORS. VERSUS RANJIT KUMAR SAHA & ANR.

I. Introduction

- The judgment deals with the jurisdiction of the General Assam Rifles Court (GARC) to try offenses under the Prevention of Corruption Act (PC Act) against members of the Assam Rifles.

- The Supreme Court allowed the appeal, setting aside the High Court's judgment, and held that the GARC has jurisdiction to try offenses under the PC Act against members of the Assam Rifles.

II. Background

- The respondents, Ranjit Kumar Saha and another, were members of the Assam Rifles and faced charges under the PC Act.

- A GARC was convened to try them.

- The respondents raised preliminary objections, arguing that the GARC lacked jurisdiction to try them under the PC Act.

- The GARC rejected their objections, and they approached the High Court, which ruled in their favour, holding that the GARC had no jurisdiction to try them under the PC Act.

III. Reasoning

- The Supreme Court analyzed the provisions of the PC Act and the Assam Rifles Act, 2006, to determine the jurisdiction of the GARC.

- The court noted that Section 4 of the PC Act provides that offenses under the Act shall be tried only by a special judge, while Section 55 of the Assam Rifles Act, 2006, provides that any civil offense committed by a member of the Assam Rifles shall be tried by the GARC.

- The court held that there is no irreconcilable conflict between the two provisions and that they can be harmoniously construed.

- The court relied on the principle that a special statute can exist as an exception to a general statute.

IV. Key Points

- The GARC has jurisdiction to try offenses under the PC Act against members of the Assam Rifles.

- There is no irreconcilable conflict between Section 4 of the PC Act and Section 55 of the Assam Rifles Act, 2006.

- A special statute can exist as an exception to a general statute.

- The Assam Rifles Act, 2006, is a special statute that applies specifically to members of the Assam Rifles, while the PC Act is a general statute that applies to all persons.

V. Conclusion

- The Supreme Court's judgment clarifies the jurisdiction of the GARC to try offenses under the PC Act against members of the Assam Rifles.

- The judgment establishes that a special statute can exist as an exception to a general statute, and that the Assam Rifles Act, 2006, is a special statute that applies specifically to members of the Assam Rifles.

RELEVANT PARAGRAPHS

Here are the relevant paragraphs from the judgment:

Paragraph 8: "Sections 55 and 56 of the 2006 Act read as follows: ... (55) Civil offences.—Subject to the provisions of section 56, any person subject to this Act who at any place in, or beyond, India commits any civil offence shall be deemed to be guilty of an offence against this Act and, if charged therewith under this section, shall be liable to be tried by an Assam Rifles Court and, on conviction, be punishable as follows, ...".

Paragraph 9: "Section 4 of the PC Act provides that an offence punishable under the PC Act shall be tried only by a special Judge. A special Judge under the Act is appointed by a notification issued under Section 3 of the PC Act either by the Central Government or the State Government....."

Paragraph 12: "We proceed to examine the provisions of the 2006 Act. Section 55 of the 2006 Act provides that any civil offence committed by a member of the Assam Rifles shall be tried by the GARC. As referred to earlier, a civil offence is defined by Section 2 (e) as an offence which is triable by a criminal court."

Paragraph 16: "Consolidation and amendment of laws relating to the prevention of corruption is the object of the PC Act whereas consolidation of laws relating to the governance of Assam Rifles for ensuring the security of the borders of India, to carry out the counter insurgency operations in the specified areas etc., is the object of the 2006 Act. Since the objects of the two Statutes are different and as the applicability of the 2006 Act is restricted to the members of the Assam Rifles, following the aforementioned principles on the presumption against implied repeal, Section 4 of the PC Act and Section 55 of the 2006 Act which are in apparent conflict can be harmoniously construed."

Paragraph 18: "In view of the aforesaid findings, we are of the opinion that the GARC has the jurisdiction to try offences under the PC Act against the members of the Assam Rifles."

2. EFFECT OF RED INK ENTRIES UNDER THE ASSAM RIFLES ACT, 1941
2.1 JUDGEMENT DATED 14.07.2022 IN CIVIL APPEAL NOS. 11473-11474 OF 2018 TITLED AMARENDRA KUMAR PANDEY VERSUS UNION OF INDIA & ORS (SUPREME COURT)

In this case, the appellant, Amarendra Kumar Pandey, who had joined the Assam Rifles as a Rifleman in 1993, was discharged from service on January 31, 2004, based on four Red Ink entries received during his service. The discharge order was initially set aside by a learned Single Judge of the Guwahati High Court, who remitted the matter for a fresh decision. However, the Union of India filed a writ appeal which was allowed by the Division Bench of the High Court, setting aside the order of the learned Single Judge.

The Supreme Court was tasked with addressing several key issues:

1. Whether the discharge from service was automatic or mandatory after receiving four Red Ink entries.

2. Whether the High Court had erred in its decision.

3. Whether Clause 5 required the Commandant to record reasons for the discharge.

4. Whether the discharge order was validly exercised. The Supreme Court ultimately ruled in favour of the appellant, stating that the order of discharge was invalid. The Court directed that the appellant be

treated as if he was in service until he completed the qualifying service for pension benefits.

Reasoning

The judgment emphasizes the importance of procedural fairness and the necessity for authorities to provide adequate reasoning for discharge decisions. - The case reflects the principle that public servants should not be discharged without a fair opportunity to contest the grounds for such actions.

RELEVANT PARARAPHS

"6. Discharge/Disposal of Undesirable/Inefficient Personnel Chapter VIII, Rules 24 of the Assam Rifles Manual invests powers to the Commandant of Assam Rifles Battalions to 'dismiss' or 'remove' any member of the Assam Rifles below the rank of Nb/Sub. This power may be invoked by a Commandant in case where a person has got four red ink entries. As far as practicable, however, discharge under this provision should be avoided as personnel sent on discharge on this account are not eligible for pension. In case it is necessary to send an individual on discharge under this provision, a notice will be served on the individual to give opportunity to explain his case. Complete case will be forwarded to Range HQ alongwith the notice and reply received from the individual, for the approval of the DIGAR. The documents will be sent to this Directorate Records (Doc)/UPAO (And the individual to Depot Coy (No.1 Constr Coy)"

"28. Where an Act or the statutory rules framed thereunder left an action dependent upon the opinion of the authority concerned, by some such expression as 'is satisfied' or 'is of the opinion' or 'if it has reason to believe' or 'if it considered necessary', the opinion of the authority is conclusive, (a) if the procedure prescribed by the Act or rules for formation of the opinion was duly followed, (b) if the authority acted bona fide, (c) if the authority itself formed the opinion and did not borrow the opinion of somebody else and (d) if the authority did not

proceed on a fundamental misconception of the law and the matter in regard to which the opinion had to be formed.

29. The action based on the subjective opinion or satisfaction, in our opinion, can judicially be reviewed first to find out the existence of the facts or circumstances on the basis of which the authority is alleged to have formed the opinion. It is true that ordinarily the court should not inquire into the correctness or otherwise of the facts found except in a case where it is alleged that the facts which have been found existing were not supported by any evidence at all or that the finding in regard to circumstances or material is so perverse that no reasonable man would say that the facts and circumstances exist. The courts will not readily defer to the conclusiveness of the authority's opinion as to the existence of matter of law or fact upon which the validity of the exercise of the power is predicated.

---

35. Thirdly, this Court can interfere if the constitutional or statutory term essential for the exercise of the power has either been misapplied or misinterpreted. The Courts have always equated the jurisdictional review with the review for error of law and have shown their readiness to quash an order if the meaning of the constitutional or statutory term has been misconstrued or misapplied. [See Iveagh (Earl of) v. Minister of Housing and Local Govt., (1962) 2 QB 147; Iveagh (Earl of) v. Minister of Housing and Local Govt. (1964) 1 AB 395]."

38. 38. At this stage, it may be apposite to refer to the Assam Rifles Regulation, 2016. We are conscious of the fact that these regulations do not apply to the case on hand as the order of discharge is of 2004. However, we deem fit to reproduce the relevant regulations, more particularly, 107(c) and 108 respectively, as these regulations seem to have been enacted and brought into force having regard to the ratio of the decision of this Court in the case of Veerendra Kumar Dubey (supra). Regulation 107(c) reads thus:

"107. Removal of undesirable, incorrigible and inefficient Subordinate Officers, Under Officers and other enrolled persons.

(a) …………

(b) …………

(c) The procedure for dismissal/discharge of unsuitable subordinate officer/under officer/enrolled person will be as under:

(i) As provided under Rules 24 and 25 of Assam Rifles Rules, the person concerned, subject to the exception mentioned therein, shall be served with a Show Cause Notice against the contemplated action.

(ii) Preliminary enquiry. Before recommending discharge or dismissal of an individual the authority concerned will ensure that an impartial enquiry (not necessarily a Court of Inquiry) has been made into the allegations against him and that he has had adequate opportunity of hearing.

(iii) Rule 24 of the Assam Rifles confers powers on the Commandants of the Assam Rifles Units/ establishment to discharge any subordinate officer/under officer/enrolled persons of Assam Rifles. However, the power of discharge by the Commandant shall be exercised with prior approval of immediate superior officer not below Sector Commander in case of Under Officers and other enrolled person and that of Inspector General Assam Rifles in case of Subordinate Officers.

(iv) After compliance of the provisions enumerated above, a show cause notice will be served on the individual affording him an opportunity to explain his case. Thereafter, the complete case file will be forwarded to next superior authority/Sector Headquarters for approval of the superior authority/Sector Commander.

(v) The authority competent to sanction the dismissal/discharge of the individual will before passing orders reconsider the case in the light of the individual reply to the show cause notice. A person who has been served a show cause notice for proposed dismissal may be ordered to be discharged if it is considered that discharge would meet the end of justice. If the competent authority accepts the reply of the individual to the show cause notice as entirely satisfactorily, he will pass orders accordingly.

108. **Discharge on ground of red ink entries.** A Subordinate Officer, Under Officer or other enrolled person who has incurred four or more red ink entries may be recommended for discharge from the service on the ground of unsuitability, subject to the following conditions:

(a) After an individual has earned three red ink entries, he shall be warned in writing that his service will be liable to be terminated by the competent authority if he earns one more red ink entry. Such a warning letter shall be issued to him by the concerned Sector Commander through Commandant of the individual.

(b) Each case of individuals having earned four or more red ink entries shall be examined on its own merit depending upon the nature and gravity of the offences and the aggravating circumstances under which these were committed. The authority competent to sanction discharge under this para shall record reasons for ordering the discharge, or otherwise.

(c) A person who has put in eighteen years of qualifying service for pension may be allowed to complete the required qualifying service for grant of pension before he is recommended for discharge on ground of four or more red ink entries, unless there are compelling reasons to sanction his discharge before completion of the qualifying service for pension, which must be specified in the discharge order.

(d) Before taking the final decision to order the discharge, the person concerned shall be informed through a show cause notice that his retention in the service is considered undesirable for having incurred four or more red ink entries, thereby also calling upon him to show cause as to why he should not be discharged from the service for being considered unsuitable for the service in the Assam Rifles. The *individual shall be given minimum fifteen days, after receipt of Show Cause Notice, to submit his reply.*

(e) After receipt of the individual's reply, if any, the case shall be put up to the authority competent to sanction the discharge alongwith recommendations of the Commandant of the unit concerned. Before passing the discharge order, the authority competent to sanction the discharge under this para may seek the advise of the Law Officer concerned.

(f) An order of discharge under this para shall be passed by an officer not less than a Sector Commander in the case of Under Officer or other enrolled persons and an officer not less than Inspector General Assam Rifles/Additional Director General Assam Rifles in case of Subordinate Officers."

39. Having regard to the nature of the misconduct alleged against the appellant we are of the view that the ends of justice would be met if we set aside the order of discharge and treat the appellant herein to have been in service till the time, he could be said to have completed the qualifying service for grant of pension. We are inclined to pass such an order with a view to do substantial justice as there is nothing on record to indicate that the nature of the misconduct leading to the award of four Red Ink entries was so unacceptable that the competent authority had no option but to direct his discharge to prevent indiscipline in the force.

40. The order of discharge passed against the appellant herein is hereby set aside. The appellant shall be treated to have been in service till the time he would have completed the qualifying service for grant of pension. We are informed that only six months were left for the qualifying service to be completed before the appellant came to be discharged. No back wages shall, however, be admissible. The benefit of continuity of service for all other purpose shall be granted to the appellant including pension. The monetary benefits payable to the

appellant shall be released expeditiously but not later than four months from the date of this order.

41. The appeals are allowed in the aforesaid terms. No order as to costs.

3. PAY PARITY WITH BSF AND CRPF

3.1 JUDGEMENT DATED 4.01.2008 IN SLP (C) 21222 OF 2005 TITLED UNION OF INDIA & ORS VS DINESHAN K.K (SUPREME COURT)

Delay condoned.

2. Leave granted.

3. This appeal by the Union of India and the Director General of Assam Rifles arises out of the judgment and order dated 11th February, 2005 rendered by the Gauhati High Court in WP (C) No.497 of 2001. By the impugned order, while allowing the writ petition, directions have been issued that the permission granted by the Union of India vide its letter dated 3rd March, 1998, to re-designate the rank of Havildar (Radio Mechanic) as Warrant Officer as recommended by the Ministry of Home Affairs shall be carried out and the pay scale as admissible to their counterparts in the Central Reserve Police Force (CRPF) and the Border Security Force (BSF) shall be granted from the same date.

4. The nub of the grievance of the writ petitioner, working in the rank of a Radio Mechanic in the Assam Rifles was that the Ministry of Home Affairs and the Director General of Assam Rifles having accepted in principle that the members of the Assam Rifles, should be given the same rank and pay structure as was given to other central paramilitary forces, yet the same had been denied to them. It was pleaded that as the Ministry of Home Affairs had conveyed its decision to rationalize the rank structure of non gazetted personnel of central paramilitary forces vide order dated 26th January, 1998, equal pay structure in other ranks, including the Radio Mechanics in the Assam Rifles could not be denied. His further grievance was that after the implementation of the Fourth Pay Commission, the pay of the Havildar/GD and Head Constable/Radio Mechanic was fixed in the pay scale of Rs.975-1660, without any discrimination between the general duty and technical categories but the discrimination surfaced when higher pay scale of Rs.1200-2040 was given to the Radio Mechanics working in the BSF, denying the same pay scale to the Radio Mechanics in the Assam Rifles. It was also pointed out that the Radio Mechanics working in the Delhi Police organization had been given a much higher pay scale on 10th October, 1997 which was being denied to the similar rank holders in the Assam Rifles.

5. The writ petition was contested by the Union of India. In the counter affidavit filed on its behalf, it was stated that on the recommendation of the Fourth Pay Commission, with effect from 1st January, 1986, the Assam Rifles personnel had been granted revised pay scales and allowances entirely on the lines of other central paramilitary forces. However, as the changes in the rank structure were not carried out in the Assam Rifles like in other central paramilitary forces, an apparent disparity in the service conditions of certain category of personnel including the rank of Radio Mechanic had arisen. It was also pointed out that the Assam Rifles Directorate had brought this disparity to the notice of the Ministry of Home Affairs in February, 1998, and had recommended the re-designation of Radio Mechanic and Head Constable in Assam Rifles as Warrant Officer and for replacement of pay scale of Rs.4000-6000 to bring them at par with their counterparts in other central police organizations. It was stated that in response to the said recommendation, the Ministry of Home Affairs vide letter dated 3rd March, 1998, had informed the Assam Rifles that they could re-designate the Head Constable (Radio Mechanic) as Warrant Officer provided their pre-revised and revised pay scales were identical to the pay scales of their counterparts in CRPF and BSF. However, the re-designation of the ranks could not be carried out in the light of the said communication as there was disparitybetween the pay scales of a Radio Mechanic in Assam Rifles and their counterparts in CRPF and BSF. It was conceded that though the academic qualification for

recruitment to the post of Radio Mechanic in Assam Rifles as well as in CRPF and BSF was the same yet there was disparity in the revised pay scales between the Assam Rifles and the said two other paramilitary forces. The claim of the petitioner for higher pay scales on the lines of the pay scales of Delhi Police organization was seriously contested on the ground that the Assam Rifles being a central police organisation, it could not claim parity with Delhi Police organization, which was not a central paramilitary force.

6. Taking note of the admission on the part of the Union of India that there was disparity between the pay scales of the members of the Assam Rifles and similarly ranked personnel of other paramilitary forces, the High Court felt that it would be unreasonable and discriminatory if the pay scales given to Radio Mechanics in CRPF and BSF were denied to the Radio Mechanics in Assam Rifles, when the qualifications and service requirements in all the three organizations were identical. Consequently, the High Court issued the aforenoted directions, which are questioned in this appeal.

7. Mr. B. Dutta, learned Additional Solicitor General, appearing for the Union of India contended that the direction given by the High Court is manifestly contrary to the settled legal position, enunciated by this Court in several decisions that pay fixation is essentially an executive function, ordinarily undertaken by an expert body like the Pay Commission, whose recommendations are entitled to a great weight though not binding on the Government. It was argued that the recommendations of an expert body are not justiciable since the Court is not equipped to take upon itself the task of job evaluation, which is a complex exercise. In support of the proposition, reliance is placed on two decisions of this Court in S.C. Chandra & Ors. Vs. State of Jharkhand & Ors. and Union of India & Ors. Vs. Hiranmoy Sen & Ors. .

8. Mr. Ranjit Kumar, learned senior counsel, appearing on behalf of the respondent, on the other hand, submitted that the petitioners having themselves admitted that there was an anomaly in the pay scales of the

personnel of Assam Rifles, particularly, the Radio Mechanics, as compared to their counterparts in other paramilitary forces, the High Court was fully justified in giving the impugned directions. It was pointed out that, in fact, the Director General, Assam Rifles, who is one of the petitioners in the present appeal, had himself recommended to the Ministry of Home Affairs that the anomalyin the pay scales of the Radio Mechanics should be rectified. Learned counsel submits that it is unfair on the part of the Director General to take a somersault and oppose the direction given by the High Court which is in consonance with his recommendation. Learned counsel, however, stated that the respondent was not pressing for parity with the personnel of the Delhi Police.

9. The principle of equal pay for equal work has been considered, explained and applied in a catena of decisions of this Court. The doctrine of equal pay for equal workwas originally propounded as part of the Directive Principles of the State Policy in Article 39(d) *of the Constitution. In* Randhir Singh Vs. Union of India & Ors. *, a bench of three learned Judges of this Court had observed that principle of equal pay for equal work is not a mere demagogic slogan but a constitutional goal, capable of being attained through constitutional remedies and held that this principle had to be read under* Article 14 *and 16 of the Constitution. This decision was affirmed by a Constitution Bench of this Court in* D.S. Nakara & Ors. Vs. Union of India *. Thus, having regard to the constitutional mandate of equality and inhibition against discrimination in* Article 14 *and 16, in service jurisprudence, the doctrine of equal pay for equal workhas assumed status of a fundamental right.*

10. Initially, particularly in the early eighties, the said principle was being applied as an absolute rule but realizing its cascading effect on other cadres, in subsequent decisions of this Court, a note of caution was sounded that the principle of equal pay for equal work had no mathematical application in every case of similar work. It has been observed that equation of posts and equation of pay structure being complex matters are generally left to the Executive and expert bodies like the Pay Commission etc. It has been emphasized that a carefully evolved pay structure ought not to be ordinarily disturbed by the Court as it may upset the balance and cause avoidable ripples in other cadres as well. (Vide: Secretary, Finance Department & Ors. Vs. West Bengal Registration Service Association & Ors. *and* State of Haryana & Anr. Vs. Haryana Civil Secretariat Personal Staff Association *. Nevertheless, it will not be correct to lay down as an absolute rule that merely because determination and granting of pay scales is the prerogative of the Executive, the Court has no jurisdiction to examine any pay structure and an aggrieved employee has no remedy if he is unjustly treated by arbitrary State action or inaction, except to go on knocking at the doors of the Executive or the Legislature, as is sought to be canvassed on behalf of the appellants. Undoubtedly, when there is no dispute with regard to the qualifications, duties and responsibilities of the persons holding identical posts or ranks but they are treated differently merely because they belong to different departments or the basis for classification of posts is ex-facie irrational, arbitrary or unjust, it is open to the Court to intervene.*

11. In State Bank of India & Anr. Vs. M.R. Ganesh Babu & Ors. *, a three-Judge Bench of this Court, dealing with the same principle, opined that principle of equal pay is dependent upon the nature of work done. It cannot be judged by the mere volume of work; there may be qualitative difference as regards reliability and responsibility. The functions may be the same but the responsibilities do make a difference. It was held that the judgment of administrative authorities, concerning the responsibilities which attach to the post, and the degree of reliability expected of an incumbent, would be a value judgment of the authorities concerned which, if arrived at bona fide, reasonably and rationally, was not open to interference by the Court.*

12. In State of Haryana & Anr. Vs. Tilak Raj & Ors. *, it has been observed that the principle of equal pay for equal workis not always easy to apply as there are inherent difficulties in comparing and* *evaluating the work of different persons in different organizations or even in the same organisation. It has been reiterated that this is a concept which requires for its applicability, complete and wholesale identity between a group of employees claiming identical pay scales and the other group of employees who have already earned such pay scales. It has been emphasized that the problem about equal pay cannot be translated into a mathematical formula.*

13. Yet again in a recent decision in State of Haryana & Ors. Vs. Charanjit Singh & Ors. , *a Bench of three learned Judges, while affirming the view taken by this Court in the cases of* State of Haryana & Ors. Vs. Jasmer Singh & Ors. , *Tilak Raj (supra), Orissa University of Agriculture & Technlogy & Anr. Vs. Manoj K. Mohanty and* Government of W.B. Vs. Tarun Roy & Ors. *has reiterated that the doctrine of equal pay for equal work is not an abstract doctrine and is capable of being enforced in a court of law. Inter alia, observing that equal pay must be for equal work of equal value and that the principle of equal pay for equal work has no mathematical application in every case, it has been held that* Article 14 *permits reasonable classification based on qualities or characteristics of persons recruited and grouped together, as against those who are left out. Of course, the qualities or characteristics must have a reasonable relation to the object sought to be achieved. Enumerating a number of factors which may not warrant application of the principle of equal pay for equal work, it has been held that since the said principle requires consideration of various dimensions of a given job, normally the applicability of this principle must be left to be evaluated and determined by an expert body and the Court should not interfere till it is satisfied that the necessary material on the basis whereof the claim is made is available on record with necessary proof and that there is equal work and equal quality and all other relevant factors are fulfilled.*

14. Tested on the touchstone of the aforenoted broad guidelines and not cast-iron imperatives, we are of the opinion that in the present case, on the pleadings and the material placed on record by the parties in support of their respective stands, the High Court was justified in issuing the impugned directions.

15. Vide order dated 10th October, 1997 passed by the Ministry of Home Affairs in pursuance of para 7 of the Ministry of Finance, Department of Expenditure Resolution dated 30th September, 1997, it was notified that the President was pleased to rationalize the rank structure and pay scales of non gazetted cadre of central police organizations and as a result of this exercise certain ranks were to be merged and the rank structure was communicated in the order along with the revised pay scales and replacement pay scales. Copy of this order was sent to all the paramilitary forces, including the Assam Rifles. On 22nd January, 1998, an office memorandum was issued by the Government of India, Ministry of Home Affairs, by way of a clarification. In the said letter, it was clarified that order dated 10th October, 1997 was equally applicable to all advertised categories. In the said letter, direction with regard to the re-designation of the three posts including Head Constable (RM) as ASI in central paramilitary forces along with their replacement pay scales were also ordered. It appears that the disparity in rank and pay in various central paramilitary forces could not be resolved and on 24th April, 2001, the Director General Assam Rifles submitted a report to the Government with regard to the progress on pay anomaly cases. Para 4 of the said letter is of some relevance to the issue at hand and it reads as follows:

Rank and pay of Technical Cadre Person RM. Ptmn, Pharma, and Compounder of AR with the same intake QR for remounts are given the rank of HAV wherein they are counterparts in CPOs are given ASI. The MHA had ordered to submit proposal in directing cadre to cadre comparison with BSF where the rank of ASI is available in other tech and also along with fin implication. The proposal alongwith fin implication has been submitted to MHA and the case is lying with MOF for approval.

16. Having failed to receive any positive response from the Government, one of the Radio Mechanics issued a Notice of Demand to the Ministry of Home Affairs and Director General of Assam Rifles, inter alia, praying for giving effect to office order dated 10th October, 1997 and office memorandum dated 22nd January, 1998. Vide order dated 26th December, 2001, the Ministry of Home Affairs informed the Director General of Assam Rifles that his proposal had been examined in consultation with Ministry of Finance and it was found that there was no point for comparison of grades and scales of pay for such posts across various central paramilitary forces. It was stated that the proposed upgradation may disturb relativities of various trades and grades within the Assam Rifles and there was no functional justification for upgrading these posts. It is evident that on rejection of the recommendation made by the Director General of the Force, the respondent herein was left with no option but to approach the High Court for redressal of his grievance.

17. As noted above, the writ petition was opposed by the petitioners herein by filing counter affidavit. For the sake of ready reference, the relevant portions in some of the paragraphs of the counter affidavit are extracted below:

That, with regards to the averments of the petitioner made in the writ petition in paragraph 5, I submit that Assam Rifles personnel were in receipt of pay and allowances on Army analogy with various groups in terms of Group A, B, C, D, & E to conform to their functional qualitative requirements of these groups which had varying pay scales. I submit that on the recommendation of the fourth pay commission w.e.f. 01.01.1986 for Force had been granted and pay and allowance entirely on the lines of Central Para Military Forces while no change in the rank structure was carried out and this difference in rank structure has resulted in an apparent disparity in their service conditions and certain category of personnel who were placed in the erstwhile higher groups including radio mechanics category have also been deprived of pay scales either at par with their counterparts in the Army or in the Central Police Organisation.

That, with regard to the averments of the petitioner made in the writ petition in paragraph 8, I beg to reiterate that Assam Rifles personnel were in receipt of pay and allowances on Army analogy with various groups in terms of Group A, B, C, D, & E, to conform to their functional and qualitative requirements of these groups which had varying pay scales in diminishing order. On the recommendation of the Fourth Pay Commission w.e.f. 1st January, 1986 the Force had been granted pay and allowances entirely on the lines of Central Para Military forces shortly called as CPMFs while no change in the rank structure was carried out, and this difference in the rank structure has resulted in an apparent disparity in their service condition.

That, with regards to the averments of the petitioner made in the writ petition in paragraphs 10 to 13, I beg to submit that on receipt of MHA letter No.27011/1103/97-PF.1/56 dated 22nd January, 1998, Assam Rifles Directorate by letter No.A/Pers/5th CPC/Vol.III/98 dated 18th February, 1998 had taken up a case with HA to redesignate Hav/RM-Gde I & II of Assam Rifles as Warrant Officer and for replacement of pay scale of Rs.4000-1000-6000/- to bring them at par with their counterparts in other Central Police Organisation. I submit that attention of MHA was also drawn regarding placement of Hav/RM Gde I and II in the lower scale of pay consequent to implementation of IV Pay Commission. In reply to the Assam Rifles Directorate letter the MHA had ruled out vide their letter No.27011/103/97-P.F.1 dated 3rd March, 1998 that Assam Rifles can redesignate HC (RM) as Warrant Officer if pre-revised and revised pay scale of Hav(RM) in Assam Rifles are identical to the pay scale of HC(RM) in BSF and CRPF. I submit that the main hurdle in implementing the said order in Assam Rifles is that there is disparity in pay scales of RM in Assam Rifles to that of BSF and CRPF. The Hav(RM) of Assam Rifles were drawing pay scales of Rs.975- 1660/- w.e.f. 1st January, 1986 and replacement scale as given in the 5th Central Pay Commission is

Rs.3200- 4900/- per month whereas in CRPF and BSF the Hav (RM) was drawing pay scale of Rs.1200-30-1560-40-2040/- per month whose replacement scale in the 5th Central Pay Commission is Rs.4000-100- 6000/-. It is also pertinent to clarify here that the qualification of HC(RM) in other Central Police Organisations that of Assam Rifles Hav (RM) is almost par.

As per averment made in Para 13 of the writ petition, the petitioner is seeking higher pay scale viz 5000-150-8000/- admissible to Delhi Police personnel. I submit that since the Assam Rifles is at par with other central police organization, the demand of the petitioner, for parity with an entirely another department is not possible. In view of the facts narrated above and to bring parity with other central police organization, it is proposed to grant warrant officers rank (Equivalent to Assistant Sub Inspector) to technical categories including radio mechanics vide Assam Rifles Directorate Letter No.A/Pers/45th CPC/Vol III/98/77 dated 6th April, 1998 and subsequent queries sought by the MHA has been replied. I submit that MHA has also informed to the LOAR (Liaison Office, Assam Rifles) that the case for introduction of Warrant Officers rank to technical categories is presently lying with Ministry of Finance (E-III) since 29th August, 2000.(Emphasis supplied)

18. From the afore-extracted paragraphs of the counter affidavit and the resume of correspondence referred to above, it clearly stands admitted by the petitioners herein that: (i) all the paramilitary forces, including Assam Rifles are at par with each other and (ii) there was apparent disparity in the pay scales of the personnel of Assam Rifles with their counterparts in other central paramilitary forces. In order to rectify this disparity, Director General Assam Rifles, petitioner No.2 herein, vide his letter dated 18th February, 1998 had, in fact, taken up the grievance of the respondent with the Ministry of Home Affairs, inter alia recommending re-designation of Havildar (RM) Gd.-I and II of Assam Rifles as Warrant Officer and for replacement of pay scale of Rs.4000-100-6000 to bring them at par with their counterparts in other

central police organization. However, the Ministry of Home Affairs vide letter dated 3rd March, 1998 while accepting the said proposal had recommended re-designation of HAV/RM as Warrant Officer but subject to the condition that the pre-revised and revised pay scales of HAV/RM in other paramilitary forces were identical to the pay scales of Head Constable (RM) in CRFP and BSF. Manifestly, in the instant case, the differentiation in the pay scales of the two paramilitary forces is sought to be achieved not on the ground of dissimilarity of academic qualification or the nature of duties and responsibilities but only on the ground that there was initial anomalyin the Fourth Central Pay Commission Report. The counter affidavit does not even attempt to explain how the case of the HAV/RM in Assam Rifles is different from that of Radio Mechanics in other central paramilitary forces.

19. In the present case, therefore, in the light of the admitted factual position, the question of examination of external comparisons, internal relativities and other factors, to be kept in view for job evaluation, considered to be a complex issue to be studied only by expert bodies, does not arise. As a necessary corollary, the issue as to whether there is a complete or wholesale identity between the said paramilitary forces, does not survive for consideration.

20. Thus, the short question requiring our consideration is whether having admitted in their affidavit referred to hereinabove, the apparent disparity and anomaly in the pay scales of Radio Mechanics, the administrative authorities, the petitioners herein, could be permitted to perpetuate apparent discriminatory differentiation in the pay scales because of the disparity in pre-revised and revised scales of the personnel of Assam Rifles prior to the recommendations of the Fourth Pay Commission, irrespective of the identity of their powers, duties and responsibilities with other paramilitary forces. In our considered opinion, in view of the total absence of any plea on the part of the Union of India that Radio Mechanics in other paramilitary forces were performing different or more onerous duties as compared to the Radio Mechanics in Assam Rifles, the impugned decision of the Government was clearly irrational and arbitrary and thus, violative of Article 14 of the Constitution.

21. On a conspectus of the factual scenario noted above, we do not find any infirmity in the impugned directions given by the High Court, warranting interference. There is no merit in this appeal and it is dismissed accordingly with costs.

CHAPTER VII

CENTRAL INDUSTRIAL SECURITY FORCE -LAW INCLUDING LEADING CASE LAWS

1. HOUSE RENT ALLOWANCE FOR OFFICERS IN CISF

1.1 JUDGEMENT DATED 08.02.2024 IN CIVIL APPEAL NO.4967/2023 TITLED UNION OF INDIA & ORS. VERSUS PARAMISIVAN M

ISSUE

These matters pertain to House Rent Allowance being provided to the Personnel Below Officer Rank (PBOR) serving in the Central Industrial Security Force (CISF).

> 5 The High Court in granting relief to the writ petitioners referred to Rule 61 of the Central Industrial Security Forces Rules, 2010 which reads as under:-

"61. Free accommodation. -

(1) Normally, the undertaking where the Force has been deputed shall provide accommodation in the township itself to all supervisory officers and at the rate of 45 per cent married and 55 per cent unmarried or as amended by the Central Government from time to time, to the enrolled members of the Force.

(2) The accommodation to the enrolled member of the Force shall be rent-free but where such facilities are not available they shall get house rent allowance in lieu thereof as applicable to other central government employees.

(3) The members of the Force shall also get compensation in lieu of married accommodation in terms of orders issued by the Government from time to time in this respect. The compensation shall be payable to that percentage of members of the Force who are entitled to get married accommodation minus those members of the Force who are allotted accommodation by the Undertaking.

(4) Supervisory officer of the Force who is provided accommodation by the Public Sector Undertakings or allotted accommodation by Directorate of Estate will pay licence fee to the Public Sector Undertakings at the rates as applicable to their own employees or the licence fee as fixed by the Central Government for genera pool accommodation from time to time with reference to plinth area of accommodation as the case may be."

6 The above Rule came to be interpreted in the case of "Jaspal Singh Mann Vs Union of India &Ors" by the High Court of Delhi in Civil Writ Petition No.1712/2006. The Court noted that the writ petitioner is employed in the CISF and was, therefore, entitled for official accommodation but the same was not given to him. Since neither rent free accommodation was provided nor House Rent Allowance (HRA), the Writ Petition came to be filed.

7. The High Court while deciding the case of Jaspal Singh (supra) held as follows:-

"13. The operation of Rule 61 of the said Rules and its interpretation has given rise to a situation where the grant of such accommodation or HRA in lieu thereof is sought to be made dependent where a person is posted.

14. It is trite to say that the transfer or posting is an incident of service. The respondents post such persons at different stations according to their requirement and thus there cannot be any discrimination on the question of the grant of accommodation or HRA in lieu thereof on the basis of such station one is posted to. Thus, merely *because the appellant comes to be posted at Delhi from Amritsar he cannot be deprived the HRA.*

15. *Another aspect to be noted is that in some of the paramilitary forces, 100 per cent of the force is being granted family accommodation or HRA in lieu thereof giving rise to discrimination between personnel of para-military forces and thus principles as laid down in Union of India Vs. Dineshan K.K. case (supra) would equally apply.*

16. *The appointment letter issued to the appellant itself stated that allowances as admissible and sanctioned by the Central Government would apply and HRA is payable as per CCS (HRA) Rules as admitted by the respondents.*

17. *We fail to appreciate either the rationale or the basis for creating an artificial category of persons who - would be disentitled to an accommodation or HRA. There can be percentages assigned between different categories of personnel for distribution of the accommodation available. This is a natural corollary of shortage of accommodation. The appellant cannot make a grievance in respect of the same. However, if a personnel is not granted a family accommodation on account of his seniority being lower in his category of persons as per the percentage of distribution of family accommodation, HRA must follow. The rule as sought to be interpreted would imply that not only is there a percentage distribution between different categories but the persons falling outside the ambit of consideration would be deprived even of the HRA. The only manner of reading the Rule which would sustain would be that Rule 61 of the said Rules would not entitle a person to claim family accommodation if in the percentage of distribution as per sub-rule 1 of Rule 61 of the said Rules, he is not of sufficient seniority but in that eventuality he is entitled to the HRA in lieu thereof as applicable to the Central Government employees. Sub-rule 2 of Rule 61 of the said Rules is unambiguous inasmuch as, it says that those who cannot be provided - with a free accommodation because of the paucity of accommodation* *which has to be distributed in the ratio of 45 per cent : 55 per cent in case of married and unmarried officials, shall be provided HRA in lieu thereof. If Rule 61 (1) and Rule 61 (3) of the said Rules are read together, the only conclusion which can be derived is, that while there may be a situation where there may not be a house available for allotment to an officer posted at a particular station, he still would be entitled to HRA. However, in case where a person is entitled to married accommodation but is provided with unmarried accommodation, then he may also be entitled to compensation in lieu of married accommodation in addition to the allotment of house available for unmarried category if he wants to occupy the said house".*

8 According to the High Court, if Rule 61 is interpreted in the manner suggested by the Union of India, it will be discriminatory and will fall foul of the principles of Article 14 of the Constitution. In fact, no rationale nexus with the object relating to grant of HRA, for discriminatory treatment was found by the Court. Consequently, Writ of mandamus was issued directing the employer to pay the HRA in lieu of family accommodation from the date the petitioner became entitled to claim such family accommodation. The Rule 61 of the CISF Rules was accordingly read down to imply that such entitlement will be within the parameters of such rules. In other words, where the employer was unable to provide family accommodation within the township to the enrolled personnel, they will be entitled to HRA. If the dues are not paid within three months, they were to carry interest @8%.

9 The above Judgment of the High Court in Jaspal Singh (supra) came to be challenged by the Union of India and the Civil Appeal No.1132/2009 came to be dismissed by this Court through an order dated 20-2-2009. In dismissing the appeal, this Court took note of the Office Memorandum dated 16-2-2009 produced by the then Additional Solicitor General.

10 The impugned Judgment of the High Court is a follow-up of the above Judgment, in Jaspal Singh Mann (supra)

11 Having considered the basis for the interpretation given in Jaspal Singh Mann (supra) and upon consideration of the rival submissions of the learned counsel for the parties, we see no reason to disturb the view taken in favour of the respondents, by the High Court.

12 The appeals are, accordingly dismissed.

13 The amount which the respondents are, therefore, entitled towards HRA, should be disbursed within three months. If it is not paid within three months, the payable amount will carry interest @8%, as was ordered by the High Court. The interest will be calculated from the date of judgment passed by the Division Bench of the High Court in favour of the respondents.

2. DISCIPLINARY PEOCEEDINGS UNDER THE CISF ACT

2.1 JUDGEMENT DATED 23.11.2022 IN CIVIL APPEAL NOS. 7939-7940 OF 2022 TITLED UNION OF INDIA AND OTHERS versus SUBRATA NATH (SUREME COURT)

2. ....the respondent joined the Central Industrial Security Force[1] as a Constable on 26th February, 1994. On 7th November, 2007, the respondent was detailed for 'C' shift duty from 21:00 hours on 7th November, 2007 to 05:00 hours on 8th November, 2007 at Alif Nagar Scrap yard situated in the Garden Reach area of the Kolkata Port. On the next day, i.e., on 8th November, 2007, the local police intercepted a Tata-407 truck loaded with approximately 800 kg. (approx.) of copper wires outside the port premises and informed the CISF about the said incident on learning that the copper wires had been removed from the Kolkata Port Trust area. It transpired that the said copper wires had been removed from the scrap yard of Alif Nagar Kolkata Port in the duration when the respondent was on duty. The respondent was placed under suspension and charge sheeted, vide Memorandum dated 7th December, 2007. Following are the two articles of charge framed against the respondent:

"STATEMENT OF ARTICLE OF CHARGE FRAMED AGAINST NO. 941400817 CONSTABLE SUBRATA NATH OF CISF UNIT KoPT KOLKATA.

Article of Charge- I

That the said No.941400817 Constable Subrata Nath of CISF Unit KoPT Kolkata ("C" Coy) while perforating "C" Shift duty from 2100 hrs on 07.11.2007 to 0500 hrs on 08.11.2007 at Alif Nagar Scrap Yard with Arms and Ammunition has failed to prevent theft of copper wire weighing about 800 Kgs which were laying with other bundles of copper wire at Alif Nagar Scrap Yard of DoPT under the security coverage of the said No. 941400817 Constable Subrata Nath.

The above act on the part of No. 941400817 Constable Subrata Nath amounts to gross negligence and dereliction of duty being member of a disciplined Force.

Article of Charge-II

That the said No. 941400817 Constable Subrata Nath of CISF Unit KoPT Kolkata during the period of his 13 years sendee in CISF has been involved himself in various delinquencies and thereby awarded 08 (Eight) punishments. Even then he did not mend himself and has developed an

incorrigible character."

4. *An Inquiry Officer was appointed to conduct the inquiry in respect of the above charges. During the inquiry, eight prosecution witnesses were examined. However, the respondent did not produce any witness in his defence. After examining the evidence and the defence of the respondent, the Inquiry Officer held that both the charges framed against the respondent were duly proved. The Disciplinary Authority issued a Notice to Show Cause to the respondent in relation to the inquiry report, in response whereto, he submitted a representation. Vide order dated 27th November, 2008, the Disciplinary Authority,* *namely, the Commandant rejected the representation of the respondent. It was observed that the statements of the prosecution witnesses corroborated with the scene of the crime and established that theft of copper wires from the Alif Nagar Scrap Yard had taken place when the respondent was on duty at the duty post. Further, the prosecution witnesses had proved that the respondent was found to be alert at the duty post by nine different checking officers, who had checked him in the intervening night on $7^{th}/8^{th}$ November, 2007, despite which, he did not report the criminal activities in his duty area.*

5. *Rejecting the plea taken by the respondent that the FIR had recorded the occurrence of the offence at 1530 hours on 8th November, 2007 which indicated that the theft had not taken place during his duty hours, the Disciplinary Authority held thus:*

*"**12**. After taking into account all the above aspect, I am of the opinion that prosecution witnesses by virtue of corroborative statements supported by documentary and circumstantial evidences has established, the Articles of charge-I proved against the charged official. On the other hand, the charged official could not come up with any convincing materials in his representation to disprove the Article of charge-I. Even he could not produce any defence witness. The defence documents produced by him during enquiry could not prove anything in his favour. The FIR copy produced by him (Defence Exhibit-6) showing occurrence of offence at about 1530 hours on 08.11.2007 by which he wanted to refute all claims of theft happening during his duty hours was examined in depth xxx   xxx   xxx*

xxx The above complain shows that the recovery of the copper wire was made by the complainant at 1515 hours on 08.11.2007 whereas the FIR shows the occurrence of offence at 1530 hours on 08.11.2007 and the offence described as theft of a vehicle TATA-407 loaded with some coils of copper wire and recovery vehicle was laid at Alif Nagar KMC Sweeper Quarters. Thus, it means that the recovery of copper wire was made before the theft occurred, which is improbable and absurd indeed. It was further observed that FIR shows time of information received at 2200 hours on 08.11.2007, occurrence of theft at 1530 hours while complaint shows recovery was made at 1515 hours on same day. All these reveal that the recovery was made well before receiving information by the concerned police official of West Port Police station and even before occurrence of theft............. Taking all these facts together it is clear that the FIR corroborates the fact of recovery of copper wire loaded in TATA- 407 vehicle and the statement of PW1, PW2 & PW8 corroborates the fact that the seized vehicle was held in police custody in the morning of 08.11.2007. In totality of all the above it is established that the theft of copper wire from Alif Nagar scrap yard has occurred in the night of 07/08.11.2007 during the duty period of the charged official and the said copper wire was later recovered by West Port police and kept at their custody loaded in TATA-407 vehicle well before the visit of PW1, PW2 and PW8 at the west port police station in the morning of 08.11.2007.............As regards Article of Charge-II, I find that statement of PW4 and documentary evidences held on record clearly establish that the charged official has developed into incorrigible character who even after awarding 08 punishments for various delinquencies in his 13 years of service in CISF has not reformed himself. From the fact and factual position as assessed, discussed and evaluated above over the prosecution version and defence version, I find that the findings drawn by the enquiry officer are fair, reasoned and judicially justified in all respect. I, therefore, fully agree with the findings of the enquiry officer and hold the charged official guilty of the Article of Charge-I and Article of Charge-II."

6. *In view of the above findings and in exercise of the powers conferred under Rule 32 read with Schedule-I and Rule 32 (1) of the Central Industrial Security Force Rules, 2001^2, the Disciplinary Authority imposed a penalty of dismissal from service on the respondent. Aggrieved by the order dated 27th November, 2008 passed by the Disciplinary Authority, the respondent preferred an appeal,* which was dismissed on 3rd February, 2009 with the following observations :

"5. I have carefully considered the appeal preferred by the appellant, the departmental proceeding files, findings of the enquiry officer and other related documents held on record and I have applied my mind to the case. I find that the Articles of charge leveled against the appellant were held proved on the basis of overwhelming evidence held on record. The enquiry officer had conducted the enquiry in a fair and judicious manner and afforded him all reasonable opportunities to rebut the adverse evidence and to submit sufficient material in support of his defence. He, however, failed to do so. There is also no material irregularity or miscarriage of justice in this case. The Disciplinary Authority has passed the final order after considering all aspects of the case held on records and awarded the penalty of "Dismissal from service" to the appellant vide Final Order No. V-15014/Maj-04/KoPT/Disc/SN/08/8271 dated 27.11.08 for his failure to prevent theft of copper wire weighing about 800 kgs which were laying with other bundles of copper wire at Alif Nagar scrap yard of KoPT under the security coverage of the appellant while he was performing 'C' shift duty from 2100 hrs on 7.11.2007 to 0500 hrs on 08.11.2007 at Alif Nagar Scrap yard duty post and nonimproving his conduct as expected from a member of disciplined force, in spite of having been penalized/punished earlier on 08 (Eight) occasions for his incorrigible habits during his short span of 13 years' service is commensurate to the gravity of offence. The appellant has not come up with any cogent and logical reason that warrants consideration. Many other pleas put forth by the appellant in his appeal do not have any merit.

6. As such, I do not find any mitigating circumstances to interfere with the order of penalty dated 27.11.2008 passed by the Disciplinary Authority, i.e., Commandant CISF Unit KoPT Kolkata. Hence, the appeal dated 05.12.2008 preferred by the appellant is rejected being devoid of merit."

7. *This was followed by a Revision Petition submitted by the respondent in the Office of the Inspector General, CISF/NES, which was dismissed vide order dated 19th May, 2009, holding inter alia that the charges levelled against him had been proved beyond doubt; that he had been afforded all the reasonable opportunities to defend himself; that there were no procedural irregularities in conducting the disciplinary inquiry by the Inquiry Officer or on the part of Disciplinary Authority in dealing with the case of the respondent and that principles of natural justice had been complied with.*

8. *Dissatisfied by the order passed by the Revisional Authority upholding the orders of the Disciplinary Authority and the Appellate Authority, the respondent filed a writ petition in the High Court of Calcutta, registered as WP No.14102 (W) of 2009. The said petition was disposed of by the learned Single Judge, vide order dated 25th June, 2018 and the punishment of dismissal imposed on the respondent was converted to that of compulsory retirement primarily on the ground that the authorities had failed to preserve the relevant records pertaining to the case and one of the vital documents of the inquiry, namely, the Beat Book, which recorded the time when the respondent had taken charge from his reliever and the items available on the spot and the time when he handed over charge to his successor, required examination. Observing that the authorities ought to have maintained the relevant records of inquiry in view of pendency of the writ petition, the learned Single Judge set aside the punishment of dismissal from service imposed on the respondent and compulsorily retired him from service w.e.f. 27th November, 2008 alongwith all consequential benefits.*

9. *The aforesaid order was challenged by the appellants – Union of India in two sets of appeals (FMA No.679 of 2019 and FMA 680 of 2019), that were disposed of by the Division Bench, vide the impugned judgment dated 9th September, 2021 whereby, the decision of the learned Single Judge of substituting the punishment of dismissal imposed on the respondent with one of compulsory retirement, was* *quashed and set aside. Instead, it was directed that the respondent would be entitled to be reinstated in service along with full back wages from the date of his dismissal. The Disciplinary Authority was further directed to issue a fresh order of punishment in respect of the respondent that should commensurate to his negligence and dereliction of duty, other than a punishment of dismissal, removal from service or compulsory retirement.*

10. *Questioning the aforesaid judgment, the present appeals have been filed by the appellants – Union of India. The respondent has also preferred Petitions for Special Leave to appeal being aggrieved by the directions issued by the High Court calling upon the Disciplinary Authority to issue a fresh order of punishment qua him upon reinstatement on a plea that there was no occasion for the Division Bench to have interfered with the order passed by the learned Single Judge whereby the punishment of removal from service had been set aside and the respondent was directed to becompulsorily retired from service.*

11. *Appearing for the appellants – Union of India, Ms. Aakanksha Kaul, learned counsel has argued that the impugned judgment is unsustainable for the reason that the High Court has acted as an Appellate Authority by directing reinstatement of the respondent, which runs contrary to the law laid down by the Supreme Court in* **<u>B.C. Chaturvedi v. Union of India and Others</u>**; *that the High Court while exercising the powers vested in it under judicial review, ought not to have stepped into the shoes of the Appellate Authority and reappreciated the evidence to arrive at independent findings on the evidence adduced; that no grievance was raised by the respondent that the rules of natural justice had been violated or the inquiry had not been conducted in a proper manner or that the findings arrived at by the Disciplinary Authority were based on no evidence. Learned counsel asserted that in the instant case, the inquiry was conducted by a competent officer, rules of natural justice were duly complied with and the findings arrived at by the Inquiry Officer were based on*

sufficient evidence. Stating that having regard to the fact that the charges against the respondent had been proved in a properly conducted departmental inquiry after giving a reasonable opportunity to the respondent to defend himself, there was no good reason for the learned Single Judge to have converted the punishment of dismissal from service imposed by the Disciplinary Authority and upheld by the Appellate Authority, to compulsory retirement and for the Division Bench to have further interfered by reassessing the evidence and directing reinstatement of the respondent in service with full back wages and only thereafter, pass a fresh order of punishment.

12. *Citing the decision in* **State of Orissa and Others v. Bidyabhushan Mohapatra³**, *it was contended that keeping in mind the gravity of the established misconduct, the Disciplinary Authority has the power to impose a punishment on the delinquent officer and such a punishment is not open for review by the High Court under Article 226 of the Constitution of India. It was also sought to be urged on behalf of the appellants that the past conduct of the respondent can be taken into consideration while awarding penalty, subject to the condition that the same is made a part of a separate charge, as was done in the instant case. In support of the said submission, learned counsel cited* **Central Industrial Security Force and Others v. Abrar Ali ⁴**.

13. *The only submission made by Mr. Ranjan Mukherjee, learned counsel for the respondent is that the learned Single Judge having directed reinstatement of the respondent with full back wages, the Division Bench was not justified in passing an order directing that a fresh order be passed by the Disciplinary Authority commensurate to the negligence and dereliction of duty on the part of the respondent. Instead, the appeals preferred by the appellants – Union of India ought to have been dismissed outright in which event, the punishment of compulsory retirement imposed by the learned Single Judge would*

have been restored and attained finality thereby entitling the respondent to claim his retiral benefits.

14. *The point that arises for our consideration is whether in the given facts of the case, the learned Single Judge and the Division Bench ought to have interfered with the punishment imposed on the respondent by the Disciplinary Authority and upheld by the Appellate Authority as also by the Revisional Authority.*

15. *It is well settled that courts ought to refrain from interfering with findings of facts recorded in a departmental inquiry except in circumstances where such findings are patently perverse or grossly incompatible with the evidence on record, based on no evidence. However, if principles of natural justice have been violated or the statutory regulations have not been adhered to or there are malafides attributable to the Disciplinary Authority, then the courts can certainly interfere.*

16. *In the above context, following are the observations made by a three-Judge Bench of this Court in **B.C. Chaturvedi** (supra) :*

"12. Judicial review is not an appeal from a decision but a review of the manner in which the decision is made. Power of judicial review is meant to ensure that the individual receives fair treatment and not to ensure that the conclusion which the authority reaches is necessarily correct in the eye of the court. When an inquiry is conducted on charges of misconduct by a public servant, the Court/Tribunal is concerned to determine whether the inquiry was held by a competent officer or whether rules of natural justice are complied with. Whether the findings or conclusions are based on some evidence, the authority entrusted with the power to hold inquiry has jurisdiction, power and authority to reach a finding of fact or conclusion. But that finding must be based on some evidence. Neither the technical rules of Evidence Act nor of proof of fact or evidence as defined therein, apply to disciplinary proceeding. When the authority accepts that evidence and conclusion receives support therefrom, the disciplinary authority is entitled to

*hold that the delinquent officer is guilty of the charge. **The Court/Tribunal in its power of judicial review does not act as appellate authority to reappreciate the evidence and to arrive at its own independent findings on the evidence.** The Court/Tribunal may interfere where the authority held the proceedings against the delinquent officer in a manner inconsistent with the rules of natural justice or in violation of statutory rules prescribing the mode of inquiry or where the conclusion or finding reached by the disciplinary authority is based on no evidence. If the conclusion or finding be such as no reasonable person would have ever reached, the Court/Tribunal may interfere with the conclusion or the finding, and mould the relief so as to make it appropriate to the facts of each case.*

*13. The disciplinary authority is the sole judge of facts. Where appeal is presented, the appellate authority has coextensive power to reappreciate the evidence or the nature of punishment. In a disciplinary inquiry, the strict proof of legal evidence and findings on that evidence are not relevant. Adequacy of evidence or reliability of evidence cannot be permitted to be canvassed before the **Court/Tribunal**. In Union of India v. H.C. Goel[5] this Court held at p. 728 that if the conclusion, upon consideration of the evidence reached by the disciplinary authority, is perverse or suffers from patent error on the face of the record or based on no evidence at all, a writ of certiorari could be issued.*

xxx xxx xxxxxx xxx xxx

18. A review of the above legal position would establish that the disciplinary authority, and on appeal the appellate authority, being fact-finding authorities have exclusive power to consider the evidence with a view to maintain discipline.

They are invested with the discretion to impose appropriate punishment keeping in view the magnitude or gravity of the misconduct. The High Court/Tribunal, while exercising the power of judicial review, cannot normally substitute its own conclusion on penalty and impose some other penalty. If the punishment imposed by the disciplinary authority or the appellate authority shocks the conscience of the High Court/Tribunal, it would appropriately mould the relief, either directing the disciplinary/appellate authority to reconsider the penalty imposed, or to shorten the litigation, it may itself, in exceptional and rare cases, impose appropriate punishment with cogent reasons in support thereof."

[Emphasis laid]

17. In **<u>State Bank of Bikaner and Jaipur v. Nemi Chand Nalwaya</u>**, *a two Judge Bench of this Court held as below :*

"7. **It is now well settled that the courts will not act as an appellate court and reassess the evidence led in the domestic enquiry, nor interfere on the ground that another view is possible on the material on record. If the enquiry has been fairly and properly held and the findings are based on evidence, the question of adequacy of the evidence or the reliable nature of the evidence will not be grounds for interfering with the findings in departmental enquiries. Therefore, courts will not interfere with findings of fact recorded in departmental enquiries, except where such findings are based on no evidence or where they are clearly perverse.** *The test to find out perversity is to see whether a tribunal acting reasonably could have arrived at such conclusion or finding, on the material on record. The courts will however interfere with the findings in disciplinary matters, if principles of natural justice or statutory regulations have been violated or if the order is found to be arbitrary, capricious, mala fide or based on extraneous considerations. (Vide B.C. Chaturvedi v. Union of India, Union of India v. G. Ganayutham, Bank of India v. Degala*

Suryanarayana and High Court of Judicature at Bombay v. Shashikant S. Patil).

[Emphasis laid]

18. *In* **Chairman & Managing Director, V.S.P. and Others v. GoparajuSri Prabhakara Hari Babu**, *a two Judge Bench of this Court referred to several precedents on the Doctrine of Proportionality of the order of punishment passed by the Disciplinary Authority and held that :*

"21. Once it is found that all the procedural requirements have been complied with, the courts would not ordinarily interfere with the quantum of punishment imposed upon a delinquent employee. The superior courts only in some cases may invoke the doctrine of proportionality. If the decision of an employer is found to be within the legal parameters, the jurisdiction would ordinarily not be invoked when the misconduct stands proved."

19. *Laying down the broad parameters within which the High Court ought to exercise its powers under Article 226/227 of the Constitution of India and matters relating to disciplinary proceedings, a two Judge Bench of this Court in* **Union of India and Others v. P. Gunasekaran** *held thus :*

"12. Despite the well-settled position, it is painfully disturbing to note that the High Court has acted as an appellate authority in the disciplinary proceedings, reappreciating even the evidence before the enquiry officer. The finding on Charge I was accepted by the disciplinary authority and was also endorsed by the Central Administrative Tribunal. In disciplinary proceedings, the High Court is not and cannot act as a second court of first appeal. The High Court, in exercise of its powers under Articles 226/227 of the Constitution of India, shall not venture into reappreciation of the evidence. The High Court can only see whether:

(a) the enquiry is held by a competent authority;

(b) the enquiry is held according to the procedure prescribed in that behalf;(c) there is violation of the principles of natural justice in conducting the proceedings;

(d) the authorities have disabled themselves from reaching a fair conclusion by some considerations extraneous to the evidence and merits of the case; (e) the authorities have allowed themselves to be influenced by irrelevant or extraneous considerations;

(f) the conclusion, on the very face of it, is so wholly arbitrary and capricious that no reasonable person could ever have arrived at such conclusion; (g) the disciplinary authority had erroneously failed to admit the admissible and material evidence;

(h) the disciplinary authority had erroneously admitted inadmissible evidencewhich influenced the finding;

(i) *the finding of fact is based on no evidence.*

13. *Under Articles 226/227 of the Constitution of India, the High Court shall not: (i) reappreciate the evidence;*

(ii) interfere with the conclusions in the enquiry, in case the same has been conducted in accordance with law; (iii) go into the adequacy of the evidence;

(iv) *go into the reliability of the evidence;*

(v) *interfere, if there be some legal evidence on which findings can be based.*

(vi) *correct the error of fact however grave it may appear to be;*

(vii)*go into the proportionality of punishment unless it shocks itsconscience."*

20.*In* **Union of India and Others v. Ex. Constable Ram Karan** *a two Judge Bench of this Court made the following pertinent observations :*

"23. The well-ingrained principle of law is that it is the disciplinary authority, or the appellate authority in appeal, which is to decide the nature of punishment to be given to the delinquent employee. Keeping in view the seriousness of the misconduct committed by such an employee, it is not open for the courts to assume and usurp the function of the disciplinary authority.

24. Even in cases where the punishment imposed by the disciplinary authority is found to be shocking to the conscience of the court, normally the disciplinary authority or the appellate authority should be directed to reconsider the question of imposition of penalty. The scope of judicial review on the quantum of punishment is available but with a limited scope. It is only when the penalty imposed appears to be shockingly disproportionate to the nature of misconduct that the courts would frown upon. Even in such a case, after setting aside the penalty order, it is to be left to the disciplinary/appellate authority to take a call and it is not for the court to substitute its decision by prescribing the quantum of punishment. However, it is only in rare and exceptional cases where the court might to shorten the litigation may think of substituting its own view as to the quantum of punishment in place of punishment awarded by the competent authority that too after assigning cogent reasons."

21. *A Constitution Bench of this Court in* **State of Orissa and Others** *(supra) held that if the order of dismissal is based on findings that establish the prima facie guilt of great delinquency of the respondent, then the High Court cannot direct reconsideration of the punishment imposed. Once the gravity of the misdemeanour is established and the inquiry conducted is found to be consistent with the prescribed rules and reasonable opportunity contemplated under the rules, has been afforded to the delinquent employee, then the punishment imposed is not open to judicial review by the Court. As long as there was some evidence to arrive at a conclusion that the Disciplinary Authority did, such an order becomes unassailable and the High Court ought to*

*forebear from interfering. The above view has been expressed in **Union of India v. Sardar Bahadur***

22. *To sum up the legal position, being fact finding authorities, both the Disciplinary Authority and the Appellate Authority are vested with the exclusive power to examine the evidence forming part of the inquiry report. On finding the evidence to be adequate and reliable during the departmental inquiry, the Disciplinary Authority has the discretion to impose appropriate punishment on the delinquent employee keeping in mind the gravity of the misconduct. However, in exercise of powers of judicial review, the High Court or for that matter, the Tribunal cannot ordinarily reappreciate the evidence to arrive at its own conclusion in respect of the penalty imposed unless and until the punishment imposed is so disproportionate to the offence that it would shock the conscience of the High Court/Tribunal or is found to be flawed for other reasons, as enumerated in **P. Gunasekaran** (supra). If the punishment imposed on the delinquent employee is such that shocks the conscience of the High Court or the Tribunal, then the Disciplinary/Appellate Authority may be called upon to re-consider the penalty imposed. Only in exceptional circumstances, which need to be mentioned, should the High Court/Tribunal decide to impose appropriate punishment by itself, on offering cogent reasons therefor.*

23. *Applying the law laid down above to the instant case, we are of the view that the High Court ought not to have interfered with the findings of fact recorded by the Disciplinary Authority. Charge-1 levelled against the respondent pertained to negligence and dereliction of duty attributed to him for having failed to prevent theft of 800 kgs of copper wires lying at Alif Nagar scrap yard under his security cover while performing duty in the late hours of 7th November, 2007 upto the early hours of 8th November, 2007. Records reveal that the Disciplinary Authority has minutely examined the entire evidence brought on record including the deposition of eight prosecution witnesses each of whom have corroborated the charges levelled against the respondent, duly supported by documentary and circumstantial evidence for arriving at*

the conclusion that the Articles of Charge-I stood proved against the respondent. Pertinently, the respondent did not produce any defence witness and the documents produced by him did not prove anything in his favour.

24. The contention of the respondent that the FIR registered against him mentioned the time of the occurrence as 15:30 hours on 8th November, 2007, when he was not on duty, was also analyzed in depth by the Disciplinary Authority, who referred to the fact that the FIR was lodged suo moto by the West Port Police Station on the basis of a complaint submitted by the Office-Incharge of the Police Station who had recovered the copper wires loaded in a commercial vehicle which was brought to the police station and kept at the police station compound. The complaint recorded that recovery of copper wires was made by the complainant at 15:15 hours on 8th November, 2007 whereas, the FIR showed the time of the information received as 22:00 hours on 8th November, 2007, and the time of the occurrence of the theft as 15:30 hours. Noting the discrepancies in the FIR which were in contradiction with the depositions of PW1, PW2 and PW8 who had stated that the information of the theft was received long before 22:00 hours on 8th November, 2007, the Disciplinary Authority discarded the version of the respondent as unacceptable and went on to hold that the evidence fairly established that the theft of the copper wires had occurred in the intervening night of $7^{th}/8^{th}$ November, 2007, during the duty hours of the respondent. Accordingly, the Disciplinary Authority concluded that Charge-I was proved against the respondent.

25. As for Charge-II, the Disciplinary Authority noted the statement of SI/Min. A.K. Dua (PW-4) who was working as incharge of the Document Section of the Unit and had been summoned to prove copies of the service documents related to the respondent and on going through the said documentary evidence, noted that the respondent had been awarded eight punishments over a period of thirteen years of service for various delinquencies but he had not reformed himself. In view of his continuous misconduct in the past coupled with the serious

offence of theft of 800 kgs. copper wires, subject matter of Charge-I, the Disciplinary Authority opined that the respondent was unfit to be retained in a disciplined force and therefore, directed his dismissal from service.

26. *We have noted above that the findings of the Disciplinary Authority had met with the approval of the Appellate Authority and the Revisional Authority. However, the learned Single Judge overturned the order of dismissal from service and converted the same to compulsory retirement on the sole ground of non-availability of the original record, more specifically, the Beat Book, while giving a go-by to the extract of the Beat Book that was produced before the Inquiry Officer and the fact that the respondent had admitted the said document. The learned Single Judge also ignored the fact that the Beat Book was not the only piece of document produced before the Inquiry Officer. There were depositions of other witnesses produced by the department to prove the charges levelled against the respondent and the said witnesses had corroborated the version of the Department. At no stage, did the learned Single Judge observe that the departmental inquiry was vitiated on account of violation of the rules of natural justice or that the inquiry had been conducted in gross violation of the statutory rules.*

27. *The Division Bench went a step further and proceeded to reappreciate the evidence and observed that it was not persuaded to conclude that such a major theft of 800 kgs comprising of 42 bundles of copper wires could have happened "in the blink of an eyelid" despite holding that the view of the learned Single Judge regarding nonproduction of the original Beat Book was unsustainable. The Court held that the allegation of connivance in the theft levelled against the respondent was presumptive and there wasn't enough evidence to conclude that theft of such a magnitude could have happened during the duty period of the respondent alone, yet charge-I pertaining to negligence and dereliction of duty on the part of the respondent was sustained. At the same time, the order passed by the learned Single*

Judge directing substitution of the punishment of dismissal with that of compulsory retirement was set aside and the respondent was directed to be reinstated in service with full back wages, while giving liberty to the Disciplinary Authority to issue a fresh order of punishment commensurate to the negligence and dereliction of duties on his part, except for punishment of dismissal or removal from service or compulsory retirement.

28. *We are unable to commend the approach of the learned Single Judge and the Division Bench. There was no good reason for the High Court to have entered the domain of the factual aspects relating to the evidence recorded before the Inquiry Officer. This was clearly an attempt to reappreciate the evidence which is impermissible in exercise of powers of judicial review vested in the High Court under Article 226 of the Constitution of India. We are of the opinion that both, the learned Single Judge as well as the Division Bench, fell into an error by setting aside the order of dismissal from service imposed on the respondent by the Disciplinary Authority and upheld by the Appellate Authority.*

29. *We find ourselves in complete agreement with the findings returned by and conclusion arrived at by the Disciplinary Authority, duly confirmed by the Appellate Authority and upheld by the Revisional Authority in respect of both the Articles of Charge levelled against the respondent and the punishment imposed on him. The respondent being a member of the disciplined force, was expected to have discharged his duty diligently. His gross negligence and dereliction of duty has resulted in theft of 800 kgs. copper wires from the spot where he was performing his duty. Further, the records reveal that the respondent did not mend his ways during thirteen years of service rendered by him and was awarded eight punishments for various delinquencies out of which, three punishments included stoppage of increment on two occasions for one year without cumulative effect twice and stoppage of increment for two years without cumulative effect on one occasion. In such circumstances, the desirability of continuing the respondent in the Armed Forces is certainly questionable and the Disciplinary Authority* *could not be expected to wear blinkers in respect of his past conduct while imposing the penalty of dismissal from service on him.*

30. *Therefore, it is deemed appropriate to quash and set aside the impugned judgment and order dated 9th September, 2021 passed by the Division Bench of the High Court of Calcutta in FMA No.679 of 2019 and FMA No. 680 of 2019 and the order dated 25th June, 2018 passed by the learned Single Judge in WP No.14102 (W) of 2009, while restoring the findings and the conclusion arrived at by the Disciplinary Authority, as elaborated in the order dated 27th November, 2008, duly upheld by the Appellate Authority, vide order dated 3rd February, 2009 and endorsed by the Revisional Authority, vide order dated 19th May, 2009. In our view, the penalty of dismissal from service imposed on the respondent is commensurate with the gross negligence and dereliction of duty on his part.*

31. *As a result, both the appeals preferred by the Union of India (arising out of Petitions for Special Leave to Appeal (C) Nos. 3524-25/2022) are allowed and appeals @ Petitions for Special Leave to Appeal (Civil) Nos. 11021-22/2022 filed by the private respondent are dismissed, while leaving the parties to bear their own expenses.*

www.ingramcontent.com/pod-product-compliance
Lightning Source LLC
LaVergne TN
LVHW061538070526
838199LV00077B/6830